The Pursuit of History

This classic introduction to the study of history invites the reader to stand back and consider some of its most fundamental questions – what is the point of studying history? How do we know about the past? Does an objective historical truth exist and can we ever access it?

In answering these central questions, John Tosh argues that, despite the impression of fragmentation created by postmodernism in recent years, history is a coherent discipline which still bears the imprint of its nineteenth-century origins. Consistently clear-sighted, he provides a lively and compelling guide to a complex and sometimes controversial subject, while making his readers vividly aware of just how far our historical knowledge is conditioned by the character of the sources and the methods of the historians who work on them.

The sixth edition has been revised and updated with key new material including:

- a brand new chapter on public history
- sections on digitized sources and historical controversy
- discussion of topics including transnational history and the nature of the archive
- an expanded range of examples and case studies
- a comprehensive companion website (found at www.routledge. com/cw/tosh) providing valuable supporting material, study questions and a bank of primary sources.

Lucid and engaging, this edition retains all the user-friendly features that have helped to make this book a favourite with both students and lecturers, including marginal glosses, illustrations and suggestions for further reading. Along with its companion website, this is an essential guide to the theory and practice of history.

John Tosh is Professor of History at the University of Roehampton, Visiting Professor at Birkbeck University of London and a Fellow of the Royal Historical Society. He is the author of several works on historiography, notably *Why History Matters* (2008) and *Historians on History* (2nd edn, 2009).

Praise for this edition:

"This exceptionally insightful book makes the study of history a joy to read. Tosh maps out the major questions and developments in historiography with extraordinary clarity, guiding the reader on debates and methods of research in concise and informative ways. His continued attention to up-dating the book without doubt makes it a critical text for undergraduates and an essential resource for postgraduates and scholars."

Catherine Dewhirst, *University of Southern Queensland, Australia*

"John Tosh's book is the most useful introduction to recent historiography now available. It surveys major trends and achievements more clearly and concisely than its main competitors, and is an excellent and easy resource for contextualising other historical writings of all kinds. It can add a great deal to students' understanding of historical writing."

Nicholas Karn, *University of Southampton, UK*

"*The Pursuit of History* has many strengths. It is extremely well-written and lucid. It strikes a very nice balance between tracing historiography, delineating historical methodology, and discussing the major historiographical developments over the last few decades. Comprehensive, insightful and conversant with the latest historiographical currents, it is essential reading in any undergraduate or graduate theory and method course."

Thomas W. Gallant, *University of California, San Diego, USA*

"John Tosh's *Pursuit of History* was so far ahead of the game on its first publication that much of the profession are only just now catching up with his wonderfully diverse and pluralistic approach to the study of the past. This new edition promises to equip and inspire the next generations of historians once again very much for the better."

Richard Sheldon, *University of Bristol, UK*

"Tosh's *Pursuit of History,* in its newest edition, remains the definitive introduction to historical criticism and historiography. Well-structured, up-to-date, highly readable and drawing on a wealth of fascinating illustrative material from the author's own research, it stands out as the best text combining fundamental method with key theoretical approaches and research trends."

William L. Chew III, *Vesalius College, Brussels, Belgium*

"The sixth edition of John Tosh's *The Pursuit of History* is a clearly written, informative and absorbing introduction to the practice of 'doing' history. While retaining the most useful features of earlier editions of the book, this latest edition introduces new, valuable material on public history, digitised sources, historical controversies, transnational history and the nature of the archive. It includes an expanded range of examples and case-studies, including additional material on American history, along with an updated reference list, making it an invaluable text for both tutors and students of history alike."

Robert James, *University of Portsmouth, UK*

Praise for previous editions:

"An excellent introduction to methodology in history which will be read with advantage by historians at any stage of their development."

History

"Tosh writes clearly and pungently... A very satisfactory as well as stimulating vade-mecum for all who work at history."

Times Higher Education Supplement

The Pursuit of History

Aims, methods and new directions
in the study of history

SIXTH EDITION

John Tosh

Routledge
Taylor & Francis Group

LONDON AND NEW YORK

Sixth edition published 2015
by Routledge

2 Park Square, Milton Park, Abingdon, Oxon, OX14 4RN
and by Routledge
711 Third Avenue, New York, NY 10017

Routledge is an imprint of the Taylor & Francis Group, an informa business

First edition published by Pearson in 1984
Fifth edition published by Pearson in 2010

British Library Cataloguing in Publication Data
A catalogue record for this book is available from the British Library

Library of Congress Cataloging in Publication Data
A catalog record for this title has been requested

ISBN: 978-1-138-80807-2 (hbk)
ISBN: 978-1-138-80808-9 (pbk)
ISBN: 978-1-315-72813-1 (ebk)

Typeset in Sabon
by Taylor & Francis Books Ltd

For Nick and Will

Contents

List of images

Preface to the Sixth Edition

The word *history* carries two meanings in common parlance. It refers both to what actually happened in the past and to the representation of that past in the work of historians. This book is an introduction to history in the second sense. It is intended for anyone who is sufficiently interested in the subject to wonder how historical enquiry is conducted and what purpose it fulfils. More specifically, the book is addressed to students taking a degree course in history, for whom these questions have particular relevance.

Traditionally, history undergraduates were offered no formal instruction in the nature of their chosen discipline; its time-honoured place in our literary culture and its non-technical presentation suggested that common sense combined with a sound general education would provide the student with what little orientation he or she required. This approach leaves a great deal to chance. It is surely desirable that students consider the functions served by a subject to which they are about to devote three years or more of study. Curriculum choice will be a hit-and-miss affair unless based on a clear grasp of the content and scope of present-day historical scholarship. Above all, students need to be aware of the limits placed on historical knowledge by the character of the sources and the working methods of historians, so that at an early stage they can develop a critical approach to the formidable array of secondary authorities that they are required to master. It is certainly possible to complete a degree course in history without giving systematic thought to any of these issues, and generations of students have done so. But most universities now recognize that the value of historical study is thereby diminished, and they therefore provide introductory courses on the methods and scope of history. I hope that this book will meet the needs of students taking such a course.

Although my own research experience has been in the fields of African history and gender in modern Britain, it has not been my intention to write a manifesto for 'the new history'. I have tried instead to convey the diversity of current historical practice, and to situate recent innovations in the context of mainstream traditional scholarship, which continues to account for a great deal of first-rate historical work and to dominate academic syllabuses. The scope of historical studies is today so wide that it has not been easy to determine the precise range of this book; but without some more or less arbitrary boundaries an introductory work of this length would lose all coherence. I therefore say nothing about the history of science or environmental history, and there are only passing references to the history of the body and the history of consumption. In general I have confined my choice to those themes which are widely studied by students today.

Even within these limits, however, my territory is something of a minefield. Anyone who imagines that an introduction to the study of history will express a consensus of expert opinion needs to be promptly disabused. One of the distinguishing features of the profession is its heated arguments concerning the objectives and limitations of historical study. This book inevitably reflects my own views, and it is appropriate to declare them at the outset. The salient points are: that history is a subject of practical social relevance; that the proper performance of its function depends on a receptive and discriminating attitude to other disciplines; and that the methods of academic history hold out the promise not of 'truth' in an absolute sense, but of incremental growth in our knowledge of the past. At the same time, I have tried to place these claims – none of which are of course original – in the context of recent debate among historians, and to give a fair hearing to views with which I disagree.

This book explores a number of general propositions about history and historians, rather than providing a point of entry into any one field or specialism. But since I anticipate that most of my readers will be more familiar with British history than any other, I have relied for my illustrative material mostly on that field, with some additional examples from Africa, Europe and the United States. The book is meant to be read as a whole, but I have included a certain amount of cross-referencing in the text to assist the reader who wishes to pursue specific themes.

The book is intended to take the reader from first principles through to some of the latest debates about the direction historical study is taking. Chapter 1 considers what it means to think historically. Chapter 2 reviews the debate about whether history has any use beyond human curiosity about the past. Chapter 3 seeks to categorize the many and varied kinds of study that sail under the banner of 'history'. Then follow two chapters (4 and 5) that itemize and analyse written primary sources. Chapter 6 examines the different kinds of writing through which historians communicate their findings. Chapter 7 reviews the intense debates that have arisen about the truth claims of history, paying special attention to postmodernism. The remainder of the book describes a number of specific approaches to history, all informed to a greater or lesser degree by theory. Chapter 8 considers Marxism and other kinds of social theory; Chapter 9 evaluates the contribution of cultural sources and the broader reorientation known as the 'cultural turn'. Chapter 10 deals with gender history and postcolonial history. Chapter 11 considers the relationship between history and memory, including oral history.

A number of changes have been made in this edition. Chapters 4 and 5 now include coverage of the place of digital sources in historical research, and they also draw on recent critical thinking about the archive. In Chapter 6, I have added a discussion about why historical writing is so taken up with controversy. The book now ends with a new chapter on public history, reinforcing my argument that history is not just for students, but for a wider audience. At various points in the text I have added additional historical examples drawn from American history, bearing in mind the substantial American readership of the book. Elsewhere I have updated the text and the reference material at numerous points.

In ranging so far beyond any one person's experience of research and writing, this book is more dependent than most on the help of other scholars. Earlier editions record my intellectual debts. This latest edition has benefited from the advice of Arianna Ciula, Sarah Longair, John Seed, Carey Watt and Caroline White.

I am particularly grateful to Seán Lang: he devised the student aids in the fourth edition, and I have incorporated most of them here in the same house style, with some additions.

John Tosh
August 2014

Acknowledgements

The publisher would like to thank akg-images, Alamy Images, Bridgeman Art Library, Corbis, Getty Images, Mary Evans Picture Library, Paul Shawcross, Matt Mindham, Photographers Direct and Topfoto for their kind permission to reproduce their images.

1 Historical awareness

This chapter looks at the difference between memory, whether individual or collective, and the more disciplined approach towards the past that characterizes an awareness of history. *All groups have a sense of the past, but they tend to use it to reinforce their own beliefs and sense of identity. Like human memory, collective or social memory can be faulty, distorted by factors such as a sense of tradition or nostalgia, or else a belief in progress through time. Modern professional historians take their cue from nineteenth-century* historicism, *which taught that the past should be studied on its own terms, 'as it actually was'. However, this more detached approach to the past can put historians in conflict with people who feel their cherished versions of the past are under threat.*

'Historical awareness' is a slippery term. It can be regarded as a universal psychological attribute, arising from the fact that we are, all of us, in a sense historians. Because our species depends more on experience than on instinct, life cannot be lived without the consciousness of a personal past; and someone who has lost this through illness or ageing is generally regarded as disqualified from normal life. As individuals we draw on our experience in all sorts of different ways – as a means of affirming our identity, as a clue to our potential, as the basis for our impression of others and as some indication of the possibilities that lie ahead. Our memories serve as both a data bank and a means of making sense of an unfolding life story. We know that we cannot understand a situation without some perception of where it fits into a continuing process or whether it has happened before. The same holds true of our lives as social beings. All societies have a collective memory, a storehouse of experience that is drawn on for a sense of identity and a sense of direction. Professional historians commonly deplore the superficiality of popular historical knowledge, but *some* knowledge of the past is almost universal; without it one is effectively excluded from social and political debate, just as loss of memory disqualifies one from much everyday human interaction. Our political judgements are permeated by a sense of the past, whether we are deciding between the competing claims of political parties or assessing the feasibility of particular policies. To understand our social arrangements, we need to have some notion of where they have come from. In that sense all societies possess 'memory'.

But 'historical awareness' is not the same thing as social memory. How the past is known and how it is applied to present need are open to widely varying approaches. We know from personal experience that memory is neither fixed nor infallible: we forget, we overlay early memories with later experience, we shift the emphasis, we entertain false memories and so on. In important matters we are likely to seek confirmation of our memories from an outside source. Collective memory is marked by the same distortions, as our current priorities lead us to highlight some aspects of the past and to exclude others. In our political life especially, memory is highly selective, and sometimes downright erroneous. It is at this point that the term 'historical awareness' invites a more rigorous interpretation. Under the **Third Reich** those Germans who believed that all the disasters in German history were the fault of the Jews certainly acknowledged the power of the past, but we would surely question the extent of their historical awareness. In other words, it is not enough to invoke the past; there must also be a belief that getting the story right matters. History as a disciplined enquiry aims to sustain the widest possible definition of memory, and to make the process of recall as accurate as possible, so that our knowledge of the past is not confined to what is immediately relevant. The goal is a resource with open-ended application, instead of a set of mirror-images of the present. That at least has been the aspiration of historians for the past two centuries. Much of this book will be devoted to evaluating how adequately historians achieve these ends. My purpose in this opening chapter is to explore the different dimensions of social memory, and in so doing to arrive at an understanding of what historians do and how it differs from other sorts of thinking about the past.

Third Reich
The technical term for the National Socialist (Nazi) regime in Germany, 1933–45. Reich (roughly 'Empire') was used to denote the original medieval German Empire and the unified German Empire (the Second Reich), which lasted from 1871 to 1919.

I

Social memory: creating the self-identity of a group

For any social grouping to have a collective identity there has to be a shared interpretation of the events and experiences that have formed the group over time. Sometimes this will include an accepted belief about the origins of the group, as in the case of many nation states; or the emphasis may be on vivid turning points and symbolic moments that confirm the self-image and aspirations of the group. Current examples include the vital significance of the **Edwardian suffrage movement** for the women's movement and the appeal of the 'molly house' sub-culture of eighteenth-century London for the gay community in Britain today.[1] Without an awareness of a common past made up of such human detail, men and women could not easily acknowledge the claims on their loyalty of large abstractions.

The term 'social memory' accurately reflects the rationale of popular knowledge about the past. Social groupings need a record of prior experience, but they also require a picture of the past that serves to explain or justify the present, often at the cost of historical accuracy. The operation of social memory is clearest in those societies where no appeal can be made to the documentary record as a corrective or higher authority. Precolonial Africa presents some classic instances.[2] In literate societies, the same was true for those largely unlettered communities that lay outside the elite, such as the peasantries of pre-modern Europe. What counted for historical knowledge here was handed down as a narrative from one generation to the next, often identified with particular places and particular ceremonies or rituals. It provided a guide for conduct and a set of symbols around which resistance to unwelcome intrusion could be mobilized. Until quite recently popular memory in a largely illiterate Sicily embraced both the Palermo rising of 1282 against the Angevins (the 'Sicilian Vespers') and the nineteenth-century Mafia as episodes in a national tradition of avenging brotherhood.[3]

But it would be a mistake to suppose that social memory is the preserve of small-scale, pre-literate societies. In fact the term itself highlights a universal need: if the individual cannot exist without memory, neither can society, and that goes for large-scale, technologically advanced societies too. All societies look to their collective memories for consolation or inspiration, and literate societies are in principle no different. Near-universal literacy and a high degree of residential mobility mean that the oral transmission of social memory is now much less important. But written accounts (such as school history books or popular evocations of the World Wars), film and television perform the same function. Social memory continues to be an essential means of sustaining a politically active identity. Its success is judged by how effectively it contributes to collective cohesion and how widely it is shared by members of the group. Sometimes social memory is based on consensus and inclusion, and this is often the function of explicitly national narratives. It can take the form of a **foundation myth**, as in the case of the far-seeing Founding Fathers of the American Republic, whose memory is still invoked today in order to shore up belief in the American nation. Alternatively, consensual memory can focus on a moment of heroism, like the story of Dunkirk in 1940, which the British recall as the ingenious

Edwardian suffrage movement
The movement in the period before the First World War to obtain the parliamentary vote ('suffrage') for women. It is best known for campaigns by the militant suffragettes, although it was the more moderate suffragists who finally obtained votes for women in 1918.

'molly house'
An eighteenth-century covert meeting house for homosexual men. Molly houses remained little known until Mark Ravenhill's play *Mother Clapp's Molly House* (2001) was staged to widespread acclaim at the Royal National Theatre in London.

foundation myth
A story, usually much-treasured, about the foundation of a group or people. One of the most famous is the biblical story of the Creation. Nations often have semi-'official' versions of their origins, usually involving national hero figures, but foundation myths can be found in schools, army regiments and even companies. 'Myth' need not imply that the story is entirely false, merely that it has developed into a simplistic, usually rosy, version of events.

THE DECLARATION OF INDEPENDENCE.
JULY 4TH 1776.

Figure 1.1 Foundation myth: the Declaration of Independence by America's 'Founding Fathers' in 1776 remains an iconic moment in American history of immense symbolic importance. American school history books still present it in resolutely heroic terms. © Bridgeman Art Library/Capitol Collection, Washington, USA.

escape that laid the foundations of victory (see Chapter 11 for fuller discussion).

Social memory of past oppression

But social memory can also serve to sustain a sense of oppression, exclusion or adversity, and these elements account for some of the most powerful expressions of social memory. Social movements entering the political arena for the first time are particularly conscious of the absolute requirement of a past. Black history in the United States has its origin in the kind of strategic concern voiced by Malcolm X in the 1960s. One reason why blacks were oppressed, he wrote, was that white America had cut them off from their past:

> If we don't go into the past and find out how we got this way, we will think that we were always this way. And if you think that you were in the condition that you're in right now, it's impossible for you to have too much confidence in yourself, you become worthless, almost nothing.[4]

The purpose of much British labour history has been to sharpen the social awareness of the workers, to confirm their commitment to political action and to reassure them that history is 'on their side' if only they will keep faith with the heroism of their forebears. David Montgomery's work on the American labour movement combined studies of shop-floor relations with the wider class environment in which workers developed their political consciousness. 'When you come right down to it', Montgomery remarked, 'history is the only teacher the workers have.'[5] In Britain the inaugural editorial of *History Workshop Journal* declared that the historical reconstruction of working people's experience was 'a source of inspiration and understanding'.[6] Working-class memories of work, locality, family and politics – with all the pride and anger so often expressed through them – were rescued before they were pushed out of popular consciousness by an approved national version.

The women's movement of the past thirty years has been if anything more conscious of the need for a usable past. For feminists, this requirement is not met by studies of exceptional women such as Elizabeth I who operated successfully in a man's world; the emphasis falls instead on the economic and sexual exploitation that has been the lot of most women, and on the efforts of activists to secure redress. According to this perspective, the critical determinant of women's history was not nation or class, but **patriarchy**: that is, the power of the household head over his wife and children and, by extension, the power of men over women more generally. Because mainstream history suppresses this truth, what it offers is not universal history but a blinkered account of half the human race. These are the themes which, to quote from the title of a popular feminist text, have been 'hidden from history'.[7] As one American feminist has put it:

> It is not surprising that most women feel that their sex does not have an interesting or significant past. However, like minority groups, women cannot afford to lack a consciousness of a collective identity, one which necessarily involves a shared awareness of the past. Without this, a social group suffers from a kind of collective amnesia, which makes it vulnerable to the impositions of dubious stereotypes, as well as limiting prejudices about what is right and proper for it to do or not to do.[8]

For socially deprived or 'invisible' groups – whether in a majority such as workers and women, or in a minority such as blacks in America and Britain – effective political mobilization depends on a consciousness of common experience in the past.

History Workshop Journal
A collaborative research venture set up by a group of left-wing historians led by Raphael Samuel (1934–96) at Ruskin College, Oxford, to encourage research and debate about working-class and women's history.

patriarchy
A social system based on the dominance of fathers, and, by extension, of men in general.

II

Historicism – liberating the past from the present

But alongside these socially motivated views of the past has grown up a form of historical awareness that starts from quite different premises. While social memory has continued to open up interpretations that satisfy new forms of political and social need, the dominant approach in historical scholarship has been to value the past for its own sake and, as far as possible, to rise above political expediency. It was only during the nineteenth century that historical awareness in this more rigorous sense became the defining attribute of professional historians. There were certainly important precursors – in the ancient world, in Islam, in dynastic China and in the West from the Renaissance onwards. But it was not until the first half of the nineteenth century that all the elements of historical awareness were brought together in a historical practice that was widely recognized as the proper way to study the past. This was the achievement of the intellectual movement known as *historicism*, which began in Germany and soon spread all over the Western world (the word comes from the German *Historismus*).

The fundamental premise of the historicists was that the autonomy of the past must be respected. They held that each age is a unique manifestation of the human spirit, with its own culture and values. For one age to understand another, there must be a recognition that the passage of time has profoundly altered both the conditions of life and the mentality of men and women – even perhaps human nature itself. Historians are not the guardians of universal values, nor can they deliver 'the verdict of history'; they must strive to understand each age on its own terms and to take on its own values and priorities instead of imposing ours. All the resources of scholarship and all the historian's powers of imagination must be harnessed to the task of bringing the past back to life – or *resurrecting* it, to employ a favourite conceit of the period. But historicism was more than an antiquarian rallying cry. Its proponents maintained that the culture and institutions of their own day could only be understood historically. Unless their growth and development through successive ages were grasped, their true nature would remain elusive. History, in short, held the key to understanding the world.

Seeing through the eyes of the past

Historicism was one facet of Romanticism, the dominant movement in European thought and art around 1800. The most influential Romantic literary figure, Sir Walter Scott, aimed to draw readers of his historical romances into the authentic atmosphere of the past. Popular interest in the surviving remains of the past rose to new heights, and it extended to not only the ancient world but also the hitherto despised Middle Ages. Historicism represented the academic wing of the Romantic obsession with the past. The leading figure in the movement was Leopold von Ranke, a professor at Berlin University from 1824 until 1872 and the author of over sixty volumes. In the preface to his first book, he wrote:

> History has had assigned to it the task of judging the past, of instructing the present for the benefit of the ages to come. To such lofty functions this work does not aspire. Its aim is merely to show how things actually were [*wie es eigentlich gewesen*].[9]

By this Ranke meant more than an intention to reconstruct the passage of events, though this was certainly part of his programme.[10] What was new about the historicists' approach was their realization that the atmosphere and mentality of past ages had to be reconstructed too, if the formal record of events was to have any meaning. The main task of the historian became to find out why people acted as they did by stepping into their shoes, by seeing the world through their eyes and as far as possible by judging it by their standards. **Thomas Carlyle** believed more fervently in historical recreation than any other nineteenth-century writer; whatever the purpose of historical work, 'the first indispensable condition', he declared, was that 'we *see* the things transacted, picture them wholly, as if they stand before our eyes'.[11] And this obligation extended to *all* periods in the past, however alien they might seem to modern observers. Ranke himself strove to meet the historicist ideal in his treatment of the wars of religion in the sixteenth and seventeenth centuries. Others tackled the Middle Ages in the same spirit.

Ranke's much-quoted preface is also important as a disclaimer of relevance. Ranke did not maintain that historical research served no purpose outside itself; indeed, he was probably the last major historian to believe that the outcome of studies such as his own would be to reveal the hand of God in human history. But he did not look for practical lessons from the past. Indeed he believed that detachment from present-day concerns was a condition of understanding the past. His objection to previous historians was not that they lacked all curiosity or **empathy** but that they were diverted from the real task by the desire to preach, or to give lessons in statecraft or to shore up the reputation of a ruling dynasty; in pursuing immediate goals they obscured the true wisdom to be derived from historical study. In the next chapter I will consider more fully the question of whether relevance is necessarily incompatible with historical awareness. But during the first half of the nineteenth century, when Europe experienced

Thomas Carlyle (1795–1881)
A popular, though controversial, Victorian writer and historian. He was the author of a long, colourful account of the French Revolution.

empathy
The ability to enter into the feelings of others (not to be confused with sympathy, which denotes actually sharing them). The term is often used to describe a historian's approach to the 'foreignness' of past societies. In the 1980s there was an ultimately ill-fated attempt to assess children's ability to empathize with people in the past for examination purposes.

French Revolution
The tumultuous political events in late eighteenth-century France that overturned the monarchy and established a republic based upon the principles of the Rights of Man. It involved considerable violence and chronic political instability, until Napoleon staged a military coup in 1799.

Olympian
Detached and remote, like the Greek gods on Mount Olympus.

anachronism
A historical inaccuracy in which elements from one historical period (usually the present) are inserted into an earlier one, such as the use of modern language or attitudes in historical films and dramas.

a high degree of turbulence in the aftermath of the **French Revolution**, history was politically contentious, and unless a special virtue had been made of detachment, it is hard to see how a scholarly historical practice could have become established. Although very few people read Ranke today, his name continues to stand for an **Olympian** impartiality and a duty to be true to the past before all else.

The 'otherness' of the past

Historical awareness in the sense understood by the historicists rests on three principles. The first, and most fundamental, is *difference*; that is, a recognition of the gulf that separates our own age from all previous ages. Because nothing in history stands still, the passage of time has profoundly altered the way we live. The first responsibility of the historian is to take the measure of the difference of the past; conversely one of the worst sins is **anachronism** – the unthinking assumption that people in the past behaved and thought as we do. This difference is partly about the material conditions of life, a point sometimes forcibly made by the surviving remains of the past such as buildings, implements and clothing. Less obviously, but even more importantly, the difference is one of mentality: earlier generations had different values, priorities, fears and hopes from our own. We may take the beauties of nature for granted, but medieval men and women were terrified of forests and mountains and strayed from the beaten track as little as possible. In late eighteenth-century rural England, separation and remarriage were sometimes achieved by means of a public wife-sale; although this was in part a reaction to the virtual impossibility of legal divorce for the poor, it is hard for the modern reader not to dwell on the extreme patriarchal values implied in the humiliation of a wife led to market by her husband and held by a halter.[12] During the same period, public hangings in London regularly drew crowds of 30,000 or more, both rich and poor, and usually more women than men. Their motivation varied: it might be to see justice done, to draw lessons from the deportment of the condemned man or to register indignation at his death; but all shared a readiness to gaze on an act of cold-blooded cruelty from which most people today would recoil in horror.[13] More recent periods may not be so strange, but we still have to be alert to many evidences of difference. In mid-Victorian England it was possible for a thoughtful educated person to describe the teeming poor of East London as a 'trembling mass of maggots in a lump of **carrion**'.[14]

carrion
The carcasses of dead animals on which scavengers feed.

Historical empathy, which has been much vaunted in classroom practice in recent years, is often taken to mean a recognition of the common humanity we share with our forebears; but a more realistic (and also more rigorous) interpretation of empathy dwells on the effort of imagination needed to penetrate mentalities held in the past, which are irremediably removed from anything in our experience. As the novelist **L.P. Hartley** remarked, 'The past is a foreign country'.[15] Of course, like all foreign lands, the past is never entirely alien. As well as the shock of revulsion, historians experience the shock of recognition – as when they come across unaffected spontaneity in the behaviour of parents towards children in seventeenth-century England, or uncover the consumerist culture of eighteenth-century London. 'All history', it has been said, 'is a negotiation between familiarity and strangeness.'[16] But in any scholarly enquiry it is the otherness of the past that tends to come to the fore, because the passage of time has made exotic what once seemed commonplace.

One of the ways in which we measure our distance from the past is by periodization. Labelling by century has this effect, as does the recognition of centenaries. More significant are the labels devised by historians themselves, since these express a view about the characteristics of the period concerned. As Ludmilla Jordanova has observed, 'marking time is the business of historians'.[17] The most vexed of these labels is 'modern'. Until the nineteenth century it was common to refer to all history since the fall of the Roman Empire as 'modern'. In universities 'modern history' is still sometimes used in that generic sense. In most current contexts, however, 'modern' has a narrower focus. It is identified with industrialization and the coming of mass society (in consumption, politics and culture) during the nineteenth century. The intervening epochs between the ancient and modern worlds are divided up between the medieval and early modern periods, with the fifteenth century usually treated as the bridge between the two. These terms are indispensable to historians, but they are paradoxical. In one sense they signal historical difference (we are not 'early modern'); but they also impose on the people of the past labels that had no meaning for them. In other words, they represent an act of interpretation, devised with the benefit of hindsight – and patently so when historians argue about the merits of different versions. It should also be noted that these labels are Eurocentric, and that they cannot easily be applied to histories in other parts of the world.[18]

Putting 'otherness' in context

Merely to register such instances of difference across the gulf of time can give a salutary jolt to our modern assumptions. But historians aim to go much further than this. Their purpose is not only to uncover the strangeness of the past but to explain it, and that means placing it in its historical setting. What may seem bizarre or disturbing to us becomes explicable – though not necessarily less shocking – when interpreted as a manifestation of

L.P. Hartley (1895–1972)
British novelist. His novel *The Go-Between*, about a young boy who carries messages between a pair of lovers, is told through the memory of the boy grown to adulthood. The novel's opening line, 'The past is a foreign country; they do things differently there', has been adopted by historians trying to put across the dangers of imposing modern assumptions on previous ages.

a particular society. To recoil in horror from the grisly details of witchcraft accusations in early modern Europe or colonial America is certainly to acknowledge the gulf that separates that time from ours, but this is no more than a point of departure. The reason why we understand this phenomenon so much better now than we did thirty years ago is that historians have positioned it in relation to beliefs about the human body, the framework of popular religious belief outside the Church and the tensions over the position of women.[19] *Context* is thus the second component of historical awareness. The underlying principle of all historical work is that the subject of our enquiry must not be wrenched from its setting. Just as we would not pronounce on the significance of an archaeological find without first recording carefully its precise location in the site, so we must place everything we know about the past in its contemporary context. This is an exacting standard, requiring a formidable breadth of knowledge. It is often what distinguishes the professional from the amateur. The enthusiast working on family history in the local record office can, with a little technical guidance, substantiate a sequence of births, marriages and deaths, often extending over many generations; the amateur will come to grief not over factual omissions but because of an inadequate grasp of the relevant economic or social settings. To the social historian, the history of the family is not fundamentally about lines of descent, or even about plotting average family size down the ages; it is about placing the family within the shifting contexts of household production, health, religion, education and state policy.[20] Everything in the historian's training militates against presenting the past as a fixed single-track sequence of events; context must be respected at every point.

The historical continuum

scramble for Africa
The term given to the process by which, in the 1880s and 1890s, almost the entire African continent was taken over by European powers. The term, which was used at the time, reflects distaste at the naked greed with which the Europeans jostled with each other to grab vast areas of land with no thought at all for the welfare of the African peoples who lived there.

But history is more than a collection of snapshots of the past, however vivid and richly contextualized. A third fundamental aspect of historical awareness is the recognition of historical *process* – the relationship between events over time which endows them with more significance than if they were viewed in isolation. For example, historians continue to be interested in the application of steam power to cotton spinning in the late eighteenth century, not so much because it is a striking instance of technical and entrepreneurial ingenuity but because it contributed so much to what has come to be called the Industrial Revolution. Specific annexations during the **scramble for Africa** attract attention because they formed part of a large-scale imperialism by the European powers; and so on. Apart from their intrinsic interest, what lies behind our concern with these instances of historical process is the much bigger question of how we got from 'then' to 'now'. This is the 'big story' to which so many more restricted enquiries contribute. There may be a gulf between 'us' and 'them', but that gulf is actually composed of processes of growth, decay and change which it is the business of historians to uncover. Thus the fuller understanding we now have of witchcraft in the sixteenth and seventeenth centuries begs the question of how this form of belief came into decline and disrepute, to the point where in Western society today it is subscribed to by only a very few self-conscious revivalists. Historical processes have sometimes been marked by abrupt transitions when history, as it were, speeded up – as in the case of the great revolutions. At the other extreme, history may almost stand still, its flow only perceptible with the hindsight of many centuries, as in patterns of land use or **kinship systems** in many pre-industrial societies.[21]

If historical awareness rests on the notion of continuum, this cuts both ways: just as nothing has remained the same in the past, so too our world is the product of history. Every aspect of our culture, behaviour and beliefs is the outcome of processes over time. This is true not only of **venerable** institutions such as the Christian Churches or the British monarchy, which are visibly the outcome of centuries of evolution; it applies also to the most familiar aspects of every day, such as marriage or personal hygiene, which are much less often placed in a historical frame. No human practice ever stands still; all demand a historical perspective which uncovers the dynamics of change over time. This is one reason why it is so important that students should study large swathes of history. At present in British schools and universities there is so much emphasis on the virtues of documentary study and narrow specialism that major historical trends tend to disappear from view.

kinship systems
Social systems based upon the extended family.

venerable
Worthy of respect and reverence, especially by virtue of age and wisdom.

III

Are professional historical awareness and popular social memory in opposition?

In the sense understood by the historicists, then, historical awareness means respecting the autonomy of the past, and attempting to reconstruct it in all its strangeness before applying its insights to the present. The effect of this programme was to drive a bigger wedge between elite and popular attitudes to the past, which has persisted until today. Professional historians insist on a lengthy immersion in the primary sources, a deliberate shedding of present-day assumptions and a rare degree of empathy and imagination. Popular historical knowledge, on the other hand, tends to a highly selective interest in the remains of the past, is shot through with present-day assumptions and is only incidentally concerned with understanding the past on its own terms. Three recurrent features of social memory have particularly significant distorting effects.

The distorting effects of tradition

The first of these is respect for *tradition*. In many areas of life – from the law courts to political associations, from churches to sports clubs – belief and behaviour are governed by the weight of precedent: an assumption that what was done in the past is an authoritative guide to what should be done in the present. Respect for tradition is sometimes confused with a sense of history because it involves an affection for the past (or some of it) and a desire to keep faith with it. But there is very little of the historical about appeals to tradition. Following the path laid down by the ancestors has a great deal to be said for it in communities that neither experience change nor expect it; for them present and past can scarcely be distinguished. That is why respect for tradition contributed so much to the cohesion of society among small-scale pre-literate peoples – and why indeed they are sometimes referred to by anthropologists as 'traditional societies'. But such conditions no longer exist. In any society with a dynamic of social or cultural change, as indicated by external trade or social hierarchy or political institutions, an uncritical respect for tradition is counterproductive. It suppresses the historical changes that have occurred in the intervening period; indeed it positively discourages any attention to those changes and leads to the continuance of outward forms that are really

Figure 1.2 The State Opening of Parliament. Much of the ritual at this annual ceremony has strong historical resonance, but this should not be confused with a professional, analytical sense of history. Such traditions can, in fact, conjure up the past to obscure the political reality of the present. © Getty Images/AFP.

redundant – or which we might say have been 'overtaken by history'. One reason for the famed stability of parliamentary government in Britain is that Parliament itself enjoys the prestige of a 700-year history as 'the mother of parliaments'. This confers considerable legitimacy: one often hears it said that Parliament has stood the test of time, that it has been the upholder of constitutional liberties and so on. But it also results in a reluctance to consider honestly how Parliament actually functions. The ability of the House of Commons to restrain the executive has declined sharply since the Second World War, but so far the immense tradition-based prestige of Parliament has blunted the demand for fundamental reform. Such is the authority of tradition that ruling groups have at various times invented it in order to bolster their prestige. Almost all the 'traditional' ceremonial associated with the royal family was improvised during the reign of Victoria, yet this rooting in specific historical circumstances is just what the whole notion of 'tradition' denies.[22] In modern societies, tradition may hold a sentimental appeal, but to treat it as a guide to life tends to lead to unfortunate results.

The invented traditions of nationalism

The consequences of respect for tradition are particularly disturbing in the case of nationalism. Nations are of course the product of history, and the same national designation has usually meant different things at different times. Unfortunately, historians have not always kept this truth at the forefront of their minds. For all their scholarly principle, the nineteenth-century historicists found it hard to resist the demand for one-dimensional, nation-building history, and many did not even try. Europe was then the scene of bitterly contested national identities, as existing national boundaries were challenged by those many peoples whose sense of nationhood was denied – from the Germans and Italians to the Poles and Hungarians. Their claim to nationhood rested partly on language and common culture. But it also required a historical rationale, of past glories to be revived, or ancient wrongs to be avenged – in short, a tradition that could sustain the morale of the nation in the present and impress the other powers of Europe. Historians were caught up in popular nationalism like everyone else, and many saw no contradiction between the tenets of their profession and the writing of self-serving national histories. František Palacký was both a historian and a Czech nationalist. He combined his two great passions in a sequence of books that portrayed the Czechs as a freedom-loving and democratic people since the dawn of historical time; when he died in 1876 he was mourned as the father of the Czech nation.[23] Celebratory histories of this kind lend themselves to regular rituals of commemoration, when the national self-image can be reinforced in the popular mind. Every year the Serbs mark the anniversary of their epic defeat at the hands of the Turks on the field of Kosovo Polje in 1389, and in so doing reaffirm their identity as a brave but beleaguered people; they continued to do so throughout the crisis in former Yugoslavia.[24] In such instances the untidy reality of history is beside the point. Nation, race and culture are brought together as a unified constant. Other examples span the modern world; from the Nazis in Germany to the ideology of black separatism in the United States. **Essentialism** or 'immemorialism' of this kind produces a powerful sense of exclusive identity, but it makes bad history. Not only is everything in the past that contradicts the required self-image suppressed; the interval between 'then' and 'now' is telescoped by the assertion of an unchanging identity, impervious to the play of historical circumstance.

The process of tradition-making is particularly clear in newly **autonomous** nations, where the need for a legitimizing past is strongly felt and the materials for a national past are often in short supply. Within two generations of the War of Independence, Americans had come to identify with a flattering self-image: in taming the wilderness far away from the corruptions of the old society in Europe, their colonial forebears had developed the values of self-reliance, honesty and liberty that were now the heritage of all Americans: hence the enduring appeal of folk heroes such as Daniel Boone. More recently, many African countries have faced the problem that their boundaries are the artificial outcome of the European partition of the continent in the late nineteenth century. In a few cases, such as Mali and Zimbabwe, descent can be claimed from a much earlier state of the same name. Ghana adopted the name of a medieval trading empire which did not include its present territory at all. Elsewhere in the continent, political leaders have invoked timeless qualities from the precolonial past (like Julius Nyerere's *ujamaa*, or brotherhood) as a charter of identity. To forge a national identity without some such legitimizing past is probably impossible.

But appeals to an unchanging past are not confined to new or repressed nations. Nineteenth-century Britain had a relatively secure sense of nationhood, yet in the work of historians at that time is to be found an unchanging national essence as well as the idea of change over time. William Stubbs, usually regarded as the first professional historian in Britain, believed that the reasons for the growth of the English constitution through the Middle Ages lay 'deep in the very nature of the people'; in this reading parliamentary government became the expression of a national genius for freedom.[25] Essentialist categories come readily to the lips of politicians, particularly at moments of crisis. During the Second World War, Winston Churchill invoked a tradition of dogged resistance to foreign attack stretching back to Pitt the Younger and Elizabeth I. Liberal commentators were uncomfortably

---

essentialism

Relating to the basic nature (the 'essence') of people or nations.

autonomous

State of self-governing independence.

reminded of this vein of **rhetoric** at the time of the Falklands War in 1982. Pondering the lessons of the conflict, Margaret Thatcher declared:

> This generation can match their fathers and grandfathers in ability, in courage and in resolution. We have not changed. When the demands of war and the dangers to our own people call us to arms – then we British are as we have always been – competent, courageous and resolute.[26]

Nationalism of this kind rests on the assertion of tradition, rather than an interpretation of history. It suppresses difference and change in order to uphold identity.

rhetoric
Originally the ancient Greek art of public speaking, but more usually used nowadays to mean points that rely on the persuasive power of words or voice rather than actual argument.

IV

Nostalgia – history as loss

Traditionalism is the crudest distortion of historical awareness, because it does away with the central notion of development over time. Other distortions are more subtle. One that has huge influence is *nostalgia*. Like tradition, nostalgia is backward-looking, but instead of denying the fact of historical change, it interprets it in one direction only – as change for the worse. Nostalgia is most familiar perhaps as generational regret: older people habitually complain that nowadays the young are unruly, or that the country is 'going to the dogs', and the same complaints have been documented over a very long period.[27] But nostalgia works on a broader canvas too. It works most strongly as a reaction to a sense of loss in the recent past, and it is therefore particularly characteristic of societies undergoing rapid change. Anticipation and optimism are never the only – or even the main – social responses to progress. There is nearly always regret or alarm at the passing of old ways and familiar landmarks. A yearning backward glance offers consolation, an escape in the mind from a harsh reality. It is when the past appears to be slipping away before our eyes that we seek to recreate it in the imagination. This was one of the mainsprings of the Romantic movement, and within historicism itself there was a sometimes unduly nostalgic impulse, as scholars reacted against the industrialization and urbanization around them. It is no accident that the Middle Ages, with its close-knit communities and its slow pace of change, came into fashion just as the gathering pace of economic change was enlarging the scale of social life. Ever since the Industrial Revolution, nostalgia has continued to be one of the emotional reflexes of societies experiencing major change. One of its commonest expressions in Britain today is 'heritage'. When the past is conserved or re-enacted for our entertainment, it is usually (though not invariably) presented in its most attractive light. Bygone splendours, such as the medieval tournament or the Elizabethan banquet, naturally lend themselves to the pleasures of spectacle; but everyday life – such as the back-breaking routines of the early industrial craft shop or the Victorian kitchen – is also dressed up in order to be visually appealing. A sense of loss is part of the experience of visiting heritage sites.

The problem with nostalgia is that it is a very lopsided view of history. If the past is redesigned as a comfortable refuge, all its negative features must be removed. The past becomes better and simpler than the present. Thus nineteenth-century medievalism took little account of the brevity and squalor of life, or the power of a malign spirit-world. Present-day nostalgia shows a comparable **myopia**. Even a simulation of the London Blitz will prompt regret at the loss of 'wartime spirit' as much as horror at the effects of aerial bombardment. Champions of 'family values' who posit a golden age in the past (before 1939 or 1914, according to taste) overlook the large number of loveless marriages before divorce was made

myopia
Short-sightedness.

Figure 1.3 The image of the dome of St Paul's Cathedral standing intact through the devastating London Blitz of 1940 became a powerful symbol both of British defiance of Nazi Germany and of a particular approach to the distinctiveness of British history. More recent scholarship questions the extent to which the British people were united in the Blitz, but the popular social 'memory' of the 'Blitz spirit' shows no sign of diminishing. © Getty Images/Hulton Archive.

easier, and the high incidence of family breakup through the loss of a spouse or parent from natural causes. In such cases, as Raphael Samuel put it, the past functions less as history than as allegory:

> It is a testimony to the decline in manners and morals, a mirror to our failings, a measure of absence. ... By a process of selective amnesia the past becomes a historical equivalent of the dream of primal bliss, or of the enchanted space which memory accords to childhood.[28]

This kind of outlook is not only an unreliable guide to the past, but also a basis for pessimism and rigidity in the present. Nostalgia presents the past as an alternative to the present instead of as a prelude to it. It encourages us to hanker after an unattainable golden age instead of engaging creatively with the world as it is. Whereas historical awareness should enhance our insight into the present, nostalgia indulges a desire to escape from it.

V

Dismissing the past: history as progress

At the other end of the scale of historical distortion lies the belief in *progress*. If nostalgia reflects a pessimistic view of the world, progress is an optimistic creed, for it asserts not only that change in the past has been for the better, but that improvement will continue into the future. Like process, progress is about change over time, but with the crucial difference that a positive value is placed on the change, endowing it with moral content. The concept of progress is fundamental to modernity, because for 200 years it was the defining myth of the West, a source of cultural self-assurance and of outright superiority in the West's dealings with the rest of the world. In this sense, progress was essentially the invention of the Enlightenment of the eighteenth century. Hitherto a limit on human development had always been assumed, either on account of the mysterious workings of Divine Providence or because the achievements of classical antiquity were regarded as unsurpassable. The Enlightenment of the eighteenth century placed its faith in the power of human reason to transform the world. Writers such as Voltaire, Hume and Adam Smith regarded history as an unfinished record of material and moral improvement. They sought to reveal the shape of history by tracing the growth of human society from primitive barbarism to civilization and refinement. The confidence of these historians may seem naïve and grandiose today, but for 200 years some such structure has underpinned all varieties of progressive thought, including both liberal democracy and Marxism. As recently as the 1960s, representatives of these two traditions – **J.H. Plumb** and E.H. Carr – wrote widely-read manifestos for history informed

J.H. Plumb (1911–2001)
Sir John H. Plumb, a leading Cambridge historian specializing in the history of eighteenth-century Britain. Plumb was an influential figure, and many of his students went on to become high-profile historians.

by a passionate belief in progress.[29] That kind of faith is much rarer today, in the light of dire predictions of environmental and economic disaster. But few of us are happy to live in a world of nostalgic regret all the time; the yearning for a lost golden age in one sphere is often balanced by the confident disparagement of 'the bad old days' in another.

That dismissal of the past points to the limitations of progress as a view of history. Whereas 'process' is a neutral term without an implicit value judgement, 'progress' is by definition evaluative and partial; since it is premised on the superiority of the present over the past, it inevitably takes on whatever values happen to be prevalent today, with the consequence that the past seems less admirable and more 'primitive' the further back in time we go. Condescension and incomprehension are the result. If the past exists strictly to validate the achievements of the present, there can be no room for an appreciation of its cultural riches. Proponents of progress have never been good at understanding periods remote from their own age. Voltaire, for example, was notoriously unable to recognize any good in the Middle Ages; his historical writings traced the growth of rationality and tolerance and condemned the rest. So if the desire to demonstrate progress is pressed too far, it quickly comes into conflict with the historian's obligation to recreate the past on its own terms. In fact historicism took shape very much as a reaction against the present-minded devaluation of the past that characterized many writers of the Enlightenment. Ranke regarded every age as being 'next to God', by which he meant that it should not be prejudged by modern standards. Interpreting history as an overarching story of progress involves doing just that.

Tradition, nostalgia and progress provide the basic constituents of social memory. Each answers a deep psychological need for security – through seeming to promise no change, or change for the better or an escape into a more congenial past. The real objection to them is that, as a governing stance, they require the past to conform with a deeply felt and often unacknowledged need. They are about belief, not enquiry. They look for a consistent window on the past, and they end up doing scant justice to anything else.

VI

Challenging the conventional version

If social need so easily leads to distorted images of the past, it is hardly surprising that historians have on the whole kept their distance from it. At a practical level the stance of the professional historian towards social memory is not always consistent. Thus **Herbert Butterfield**, who made his name in the 1930s with an attack on present-minded history, wrote an impassioned evocation of the English historical tradition in 1944 which was clearly intended to contribute to wartime morale.[30] Today the newspapers quite often publish articles by leading historians who are tempted by the opportunity to influence popular attitudes towards the past. But the profession as a whole prefers to emphasize how different the purpose and approach of scholarly historical work are. Whereas the starting point for most popular forms of knowledge about the past is the requirements of the present, the starting point of historicism is the aspiration to re-enter or recreate the past.

It follows that one important task of historians is to challenge socially motivated misrepresentations of the past. This activity has been likened to 'the eye surgeon, specializing in removing cataracts'.[31] But whereas patients are only too glad to have their sight corrected, society may be deeply attached to its faulty vision of the past, and historians do not make themselves popular in pointing this out. Many of their findings incur the odium of undermining hallowed pieties – as in the case of historians who question the efficacy of Churchill's wartime leadership, or who attempt a **non-sectarian** approach to the history of Northern Ireland. There is probably no official nationalist history in the world that is proof against the deflating effect of academic enquiry. The same is true of the kind of engaged history that underwrites the conflict between Left and Right. Politically motivated labour history in Britain has tended to emphasize political radicalism and the struggle against capital; yet if it is to provide a realistic historical perspective in which political strategies can be planned, labour history cannot afford to ignore the equally long tradition of working-class Toryism, still very much alive today. When Peter Burke told a conference of socialist historians, 'although I consider myself a socialist and a historian, I'm not a socialist historian', he meant that he wanted to study the real complexity of the historical record, not reduce it to an overdramatized confrontation between Us and Them.[32] The same argument can be made with regard to distortion emanating from the Right. During the mid-1980s, Margaret Thatcher tried to make political capital out of a somewhat self-serving image of nineteenth-century England. When she applauded 'Victorian values', she meant that **untrammelled** individualism and a **rolling back of the state** might once again make Britain great. She omitted to say that the essential pre-condition of the Victorian economic miracle had been Britain's global strategic dominance, and she did not dwell on the appalling social costs in terms of destitution and environmental damage. Historians were quick to point out that her vision was both unrealistic and undesirable.[33]

Herbert Butterfield (1900–79)
Cambridge historian specializing in the eighteenth century. His analysis of *The Whig Interpretation of History* (1931) attacked the tendency of 'Whig' historians to see history in terms of progress, thereby unjustly (and anachronistically) criticizing earlier ages as 'backward'.

non-sectarian
Avoiding allegiance to any particular religious group.

untrammelled
Unhindered.

rolling back of the state
The role of the state grew enormously in twentieth-century Britain, especially after Clement Attlee's post-war Labour government (1945–51) nationalized heavy industry and the health service. The Conservative governments of Margaret Thatcher (1979–90) reversed this policy by returning nationalized industry to private ownership.

The overlap between history and social memory

If this debunking activity would seem to put historians in the opposite camp from the keepers of social memory, it needs to be stressed that the distinction is by no means as hard and fast as I have depicted it up to this point. One strand of opinion (particularly associated with Postmodernism) holds that there is in fact no difference between history and social memory. According to this view, the aspiration to recreate the past is an illusion, and all historical writing bears the indelible impression of the present – indeed tells us more about the present than the past. I will evaluate the merits of this radically subversive position in Chapter 7. Here it is enough to point out that the collapsing of history into social memory appeals to a particular kind of sceptical theorist but commands very little support from historians. However, there are significant areas of overlap. It would be wrong to suppose that accuracy of research is the exclusive property of professional historians. As Raphael Samuel pointed out, there is an army of enthusiastic amateurs in this country, investigating everything from family genealogy to steam locomotives, whose fetish for accuracy is unsurpassed.[34] Academic historians may distance themselves from the distortions of social memory, but many well-established historical specialisms today have their origin in an explicit political need: one thinks of labour history, women's history and African history. It is not always possible to distinguish completely between history and social memory, because historians perform some of the tasks of social memory. Perhaps most important of all, social memory itself is an important topic of historical enquiry. It is central to popular consciousness in all its forms, from democratic politics to social mores and cultural taste, and no comprehensive social history can afford to ignore it; oral history represents in part an attempt to take account of this dimension (see below, Chapter 11). In all these ways history and social memory feed on each other. As Geoffrey Cubitt puts it, 'History and memory are proximate concepts: they inhabit a similar mental territory.'[35]

Yet for all these points of convergence, the distinction that historians like to make between their work and social memory remains important. Whether social memory services a totalitarian regime or the needs of interest groups within a democratic society, its value and its prospects of survival are entirely dependent on its functional effectiveness: the content of the memory will change according to context and priorities. Of course historical scholarship is not immune from calculations of practical utility. Partly this is because we understand more clearly than Ranke did that historians cannot detach themselves completely from their own time. Partly also, as I will argue in the next chapter, the richness of history is positively enhanced by responding to topical agendas. Where most historians will usually part company from the keepers of social memory is in insisting that their findings should be guided by the historicist principles described in this chapter – that historical awareness should prevail over social need. This is a principle that can be defended on its own merits. But it must also be sustained if we are to have any prospect of learning from history, as distinct from finding there the mirror image of our own immediate concerns. To that possibility I now turn.

Further reading

Michael Bentley, *Modern Historiography*, Routledge, 1999.

J.H. Plumb, *The Death of the Past*, Macmillan, 1969.

George G. Iggers and James Powell (eds), *Leopold Ranke and the Shaping of the Historical Discipline*, Syracuse University Press, 1990.

Geoffey Cubitt, *History and Memory*, Manchester University Press, 2007.

Stefan Berger (ed.), *Writing National Histories*, Routledge, 1998.

David Lowenthal, *The Past is a Foreign Country*, Cambridge University Press, 1985.

Raphael Samuel, *Theatres of Memory*, vol. I: *Past and Present in Contemporary Culture*, Verso, 1994.

Sam Wineberg, *Historical Thinking and Other Unnatural Acts: Charting the Future of Teaching the Past*, Temple University Press, 2001.

Notes

1 Rictor Norton, *Mother Clap's Molly House: the Gay Subculture in England, 1700–1830*, Gay Men's Press, 1992.
2 Jan Vansina, *Oral Tradition as History*, James Currey, 1985.
3 James Fentress and Chris Wickham, *Social Memory*, Blackwell, 1992, ch. 5.
4 Malcolm X, *On Afro-American History*, 3rd edn, Pathfinder, 1990, p. 12.
5 Interview with David Montgomery, in MAHRO (the Radical Historians Organization) (ed.), *Visions of History* (Pantheon, 1984), p. 180.
6 *History Workshop Journal*, I, 1976, p. 2 (editorial).
7 Sheila Rowbotham, *Hidden from History*, Pluto Press, 1973.
8 Sheila R. Johansson, '"Herstory" as history: a new field or another fad?', in Berenice A. Carroll (ed.), *Liberating Women's History*, Illinois University Press, 1976, p. 427.
9 L. von Ranke, *Histories of the Latin and German Nations from 1494 to 1514*, extract translated in G.P. Gooch, *History and Historians in the Nineteenth Century*, 2nd edn, Longman, 1952, p. 74.
10 Unfortunately this is the impression conveyed by the most frequently cited translation, 'what actually happened': see Fritz Stern (ed.), *The Varieties of History*, 2nd edn, Macmillan, 1970, p. 57.
11 Thomas Carlyle, quoted in J.R. Hale (ed.), *The Evolution of British Historiography*, Macmillan, 1967, p. 42.
12 E.P. Thompson, *Customs in Common*, Penguin, 1993, ch. 7.
13 V.A.C. Gatrell, *The Hanging Tree: Execution and the English People, 1770–1868*, Oxford University Press, 1994.

14 Quoted in Gareth Stedman Jones, *Outcast London*, Penguin, 1976, p. 258.

15 L.P. Hartley, *The Go-Between*, Penguin, 1958, p. 7.

16 Simon Schama, 'Clio at the Multiplex', *The New Yorker*, 19 January 1998, p. 40.

17 Ludmilla Jordanova, 'Marking time', in Holger Hoock (ed.), *History, Commemoration and National Preoccupation*, Oxford University Press, 2007, p. 7.

18 Penelope J. Corfield, *Time and the Shape of History*, Yale University Press, 2007, pp. 131–49.

19 See, for example, James Sharpe, *Instruments of Darkness: Witchcraft in England, 1550–1750*, Hamish Hamilton, 1996; Jonathan Barry, Marianne Helster and Gareth Roberts (eds), *Witchcraft in Early Modern Europe*, Cambridge University Press, 1996.

20 See, for example, John Gillis, *For Better, For Worse: British Marriages, 1600 to the Present*, Oxford University Press, 1985.

21 Fernand Braudel, 'History and the social sciences: *la longue durée*', in his *On History*, Weidenfeld & Nicolson, 1980, pp. 25–52.

22 E.J. Hobsbawm and T.O. Ranger (eds), *The Invention of Tradition*, Cambridge University Press, 1982.

23 Richard G. Plaschka, 'The political significance of František Palacký', *Journal of Contemporary History*, VIII, 1973, pp. 35–55.

24 Noel Malcolm, *Kosovo: A Short History*, Macmillan, 1998.

25 William Stubbs, quoted in Christopher Parker, *The English Historical Tradition since 1850*, Donald, 1990, pp. 42–3.

26 Margaret Thatcher, speech in Cheltenham, 3 July 1982, reprinted in Anthony Barnett, *Iron Britannia*, Allison & Busby, 1982.

27 Geoffrey Pearson, *Hooligan: A History of Respectable Fears*, Macmillan, 1983.

28 Raphael Samuel, *Theatres of Memory*, vol. II: *Island Stories: Unravelling Britain*, Verso, 1998, pp. 337–8.

29 J.H. Plumb, *The Death of the Past*, Macmillan, 1969; E.H. Carr, *What Is History?*, Macmillan, 1961.

30 H. Butterfield, *The Englishman and His History*, Cambridge University Press, 1944.

31 Theodore Zeldin, 'After Braudel', *The Listener*, 5 November 1981, p. 542.

32 Peter Burke, 'People's history or total history', in Raphael Samuel (ed.), *People's History and Socialist Theory*, Routledge & Kegan Paul, 1981, p. 8.

33 Eric M. Sigsworth (ed.), *In Search of Victorian Values*, Manchester University Press, 1988; T.C. Smout (ed.), *Victorian Values*, British Academy, 1992.

34 Raphael Samuel, 'Unofficial knowledge', in his *Theatres of Memory*, vol. I: *Past and Present in Contemporary Culture*, Verso, 1994, pp. 3–39.

35 Geoffrey Cubitt, *History and Memory*, Manchester University Press, 2007, p. 4.

2 The uses of history

*This chapter looks at some of the different ways in which histor-
ians have tried to explain the purpose of their work. Some see
history as a study in itself which needs no wider justification;
others see it in terms of the inexorable march across time of great
forces, human or even divine, which explain both how we got to
where we are and where we might be heading; others deny that
history has any lessons for us at all. Historians explain the past in
response to present-day concerns and questions. History can certainly allow us to experience situations and face alternatives that
we would not otherwise encounter, and in that sense it serves a
useful purpose; it can also reveal that aspects of modern life are
not as old, or as new, as we have assumed. But how can we learn
any useful lessons from history – especially for the future – when
so much depends on the details of the historical context? And if
history does not repeat itself, what sort of a guide can it provide
for the present?*

None of the issues discussed in this book has drawn a greater
variety of answers than the question 'what can we learn from
history?' The answers have ranged from Henry Ford's celebrated
aphorism 'history is bunk' to the belief that history holds the clue
to human destiny. The fact that historians themselves give very
different responses suggests that this is an open-ended question
which cannot be reduced to a tidy solution. But anyone proposing
to spend several years – and in some cases a lifetime – studying
the subject must reflect on what purpose it serves. And one
cannot get very far in understanding how historians set about
their work, or in evaluating its outcome, without first considering
the rationale of historical enquiry.

I

Metahistory – history as long-term development

At one extreme lies the proposition that history tells us most of
what we need to know about the future. Our destiny is disclosed

trajectory
The line of an object in flight. It can be applied, as here, to a perceived 'path' of a theme traced over a long period of time.

Divine Providence
The idea of a benevolent God who watches over and protects people on earth.

Last Judgement
In Christian, especially Catholic, theology the Last Judgement is the moment at the end of time when all humans come before God for judgement of their lives on earth, some being allowed to enter heaven, others being condemned for eternity to hell. It was a common theme in medieval art and is dramatically presented in Michelangelo's frescos in the Sistine Chapel in the Vatican.

Enlightenment belief in moral progress
The eighteenth-century Enlightenment believed that the exercise of human reason would liberate people from the mental and political oppression of organized religion and superstition. By aiming for greater human liberty and happiness, reason was thereby equated with moral progress.

totalitarianism
Dictatorship, associated particularly with European regimes of the 1920s and 1930s, which stressed the all-encompassing role of the state.

in the grand **trajectory** of human history, which reveals the world today as it really is, and the future course of events. This belief requires a highly schematic interpretation of the course of human development, usually known as *metahistory*. A spiritual version of it predominated in Western culture until the seventeenth century. Medieval thinkers believed that history represented the inexorable unfolding of **Divine Providence**, from the Creation through the redeeming life of Christ to the **Last Judgement**: the contemplation of the past revealed something of God's purposes and concentrated the mind on the reckoning to come. This view became less tenable with the gradual secularization of European culture from the eighteenth century onwards. New forms of metahistory developed, which attributed the forward dynamic of history to human rather than divine action. The **Enlightenment belief in moral progress** was of this kind. But the most influential metahistory of modern times has been Marxism. The driving force of history became the struggle by human societies to meet their material needs (which is why the Marxist theory is known as 'historical materialism'). Marx interpreted human history as a progression from lower to higher forms of production; the highest form was currently industrial capitalism, but this was destined to give way to socialism, at which point human needs would be satisfied abundantly and equitably (see Chapter 8). Since the fall of international communism, belief in historical materialism has sharply declined, but metahistorical thinking continues to hold an appeal: Marxism has been turned on its head by certain free-market theorists, for whom the 1990s signalled the global triumph of liberal democracy, or 'the end of history'.[1]

The rejection of history

At the other extreme is the view that *nothing* can be learned from history: not that history is beyond our reach, but that it offers no guidance. This rejection of history takes two forms. The first is essentially a defence against **totalitarianism**. For many intellectuals during the Cold War, the practical consequences of invoking the past to legitimize communist ideology had been so appalling that any idea that history might hold clues for the present became completely discredited; some historians recoiled so far from any idea of pattern or meaning that they refused to find in history anything more than accident, blunder and contingency.[2]

The second basis for rejecting history is a commitment to modernity: if one is committed to the new, why bother with the past? This point of view has a much longer pedigree. The equation of modernity with a rejection of the past was first put into effect during the French Revolution of 1789–93. The revolutionaries executed the king, abolished the aristocracy, attacked religion and declared 22 September 1792 the beginning of Year 1. All this was done in the name of reason, untrammelled by precedent or tradition. The early twentieth century was another high point in the **modernist** rejection of history. In **avant-garde** thinking, human creativity was seen as opposed to the achievements of the past, rather than growing out of them; ignorance of history liberated the imagination. During the inter-war period these ideas became the dominant strand in the arts, under the banner of 'modernism'. Fascism and Nazism adapted this language to the political sphere. They reacted to the catastrophe of the First World War and the **alarming instability of the world economy** by claiming the virtue of a complete break with the past. They lambasted the corruption of the old society and demanded the conscious creation of a 'new man' and a 'new order'.[3] Today, **root-and-branch** totalitarianism is completely discredited. But 'modernism' retains some of its allure. It validates a technocratic approach to politics and society and underwrites the fascination with the new in the arts.

Neither metahistory nor the total rejection of history commands much support among practitioners of history. Metahistory may cast the historian in the gratifying role of prophet, but at the cost of denying, or drastically curtailing, the play of human agency in history. Marxism has had great influence on the writing of history over the past fifty years, but as a theory of socio-economic change rather than as the key to human destiny. Ultimately the choice between free will and determinism is a philosophical one. There are many intermediate positions. If most historians would tip the balance in favour of free will, this is because determinism sits uncomfortably with the contingencies and rough edges that loom so large in the historical record. Metahistory involves holding on to one big conviction at the expense of many less ambitious insights. It is an outlook profoundly at odds with the experience of historical research.

Historians are no happier to have their findings dismissed as a complete irrelevance. The rejection of history would obviously limit its study to a self-indulgent **antiquarian** pursuit. In fact, the claims for historical awareness have for 200 years been asserted in a continuing **dialectic** with the modernist rejection of history. Historicism itself was to a considerable extent a reaction against the French Revolution. To conservatives such as Ranke, the political excesses in France were a terrifying instance of what happens when radicals turn their backs on the past; to apply first principles without respect for inherited institutions was a threat to the very fabric of the social order. As the Revolution went off course, many of the radicals acquired a new respect for history too. Those who still believed in freedom and democracy came to realize that humans were not so free from the hand of the past as the revolutionaries had supposed, and that progressive change must be built on the cumulative achievements of earlier generations.

modernists
In this context, those whose concerns are concentrated on the modern day to the exclusion of any consideration of the past.

avant-garde
(French) The troops at the front who spearhead an army's advance into battle. The term was applied to radical and pioneering artistic movements in the early twentieth century and has since come to denote any new or radical ideas.

alarming instability of the world economy
The international economic slump of the 1930s that followed on from the New York Stock Exchange crash of October 1929.

root-and-branch
Thorough-going. The term derives from a seventeenth-century religious group who wanted a comprehensive reform of the Church of England.

antiquarian
Interest in historical details and artefacts without reference to their wider context or significance.

dialectic
The conflict of one idea (the thesis) and another diametrically opposed to it (the antithesis). The resulting amalgamation of the two is known as the synthesis.

Only a visionary would accept the full implications of meta-history; only an antiquarian would be content to surrender all claim to practical utility. The most convincing claims of history to offer relevant insights lie somewhere between these two extremes. And they hinge on taking seriously the principles of historical awareness established by the nineteenth-century founders of the discipline. The historicists have become a by-word for disinterested historical enquiry without practical application, but this is not an accurate picture of their position. They did not disclaim all claims to practical relevance, but merely insisted that the faithful representation of the past must come first. In fact the three principles of difference, context and process (discussed in the previous chapter) point to the specific ways in which the scholarly study of history can yield useful knowledge. The end result is not a master key or an overall schema, but rather an accumulation of specific practical insights consistent with a sense of historical awareness.

II

The uses of history – an inventory of alternatives

Historical *difference* lies at the heart of the discipline's claim to be socially relevant. As a memory-bank of what is unfamiliar or alien, history constitutes our most important cultural resource. It offers a means – imperfect but indispensable – of entering into the kind of experience that is simply not possible in our own lives. Our sense of the heights to which human beings can attain, and the depths to which they may sink, the resourcefulness they may show in a crisis, the sensitivity they can show in responding to each other's needs – all these are nourished by knowing what has been thought and done in the very different contexts of the past. Art historians have long been familiar with the idea that the creative achievements of the past are an inventory of assets whose value may be realized by later generations – witness the way that Western art has repeatedly reinvented and rejected the **classical tradition** of Greece and Rome. But creative energy can be drawn from the past in many other fields. History reminds us that there is usually more than one way of interpreting a predicament or responding to a situation, and that the choices open to us are often more varied than we might have supposed. Theodore Zeldin has written a magpie's feast of a book, called *An Intimate History of Humanity* (1994), ranging over such subjects as loneliness, cooking, conversation and travel. His aim is not to lay bare a pattern, still less to predict or prescribe, but to open our eyes to the range of options that past experience places at our disposal. Most historians probably have serious misgivings about a fragmented exposition such as Zeldin's, which lacks any topographical or chronological coherence. But his rationale is not unusual. Natalie Zemon Davis – a leading

classical tradition
'Classical' refers to the ancient world of Greece and Rome. Their ideas and philosophy were often revived by later ages, notably during the fifteenth- and sixteenth-century Renaissance and again in the eighteenth century.

cultural historian of early modern Europe – has said, 'I let [the past] speak and I show that things don't have to be the way they are now. ... I want to show that it could be different, that it was different, and that there are alternatives.'[4] As the process of historical change unfolds, old arguments or programmes may once more become relevant. This has been a persistent theme in the work of the foremost historian of the English Revolution, Christopher Hill:

> Since capitalism, the **Protestant ethic, Newtonian physics,** so long taken for granted by our civilization, are now at last coming under general and widespread criticism, it is worth going back to consider seriously and afresh the arguments of those who opposed them before they had won universal acceptance.[5]

The point is not to find a precedent but to be alert to possibilities. History is an inventory of alternatives, all the richer if research is not conducted with half an eye to our immediate situation in the present.

Lessons from the familiar

Of course not all the past is exotic. In practice our reaction to a particular moment in the past is likely to be a mixture of estrangement and familiarity. Alongside features that have changed out of all recognition, we may encounter patterns of thinking or behaviour that are immediately accessible to us. The juxtaposition of these two is an important aspect of historical perspective, and it is often the point at which the more thoughtful professional scholar engages most directly with the claims of social relevance. Peter Laslett's path-breaking work on the history of the English family offers a striking instance. Since the 1960s – beginning with *The World We Have Lost* (1965) – he has written a succession of books about the nature of early modern English society. He emphasizes two general conclusions. First, the residential extended family, which we fondly believe existed in the pre-modern world, is a figment of our nostalgic imagination: our forebears lived in nuclear households seldom spanning more than two generations. Second, the care of the elderly was not notably more family-based than it is today, but the scale of the problem was vastly different – indeed old age was not regarded as a problem at all because few people survived for very long after their productive life was over. Our view of the nuclear family is changed when we recognize that it was not a response to industrialization but was rooted in much earlier English practice. On the other hand, policy towards the old will get nowhere if it is guided by past models: 'Our situation remains irreducibly novel', writes Laslett; 'it calls for invention rather than imitation'.[6] He does not trace the evolution of family forms over time – the eighteenth and nineteenth centuries are missed out

Protestant ethic
Also known as the Protestant work ethic. First analysed in detail by Max Weber in *The Protestant Ethic and the Spirit of Capitalism* (1905), this held that Protestant theology, with its stress upon an individual relationship with God (as opposed to the Catholic stress on the collective community of the Church), was uniquely well suited to the development of an independent, self-reliant approach to work.

Newtonian physics
The understanding of the operation of the natural world developed by Sir Isaac Newton (1642–1727). Newton's theories were unchallenged until the writings of Albert Einstein (1879–1955).

entirely. His point is rather that the first step to understanding is comparison *across* time, which throws into relief what is transient and what is enduring about our present circumstances.

The ability to distinguish between the enduring and the transient is vital to any realistic programme of social action in the present. Consider, for example, another aspect of the history of old people – state provision in the form of a pension. Historical perspective is usually limited to the establishment of the Welfare State after the Second World War, with perhaps a backward glance to the introduction of old age pensions by Lloyd George in 1908. But these antecedents do not explain why the level of the pension has consistently been fixed at below subsistence level. Here, as Pat Thane explains, the relevant past is the nineteenth-century Poor Law administration, accountable to local rate-payers and concerned to allocate the barest minimum to every category of claimant.[7] History here is not being quarried for 'meaning' to validate particular values but is treated as an instrument for maximizing our control over our present situation. To be free is not to enjoy total freedom of action – that is a Utopian dream – but to know how far one's action and thought are conditioned by the heritage of the past. This may sound like a prescription for conservatism. But what it offers is a realistic foundation for radical initiatives. We need to know when we are pushing against an open door and when we are beating our heads against a brick wall. Grasping what one historian has called 'the distinction between what is necessary and what is the product merely of our own contingent arrangements' offers important practical dividends.[8]

Idi Amin (1925–2003)
General Amin seized power in Uganda in 1971 in a military coup. He proved a brutal dictator and massacred large numbers of his own people. He expelled Uganda's entire Asian population and was finally overthrown by a military invasion by neighbouring Tanzania in 1979.

Pol Pot (1925–98)
Communist leader of Cambodia 1975–9. He instituted a reign of terror in which the entire urban population was forced into the countryside and some two million people were massacred. He was overthrown by an invasion from neighbouring Vietnam.

Facing up to pain: history as therapy

The concept of historical difference has one other rather surprising application – as a means of grappling with aspects of the very recent past that we might prefer to forget. It is a measure of the almost incredible extremes of human behaviour over the past century that a real effort of the imagination is now needed to understand what happened under the Third Reich or in the Soviet Union under Stalin (more recent instances include **Idi Amin's** Uganda and **Pol Pot's** Cambodia). In cases such as these, the gulf between present and past is, as it were, compressed into a single life-span. Those who lived through these experiences of mass death, incarceration and forced removal suffer from a collective trauma. The line of least resistance may be to leave the past alone, and in the Soviet Union 'forgetting' was the official line for most of the period between the death of Stalin and the collapse of communism. Individuals did not forget, but there was no way in which their pain could be shared or publicly marked. A nation that cannot face up to its past will be gravely handicapped in the future. This understanding was central to the policy of *glasnost* ('openness') proclaimed by **Mikhail Gorbachev** in the late 1980s. He realized how crippling the psychological burden of the past was as long as it remained buried. After some initial hesitation, he opened up the archives to historians and allowed the Soviet people to acknowledge publicly the terrible sufferings of the Stalin era. Whatever else happens in Russia in the future, that collective owning of the past cannot be undone. James Joll saw this kind of painful engagement with the recent past in therapeutic terms:

> Just as the psychoanalyst helps us to face the world by showing us how to face the truth about our own motives and our own personal past, so the contemporary historian helps us to face the present and the future by enabling us to understand the forces, however shocking, which have made our world and our society what it is.[9]

Historical difference provides an indispensable perspective on the present, whether as an inventory of experience, as evidence of the transience of our own time or as a reminder of the deeply alien elements in our recent past.

III

Understanding behaviour in its context

The practical applications of historical *context* are much less likely to make the headlines, but they are no less important. As explained in Chapter 1, the discipline of context springs from the historian's conviction that a sense of the whole must always inform our understanding of the parts. Even when historians write about specialized topics in economic or intellectual history, they should respect this principle, and they open themselves to major criticism if they fail to do so. The same principle informs the practice of **social anthropology**, where fieldwork is concerned as much with the entire social structure or cultural system as with particular rituals or beliefs. The problem both history and anthropology face is how to interpret behaviour that may be founded on quite different premises from our own. It would, for example, be a great mistake to suppose that commercial transactions in thirteenth-century England – or twentieth-century Polynesia – were guided solely by what we define as economic rationality; looking at these societies as wholes will give us a grasp of how trade and exchange were informed by religion, social morality and social hierarchy (to specify only the most likely dimensions). The reason why this mode of thinking has contemporary application

Mikhail Gorbachev (1931–)
Soviet leader 1985–91. Gorbachev instituted the policy of *glasnost* (openness) in discussing the failures of the Soviet system, and of fundamental reconstruction (*perestroika*) of Soviet society. This precipitated the collapse of the Soviet Union, and Gorbachev resigned in the aftermath of an attempted coup in 1991.

social anthropology
Academic discipline that analyses small-scale societies by the techniques of participant observation.

is not, of course, that our own society is alien or 'different'. Rather, the problem today is the baffling complexity of society, which leads us to place exaggerated faith in specialist expertise, without proper regard to the wider picture. E.J. Hobsbawm deplores how modern policy-making and planning are in thrall to 'a model of scientism and technical manipulation'.[10] This is more than prejudice born of a demarcation dispute between arts and sciences (Hobsbawm himself has always been respectful of science and technology). The argument here is that the technical approach to social and political problems compartmentalizes human experience into boxes marked 'economics', 'social policy' and so on, each with its own technical lore, whereas what is really required is an openness to the way in which human experience constantly breaks out of these categories.

The lateral links between different aspects of society are much easier to discern with the benefit of hindsight. In our own time it is clearly harder to spot the connections, given our lack of detachment and our lack of hindsight. But at the very least, a historical training should encourage a less blinkered approach to current problems. The **Gulf War** in 1991 illustrates this point – if in a regrettably negative way. The history of Western imperialism has been the subject of some highly sophisticated analysis over the past forty years. Historians do not see the process of European expansion merely as an expression of maritime flair and technical superiority. They link it to economic structures, patterns of consumption and international relations – and increasingly to codes of masculinity and constructions of racial difference as well. All too little of this kind of contextualization was applied by the media to the escalation of conflict in the Gulf. For most commentators it was hardly seen outside the frame of international law and the politics of oil. Historians can claim with some justice to be specialists in lateral thinking, and this has underpinned their traditional claim to train graduates for management and the civil service, where the ability to think beyond the boundaries of particular technical perspectives is at a premium. A similar case can be made in relation to the education of the participating citizen, who inevitably approaches most public issues as a non-specialist.[11]

Gulf War
In 1990 President Saddam Hussein of Iraq invaded and annexed the small oil-rich kingdom of Kuwait. The invasion was condemned by the United Nations, and the Iraqis were forced out of Kuwait the following year by a counter-invasion by a broad international coalition led by the United States.

Does history repeat itself?

Context is also the principle that historians invoke against the common, but mistaken, belief that history repeats itself. Human beings strive to learn from their mistakes and successes in their collective life just as they do in everyday individual experience. Historical biography is said to feature prominently in the leisure reading of British politicians. Indeed a few of them have written distinguished works of this kind – **Winston Churchill** and **Roy Jenkins**, for example.[12] That politicians have a lively interest in the historical context in which posterity will judge their own standing is only part of the explanation. The real reason for their study of history is that politicians expect to find a guide to their conduct – in the form not of moral example but of practical lessons in public affairs. This approach to history has a long pedigree. It was particularly pronounced during the Renaissance, when the record of classical antiquity was treated as a storehouse of moral example and practical lessons in statecraft. **Machiavelli**'s prescriptions for his native Florence and his famous political maxims in *The Prince* (1513) were both based on Roman precedent. He was justly rebuked by his younger contemporary, the historian Francesco Guicciardini:

> How wrong it is to cite the Romans at every turn. For any comparison to be valid, it would be necessary to have a city with conditions like theirs, and then to govern it according to their example. In the case of a city with different qualities, the comparison is as much out of order as it would be to expect a jackass to race like a horse.[13]

Guicciardini put his finger on the principal objection to the citing of precedent, that it usually shows scant regard for historical context. For the precedent to be valid, the same conditions would have to prevail, but the effect of the passage of time is that what looks like an old problem or a familiar opportunity requires a different analysis because the attendant circumstances have changed. The gulf that separates us from all previous ages renders the citing of precedents from the distant past a fruitless enterprise.

Only in the case of the recent past have historians seriously attempted to draw on historical analogies, on the grounds that much of the context may remain essentially the same over a short period and that the changes which have occurred are comparatively well documented. During the later stages of the Cold War there was something of a vogue for 'applied' history of this kind.[14] But even here the task is a daunting one. Consider the case of the arms race. The decade before the Second World War is commonly regarded as an object lesson in the dangers of military weakness and of appeasing an aggressive power. But one could equally cite the precedent of the First World War, one of whose causes was the relentless escalation in armaments from the 1890s onwards. Which precedent is valid? The answer must be: neither as it stands. Even within the time-span of a hundred years, history does not repeat itself. No one historical situation has been, or ever can be, repeated in every particular. If an event or tendency recurs, as the arms race has done, it is as a result of a unique combination of circumstances, and the strategies we adopt must have regard primarily to those circumstances.[15] The key historicist notion of the 'otherness'

Winston Churchill (1874–1965)
As well as his multi-volume histories of the two World Wars, Churchill also wrote a detailed biography of his famous ancestor, John Churchill, Duke of Marlborough.

Roy Jenkins (1920–2003)
Served as Home Secretary and Chancellor of the Exchequer under the Labour Prime Ministers Wilson and Callaghan, as President of the European Commission, and was one of the founders of the short-lived Social Democratic Party (SDP). He also found time to write critically acclaimed biographies of Gladstone and Churchill.

Machiavelli (1469–1527)
Niccolò Machiavelli, Florentine statesman and philosopher. When Florence overthrew the ruling Medici dynasty and declared itself a republic in 1493, Machiavelli served the new regime, but he was arrested and tortured when the Medici returned. Machiavelli is best known for his book of advice for rulers, *The Prince*, which suggests that the most successful rulers should know how to deceive and dissemble. It earned him a quite unjust reputation as a promoter of unprincipled tyranny.

of the past is not suspended merely because we stand at only two or three generations' distance from our object of study. As Hobsbawm reminded us, the atmosphere of the 1930s (through which he lived) was utterly different from today's, which makes any comparison between the original Nazis and their imitators today pretty point-less.[16] At the same time, the drawing of historical analogies, often half consciously, is a habitual and unavoidable part of human reasoning to which people in public life are especially prone. It is not necessarily futile, provided we do not look for a perfect fit between past and present, or treat precedent as grounds for closing critical debate about the options available now.

The truth that history never repeats itself also limits the con-fidence with which historians can predict. However probable it may seem that a recurrence of this or that factor will result in a familiar outcome, the constant process of historical change means that the future will always be partly shaped by additional factors that we cannot predict and whose bearing on the problem in hand no one could have suspected. Moreover, when people do perceive their situation as 'history repeating itself', their actions will be affected by their knowledge of what happened the first time. As E.H. Carr pointed out, historical precedent gives us some insight into what kind of conditions make for a revolution, but whether and when the revolution breaks out in a specific instance will depend on 'the occurrence of unique events, which cannot themselves be pre-dicted'.[17] The dismal record of well-informed intelligent people

Figure 2.1 South Africa's Truth and Reconciliation Commission provided a forum where those who had committed crimes in the name of apartheid could admit openly what they had done and receive forgiveness from their victims. This process of facing up to a painful recent past proved helpful in allowing South Africans to work together to face the future.
© Topfoto/Image Works.

who have made false predictions, or have failed to predict what with hindsight seems obvious, does however suggest one lesson of history: that control of the future is an illusion, and that living with uncertainty is part of the human condition.

IV

The way ahead: history and sequential prediction

Process – the third principle of historicism – is more productive of insights into the present day. Identifying a process does not mean that we agree with it, or believe that it made for a better world. But it may help to explain our world. Situating ourselves in a trajectory that is still unfolding gives us some purchase on the future and allows a measure of forward planning. In fact, this mode of historical thinking is deeply rooted in our political culture. As voters and citizens, almost instinctively, we interpret the world around us in terms of historical process. Much of the time our assumptions are not grounded in historical reality; they may amount to little more than wishful thinking projected backwards. But if conclusions about historical process are based on careful research, they can yield modest but useful predictions. We might call these *sequential* predictions, in order to distinguish them from the discredited *repetitive* or *recurrent* variety. These prevailing beliefs about historical process need to be brought into the light of day, tested against the historical record, and if necessary replaced by a more accurate perspective.

One prediction based on historical process which has stood the test of time concerns the political destiny of South Africa. During the 1960s, when most colonies in tropical Africa were securing their political independence, it was widely assumed that majority rule would shortly come about in South Africa too. Despite the weight of white oppression, mass nationalism was visibly the outcome of a process that dated back to the foundation of the **African National Congress** in 1912, and that had been marked by a growing sophistication in both political discourse and techniques of mass mobilization. Moreover, the South African case could be seen as part of a worldwide phenomenon of anti-colonial nationalism which had been building up since the late nineteenth century. In that sense history might be said to be 'on the side' of African nationalism in South Africa. What could not be predicted was the form of the succeeding political order, and the manner in which it would be achieved, whether by revolution from below or by devolution from above: those were matters of detail which only the future could divulge. But the direction in which the historical process was unfolding in South Africa seemed clear. The time-scale turned out to be more extended than had been supposed – thus demonstrating the crab-like way in which a

African National Congress
The black South African political party, founded in 1912, which led resistance to apartheid.

historical process may unfold – but the general prediction was accurate enough.[18]

Sometimes identifying the valid and appropriate historical process is complicated by the presence of more than one possible trajectory. Take the current debate about the 'breakdown' of the family. Processual thinking is certainly very evident in the way the media handle this issue. The relevant process is generally seen to be the decline of personal morality, aided and abetted by misguided legislation, beginning with the **Matrimonial Causes Act** of 1857, which set in train the liberalization of divorce.[19] Historians, on the other hand, bring into play a much more fundamental and long-term process, namely the changing role of the home in production. Some 250 years ago, most work was done in or adjacent to the home. In selecting a mate, prospective spouses were influenced as much by the home-making and bread-winning skills of their partners as by their personal attractions; the ending of a marriage through separation or desertion meant the end of a productive unit, and for this reason most marriages endured until death. The Industrial Revolution changed all this: the growth of the factory (and other large firms) meant that most production no longer took place in a domestic setting, and control over domestic dependants ceased to be economically central. Now that personal fulfilment is by far the most compelling rationale of marriage, there is far less reason for people to stay in family relationships that no longer bring them happiness. The decline of the productive household, rather than a collapse of individual morality, would seem to be the critical historical process involved here; and given that the separation of work from home shows little sign of being reversed, it is a reasonable prediction that our society will continue to experience a comparatively high rate of marital breakdown.[20]

Matrimonial Causes Act

This act of 1857 enabled couples to seek divorce through the newly created divorce courts. Previously, it had only been obtainable through a specially passed Act of Parliament.

Union of Scotland and England

The Act of Union between England and Scotland was passed by both countries' Parliaments in 1707. Although there were economic advantages to both sides, the English wanted it primarily to prevent the Catholic pretender, Prince James Edward Stuart, becoming king of Scotland. The act only passed through the Scottish Parliament with the help of wholesale bribery.

Questioning assumptions

However, the most important role of processual thinking is in offering an alternative to the assumptions of permanence and timelessness that underpin so many social identities. As we saw in the last chapter, nations tend to imagine themselves as unchanged by the vicissitudes of time. The fallacy of essentialism does not hold up well against historical research. 'British', for example, was in the eighteenth century a newly minted category to take account of the recent **Union of Scotland and England**, and it was built on the exclusion of Roman Catholics and the French. At the beginning of the twenty-first century, the cultural meaning of Britishness is probably less certain than it has ever been, while the British state seems set for disintegration as Scotland edges closer to independence.[21] In the same way, any notion of what it means to be German has to come to terms not only with the multitude of states under which most Germans lived until the mid-nineteenth century but also with the political calculations that led to the exclusion of many German-speaking lands (notably Austria) from the German Empire in 1871. A historical perspective requires us to abandon the idea that nations are organic; it is nearer the truth to regard them, in the words of an influential text, as 'imagined communities'.[22]

The term 'race' raises similar problems. In its modern form, 'race' was originally developed as a category that justified the growing ascendancy of the West over other peoples. It treated as fixed and biologically-determined what is socially constructed, and it has been most strongly developed as a means of reinforcing political and economic control over subordinate groups (as in colonial Africa and Nazi Germany). The way in which an earlier generation of historians wrote about Western global expansion strongly implied that the 'native' peoples at the receiving end were inferior both in their indigenous culture and in their capacity to assimilate Western techniques; and these negative stereotypes served in turn to sustain a flattering self-image of the British – or French or German – 'race'. More recently, minorities with a strong ethnic identity have constructed what might be called a 'reverse discourse'; they too embrace the concept of 'race', because the term brings biological descent and culture together in a powerful amalgam that maximizes group cohesion and emphasizes distance from other groups. Among blacks in America and Britain there is today rising support for Afrocentrism – the belief in an absolute sense of ethnic difference and in the transmission of an authentic cultural tradition from Africa to blacks of the modern **diaspora**. A stress on common ancestry and a downplaying of outside influences lead to a kind of 'cultural insiderism'. The appropriate response is to point out that no nation has ever been ethnically **homogeneous** and to stress the formative experience of slavery and other forms of cultural contact between black and white in Europe and the New World. The purpose of historical work is not to undermine black identity but to anchor it in a real past instead of a mythical construction. The outcome is likely to bear a rather closer relation to the circumstances in which black and white people live today. The formation of racial and national identities is never a once-and-for-all event, but a continuous and contingent process.[23]

diaspora
The dispersal of a
people over a wide area.

homogeneous
All of the same sort.

Challenging notions of 'natural'

What is true of the nation applies still more to the 'natural'. When unwelcome changes in our social arrangements are afoot, we often express our attachment to what is being replaced by asserting that it has always been there – that what is changing is not one particular phase with a limited time-span but something

entrepreneurial widow
We now know that
many widows in
seventeenth- and
eighteenth-century
England ran their own
businesses, and that it
was by no means
unusual for women to
assume positions of
influence that historians
had long assumed were
reserved for men.

abolition of slavery
The campaign for the
abolition first of the
transatlantic slave
trade, then of slavery
itself, and later of the
internal African slave
trade, constituted one
of the most important
and influential lobbying
movements of the
nineteenth century.
Church groups and
women played a
prominent role in the
process on both sides
of the Atlantic.

traditional, or fundamental, or 'natural'. This is especially true of gender. The 'traditional' role of women looks less and less tenable when we read about the **entrepreneurial widow** of seventeenth-century England, or the groundswell of women's organizations that worked for the **abolition of slavery** in the nineteenth century, well ahead of the agitation for women's suffrage.[24] The new history of men and masculinity is equally unsettling of received truths. Traditional fatherhood is often thought to have combined an emotionally hands-off approach with a distinctly hands-on approach to family discipline. That is usually what is meant by 'Victorian' fatherhood. But insofar as the Victorians kept their distance from their children and meted out harsh punishments to them, this was a reaction *against* the past, rather than the climax of a long tradition. The celebrated political journalist William Cobbett recalled that his time as a young father was spent 'between the pen and the baby'; he remembered how he had fed and put his babies to sleep 'hundreds of times, though there were servants to whom the task might have been transferred'.[25] Cobbett was writing in 1830, just when the tide was beginning to turn against the close paternal involvement with young children that had been so common when he was a young man thirty years before. It makes a difference now to know that a fully engaged fatherhood today is not some Utopian fantasy but a pattern that has existed within English culture in the comparatively recent past. In fact, codes of fatherhood have been in continuous flux throughout the past 200 years, and probably for longer.[26] One of the most salutary influences on the practice of history in recent years has been the French historian and philosopher Michel Foucault. His cardinal principle was that no aspect of human culture is God-given or lies outside history, and in his historical work he plotted some of the major shifts that have occurred in the human experience of sexuality, sickness and insanity. In selecting major themes of this kind in pursuit of what he called 'an archaeology of the present', Foucault achieved an influence that extended far beyond academia.[27]

V

History for its own sake?

Granted, then, that history has a varied and significant practical relevance, the question remains whether this should influence the way in which historians set about their work. Prior to the Rankean revolution, this question could hardly have arisen. Historians believed what their audience assumed, that a historical education offered a training for citizens and statesmen alike. They took it for granted that history furnished the basis for a rational analysis of politics; indeed, many of the best historians, from Guicciardini in the sixteenth century to **Macaulay** in the nineteenth, were active in public life. All this was changed by the professionalization of history. By the late nineteenth century the subject featured prominently in the university curriculum all over Europe, controlled by a new breed of historians whose careers were largely confined to academic life. Their subject's traditional claim to offer practical guidance seemed irrelevant – almost an embarrassment. They adhered strictly to the central tenet of historicism, that history should be studied for its own sake, without paying much attention to the practical benefits that could accrue from this approach. This attitude has been very influential with the historical profession in Britain. A generation of conservative historians was inspired by the philosopher Michael Oakeshott, who deplored what he called the 'practical attitude to the past'; he regarded it as 'the chief undefeated enemy of "history"'.[28] G.R. Elton was an outspoken champion of the prevailing orthodoxy:

> Teachers of history must set their faces against the necessarily ignorant demands of 'society' ... for immediate applicability. They need to recall that the 'usefulness' of historical studies lies hardly at all in the knowledge they purvey and in the understanding of specific present problems from their prehistory; it lies much more in the fact that they produce standards of judgement and powers of reasoning which they alone develop, which arise from their very essence and which are unusually clear-headed, balanced and compassionate.[29]

Apart from providing an intellectual training, the study of history is represented as a personal pursuit which at most enables the individual to achieve some self-awareness by stepping outside his or her immediate experience; in the austere formulation of V.H. Galbraith, 'the study of history is a personal matter, in which the activity is generally more valuable than the result'.[30] Neither of these justifications is peculiar to history: training the mind is part of all academic disciplines worth the name, while the claim to enlarge the individual's experience can be argued with equal, if not greater, conviction by teachers of literature.

It should be noted that there was a political context to this fastidious recoil from 'relevance'. Both Elton and Galbraith had in mind the excesses of propaganda to which relevant history had led under the regimes of Hitler and Stalin (Elton was a refugee from Nazi Germany): Nazi and Soviet historians were state employees, expected to repeat crude party dogma about the past. In Europe, totalitarian excesses on that scale are a thing of the past, but in many countries historical scholarship is still vulnerable to political pressure, especially of a nationalist kind. Against that background, scholarly detachment can seem virtuous. As Peter Mandler has suggested, 'historians shy away from considering the uses of their discipline for fear of stirring up dying chauvinist embers'.[31]

Macaulay (1800–59)
Thomas Babington Macaulay, British historian, poet and administrator. As well as writing a bestselling *History of England*, Macaulay served on the Council of the Governor-General of India, as MP for Edinburgh, and as Secretary at War in the government of Lord Melbourne.

One positive result of 'history for its own sake' is a whole-hearted commitment to the recreation or resurrection of the past in every material and mental dimension. There are historians for whom a fascination with the past as it was really lived and experienced overrides all other considerations. A notable case was Richard Cobb, a leading historian of the French Revolution:

> The historian should, above all, be endlessly inquisitive and prying, constantly attempting to force the privacy of others, and to cross the frontiers of class, nationality, generation, period and sex. *His principal aim is to make the dead live.* And, like the American 'mortician', he may allow himself a few artifices of the trade: a touch of rouge here, a pencil-stroke there, a little cotton wool in the cheeks, to make the operation more convincing.[32] [emphasis added]

Death in Paris
Richard Cobb (1917–96) was a colourful British authority on the history of France. *Death in Paris* gives a glimpse of the social history of nineteenth-century Paris through a collection of police records relating to dead bodies fished out of the Seine.

New Model Army
The highly trained professional army created by Parliament during the English Civil Wars (1642–9). It is usually credited with having turned the tide of the war against King Charles I.

Anglo-Zulu War
Also known as the Zulu War (1879). It began with a completely unprovoked British military invasion of Zululand in South Africa, after which an entire British army column was wiped out by the Zulu at Isandhlwana. In the end, superior technology and firepower enabled the British to defeat the Zulu.

Cobb's marvellously evocative studies of the seamy side of life in revolutionary France, notably *Death in Paris* (1978), certainly vindicate his approach. Probably all historians can trace their vocation back to a curiosity about the past for its own sake, often aroused in childhood by the visible relics of the past around them. And there will always, one hopes, be historians like Cobb with special gifts in the recreation of the past. But it is quite wrong to suppose that historians in general should be content with this. For most of them it is the essential preliminary to *explaining* the past. Their purpose is to identify trends, to analyse causes and consequences – in short to interpret history as a process and not just as a series of brightly coloured lantern-slides. Thus historians of the English Revolution approach their work with a view to discovering not only what happened in the Civil War or what it felt like to be a soldier in the **New Model Army** but also why the war occurred and what changes it brought about in the nature of English politics and society. Or to take a more distant example: the events of the **Anglo-Zulu War** of 1879, which saw the dissolution of the Zulu kingdom and the destruction of an entire British regiment, were tragic enough; but a whole other dimension of irony and pathos is revealed when we consider the betrayals, the mutual misunderstandings and the culture conflict that set the two sides on a collision course.[33] This represents the other side of historicism. Without it, history's practical explanatory functions could not be fulfilled at all. (The distinction between recreation and explanation is further explored in Chapter 6.)

The rejection of relevance

However, it is perfectly possible for historical explanation to be pursued without reference to the claims of social relevance, and this, rather than the strictly 'resurrectionist' position, represents the mainstream academic view. For explanation, too, can be sought 'for its own sake'. Topics such as the origins of the First World War or the social welfare provision of the Victorians can be tackled in an entirely self-contained way without any recognition that they might have a bearing on the choices available to us today. Academic syllabuses are sometimes drawn up on the assumption that history consists of a number of core themes and episodes of permanent significance which, because they have generated extensive research and debate, offer the best material for training the intellect. New areas of study such as the history of Africa or the history of the family are dismissed as passing fancies peripheral to 'real history'. Commenting on the gradual retreat from big, contentious topics in university teaching, David Cannadine writes:

> The belief that history provides an education, that it helps us understand ourselves in time, or even that it explains something of how the present world came into being, has all but vanished.[34]

It is hard not to detect a fundamental conservatism in these attitudes: if history is defined to exclude anything that smacks of 'relevance', it is less likely to call into question the dominant mythologies of today or suggest radical alternatives to current institutions. This explains why 'relevant' historical enquiry attracts charges of irreverent muckraking.[35] There can be little doubt that conservatives are disproportionately represented in the ranks of the historical profession. As noted earlier, the triumph of historicism during the nineteenth century owed much to the strength of the conservative reaction to the French Revolution. It remains the case that the study of the past often attracts those who are hostile to the direction of social and political change in their own day and who find comfort in an earlier and more congenial order. This outlook has been marked in English local history: the writings of W.G. Hoskins, a formative influence on this field, are suffused with a nostalgic regret for the passing of the old English rural society.[36]

Disclaimers of social relevance are not, however, usually couched in explicitly conservative terms. They are more commonly defended on the grounds that 'relevant' history is incompatible with the historian's primary obligation to be true to the past, and with the requirements of scholarly objectivity. This argument has a wide currency among academic historians, being supported by many who are not conservative in other respects but who see their professional integrity at stake. But whether grounded in a conservative attitude or not, the denial of practical relevance is unduly cautious. It is entirely understandable that the original champions of the new historical consciousness should have distanced themselves from topicality, because they were only too aware how severely their subject had suffered at the hands of prophets and propagandists in the past. But the battle for scholarly standards of historical enquiry within the profession has long since been won. Practical purposes can be entertained without sacrificing standards of scholarship – partly because professional historians are so zealous in scrutinizing each other's work for bias.

Relevant fields of historical study

Historians should, of course, strive to be true to the past; the question is, which past? Faced with the almost limitless evidence of human activity and the need to select certain problems or periods as more deserving of attention than others, the historian is entirely justified in allowing current social concerns to affect his or her choice. International history originated in the 1920s as a very positive contribution by historians to the new – if short-lived – ethos of internationalism. The notable broadening of the scope of historical enquiry during the past fifty years is largely the result of a small minority of historians responding to the demands of topicality. The **crisis in America's cities** during the 1960s brought into being the 'new urban history', with its stress on the history of social mobility, minority group politics and inner-city deprivation. African history was developed at about the same time in Africa and the West by historians who believed that it was indispensable both to the prospects of the newly independent states and to the outside world's understanding of the **'dark continent'**. More recently, women's history has grown rapidly, as traditional gender roles have been modified in the family, the workplace and public life. In each of these areas the door has been opened to alternative possibilities, to paths not taken, and to conditioning factors whose influence still weighs on the present. In none of these areas has historical enquiry simply confirmed the obvious. As Harold James has put it, 'history has a peculiar legitimacy when it tells us something unexpected about current problems'.[37]

Obviously, new areas of history which proclaim their relevance run the risk of being manipulated by ideologues. But the responsibility of historians in these cases is clear: it is to provide a historical perspective that can inform debate rather than to service any particular ideology. Responding to the call of 'relevance' is not a matter of falsifying or distorting the past, but rather of rescuing from oblivion aspects of that past that now speak to us more directly. Historians of Africa, for example, should be concerned to explain the historical evolution of African societies, not to create a nationalist mythology, and one of the consequences of five decades of research and writing is that it is now much easier to distinguish between the two than it used to be. Our priorities in the present should determine the questions we ask of the past, but not the answers. As will be shown later in the book, the discipline of historical study makes this a meaningful distinction. At the same time, it is a fallacy to suppose that the aspiration to reconstruct

Crisis in America's cities
The mid-1960s saw serious rioting in a large number of American cities. The riots began in 1965 in the Watts district of Los Angeles, where young working-class blacks were protesting against the poverty and squalor in which they lived, but soon spread across the whole nation. The country erupted in further violence after the assassination of Dr Martin Luther King in 1968.

'dark continent'
The standard Victorian nickname for Africa. It referred both to the colour of Africans' skin and to the fact that so little was known in the West about the interior of the continent.

the past in its own terms carries the promise of objectivity: no essay in historical recreation is proof against the values of the enquirer (see Chapter 7).

But historians who renounce relevance in the cause of objective knowledge are not only pursuing a **chimera**; they are also evading a wider responsibility. Intellectual curiosity about the past for its own sake is certainly one reason why people read history, but it is not the only one. Society also expects an interpretation of the past that is relevant to the present and a basis for formulating decisions about the future. Historians may argue that since their expertise concerns the past not the present, it is not their job to draw out the practical import of their work. But they are in fact the only people qualified to equip society with a truly historical perspective and to save it from the damaging effects of exposure to historical myth. If professionally trained historians do not carry out these functions, then others who are less well informed and more prejudiced will produce ill-founded interpretations. What Geoffrey Barraclough, a veteran champion of contemporary values in history, said more than fifty years ago applies with equal force today:

> Man is an historical animal, with a deep sense of his own past; and if he cannot integrate the past by a history explicit and true, he will integrate it by a history implicit and false. The challenge is one which no historian with any conviction of the value of his work can ignore; and the way to meet it is not to evade the issue of 'relevance', but to accept the fact and work out its implications.[38]

chimera
A creature of the imagination, an illusion.

The need for contemporary history

One clear implication is that the recent past has a strong claim on historians. This is the province of *contemporary history*, usually defined as the period within living memory (a favoured starting point is the end of the Cold War in 1989–92). It can be argued that scholars today are too close to the events of this period to achieve sufficient detachment, and that they are further handicapped by their limited access to confidential records (see Chapter 4). But although the job cannot be done as well as historians would like, it is important that they do it to the best of their ability. For it is the recent past on which people draw most for historical analogies and predictions, and their knowledge of it needs to be soundly based if they are to avoid serious error.

Two examples will amplify this point. The first concerns the American deployment of military power overseas. The many interventions made by the US since the end of the nineteenth century are widely seen as being either defensive, or intended to promote liberty. As President Reagan declared, 'Our country has never started a war. Our whole objective is deterrence, the strength and capability it takes to prevent war.'[39] This is a selective reading of history, which while it bolsters national morale, fails to account for the bitter resentment shown towards the USA in parts of Latin America and the Caribbean. The second example is the Israel/Palestine conflict. In Britain and the USA, most people's understanding of the historical background does not extend beyond the war which the Arab states declared on Israel in 1967 (the Six Days' War) and the successive manifestations of Palestinian resistance since then. Partly on account of the foreshortened perspective of the media, few people understand that the Palestinian sense of loss arose from their forcible expulsion from Israel proper by the forces of the new Israeli state in 1948. The starting point for understanding the conflict must be the formative experience of all parties.[40] Academic study of contemporary history is an important contribution to some of the most contentious issues of current politics.

But the fulfilment of history's practical functions does not mean the abandonment of more distant periods – far from it. So many facets of the contemporary scene are rooted in the remote past that the tradition of studying the classical, medieval and early modern epochs can never be given up: without it our historical perspective on current problems would be seriously defective. And as evidence of the range of human achievement and mentality in the past, those periods are indispensable. Responding to society's expectations does not, therefore, impose a limitation as regards periods – or as regards countries. But it does suggest that the selection of themes for research should be influenced by a sensitivity to those areas of current concern that stand most in need of a historical perspective.

VI

A cultural subject, or a social science?

The argument of this chapter can be briefly summed up by situating history in the context of its neighbours among the academic disciplines. Traditionally, history has been counted, along with literary and artistic studies, as one of the humanities. The fundamental premise of these disciplines is that what mankind has thought and done has an intrinsic interest and a lasting value irrespective of any practical implications. The recreation of episodes and ambiences in the past has the same kind of claim on our attention as the recreation of the thought expressed in a work of art or literature. The historian, like the literary critic and art historian, is a guardian of our cultural heritage, and familiarity with that heritage offers insight into the human condition – a means to heightened self-awareness and empathy with others. In this sense history is, in Cobb's phrase, 'a cultural subject, enriching in itself'[41] and any venture in historical reconstruction is worth doing.

By contrast the social sciences owe their position to their promise of practical guidance. Economists and sociologists seek to understand the workings of economy and society with a view to prescribing solutions to current problems, just as scientists offer the means of mastering the natural world. Historians who believe in their subject's practical functions habitually distance it from the humanities and place it alongside the social sciences. E.H. Carr did so in *What is History?* (1961):

> Scientists, social scientists, and historians are all engaged in different branches of the same study: the study of man and his environment, of the effects of man on his environment and of his environment on man. The object of the study is the same: to increase man's understanding of, and mastery over, his environment.[42]

On this reading, historical recreation has value primarily as a preliminary to historical explanation, and the kinds of explanation that matter are those which relate to questions of social, economic and political concern.

In this discussion I have given pride of place to the practical uses of history because these continue to arouse such strong resistance among many professional historians. But the truth is that history cannot be defined as either a humanity or a social science without denying a large part of its nature. The mistake that is so often made is to insist that history be categorized as one to the exclusion of the other. History is a hybrid discipline which owes its endless fascination and its complexity to the fact that it straddles the two. If the study of history is to retain its full vitality, this central ambivalence must continue to be recognized, whatever the cost in logical coherence. The study of history 'for its own sake' is not mere antiquarianism. Our human awareness is enhanced by the contemplation of vanished eras, and historical recreation will always exercise a hold over the imagination, offering as it does vicarious experience to writer and reader alike. At the same time, historians also have a more practical role to perform, and the history that they teach, whether to students in schools and colleges or through the media to the wider public, needs to be informed by an awareness of this role. In this way a historical education achieves a number of goals at once: it trains the mind, enlarges the sympathies *and* provides a much-needed perspective on some of the most pressing problems of our time.

Further reading

John Tosh, *Why History Matters*, Palgrave Macmillan, 2008.
Beverley Southgate, *Why Bother With History? Ancient, Modern and Postmodern Motivations*, Routledge, 2000.

Jeremy Black, *Using History*, Arnold, 2005.

Michael Howard, *The Lessons of History*, Oxford University Press, 1989.

Eric Hobsbawm, *On History*, Weidenfeld & Nicolson, 1997.

Peter Mandler, *History and National Life*, Profile, 2002.

Marc Ferro, *The Use and Abuse of History*, Routledge & Kegan Paul, 1984.

Raphael Samuel, *Island Stories: Unravelling Britain*, Verso, 1998.

Margaret Macmillan, *The Uses and Abuses of History*, Profile, 2009.

Richard E. Neustadt and Ernest R. May, *Thinking in Time: The Uses of History for Decision-Makers*, Free Press, 1986.

Stuart Macintyre (ed.), *The History Wars*, Melbourne University Press, 2001.

Notes

1 Francis Fukuyama, *The End of History and the Last Man*, Hamish Hamilton, 1992.

2 A.J.P. Taylor, *War by Timetable: How the First World War Began*, Macdonald, 1969, p. 45; Richard Cobb, *A Second Identity*, Oxford University Press, 1969, p. 47.

3 George L. Mosse, *The Image of Man: The Creation of Modern Masculinity*, Oxford University Press, 1996, ch. 8.

4 Interview with N.Z. Davis in Henry Abelove et al. (eds), *Visions of History*, Manchester University Press, 1984, pp. 114–15.

5 Christopher Hill, *Change and Continuity in Seventeenth-Century England*, Weidenfeld & Nicolson, 1974, p. 284.

6 Peter Laslett, *Family Life and Illicit Love in Earlier Generations*, Cambridge University Press, 1977, p. 181.

7 Pat Thane, *Old Age in English History: Past Experiences, Present Issues*, Oxford University Press, 2000.

8 Quentin Skinner, 'Meaning and understanding in the history of ideas', *History & Theory*, VIII, 1969, p. 53.

9 James Joll, *Europe Since 1870*, Penguin, 1976, p. xii.

10 Eric Hobsbawm, *On History*, Weidenfeld & Nicolson, 1997, p. 27.

11 Gordon Connell-Smith and Howell A. Lloyd, *The Relevance of History*, Heinemann, 1972, pp. 29–31, 123.

12 W.S. Churchill, *Marlborough: His Life and Times*, 4 vols, Harrap, 1933–8; Roy Jenkins, *Asquith*, Collins, 1964.

13 Francesco Guicciardini, *Maxims and Reflections of a Renaissance Statesman (Ricordi)*, Harper & Row, 1965, p. 69.

14 See, for example, Richard E. Neustadt and Ernest R. May, *Thinking in Time: The Uses of History for Decision-Makers*, Free Press, 1986; Paul Kennedy, *The Rise and Fall of the Great Powers*, Unwin Hyman, 1988.

15 David H. Fischer, *Historians' Fallacies*, Routledge & Kegan Paul, 1971, ch. 9.

16 Hobsbawm, *On History*, pp. 29, 233.

17 E.H. Carr, *What is History?*, 2nd edn, Penguin, 1987, p. 69.

18 These assumptions underpinned Donald Denoon, *Southern Africa Since 1800*, Longman, 1972, and many other texts of the time.

19 Mary Lyndon Shanley, *Feminism, Marriage and the Law in Victorian England, 1850–1895*, Princeton, 1989.

20 Michael Anderson, 'The relevance of family history', in Chris Harris (ed.), *The Sociology of the Family*, Keele, 1980.

21 Linda Colley, *Britons: Forging the Nation, 1707–1837*, Yale University Press, 1992; Raphael Samuel, *Theatres of Memory*, vol. II: *Island Stories: Unravelling Britain*, Verso, 1998, pp. 41–73.

22 Benedict Anderson, *Imagined Communities*, Verso, 1983.

23 Paul Gilroy, *The Black Atlantic: Modernity and Double Consciousness*, Verso, 1993.

24 Amy Louise Erickson, *Women and Property in Early Modern England*, Cambridge University Press, 1993; Clare Midgley, *Women Against Slavery*, Routledge, 1992.

25 William Cobbett, *Advice to Young Men*, Peter Davies, 1926, p. 176.

26 John Tosh, *A Man's Place: Masculinity and the Middle-Class Home in Victorian England*, Yale University Press, 1999.

27 For an introductory selection, see P. Rabinow (ed.), *The Foucault Reader*, Pantheon, 1984.

28 Michael Oakeshott, *Rationalism in Politics and Other Essays*, Methuen, 1962, p. 165.

29 G.R. Elton, 'Second thoughts on history at the universities', *History*, LIV, 1969, p. 66. See also his *The Practice of History*, Fontana, 1969, pp. 66–8.

30 V.H. Galbraith, in R.C.K. Ensor et al. (eds), *Why We Study History*, Historical Association, 1944, p. 7; see also his *An Introduction to the Study of History*, C.A. Watts, 1964, pp. 59–61.

31 Peter Mandler, *History and National Life*, Profile, 2002, p. 10.

32 Richard Cobb, *A Second Identity*, Oxford University Press, 1969, p. 47.

33 Jeff Guy, *The Destruction of the Zulu Kingdom*, Longman, 1979.

34 David Cannadine, 'British history: past, present – and future?', *Past & Present*, cxvi, 1987, p. 180.

35 See, for example, G.R. Elton, *Return to Essentials*, Cambridge University Press, 1990, pp. 84–7.

36 See W.G. Hoskins, *The Making of the English Landscape*, Penguin, 1970.

37 Harold James, in Pat Hudson (ed.), *Living Economic and Social History*, Economic History Society, 2001, p. 166.

38 Geoffrey Barraclough, *History in a Changing World*, Blackwell, 1955, pp. 24–5.

39 Ronald Reagan, quoted in Margaret Macmillan, *The Uses and Abuses of History*, Profile, 2009, pp.146–7.

40 Ilan Pappe, *Ethnic Cleansing of Palestine*, Oneworld, 2011; Greg Philo and Mike Berry, *Bad News from Israel*, Pluto, 2004.

41 Richard Cobb, *A Sense of Place*, Duckworth, 1975, p. 4.

42 Carr, *What is History?*, p. 86.

3 Mapping the field

Much of the history students encounter is concerned with political events, but that is far from the limit of the historian's interest or concerns. Historians have greatly widened the range of their studies since the heyday of Victorian constitutional history. Today, no aspect of human thought and activity is excluded from the scope of historical study. Economy, society, mentality and culture all have their place in the curriculum. This chapter describes and classifies this richness.

Whether history is studied for practical purposes or on account of its intrinsic value as a cultural resource, it is almost impossible to set limits on its scope. The implications are truly formidable if history is defined as the study of the entire past of humankind; they are only marginally less so if we limit this definition to the periods and places for which there is a written record. All history has some claim on our attention, but making sense of history demands that we categorize the very wide range of approaches that can be taken in studying the past. Nearly all historians accept a defining label; even those who call themselves world historians or global historians are not claiming omniscience, but are foregrounding one perspective at the expense of a great many others. Several labelling schemes are in use. Historians have for a long time identified themselves by the period they study, as for example, 'medievalists', 'early modernists' or 'contemporary historians', and in practice the period for which they have an acknowledged expertise is likely to be limited still further – to a century perhaps in the case of a medievalist, and often no more than a decade in the case of a specialist in the nineteenth or twentieth centuries. Then there is specialization by locality. Particular periods are generally studied in relation to one country or region only. The specialist in the English Revolution of the seventeenth century, for example, would naturally be interested in those countries of Western Europe which, like France and the Netherlands, experienced their own political crises at the same time, but his or her knowledge of them would probably not be founded on anything more than a reading of the secondary literature – and regrettably in many cases only the literature in English and one other European language. Those historians with firsthand research experience in more than one country or period are a small minority.

In addition to the specialization of time and place, there is also the specialization of theme. Whereas modern historical scholarship achieves a more or less steady output for all the periods and countries that are reasonably well documented, its choice of theme is much more subject to changing fashion. The claims of social relevance, the development of new techniques of research and the theoretical insights of other disciplines all influence historians in determining which aspects of the past should enjoy research priority. For these reasons, choice of theme gives a much clearer indication of the actual content of historical enquiry than does choice of period or country. It is also much the best way of conveying the richness of contemporary scholarship, since the range of historical themes has greatly expanded over the past fifty years. I begin with what might be regarded as the senior branch of historical study, though it is no longer the dominant one.

I

Political history

Political history is conventionally defined as the study of all those aspects of the past that have to do with the formal organization of power in society, which for the majority of human societies in recorded history means the state. It includes the institutional organization of the state, the competition of factions and parties for control over the state, the policies enforced by the state and the relations between states. To many people, the scope of history would appear to be exhausted by these topics, mainly because that was what they studied in school. In recent years both the National Curriculum and television programmes have reflected a broader range of interest. But political history has not lost its appeal, and it capitalizes on its central place in historical scholarship since ancient times.

The reasons for this traditional dominance are clear enough. Historically, the state itself has been much more directly involved in the writing of history than with any other literary activity. On the one hand, those who exercised political power looked to the past for guidance as to how best to achieve their ends. At the same time, political elites had an interest in promoting for public consumption a version of history that legitimized their own position in the body politic, either by emphasizing their past achievements, or by demonstrating the antiquity of the constitution under which they held office. Moreover, political history has always found an avid **lay readership**. The rise and fall of statesmen and of nations or empires lends itself to dramatic treatment in the grand manner. Political power is intoxicating, and for those who cannot exercise it themselves, the next best thing is to enjoy it vicariously in the

lay readership
Readers outside the academic historical profession.

pages of a gifted writer. The consequences of pandering to this popular preference have long been deplored. **Arthur Young**, the English agronomist famous for his descriptions of the French countryside on the eve of the Revolution, was blunt:

> To a mind that has the least turn after philosophical inquiry, reading modern history is generally the most tormenting employment that a man can have: one is plagued with the actions of a detestable set of men called conquerors, heroes and great generals; and we wade through pages loaded with military details; but when you want to know the progress of agriculture, or commerce and industry, their effect in different ages and nations on each other ... all is a blank.[1]

Political history in turbulent times

In fact, during the Enlightenment of the eighteenth century, a 'philosophical' turn of mind was rather more evident than Young allowed for. **Voltaire**'s historical works ranged over the whole field of culture and society, and even Gibbon did not confine himself to the dynastic and military fortunes of the Roman Empire. But the nineteenth-century revolution in historical studies greatly reinforced the traditional preoccupation with statecraft, **faction** and war. German historicism was closely associated with a school of political thought, best represented by Hegel, which endowed the concept of the state with a moral and spiritual force beyond the material interests of its subjects; it followed that the state was the main agent of historical change. Equally, the nationalism that inspired so much historical writing at this time led to an emphasis on the competition between the great powers and the struggles of submerged nationalities for political self-determination. Few historians would have quarrelled with Ranke when he wrote, 'the spirit of modern times ... operates only by political means'.[2] The Victorian historian, E.A. Freeman, put it more simply: 'History is past politics'.[3] The new university professors in the Rankean mould were essentially political historians.

What should political history be about?

Yet, as the definition given earlier would suggest, political history can mean different things, and its content has been almost as varied and as subject to fashion as any other branch of history. Ranke himself was chiefly interested in how the great powers of Europe had acquired their strongly individual characters during the period between the Renaissance and the French Revolution. He looked for explanations less to the internal evolution of those states than to the unending struggle for power between them. One of Ranke's legacies, therefore, was a highly professional approach to the study of foreign policy. *Diplomatic history* has been a staple pursuit of the profession ever since, its appeal periodically reinforced as historians have responded to a public demand to understand the origins of the latest war. In the aftermath of the First World War especially, much of this work verged on nationalist propaganda and it was too heavily dependent on the archives of a single country. At times, diplomatic history has been reduced to scarcely more than a record of what one diplomat or foreign minister said to another, with little awareness of the wider influences that so often shape foreign policy – financial and military factors, the influence of public opinion, and so on. Nowadays the best diplomatic history deals with international relations in the most comprehensive sense, rather than the diplomacy of a particular nation. In her book *Peacemakers* (2001), Margaret Macmillan provides a masterly account of the six months of negotiation that led up to the Treaty of Versailles in 1919. Her account revolves around the intense negotiations between the three key players: Woodrow Wilson of the United States, Clemenceau of France and Lloyd George of Britain. But

Figure 3.1 The 'Big Four' at the Paris Peace Conference, 1919: seated left to right: Orlando (Italy), Lloyd George (Britain), Clemenceau (France) and Woodrow Wilson (United States). Most of the business of the conference was settled in meetings between them. They were subject to incessant lobbying by the many other powers represented at the conference. © Getty Images/Time & Life Pictures.

Macmillan shows how their decisions were conditioned not only by the disposition of forces at the end of the war, but by the strength of popular feeling in their respective countries.

Many of Ranke's contemporaries and followers emphasized instead the internal evolution of the European nation states, and *constitutional history* was largely their creation. This emphasis was most pronounced in Britain, where history became an academically respectable subject during the 1860s and 1870s almost entirely on the strength of constitutional history. Its central theme was of course the evolution of Parliament, considered by the Victorians to be England's most priceless contribution to civilization, and thus the appropriate focus for a national history. England's constitutional history was seen as a sequence of momentous conflicts of principle, alternating with periods of gradual change, stretching back to the early Middle Ages; it was enshrined in a succession of great state documents (Magna Carta and the like) which required disciplined textual study. For fifty years after the publication of Stubbs's three-volume *Constitutional History of England* (1873–8), constitutional history carried the greatest academic prestige in Britain, and major revisionist work continues to be done to this day. In the hands of Stubbs's followers – most of them medievalists, as he was – the subject was diversified to encompass two closely related specialisms: the history of law, and administrative history. Legal history enjoys relatively little interest today, but administrative history shows every sign of enjoying a new lease of life as historians seek to interpret the massive increase in the functions and personnel of government that took place in all Western societies during the last century.

The fine grain of politics

It would be very misleading, however, to suggest that the practice of political history remains wedded to the categories marked out in the nineteenth century. In Britain especially, reaction against the traditional forms of political history has turned on the contention that none of them directly confronts what ought to be a central issue in any study of politics, namely the acquisition and exercise of political power and the day-to-day management of political systems. From this perspective, the Stubbs tradition, with its emphasis on constitutional principles and the formal institutions of government, seems unhelpful.

The most influential spokesman for this reaction was L.B. Namier, whose writings on eighteenth-century England marked something of a turning point. What interested Namier was not primarily the great political issues of the time or the careers of the leading statesmen, but the composition and recruitment of the political elite as revealed by the personal case histories of ordinary MPs. In *The Structure of Politics at the Accession of George III* (1929) and later works, Namier asked why men sought a seat in the Commons, how they obtained one and what considerations guided their political conduct in the House. He cut through the ideological pretensions with which politicians clothed their behaviour (aided and abetted by later historians), and neither their motives nor their methods emerged with much credit. As a result, most of the accepted picture of eighteenth-century English politics was demolished – the two-party system, the packing of the Commons with government placemen and the assault on the constitution by the young George III. Namier's method was quickly taken up by historians working on other periods, and towards the end of his life he enshrined it in the officially sponsored *History of Parliament*, which will eventually comprise biographies of everyone who sat in the House of Commons between 1485 and 1901: so far 21,420 biographies have been published, with free online access.[4]

STREET FIGHTING IN THE RUE DE RIVOLI

Figure 3.2 One of the most significant ideas to come out of the French Revolution was the concept of the nation as a focus for group identity, instead of loyalty to a dynastic ruler. Nationalism was often linked to liberalism, although it was also taken up by illiberal conservatives. Nineteenth-century Europe saw a number of revolutionary nationalist risings, although Italy and Germany, the two main examples of nineteenth-century states established along nationalist lines, both owed their existence more to the manoeuvres of statesmen than they did to revolutionaries. The nation state was at the heart of President Woodrow Wilson's policy of national self-determination at the Paris Peace Conference of 1919. © Mary Evans Picture Library.

Such an approach, in which the analysis of motive and manoeuvre is allowed full play, makes for a fascinating study in the psychology of political conflict. But it illuminates the surface only. As soon as it is conceded that politics is not only about personalities but also about the clash of competing economic interests and rival ideologies, then the wider society outside the rarefied atmosphere of court or Parliament becomes critically important. This is self-evident in the case of periods of revolutionary change when the political system broke down as a result of changes in the structure of economy or society. In more stable political situations, the dimensions of class and ideology may not be so clearly articulated, but they are present nonetheless, and any analysis of political trends beyond the short term demands that they be understood. At the very least, historians have to be aware of the social and economic background of the political elite and the role of public opinion. More than any other branch of history, political history depends for its vitality on a close involvement with its intellectual neighbours, and particularly with the fields of economic and social history.

II

History beyond the elite

It is hardly an exaggeration to say that for Ranke's generation, economic and social history did not exist. By the late nineteenth century, however, Western Europe and the United States were emerging from a major economic and social transformation which historical study as then practised was manifestly incapable of explaining. Although Marx's thought has been rigorously applied to historical research in the West on a large scale only during the past fifty years (see Chapter 8), his emphasis on the historical significance of the means of production and of relations between classes had already gained wide currency among politically literate people by the early twentieth century. Moreover, the effect of the rise of organized labour and the mass socialist parties was to push issues of economic and social reform more insistently into the centre of the political stage than ever before. Developments in the early twentieth century pointed in the same general direction. For many, the First World War dealt a fatal blow to the ideal of the nation state, whose rise had been the great theme of nineteenth-century **historiography**, while the recurrent slumps and depressions in the world economy confirmed the need for a more systematic grasp of economic history.

historiography
The study of the writing of history, although the term is sometimes also used to denote the range of historians' writings on a particular theme.

Around the turn of the century, the narrowly political focus of academic history came under increasing attack from historians themselves. Manifestos calling for a new and broader approach were launched in several countries – most self-consciously in the United States, where they sailed under the flag of the 'New History'.

In Britain the connection between historical study and current social issues was particularly evident in the careers of **Sidney and Beatrice Webb**, social reformers and historians of the British Labour movement; economic history featured from the start in the curriculum of the London School of Economics, which they founded in 1895.

Learning from other disciplines: the Annales *school*

It was, however, in France that the implications of broadening history's scope were most fully worked out. This was the achievement of Marc Bloch, a medievalist, and Lucien Febvre, a specialist in the sixteenth century, whose followers today probably command greater international prestige in the academic world than any other school. In 1929, Bloch and Febvre founded a historical journal called *Annales d'histoire sociale et économique*, usually known simply as *Annales*.[5] In the first issue they demanded of their colleagues not just a broader approach but an awareness of what they could learn from other disciplines, especially the social sciences – economics, sociology, social psychology and geography (a particularly strong enthusiasm of the *Annales* historians). While conceding that the practitioners of these disciplines were primarily concerned with contemporary problems, Bloch and Febvre maintained that only with their help could historians become aware of the full range of significant questions that they could put to their sources. And whereas earlier reformers had called for an interdisciplinary method, it was systematically put into practice by the *Annales* historians in a formidable corpus of publications, of which Marc Bloch's *Feudal Society* (1940) is probably the best known outside France. From this basic premise, historians of the *Annales* school have continued to broaden and refine the content and methodology of history, with the result that many of the new directions that the discipline has taken in the past fifty years owe much to their contribution. At the same time, the *Annales* school heaped considerable scorn on the traditional pursuit of political narrative – a reaction that was shared by many economic and social historians in Britain: in R.H. Tawney's words, politics was 'the squalid scaffolding of more serious matters'.[6]

It is mainly because of the initiatives taken by the *Annales* historians and their contemporaries that the range of history writing is today so vast. The vitality of economic, social and cultural history is testimony to those efforts. Meanwhile, new specialisms continue to be added, such as global history, environmental history, the history of the body and the history of the book, and none of the more established approaches is wholly abandoned. An inventory of what historians do can easily read like a dizzying catalogue in which all coherence is lost. The confusion is compounded when we recognize that work in one area may be divided by theoretical

Sidney (1859–1947) and Beatrice (1858–1943) Webb British social historians and reformers, prominent in the 1910s and 1920s. They took a leading role in the socialist Fabian Society and in the trade union movement. Convinced of the importance of social and economic history, they published a *History of Trade Unionism* and in 1895 they helped to found the London School of Economics.

approaches, and these same theories may be found in other areas (Marxism being an obvious example). In order to make sense of this diversity in what follows I pursue the metaphor of 'field' by taking three different cross-sections; each is composed of paired opposites. Together they capture something of the range of historical study, and they provide a grid on which any individual historical work can be placed. The first cross-section contrasts the individual with society or the mass of the people. The second contrasts the material world with the mental or cultural aspects of experience. And the third juxtaposes the local with the global, reflecting the very different spatial frames employed by historians.

III

Biography

Focusing on eminent individuals of the past might seem to be a self-evident concern of historians, but it has not always been so. The common factor behind the new histories that came to the fore during the twentieth century was that they were about 'society'. The traditional conventions of academic history stood condemned for their concern with small elites and with individuals – the makers of foreign policy, the statesmen who promoted or resisted constitutional change and the leaders of revolutionary movements. Yet such figures continued to attract both academic study and a popular readership. This human curiosity has been indulged by historians in the form of *biography* for as long as history has been written. It has, however, often been overlaid by intentions that are inconsistent with a strict regard for historical truth. During the Middle Ages and the Renaissance many biographies were frankly **didactic**, designed to present the subject as a model of Christian conduct or public virtue. In Victorian times, the characteristic form of biography was commemorative: for the heirs and admirers of a public figure the most fitting memorial was a large-scale 'Life', based almost exclusively on the subject's own papers (many of them carefully preserved for this very purpose) and so taking the subject at his or her own valuation. Figures in the more distant past were treated hardly less reverently. Honest, **'warts-and-all'** biography was practised by only a few brave spirits. The Victorian reader of biographies was therefore confronted by a gallery of worthies, whose role was to sustain a respect for the nation's political and intellectual elite.

For historians, the essential requirement in a biography is that it understands the subject in his or her historical context. It must be written by someone who is not merely well grounded in the period in question but who has examined all the major collections of papers that have a bearing on the subject's life – including those of adversaries and subordinates as well as friends and family. A historical biography is, in short, a major undertaking.

didactic
With an overtly educational purpose.

'warts-and-all'
Honest, showing the bad points as well as the good. The term comes from a portrait of Oliver Cromwell by the painter Sir Peter Lely. Cromwell, who had one or two warts on his face, told Lely he did not want a falsely flattering portrait, but wanted to be painted 'warts and all'.

Yet even biography that meets the requirements of modern scholarship is not without its critics. Many historians believe that it has no serious place in historical study. The problem of bias cannot be lightly disposed of. Although there has been a vogue for debunking biography ever since **Lytton Strachey** exposed the human frailties of his ironically named *Eminent Victorians* (1918), anyone who devotes years to the study of one individual – something that Strachey never did – can hardly escape some identification with the subject and will inevitably look at the period to some extent through that person's eyes. Furthermore, biographical narrative encourages a simplified, linear interpretation of events. Maurice Cowling, a leading specialist in modern British political history, argued that political events can only be understood by showing how members of the political establishment reacted to one another. 'For this purpose', he wrote:

> biography is almost always misleading. Its refraction is partial in relation to the [political] system. It abstracts a man whose public action should not be abstracted. It implies linear connections between one situation and the next. In fact connections were not linear. The system was a circular relationship: a shift in one element changed the position of all the others in relation to the rest.[7]

It is hard to deny that, with the best will in the world, biography nearly always entails some distortion, but there are good grounds for not dismissing it. First, Cowling's objection carries much less weight in the case of political systems where power is concentrated in one man. Ian Kershaw, author of the most substantial biography of Hitler, has recounted how reluctant he was initially to attempt the task, since in his previous work he had focused on the structure of Nazi power in German society. But he came to realize that a structural approach required 'increased reflection on the man who was the indispensable fulcrum and inspiration of what took place, Hitler himself'.[8] Second, at the other extreme, biographies of people who were in no way outstanding can sometimes, if the documentation is rich enough, bring to light neglected features of the past. Linda Colley has written the life of an obscure eighteenth-century woman called Elizabeth March. Because her experiences included capture in Morocco and marriage in India, as well as visits to many far-flung ports, the narrative sheds light on a global maritime world that featured trade, migration and slavery; the book is 'a biography that crosses boundaries'.[9]

Lastly, and perhaps most important of all, biography is indispensable to the understanding of motive and intention. There is much dispute among historians as to how prominently matters of motive – as distinct from economic and social forces – should feature in historical explanation, and they certainly receive less

Lytton Strachey (1880–1932)
British writer and member of the famous group of literary figures known from the area of London where many of them lived as the Bloomsbury group. Strachey's *Eminent Victorians* (1918) shocked many readers by taking a satirical, sarcastic approach to four revered figures from the previous century, including Florence Nightingale and General Gordon.

emphasis now than they did in the nineteenth century; but plainly the motives of individuals have *some* part to play in explaining historical events. Once this much is conceded, the relevance of biography is obvious. The actions of an individual can be fully understood only in the light of his or her emotional make-up, temperament and pre-judices. Of course in even the best-documented lives a great deal remains a matter of conjecture: the writings of public figures especially are often coloured by self-deception as well as deliberate calculation. But the biographer who has studied the development of his or her subject from childhood to maturity is much more likely to make the right inferences. It is for this reason that during the pre-sent century biographers have increasingly stressed the private or inner lives of their subjects as well as their public careers. From this perspective, the personal development of important individuals in the past is a valid subject of historical enquiry in its own right.

IV

What is social history?

No branch of history proclaims its indifference to the individual more clearly than *social history*. That label always indicates a focus on society as a whole – even if only a small fragment has actually been investigated. In fact, the full ambition of social history was not immediately apparent. There was, first, the history of social problems such as poverty, ignorance, insanity and disease. Historians focused less on the experience of people afflicted by these conditions than on the 'problem' that they posed to society as a whole; they studied the reforming efforts of private **philanthropy**, as seen in charitable institutions such as schools, orphanages and hospitals, and the increasingly effective intervention of the state in the social field from the mid-nineteenth century onwards. The limitations of this genre of social history can be illustrated in the case of Ivy Pinchbeck and Margaret Hewitt's two-volume study, *Children in English Society* (1969, 1973); they documented in detail the achievements of organized charity and government concern over a period of four hundred years, but the recipients of all this care and attention are only occasionally heard, while children who were not in need are entirely absent from their account.

Social history meant, second, the history of everyday life in the home, the workplace and the community. As **G.M. Trevelyan** put it, 'social history might be defined negatively as the history of a people with the politics left out'.[10] His *English Social History* (1944), for long a standard work, took little account of economics either, and much of it reads like a catch-all for the miscellaneous topics that did not fit into his earlier (and largely political) *History of England* (1926); there is a great deal of descriptive detail, but little coherence of theme. Much of this kind of writing

philanthropy
Charitable work.

**G.M. Trevelyan
(1876–1962)**
George Macaulay Trevelyan, British historian and great-nephew of the celebrated historian Thomas Babington Macaulay. A prolific writer, he is best known for his popular *English Social History*, which reflected a wartime regret for the passing of a more stable society.

had an **elegiac** tone: a regret for the passing of the pre-industrial order when everyday life was on a human scale and geared to natural rhythms, and a revulsion from the anomie and ugliness of modern urban living.

elegiac
Lyrical, poetic evocation of times past.

Labour history and history from below

Lastly, there was the history of the common people, or working classes, who were almost entirely absent from political history. In Britain this kind of social history was from the end of the nineteenth century dominated by historians who were sympathetic to the labour movement. Although often passionately committed to the workers' cause, their writings were at this stage hardly affected by Marxist influence. Their main concern was to furnish the British labour movement with a collective historical identity, and they sought it not through a new theoretical framework (for which Marxism was of course well suited), but in the historical experience of the working class itself during the preceding century – the material and social deprivation, the tradition of self-help and the struggles for improved wages and conditions of employment. For G.D.H. Cole, the leading British labour historian during the 1930s and 1940s, nothing seemed more important than that 'as the working class grows towards the full exercise of power, it should look back as well as forward, and shape its policy in the light of its own historic experience'.[11]

This tradition of social history was revived and expanded during the 1960s under the banner of *history from below*. But whereas labour history was characterized by a strong institutional bias, history from below concentrates on the unorganized and the marginal who have been least visible in the historical record. Seeing history from the bottom up does not just mean recreating the rhythms of everyday life. It means seeing the past from the point of view of ordinary people and identifying with their politics. Above all, history from below contests the passivity to which ordinary people have been consigned by so many historians. Popular agency and resistance are its hallmarks. An early exponent of this approach was George Rudé, who studied the urban crowd in both eighteenth-century London and revolutionary Paris; he rejected the use of the word 'mob', and instead reconstructed the motives and methods of those who took to the streets to voice their grievances. His study of the Gordon Riots of 1780, when the government lost control of the streets of London for an entire week, is a classic of its kind.[12] Rudé's agenda was broadened still further in the 1970s by the History Workshop movement. Though based at Ruskin, the trade-union-sponsored college at Oxford, History Workshop quickly extended its range from organized workers to encompass all groups in society that stood outside – or 'below' – the elites on which traditional histories had focused. Women's history and the history of immigrant communities soon made their appearance.[13] History Workshop has been particularly notable in drawing in amateur and community historians, alongside the left-wing academics who form its core.

History and social structure

But none of the approaches mentioned so far entirely explains why social history, for so long the poor relation, came to enjoy such prominence. What happened in the 1960s and 1970s was that its subject matter was redefined in a much more ambitious manner. Social history now aspired to offer nothing less than the history of social structure. The notion of 'social structure' is a sociological abstraction of a conveniently indeterminate kind, which can be – and has been – clothed in any number of theoretical garbs. But what it essentially means is the sum of the social relationships between the many different groups in society. Under the influence of Marxist thought, class has had the lion's share of attention, but it is by no means the only kind of group to be considered: there are also the cross-cutting ties of age, gender, race and occupation.

Social structure may seem to be a static, timeless concept, partly because it has been treated in this way in the writings of many sociologists. But it need not be so, and historians tend naturally to adopt a more dynamic approach. As Keith Wrightson, a leading social historian of early modern England, puts it:

> Society is a process. It is never static. Even its most apparently stable structures are the expression of an equilibrium between dynamic forces. For the social historian the most challenging of tasks is that of recapturing that process, while at the same time discerning long-term shifts in social organization, in social relations and in the meanings and evaluations with which social relationships are infused.[14]

Against the background of a durable social structure, those individuals or groups who move up or down are often particularly significant, and social mobility has been much studied by historians. Beyond a certain point, social mobility is incompatible with the maintenance of the existing structure, and a new form of society may emerge, as happened most fundamentally during the Industrial Revolution. Urbanization, in particular, needs to be studied not just in its economic aspects, but as a process of social change, including the assimilation of immigrants, the emergence of new forms of social stratification, the hardening distinction between work and leisure and so on; important work along these lines has been pioneered in America, and urban history is a significant specialism in Britain too.[15] The analysis of social structure and social change can have major implications for economic and political history, and social historians in recent years have staked out large claims in these areas. The long-drawn-out 'gentry controversy' was mainly a dispute about the connection between changing social structure and political conflict in England during the hundred years before the Civil War.[16] The origins of the Industrial Revolution are now sought not only in economic and geographical factors, but in the social structure of eighteenth-century England – especially the 'open aristocracy', with a two-way flow of men and wealth into and out of its ranks.[17] At this point, social history begins to approximate to the 'history of society' in its broadest sense which, it has been argued, is its proper domain.[18]

Much of the earlier, less ambitious social history is relevant to this new concern, provided its terms of reference are revised. The new social historians include many who started within the more limited horizons of one or other of the established categories. E.P. Thompson, the best-known social historian during the 1960s and 1970s, had his roots deep in the labour history tradition, but in *The Making of the English Working Class* (1963) he stepped outside it; the growth of a working-class awareness during the Industrial Revolution is placed in the widest possible context, including religion, leisure and popular culture, as well as the factory system and the origins of trade unionism; and, so far from politics being 'left out', the presence of the state is both constant and menacing, as an instrument of class control.

As well as being formative in the social history of Britain, the period covered by Thompson was rich in distinguished individuals. Thompson's own last published work was a study of the visionary painter and poet, William Blake.[19] Historians do not divide neatly between students of the mass and students of the individual. Biography and social history may represent sharply divergent perspectives, but both are needed, and both feature prominently in contemporary historical practice.

V

Economic history

My second pairing contrasts the material and mental worlds. The one deals with the external requirements of life; the other probes the internal world of thought and emotion. Both must feature in a comprehensive recovery of the past. *Economic history* focuses on 'earthly necessities' – the title of an outstanding economic history of early modern England.[20] It seeks to reconstruct production, exchange and consumption. Such activities are for the most part a matter of external observation, and in many cases they can be measured. This approach can be contrasted with one that seeks to

'gentry controversy'
A long-running argument in academic circles about the development of social change in early seventeenth-century England and its bearing on the origins of the English Civil War. The argument was over whether the lesser landowning class (the gentry) was 'rising' in social and economic status at the expense of the older, landed aristocracy, or whether the opposite was true. The argument raged for many years and was a staple feature of undergraduate essays; however, since it is not easy to come up with a clear-cut definition of 'gentry' and 'aristocracy', or exactly what is meant by a class 'rising', no clear conclusion was ever reached.

E.P. Thompson (1924–93)
British Marxist historian. Thompson was also active in socialist politics. His *Making of the English Working Class* was the first attempt to tell the story of the development of a distinctive working-class culture and identity in the late eighteenth and early nineteenth centuries.

reconstruct mental processes, including formal thought, religious belief and emotional states. These cannot be measured or observed, and they call for a considerable degree of empathy and an ability to tease out the latent meanings of texts and images.

Economic history was the first specialism to gain recognition outside political history. By 1914 it had emerged as a sharply defined area of study in several countries, including Britain and the United States. The relevance of economic history to contemporary problems largely explains its head-start over other contenders; indeed, in many universities, especially in America, economic history was studied not as part of general history, but in conjunction with economics, a discipline whose own claims to academic respectability had only just won general recognition by the end of the nineteenth century. Both in Britain and in the rest of Europe, much of the pioneer work concerned the economic policies of the state – an approach that required the minimum adaptation on the part of historians schooled in political history. But this was clearly an inadequate base on which to come to grips with the historical phenomenon of industrialization, which from the start loomed large on the agenda of economic historians. It resulted in a special emphasis on Britain, the first country to experience an industrial revolution, and attracted continental as much as British historians. Their work was particularly strong on local studies of particular industries, such as Lancashire cotton textiles or Yorkshire woollens, and it highlighted individual initiative and technical innovation. A pale reflection of this approach is still to be seen in those old-fashioned textbooks which chronicle Britain's Industrial Revolution as a sequence of inventions made in the late eighteenth century.

The difficult interplay of economic and political history

In many ways economic history offers about the biggest contrast to political history that can be imagined. Its chronology is quite different. It often makes light of differences of political culture and national tradition, particularly in studies of the modern global economy. And it gives minimal scope to personality and motive, the classic preoccupations of historians; instead 'impersonal' forces such as inflation or investment tend to hold the centre of the stage. Furthermore, economic historians delight in undermining the bedrock assumptions of their non-specialist colleagues – most provocatively in several works that deny that Britain experienced an industrial revolution at all.[21] For all these reasons many political historians would prefer to hold economic history at arm's length. But in practice their own agenda has been influenced by the findings of economic history in very positive ways. For example, the financial predicament of Tudor governments – and the political difficulties with Parliament that this brought in its train – cannot be grasped without an understanding of the great inflation of the sixteenth century.[22] Similarly, interpretations of the origins of the Boer War, which broke out in 1899 between Britain and the gold-rich Transvaal, have been modified in the light of precise information about the vicissitudes of the international gold standard at that time.[23]

Enterprise and economic growth

Two trends stand out in current writing on modern economic history, although they do not define its entire scope. The first one is business history – the systematic study of individual firms on the basis of their business records. The source materials are usually manageable, and firms that allow access to them sometimes foot the bill for research as well. Whether or not the historian identifies with the values of capitalist entrepreneurship, what comes out best from these studies is a keener understanding of the mechanisms of economic expansion, often at a critical juncture in the history of an industry. The implications of research in business history can be wider still. How far the beginning of Britain's economic decline in the period 1870–1914 was caused by a failure of entrepreneurship is a major issue to which business historians have much to contribute.

Business history may be regarded as economic history on the ground. The second approach, by contrast, seeks to explain the dynamics of growth or decline of an entire economy. This is quite simply the biggest issue in economics today, both for professional economists and for the lay public, and since it has been present in a recognizably modern form since the onset of industrialization 200 years ago, it is hardly surprising that historians should be interested too. But in seeking to contribute to a wider debate they have been compelled to sharpen their analytical tools. The older economic histories, such as J.H. Clapham's *Economic History of Modern Britain* (1926–38), were essentially descriptive: they reconstructed the economic life of a particular period, sometimes in vivid detail, but in explaining how one phase gave way to the next they showed little interest in the actual mechanisms of economic change. The current debates are very largely about those mechanisms, and they are conducted in the context of the highly sophisticated theoretical work on growth that economists have been carrying out since the 1950s. If historians are to do justice to their material in this area, they have to be much more versed in the competing theoretical explanations than they used to be; and since the testing of these theories depends on the accurate measurement of indices of growth, historians must also become quantifiers. In this field, the breaking down of those inter-disciplinary barriers which the *Annales* school called for half a century ago has been more complete than in any other.

VI

Getting into the mind of the past

Economic history, with its emphasis on externally observed behaviour, can be contrasted with the study of intellectual, emotional and psychological states. It is one thing to categorize people according to their place in a given structure by indicating their occupation, status and wealth. It is quite another to enter into their assumptions and attitudes, to see them as 'sentient reflecting beings'.[24] This approach includes themes as varied as political thought, religion and mass psychology. They have never been brought together under a single label, but what they have in common is a concern with mental process. Individual and collective behaviour still count, but as a basis for making inferences about mentality or belief.

Given the political orientation of historical scholarship as it matured during the nineteenth century, it comes as no surprise that the history of political thought has the longest pedigree. The works of writers like Plato, Machiavelli and Hobbes were seen as building blocks in a single Western tradition. Today, however, scholars place much more emphasis on understanding these thinkers in their historical context – forming their ideas in response to the events unfolding around them, and restricted by the cultural resources available to them. A much keener awareness is also shown of the fact that the intellectual landscape of a period is not primarily composed of the handful of great works that have inspired posterity; almost by definition, these were inaccessible to all but a few. The common wisdom of the day against which the great names were judged (and in many instances condemned) was what contemporaries had retained, often selectively and incoherently, from earlier traditions of thought. For the political historian especially, what counts is the set of ideas within which people with no claims to intellectual originality operated, and from this perspective the diffusion of new ideas through derivative and ephemeral literature is as important as their genesis in the mind of a great thinker. The intellectual context of periods of revolutionary change when ideas are often particularly potent can be properly understood in no other way. In *The Intellectual Origins of the American Revolution* (1967), for example, Bernard Bailyn reconstructed the political culture of ordinary Americans from 400 or so pamphlets bearing on the Anglo-American conflict which were published in the thirteen colonies between 1750 and 1776. His research revealed the influence of not only the New England Puritan tradition and the thought of the Enlightenment, which had long been taken for granted, but also the anti-authoritarian political thought of the Civil War period in England, kept alive by English radical pamphleteers of the early eighteenth century and transmitted across the Atlantic. At this point the history of ideas enters the market-place, as it were, and becomes part of the common culture of the day.

The history of religion

Comparable issues are raised by the history of religion. At one level, this is about the life and writings of great religious leaders like **Martin Luther** or **Ignatius Loyola**. There is also a strong tradition of studying the history of religious institutions, given the immense power of the Christian Churches throughout most of their history. But increasingly historians have turned to the study of popular religion: what did people believe, and how did their beliefs affect their lives? Conversion is a promising place to start. In *Pulling the Devil's Kingdom Down* (2001) Pamela Walker examines the Salvation Army in late Victorian Britain. At the heart of her account is the conversion experiences of early Salvationists recruited from the poorest neighbourhoods of London, based on their published biographies and on the *War Cry* (the Army's journal). At the same time, organized religion has often had to co-exist with unofficial belief systems. In *Religion and the Decline of Magic* (1971), Keith Thomas assessed the ebb and flow of witchcraft, prophecy and astrology during the era of the Reformation and the English Revolution. 'I hope', says Thomas, 'to have contributed to our knowledge of the mental climate of early modern England.'[25]

Some works of history can be clearly allocated to either the 'material' or the 'mental' camp. An economic study based on statistics is clearly in a different category from an investigation of popular magic based on the close reading of court depositions. But it is important to stress that the material and the mental are not irreconcilable opposites. They are better regarded as compass points, around which we can take our bearings when placing a work of history. In fact some of the most illuminating work places the material and the mental on a continuum and brings them together in an integrated analysis. A notable example is the history of consumption. Shopping satisfies material wants. But the choice of purchases may be influenced by a culturally informed taste and by the requirements of status. Moreover, by the late nineteenth century, middle-class women in the major Western economies experienced shopping as romance and glamour, promoted by the new department stores: *Shopping For Pleasure*, as the title of one study aptly puts it.[26]

Martin Luther (1483–1546)
One of the most influential figures in the history of Christianity. His protest against the authority of the Pope in 1517 began the Protestant Reformation and the split in the Western Church. His ideas rapidly spread under the patronage of rulers in Germany and elsewhere.

Ignatius Loyola (1491–1556)
Founder of the Jesuit order, based on spiritual discipline and missionary work. His life and achievements symbolized the resolve of the Catholic Church to reinvigorate itself against the Protestant challenge (known as the Counter-Reformation).

VII

Transnational history

Finally, historians deploy a variety of spatial perspectives, ranging from the local at one extreme to the global at the other. Once again, the two ends of the spectrum may seem to have little in common, but both are a reaction against the traditional assumption that history is about the nation state and nothing else. Both local history and world history question the nation state as the default framework for historical enquiry – the first on the grounds that it fails to engage with the communities in which ordinary people lived; the second because it ignores the global networks that have explained – and constrained – many aspects of the nation's development.

Historians of the nation have long taken account of external relations: textbooks habitually feature substantial sections on foreign policy. But there has been less attention to the full range of contacts and influences from abroad which have shaped the development of the nation, if in less obvious ways. *Transnational history* is the label adopted by historians committed to reversing this neglect. In some countries it is almost an article of faith that the nation is unique, autonomous and self-directed. The most striking instance is the United States. From the Revolution onwards, Americans emphasized their difference from Europe, based on the proposition that perfect liberty was only to be found in the US. The long-drawn-out expansion of American society from the Atlantic to the Pacific was believed to demonstrate the national virtues of individualism, self-reliance and entrepreneurial flair. In this 'exceptionalist' version of the American past there was little allowance for external factors, even though the country has been a global presence for a hundred years. Yet to deny the importance of those factors is to produce a lopsided picture of the American past. Political thought, religion, trade and investment are some of the key areas in which American developments were locked into extra-continental events. Ian Tyrrell calls his revisionist account of American history *Transnational Nation* (2007).

World history

Yet a transnational focus is a comparatively modest step towards large-scale history. For historians impatient with the traditional prioritization of the nation, the ultimate goal is *world history*. At first glance this sounds like an impossibility. How could anyone 'know everything' about what has happened on the planet? But world history is not about piling up detail. More than any other branch of history, it depends on selection, and the principle of selection is dictated by themes and developments which have occurred in different parts of the world, and in some cases all over the world. Examples include the spread of world religions like Christianity and Islam; the diffusion of New World food crops; and the rise and fall of global commercial systems. Two important general points can be made here. First, world history breaks the identification of academic history with the history of the

West; to employ a global perspective means taking seriously the history of Third World societies – recognizing indeed that prior to the late eighteenth century regions like India and China were at least as powerful and as sophisticated as their Western counterparts (see Chapter 10). Second, because world history involves juxtaposing societies and cultures that are usually studied in separate compartments, it makes considerable use of the comparative method (discussed more fully in Chapter 6). For example, to ask why Christianity expanded more rapidly than Islam in the second half of the nineteenth century (or why the balance between them was reversed in the second half of the twentieth century) requires a highly demanding comparative approach, encompassing not just the distinctive features of each faith, but the societies in which believers lived.

Globalization

Further precision is added to world history when its subject matter is defined as the origins of today's increasingly globalized world. Globalization refers to the processes whereby our world has

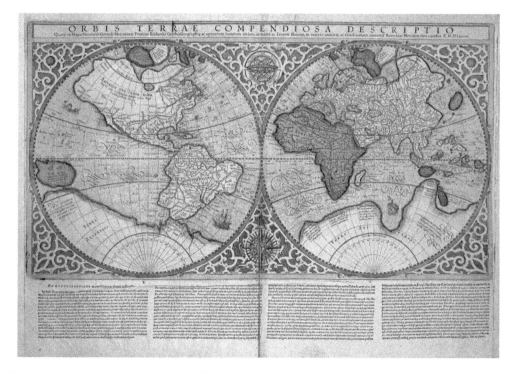

Figure 3.3 Mercator's map of the world, 1587. The circumnavigation of the globe enabled European map-makers to represent the world as a whole. But there were still limits to their knowledge, as the depiction here of Antarctica shows. The eighteenth century was the watershed in accurate map-making. © Bridgeman Art Library/Private collection.

become more integrated and uniform, shrinking both time and distance, and absorbing production and trade into a single international capitalist system. National histories can cast only a fitful light on this theme. *Global history* signifies an effort to make sense of our globalizing world (though it can also mean world history in a broader sense). This is all the more necessary as a topic for historians, because contemporary comment often overplays the novelty of globalization, with its single market, rapid communications and homogenized culture. Like nearly everything else in the modern world, globalization has evolved over a considerable period. Critical features can be traced back to the period of British ascendancy in the nineteenth century, to the earlier maritime empires of the Dutch, the Portuguese and the Spanish, and even to the 'world economy' linking all the lands between China and Western Europe in the thirteenth century.[27] It is seldom recognized that in some ways global integration is less complete now than in the past. Historians refer to the late nineteenth century as the period of 'high globalization', when the telegraph and the steamship had transformed communications, when all the major currencies were convertible at a fixed rate, and when – a highly significant variation from today – there was little impediment to the free movement of labour across the oceans.[28]

One of the most impressive works of global history to date is C.A. Bayly's *The Birth of the Modern World* (2004). His declared aim is to rescue history from the nation and to bring to light the multi-centred character of modernity. This means seeing the world beyond the West not as passive recipients of European expansion, but as dynamic societies which made their own adjustments to changing global conditions. Before the nineteenth century Europe was just one region, along with Japan, China, Mughal India, Persia and the Ottoman Empire, whose worldwide links Bayly calls 'archaic globalization'.[29] Europe's lead over the rest of the world became clear in the course of the nineteenth century, especially in the spheres of technology and production. But today's world is also to be explained by creative reactions in the Third World: in religion, and also (more surprisingly perhaps) in national identity and social organization. Modernity, in short, was a truly global phenomenon, requiring a global reach of scholarship such as Bayly possesses in full measure.

VIII

Local history

Like world history, *local history* has until relatively recently been disdained by the academic profession, but for different reasons. The greatest interest in a specific locality is felt by those who live there. Hence, especially in England, local history used to be dominated by local amateurs who were prepared to work at the sources without necessarily being able to recognize their wider significance. Typically they were preoccupied by the doings of the squire and the parson, to the exclusion of the rest of the population. Their publications were dismissed as being of antiquarian rather than academic interest.

The past fifty years have seen a complete reversal of this outlook. Local history in England has become a kind of in-depth microcosmic social history. During the 1950s the 'Leicester school' of historians, led by W.G. Hoskins, reinterpreted English local history as the reconstruction of historic communities. Hoskins laid special emphasis on visual evidence, such as field patterns, abandoned settlement sites and vernacular architecture. Other historians pursued every scrap of evidence in order to follow the fortunes of individual households over a century or more. Intensive study of this kind assumed a small unit with a maximum population of 2,000; in other words a village. But in the best-documented cases the outcome was a study that brought together every dimension of community life: land use, economy, social structure and religion. Hoskins was drawn to pre-industrial villages, which approximated to his nostalgic pastoralism. But the method is equally valuable as a means of investigating the human realities of social change. *The Making of an Industrial Society* by David Levine and Keith Wrightson shows how the Tyneside village of Whickham adapted to the requirements of coal mining during the seventeenth and eighteenth centuries.[30]

Microhistory and total history

In community studies knowing the names does not necessarily mean knowing the people: family size, occupation and church membership often do little more than enable us to categorize the inhabitants of a village. But in exceptional cases the surviving sources bring individuals to life, allowing us the illusion of a direct encounter, like in a novel. Work of this kind is usually known as *microhistory* – a term coined by the Italian scholars who pioneered it in the 1970s.[31] The most celebrated example is Emmanuel Le Roy Ladurie's account of life in fourteenth-century Montaillou. Drawing mainly from the records of the Inquisition, Ladurie was able to reconstruct the everyday life of the peasants of Montaillou – their social relationships, their religious and magical observances, and not just their attitudes to sex but much of their actual sex life. We are able to follow individuals through the book, notably the parish priest, Pierre Clergue, whose ready access to people's homes enabled him to engage in many extra-marital liaisons. This is a 'microhistory' in the sense that it fills out in small-scale and human detail some of the social and cultural features that are otherwise known only as generalizations.[32]

Local history not only breathes life into abstractions; it can also bring together on a single canvas the varied themes that are usually treated separately by specialists. The proliferation of approaches described in this chapter presents a major problem of integration: how can we see a society in the round if historians give us only partial perspectives on, say, economy or religion? Focusing on a single community of a few hundred people enables the researcher not only to investigate every dimension of life, but to see how they were linked together as a whole experience. The many local histories that have travelled some way along this road have acted as a powerful solvent of the rigidities to which conventional specialists working on a larger canvas are so prone. For political historians particularly, local history serves as a reminder that their subject is about not only the central institutions of the state, but also the assertion of authority over ordinary people. As W.G. Hoskins put it, 'the local historian is in a way like the old-fashioned GP of English medical history, now a fading memory confined to the more elderly among us, who treated Man as a whole'.[33] This has important implications for the goal of historians to integrate their specialist studies into a fully integrated picture of the past. On a grand scale it is an impossible task. But it is practicable within the confines of town or village. Paradoxically, 'total history' turns out to mean local history. That explains its high academic standing today.

IX

In many ways the local historian and the global historian stand further away from each other than any of the other specialists discussed in this chapter; but even here there are illuminating links to be made. It is a mistake to suppose that the village community was ever completely isolated. Economic and cultural influences always impinged from the outside. Perhaps the most striking demonstration of the links between the local and global is Donald Wright's book, *The World and a Very Small Place in Africa* (2004). The subject is the tiny West African kingdom of Niumi at the mouth of the Gambia river. Wright analyses the impact of its global links from the trans-Saharan trade of the late medieval era up to the drive for development in independent Gambia. His study demonstrates that it makes little sense for historians or anthropologists to study small communities as if they were cut off from the outside world.

Every work of history strikes some kind of balance between the individual and society, between the material and the mental, and between the local and the global. Where that balance is struck is the choice of the researcher. Academic fashion often influences the outcome, since historians are keen to ride the crest of a wave, or better still to anticipate it. It is also more common today for researchers to be recruited into teams with a collective brief and research funding to match. Even so, the range of options is still extraordinarily wide, reflecting the fact that history knows no disciplinary bounds. More than ever before, the generic occupational label 'historian' gives little clue as to what an individual scholar actually does. The range of possibilities is sometimes experienced as overwhelming. It is also what makes the study of history such a stimulating pursuit.

Further reading

David Cannadine (ed.), *What is History Today?* Palgrave, 2003.

Peter Burke (ed.), *New Perspectives on Historical Writing*, Polity Press, 1991.

Anna Green and Kathleen Troup (eds), *The Houses of History: A Critical Reader in Twentieth-Century History and Theory*, Manchester University Press, 1999.

Peter Burke, *The French Historical Revolution: The Annales School 1929–89*, Polity Press, 1990.

Fernand Braudel, *On History*, Weidenfeld & Nicolson, 1980.

Carlo M. Cipolla, *Between History and Economics: An Introduction to Economic History*, Blackwell, 1991.

Miles Fairburn, *Social History: Problems, Strategies and Methods*, Routledge, 1999.

Kate Tiller, *English Local History: An Introduction*, 2nd edn, Sutton, 2002.

Maxine Berg (ed.), *Writing the History of the Global: Challenges for the Twenty-First Century*, Oxford University Press, 2013.

Notes

1 Arthur Young writing from Florence in 1789, quoted in J.R. Hale (ed.), *The Evolution of British Historiography*, Macmillan, 1967, p. 35.

2 Leopold von Ranke, *History of Serbia*, 1828, quoted in Theodore H. von Laue, *Leopold Ranke: The Formative Years*, Princeton University Press, 1950, p. 56.

3 Edward A. Freeman, *The Methods of Historical Study*, Macmillan, 1886, p. 44.

4 Sir Lewis Namier and John Brooke, *The House of Commons 1754–1790*, 3 vols, HMSO, 1964, marked the first stage in this massive enterprise. Online access is at www.historyofparliamentonline.org.

5 The journal was renamed *Annales: économies, sociétés, civilisations* in 1946.

6 R.H. Tawney, obituary of George Unwin (1925), quoted in N.B. Harte (ed.), *The Study of Economic History*, Frank Cass, 1971, p. xxvi.

7 Maurice Cowling, *The Impact of Labour, 1920–1924*, Cambridge University Press, 1971, p. 6.

8 Ian Kershaw, *Hitler*, vol I: *Hubris*, Allen Lane, 1998, p. xii.

9 Linda Colley, *The Ordeal of Elizabeth Marsh: A Woman in World History*, Harper, 2007, p. xix.

10 G.M. Trevelyan, *English Social History*, Longman, 1944, p. vii. An almost identical definition is given in G.J. Renier, *History: Its Purpose and Method*, Allen & Unwin, 1950, p. 72.

11 G.D.H. Cole, *A Short History of the British Working-Class Movement, 1789–1947*, Allen & Unwin, 1948, pp. v–vi.

12 George Rudé, *Paris and London in the 18th Century*, Fontana, 1970, pp. 268–92.

13 For a representative collection of work done under the auspices of History Workshop in its early years, see Raphael Samuel (ed.), *People's History and Socialist Theory*, Routledge, 1981.

14 Keith Wrightson, *English Society 1580–1680*, Hutchinson, 1982, p. 12.

15 See Stephan Thernstrom, 'Reflections on the new urban history', *Daedalus*, C, 1971, pp. 359–75. For British developments, see H.J. Dyos, *Exploring the Urban Past*, Cambridge University Press, 1982.

16 For a review of the literature, see Lawrence Stone, *The Causes of the English Revolution, 1529–1642*, Routledge & Kegan Paul, 1972.

17 Harold Perkin, *The Origins of Modern English Society, 1780–1880*, Routledge & Kegan Paul, 1969.

18 E.J. Hobsbawm, 'From social history to the history of society', *Daedalus*, C, 1971, pp. 20–45.

19 E.P. Thompson, *Witness Against the Beast: William Blake and the Moral Law*, Cambridge University Press, 1994.

20 Keith Wrightson, *Earthly Necessities: Economic Lives in Early Modern Britain*, Yale University Press, 2000.

21 R.C. Floud and D. McCloskey (eds), *The Economic History of Britain since 1700*, 2 vols, Cambridge University Press, 1981.

22 R.B. Outhwaite, *Inflation in Tudor and Early Stuart England*, 2nd edn, Macmillan, 1982.

23 J.J. Van-Helten, 'Empire and high finance: South Africa and the international gold standard, 1890–1914', *Journal of African History*, XXIII, 1982, pp. 529–48.

24 I have taken this phrase from Margaret Spufford, *Contrasting Communities: English Villagers in the Sixteenth and Seventeenth Centuries*, Cambridge University Press, 1974, p. xxiii.

25 Keith Thomas, *Religion and the Decline of Magic*, Weidenfeld & Nicolson, 1971, p. ix.

26 Erika Rappaport, *Shopping For Pleasure: Women in the Making of London's West End*, Princeton University Press, 2001.

27 Janet L. Abu-Lughod, *Before European Hegemony: The World System, A.D. 1250–1350*, Oxford University Press, 1989.

28 Martin Daunton, 'Britain and globalization since 1850, I: Creating a global order. 1850–1914', *Transactions of the Royal Historical Society*, 6th series, XVI, 2006.

29 C.A. Bayly, *The Birth of the Modern World, 1780–1914*, Blackwell, 2004, pp. 41–47.

30 David Levine and Keith Wrightson, *The Making of an Industrial Society: Whickham, 1560–1765*, Oxford University Press, 1991.

31 See especially Carlo Ginzburg, *The Cheese and the Worms: The Cosmos of a Sixteenth-Century Miller*, Routledge & Kegan Paul, 1980.

32 Emmanuel Le Roy Ladurie, *Montaillou: Cathars and Catholics in a French Village, 1294–1324*, Penguin, 1976.

33 W.G. Hoskins, *English Local History: The Past and the Future*, Leicester University Press, 1966, p. 21.

4   The raw materials

Students rarely work with historical sources in their original state. Examination papers and textbooks contain short, labelled extracts, which bear little resemblance to the originals. What sort of sources are available to the historian? How did they come to be made available, and how might this affect their usefulness? This chapter gives a fuller idea of the provenance of, and problems with, the sort of sources historians habitually use.

Such is the range of motives and the variety of interests that draw people to the past that history can be said to embrace the human experience of every place and period. No part of that past can be dismissed as falling outside the proper domain of historical knowledge. But how far it can be made the subject of well-founded research depends on the availability of historical evidence. Whether the historian's main concern is with recreation or explanation, with the past for its own sake or for the light it can shed on the present, what he or she can actually achieve is determined in the first instance by the extent and character of the surviving sources. Accordingly, it is with the sources that any account of the historian's work must begin. This chapter describes the main categories of documentary material, showing how they came into being, how they have survived down to the present, and in what form they are available to the scholar.

I

Specialist sources and skills

Historical sources encompass every kind of evidence that human beings have left behind of their past activities – the written word and the spoken word, the shape of the landscape and the material **artefact**, the fine arts as well as photography and film. Among the humanities and social sciences, history is unique in the variety of its source materials, each calling for specialist expertise. The military historian of the English Civil War can examine the arms and armour surviving from the seventeenth century and the terrain over which the battles were fought, as well as the military

artefact
Any object left over from the past.

General Strike
A major industrial dispute that brought virtually all of Britain's industry to a halt in May 1926. The dispute began in the mining industry, but spread when other trade unions came out in support of the miners.

dispatches of each side. A rounded picture of the **General Strike** of 1926 calls for a study of government and trade union records, the press and broadcasting, together with the collection of testimonies from survivors. The reconstruction of a pre-colonial kingdom in black Africa is likely to depend not only on the excavation of its capital but also on the contemporary observations of European or Arab visitors and the oral traditions handed down over many generations. No single historian can possibly master all these tools. The more technical of them have become the province of distinct specialisms. The excavation of ancient sites and the interpretation of the material remains found there is the business of the archaeologist, assisted these days by the aerial photographer and the chemical analyst. In the case of the visual arts the equivalent specialist is the art historian, though there is an increasing overlap with the discipline of history (considered in Chapter 9).

During the past forty years, the range of sources in which historians claim expertise has certainly increased. It now includes place names, landscape patterns and – for recent history – film. Oral testimony is now fully established as a legitimate source for historians (see Chapter 11). The fact remains, however, that the study of history has nearly always been based squarely on what the historian can read in documents or printed material. That emphasis was confirmed when historical research was placed on a professional footing during Ranke's lifetime. For the majority of historians, research is an activity that goes on in libraries and archives.

Figure 4.1 Archival holdings are essential to historical scholarship. Not only do historians have to treat their sources carefully, they have to remember how it is that some sources made their way into the archives while others did not. © Getty Images/Time & Life Pictures.

The written word

The reason is not just academic conservatism. From the High Middle Ages (*c*.1000–1300) onwards, the written word survives in greater abundance than any other source for Western history. The fifteenth and sixteenth centuries witnessed not only a marked growth in record-keeping by the state and other corporate bodies but also the rapid spread of printing, which encouraged literate production of all kinds and transformed its prospects of survival. Written sources are usually precise as regards time, place and authorship, and they reveal the thoughts and actions of individual men and women as no other source can do. One has only to read an account of a society for which virtually no written records exist – for example Iron Age Britain or **medieval Zimbabwe** – to see how lacking in human vitality history can be when denied its principal source material. Moreover, the written word has always served many different purposes – information, propaganda, personal communication, private reflection and creative release – all of which may have relevance for the historian. The interpretation of texts serving a variety of functions from an age whose habits of mind differed sharply from our own calls for critical abilities of a very high order. Written sources are at the same time the most rewarding and (in most cases) the most plentiful. Small wonder, then, that historians seldom look elsewhere.

The use of written materials as the principal historical source is complicated by the fact that historians communicate their findings through the same medium. Both in their choice of research topic and in their finished work, historians are influenced to a greater or lesser extent by what their predecessors have written, accepting much of the evidence they uncovered and, rather more selectively, the interpretations they put upon it. But when we read the work of a historian we stand at one remove from the original sources of the period in question – and further away still if that historian has been content to rely on the writings of other historians. The first test by which any historical work must be judged is how far its interpretation of the past is consistent with all the available evidence; when new sources are discovered or old ones are read in a new light, even the most prestigious book may end on the scrapheap. In a real sense, the modern discipline of history rests not on what has been handed down by earlier historians, but on a constant reassessment of the original sources. It is for this reason that historians regard the original sources as *primary*. Everything that they and their predecessors have written about the past counts as a *secondary* source. Most of this book is concerned with secondary sources – with how historians formulate problems and reach conclusions, and how we as readers should evaluate their work. But first it is necessary to examine the raw materials a little more closely.

medieval Zimbabwe
The medieval kingdom of Zimbabwe was a major power in southern Africa from the thirteenth to the fifteenth century. The impressive stone ruins of its royal palace at Great Zimbabwe posed a serious challenge to those white settlers who dismissed indigenous African culture as intrinsically inferior to that of Europeans.

Primary and secondary sources

contemporary
Literally 'at the same time as'. In historical terminology it usually refers to events or people from the period being studied.

British reactions to the French Revolution
When the French Revolution broke out in 1789, opinion in Britain was initially supportive. However, it quickly became implacably hostile as events in France descended into rule by violence and terror. A small group of political radicals, however, remained consistently supportive of the Revolution. These two responses continue to be mirrored in the attitudes of British historians of the period.

medieval chronicles
Medieval chronicles were written narratives, often skilfully crafted into a highly readable form. We do not know how much research went into their writing, though they were often consulted by later chroniclers and writers.

Macaulay's *History of England*
Although called a *History of England*, Macaulay's work in fact concentrates almost entirely on the important constitutional changes following the overthrow of King James II in 1688 and the accession of the first Hanoverian king, George I, in 1714.

The distinction between primary and secondary sources, fundamental though it is to historical research, is rather less clear-cut than it might appear at first sight, and the precise demarcation varies among different authorities. By 'primary sources', it is generally meant evidence **contemporary** with the event or thought to which it refers. But how far should our definition of 'contemporary' be stretched? No one would quibble about a conversation reported a week or even a month after it took place, but what about the version of the same episode in an autobiography composed twenty years later? And how should we categorize an account of a riot written shortly afterwards, but by someone who was not present and relied entirely on hearsay? Although some purists regard the testimony of anyone who was not an eyewitness as a secondary source,[1] it makes better sense to apply a broad definition but to recognize at the same time that some sources are more 'primary' than others. The historian will usually prefer those sources that are closest in time and place to the events in question. But sources more remote from the action have their own significance. The historian is often as much interested in what contemporaries *thought* was happening as in what actually happened: **British reactions to the French Revolution**, for example, had a profound influence on the climate of politics in Britain, and from this point of view the often garbled reports of events in Paris which circulated in Britain at the time are an indispensable source. As this example suggests, to speak of a source as 'primary' implies no judgement of its reliability or freedom from bias. Many primary sources are inaccurate, muddled, based on hearsay or intended to mislead, and (as the next chapter will show) it is a vital part of the historian's work to scrutinize the source for distortions of this kind.

The distinction between primary and secondary is further complicated by the fact that sometimes primary and secondary material appear in the same work. **Medieval chronicles** usually began with an account of world history from the Creation to the life of Christ, based on well-known authorities; but what modern historians value them most for is the entries that they recorded year by year concerning current events. Equally, a work can be primary in one context and secondary in another: **Macaulay's *History of England*** (1848–55) is a secondary source whose reputation has been much undermined by modern research; but for anyone studying the political and historical assumptions of the early Victorian elite, Macaulay's book, in its day a bestseller, is a significant primary source. These examples might suggest what is often assumed, that 'historical documents' are the formal, dignified records of the past. It is true that records of this kind are more likely to endure, but the term should carry the widest possible reference. Every day all of us create what are potentially historical documents – financial accounts, private correspondence, even shopping lists. Whether they actually become historical documents depends on whether they survive and whether they are used as primary evidence by scholars of the future.

In order to make sense of the vast mass of surviving primary sources, the first requirement is some system of classification. Two types are in common use. The first draws a distinction between the published – which in the modern period has usually meant printed – and the unpublished or manuscript source. The second emphasizes instead the authorship of the sources, drawing a distinction between those produced by governments and those produced by corporations, associations or private individuals. Each of these methods lends itself to the precision required by the cataloguer, and bibliographies published by historians at the end of their works are normally arranged along these lines. But the criteria that historians actually apply in the course of their research, although related to these two types of classification, are rather less cut and dried. In the historian's hierarchy of sources, those that carry most weight are the ones that arise directly from everyday business or social intercourse, leaving open the task of interpretation. In every recent age men and women have sought to make sense of their times, and to interpret the pattern of events through books, **broadsheets** or newspapers. Such statements offer valuable insights into the mentality of the age, but for the historian they are no substitute for the direct, day-to-day evidence of thought and action provided by the letter, the diary and the **memorandum**: these are the 'records' of history *par excellence*. Historians wish to be as nearly as possible observers of the events in question; they do not want to deliver themselves into the hands of a narrator or commentator. The most revealing source is that which was written with no thought for posterity. **Marc Bloch** called this 'the evidence of witnesses in spite of themselves';[2] it has all the fascination of eavesdropping.

II

Narratives and memoirs

We begin, however, with primary sources written for the benefit of posterity. These tend to be the most accessible because their survival was seldom left to chance. Often they have a literary quality that makes them a pleasure to read. They provide a ready-made chronology, a coherent selection of events, and a strong sense of period atmosphere. Their drawback is that they recount only what people found worthy of note about their own age – which may not be what interests us today. Prior to the Rankean revolution in the nineteenth century, it was on primary sources of this kind that historians tended to rely. For Roman history they turned to Caesar, Tacitus and Suetonius, while medievalists drew

broadsheets
A form of early newspaper designed to be pinned up in a public place.

memorandum
An internal message or note sent within an office or institution. Memoranda from government offices can give a very detailed picture of the development of policy.

Marc Bloch (1886–1944)
French medievalist historian. He was one of the founders of the *Annales* school, which sought to link the study of history with an in-depth appreciation of the role of geography and other disciplines. He also wrote a perceptive study of *The Historian's Craft*. During the Second World War he fought in the French resistance, but was captured and shot shortly before the D-Day landings.

Figure 4.2 Vincenz of Beauvais, medieval polyhistorian. Although medieval chroniclers did consult documents and were sometimes able to speak with some of the major figures they wrote about, their priority was to provide a lively narrative. The historical discipline of measured analysis of source material was a much later, nineteenth-century development. © akg-images, London.

Anglo-Saxon Chronicle

A detailed yearly chronicle of major events in Anglo-Saxon England compiled by monks at different monasteries and abbeys and brought together on the orders of King Alfred the Great. It was long thought to be an objective account of events, but historians now see it as heavily slanted in King Alfred's favour, possibly on his instructions.

on the **Anglo-Saxon Chronicle** and the works of writers such as **Matthew Paris** in the thirteenth century and **Jean Froissart** in the fourteenth. Nor do modern historians disparage these narrative sources. They owe their continuing importance to the fact that they survive from periods that have left only a limited amount of record sources. In the Middle Ages most of the early chronicles were written by monks without personal experience of public affairs, but increasingly from the twelfth century they were joined by **secular clergy** who had served the king in responsible positions and could to some extent record political history from the inside. **Gerald of Wales** was a royal chaplain who became acquainted with **Henry II** towards the end of his reign in the 1180s. The following passage well conveys the restless energy of one of England's most remarkable kings:

> Henry II, king of England, was a man of reddish, freckled complexion with a large round head, grey eyes which glowed fiercely and grew bloodshot in anger, a fiery countenance and a harsh, cracked voice. His neck was somewhat thrust forward from his shoulders, his chest was broad and square, his arms strong and powerful. His frame was stocky with a

pronounced tendency to corpulence, due rather to nature than to indulgence, which he tempered by exercise. ... In times of war, which frequently threatened, he gave himself scarcely a modicum of quiet to deal with those matters of business which were left over, and in times of peace he allowed himself neither tranquillity nor repose. He was addicted to the chase beyond measure; at crack of dawn he was off on horseback, traversing waste lands, penetrating forests and climbing the mountain-tops, and so he passed restless days. At evening on his return he was rarely seen to sit down either before or after supper. After such great and wearisome exertions he would wear out the whole court by continual standing.[3]

The autobiography is essentially a modern variant of the chronicle, with the personality of the author brought centre stage. Invented by the self-conscious Italians of the Renaissance,[4] this form is favoured by artists, writers and perhaps most of all by politicians. The fascination of autobiographies derives from the fact that they are the recollections of an insider. Indeed they often provide the only available first-hand account, because in all countries recent government records are closed to public inspection (see p. 92); in Britain former Cabinet ministers, when writing their memoirs, are permitted to consult official papers relating to their term of office, though they may not cite or quote from them. But the author's purpose is less to offer an objective account than to justify his or her actions in retrospect and to provide evidence for the defence before the bar of history. Autobiographies may be very revealing of mentality and values, but as a record of events they are often inaccurate and selective to the point of distortion. This was pre-eminently true of Winston Churchill who, even while he was Prime Minster, intended to write the definitive record of his war-time leadership. Through his voluminous memoirs, published soon after the Second World War, he successfully established his own somewhat self-aggrandizing version of events. It was many years before the extent of the distortion became clear to historians. Even today, Churchill's popular image remains pretty much what he himself planted in the public mind during and after the war.[5]

At the same time it would be a mistake to think of the published memoir as an upper-class preserve. In Britain by the mid-nineteenth century it had become a recognized means of expression for the literate artisan as well. As David Vincent has shown, autobiographies were written in order to convey the humanity of the working man (and, more rarely, the working woman), and also to challenge common misconceptions about working-class life. The pride and resentment are evident in the

Matthew Paris (c.1200–c.1259)
Monk of St Albans and author of one of the most important chronicles of medieval England. Paris seems to have spoken to leading figures in the course of compiling his chronicle.

Jean Froissart (c.1335–c.1404)
French chronicler, he spent long periods in England at the court of King Edward III. His chronicle covers the early period of the Hundred Years' War between England and France. His early version was more sympathetic to the English than his later accounts.

secular clergy
Priests who do not belong to a monastic order.

Gerald of Wales (1146–1223)
Gerald de Barri, Bishop of St Davids and writer of descriptions of Wales and Ireland. Frustrated ambition led him to turn against his English patrons and fight for Welsh independence against King Edward I.

Henry II (1135–89)
First of the Plantagenet Kings of England (also known as Angevins, from their native Anjou in France). Henry is best known for his disastrous feud with Archbishop Thomas à Becket, but he also instituted major reforms in the legal system.

**Thomas Hardy
(1752–1832)**
Scottish radical. He was accused and acquitted of high treason in 1794, during the wars with Revolutionary France. Not to be confused with the novelist of the same name.

opening lines of the radical **Thomas Hardy**'s autobiography, published in 1832:

> As every man whose actions, from whatever cause, have acquired publicity, is sure, in many things, to be misrepresented, such a man has an undoubted right, nay, it becomes his duty, to leave to posterity a true record of the real motives that influenced his conduct. The following Memoir, therefore, requires no apology, and none is offered.[6]

Over 140 such works have survived from the period 1790–1850 alone.

Official papers and newspapers

The chronicles and memoirs that people write for future genera-tions are, of course, only a small minority of what is published in any period. Most publications are issued with little thought for posterity; they are rather intended to inform, influence, mislead or entertain contemporaries. The invention of printing in the fifteenth century greatly facilitated the dissemination of such writings, while the growth of literacy among the laity increased the demand for them. Governments were quick to profit from the revolution in communications, and by the nineteenth century statements of policy, propaganda and digests of information on trade, revenue and expenditure were flowing from the official presses. In Britain, perhaps the most impressive of these publica-tions were the **census reports** published every ten years from 1801, and the reports of **royal commissions** set up from the 1830s onwards to take evidence about and make recommendations on major social problems such as public health and conditions of work. Another official publication of great interest is that of the reports of parliamentary proceedings. Thomas **Hansard** began publication of the debates in the Lords and Commons as a private venture in 1812 (though not quite the first of its kind). The series assumed its modern format in 1909, when the government, through His Majesty's Stationery Office, took it over; first-person, **verbatim** reporting became the rule. Few other sources convey so well the public face of political discourse.

census reports
The census has been held in Britain at regular ten-year intervals ever since 1801, except for 1941, when the demands of war made it impossible. Census reports include detailed commentary as well as statistical tables, which make them peculiarly useful to social historians.

royal commissions
A committee of inquiry set up at the command of the monarch (i.e. of the government) to investigate an issue. Commissions take evidence from witnesses and then produce detailed reports. Both the transcriptions of questioning of witnesses and the reports are usually published.

However, the most important published primary source for the historian is the press, which in Britain has a continuous history dating back to the early eighteenth century, the first daily newspaper having been founded in 1702. Newspapers have a threefold value. First, they record the political and social views that made most impact at the time; indeed in Britain the earliest newspapers, which had developed out of the vigorous tradition of pamphleteer-ing during the Civil War and **Commonwealth** (1642–60), contained little else and are remembered now for the brilliant polemics of Addison, Steele and Swift. To this day the leaders and correspondence columns of the great London dailies offer the best entry into the current state of **establishment** opinion – provided due allowance is made for the editorial bias of the paper in question. Second, newspapers provide a day-to-day record of events. During the nineteenth century, this function began to be filled much more fully, particularly when the development of the electric telegraph in the 1850s enabled journalists in distant postings to **file their copy** home as soon as it was written. W.H. Russell of *The Times* was one of the first to take advantage of this revolution in communications. His celebrated dispatches from the **Crimea** during the war of 1854–6, which provided shocking evidence of the disarray of the British forces, had a major impact on public opinion at home.[7] As sources of straight reporting, newspapers are likely to become even more valuable to historians in the future. For despite the vast archives that governments and corporations continue to amass, important decisions are increasingly communicated by telephone and e-mail rather than by letter, and information obtained informally by journalists at the time may provide the only contemporary written record of what has taken place. Lastly, newspapers from time to time present the results of more thorough enquiries into issues that lie beyond the scope of routine news reporting. The founder of this tradition was Henry Mayhew, an **impecunious** writer briefly employed by the *Morning Chronicle* in 1849–50. As 'Special Correspondent for the Metropolis' he wrote a series of articles exposing social conditions among the London poor in the aftermath of the great cholera epidemic of 1849, which later formed the basis of his book *London Labour and the London Poor* (1851). Few investigative journalists since then have equalled Mayhew in the thoroughness of his research or in his impact on contemporary opinion.[8]

Literature as historical source material

There is one other kind of source intended for the eyes of contemporaries (and often for posterity too) that historians have to consider, though it is rather a special case: this is creative literature. Novels and plays cannot, of course, be treated as factual reports, however great the element of autobiography or social observation may be. Nor, needless to say, do historical novels – or Shakespeare's history plays for that matter – carry any authority as historical statements about the periods to which they refer. But all creative literature offers insights into the social and intellectual milieu in which the writer lived, and often vivid descriptions of the physical setting as well. The success of an author is often attributable to the way in which he or she articulates the values and preoccupations of literary contemporaries.

Hansard
Named after its founder, Thomas Hansard (1776–1833), this is the name given to the daily written reports on proceedings in Parliament. In its early versions, the *Parliamentary History* wrote in reported speech ('He said he would ... ') and sometimes described the scene in the chamber rather than reproducing the exact word. The development of shorthand enabled reporters to reproduce the exact words spoken.

verbatim
Reported word for word.

Commonwealth
From 1649 to 1654 England was ruled as a republic, known as the Commonwealth, and from 1654 to 1659 as a Protectorate under Oliver Cromwell. The constitutional and political uncertainty of the period saw the production of a huge number of pamphlets laying out conflicting political and religious theories about the direction in which the country ought to move.

establishment
A term originally coined by young satirists and radical writers in the 1960s to denote all those persons, institutions and attitudes that do well out of the status quo and wish therefore to preserve it.

file their copy
'To file copy' is a journalistic term for submitting the text of an article.

Crimea
The Crimean War (1854– 6), in which Britain fought alongside France and Turkey against Russia, was marked by serious administrative inefficiency and incompetence in British military administration. As a result, the figures who emerged with most credit from the war were those, like the journalist William Howard Russell or the nursing administrator Florence Nightingale, who exposed its shortcomings, and the ordinary British soldier who suffered from them.

impecunious
Poor, short of money.

Chaucer (c.1340–1400)
Geoffrey Chaucer, English poet and author of *The Canterbury Tales*. The tales cover a wide range of subjects and social classes, and are therefore heavily used by historians of the late Middle Ages.

'condition of England' question
A phrase used in the 1840s to denote the questions surrounding the problems of poverty, squalor and relations between the rich and the poor.

So it makes good sense to cite **Chaucer** as a spokesman for the attitudes of the fourteenth-century laity to abuses in the Church, or Dickens as evidence of the frame of mind in which middle-class Victorians considered the **'condition of England' question**.

III

Record sources: memos, minutes and official correspondence

Because newspapers, official publications and parliamentary speeches are composed mostly with a view to their impact on contemporary opinion, historians attach greater weight to them than to the chronicles and memoirs written with the requirements of posterity in mind. But the very fact of publication sets a limit on the value of all these sources. They contain only what was considered to be fit for public consumption – what governments were prepared to reveal, what journalists could elicit from tight-lipped informants, what editors thought would gratify their readers, or MPs their constituents. In each case there is a controlling purpose which may limit, distort or falsify what is said. The historian who wishes, in Ranke's phrase, 'to show how things actually were' (see p. 7) must go behind the published word, and that is why the greatest advances in modern historical knowledge have been based on research into 'records' – confidential documents such as letters, minutes and diaries. It is in these forms that men and women record their decisions, discussions and sometimes their innermost thoughts, unmindful of the eyes of future historians. Time and again, historians have found that a careful study of the record sources reveals a picture very different from the confident generalizations of contemporary observers. In nineteenth-century England, the medical writer William Acton declared that respectable women experienced no sexual feelings of any kind, and his view has been much cited as evidence of Victorian repression; only when the letters and diaries between spouses were examined did it become clear that a much wider range of sexual responses existed among married women.[9] Whether the question at issue is the motives of the participants in the English Civil War, or the impact of the Industrial Revolution on standards of living, or the volume of the Atlantic slave trade, there is no substitute for the painstaking accumulation of evidence from the record sources of the period.

In most countries the largest single body of unpublished records is that belonging to the state, and since Ranke's day more research has been devoted to government archives than to any other kind of source. In the West, the oldest surviving state archives took shape during the twelfth century, which saw a marked advance in the sophistication of government organization all over Europe. In England a continuous series of revenue records – the

Pipe Rolls of the Exchequer – extends back to 1155, and the records of the royal courts (King's Bench and Common Pleas) to 1194. The beginning of systematic record-keeping can be dated precisely to 1199. In that year, King John's Chancellor, Hubert Walter, began the practice of making copies on parchment rolls of all the more important letters dispatched from the **Chancery** in the king's name. Even after the emergence of other departments in the thirteenth and fourteenth centuries, the Chancery remained the nerve centre of royal administration, and its enrolments are the most important archival source for the Middle Ages in England.

Chancery
The royal secretariat in medieval times, administered by the King's Chancellor.

The records of bureaucracy

During the period 1450–1550, the medieval system was superseded by a more bureaucratic structure controlled by the Privy Council. The most powerful single official within this structure was the King's Secretary (later called the Secretary of State), and from the reign of Henry VIII his records, known as the State Papers, become the most rewarding source for information about the policies and actions of the government. In contrast to Chancery records the State Papers, to quote Galbraith,

> are not the routine products of an office, but the intimate and miscellaneous correspondence of an official whose duties knew no fixed limits. ... The veil that separates us from character and personality in the Middle Ages is torn aside.[10]

Among the State Papers for 1536 there survives this letter summoning an unfortunate priest from Leicestershire to an interrogation, probably in connection with treason; the menacing tone is unmistakable:

> I commend me unto you. Letting you wit the King's pleasure and commandment is that, all excuses and delays set apart, ye shall incontinently upon the sight hereof repair unto me wheresoever I shall chance to be, the specialties whereof ye shall know at your coming. Without failing thus to do, as ye will answer at your peril. From the Rolls, the 8th day of July. Thomas Crumwell [*sic*].[11]

Thomas Cromwell (c.1485–1540)
Secretary successively to Cardinal Wolsey and to King Henry VIII. Cromwell oversaw the dissolution of the monasteries, which involved rigorous examination of the internal affairs of monasteries, convents and abbeys.

It is this category of document that proliferated in the following centuries, as additional Secretaries of State were appointed to run new departments that could keep abreast of the expanding scope of government. By the nineteenth century, each department of state was keeping a systematic record of letters and papers received, copies of letters sent out and memoranda circulating within the department. At the apex of this complex bureaucratic structure stands the Cabinet. For the first 200 years of its existence, its deliberations were entirely 'off the record', but since 1916 the Cabinet Secretariat has kept minutes of the Cabinet's weekly meetings and prepared papers for its use.

Another aspect of the enlargement of government under the Tudors was the beginning of routine diplomacy conducted by resident ambassadors. The Italian states set the pattern in the 1480s and 1490s; other countries soon followed, and England's diplomatic network had taken shape by the 1520s. The Venetian ambassador who, in the course of twelve months in 1503–4, sent back from Rome 472 dispatches, was more industrious than most,[12] but regular reporting home was from the start an essential part of the ambassador's duties. These reports not only document the conduct of foreign policy more fully than ever before; they also record the diplomat's appraisal of the court and country to which he was accredited. Ranke relied on them heavily for both political and diplomatic history, and since then there have been many historians whose expertise is almost entirely limited to diplomatic documents. By the late nineteenth century – often thought of as the 'golden age' of diplomacy – the documentary record is so full that the historian can reconstruct every stage of a diplomatic initiative from the first tentative proposal of a ministry official to the completed report on the negotiations.

The nineteenth century was also the period when government began to make systematic records of the entire population. The census aims to list all the members of a country or community alive at any one time; without it absolute numbers cannot be determined, nor whether the population is increasing or declining. In Britain, a census has been taken at ten-yearly intervals since 1801, and it is generally conceded that after 1841 (when the name of each individual was noted for the first time), errors in the totals are statistically insignificant. Other listings survive from earlier periods – tax returns, returns of church communicants, declarations of political loyalty and the like. But, though comprehensive in intent, these were seldom so in practice, and the margin of error is very uncertain and inconsistent. At the same time as the census was being developed, Britain set up a comprehensive system of civil registration to record all 'vital' events, i.e. births, marriages and deaths, on the basis of which much more accurate demographic projections could be made. Since then, the range and volume of data amassed by government about the population as a whole has steadily increased.

Church records

Two other types of record share the official character of central government records. First, during the Middle Ages the Church wielded as much, if not more, authority than the state, and in most European countries it retained many of its powers in the secular sphere until the early nineteenth century. Its history is fully documented by the immense quantity of Church records that are available to historians today, many of them still virtually untouched. Royal charters granting land and privileges to the Church have been preserved from the early Middle Ages, and copious records document the efficiency of **episcopal** and monastic administration. The records of the **Church courts** are more interesting than might seem likely at first glance, because so many moral misdemeanours of ordinary people came within their jurisdiction. In sixteenth- and early seventeenth-century England, for example, when the established Church's position vis-à-vis the Puritan sects was under threat, strenuous efforts were made through the Church courts to discipline the **laity**, and the records of these courts are therefore an important source for the social historian, particularly as regards sexual misdemeanours and sexual defamation.[13] The Church courts also retained jurisdiction over wills in England until 1858, and from Elizabeth I's reign onwards they insisted on detailed inventories of all movable property, which can now tell the historian a great deal about wealth, status and standards of living.

episcopal
Pertaining to bishops.

Church courts
Church courts dealt with offences against canon (i.e. Church) law, rather than civil offences, which were dealt with in the king's courts. Church courts often dealt with cases of sexual immorality.

laity
'Lay' people, i.e. those who are not members of the clergy.

Local government and private firms

Second, there are the records of local government. During the thirteenth century in England, lords of the manor began to follow the king's example and keep records – and particularly judicial records, since they had legal jurisdiction over their tenants and servants. One result is that changes in landholding are relatively well documented for rich and poor alike. The first Justices of the Peace were commissioned by the Crown in the fourteenth century, and under the Tudors they were saddled with a mounting load of responsibility – for matters as various as policing, poor relief, wage regulation and military recruitment. Much of this burden was discharged during quarter sessions held at three-monthly intervals in each county, and recorded by a Clerk of the Peace. This remained the basis of local government in England until the modern system of county and borough councils was established during the nineteenth century. Until that time a high proportion of local records are legal: the same individuals – whether lords of the manor or Justices of the Peace – were charged with judicial as well as administrative duties. Of all public records, the court records of everyday and often trivial disputes and offences shed most light on the wider society beyond the small world of government.

The records of the Church and local administration might seem to be of marginal interest. In fact they are crucial to the prospects of social history. The limited scope of the first ventures in social history is partly explained by the tendency of historians to take the line of least resistance and follow the trail through the records of institutions with an avowedly 'social' function – schools, hospitals, trade unions and such; the result was all too often work of a narrowly institutional character. But social history as it is now understood demands a great deal more. Social groups do not leave corporate records. Their composition and their place in the social structure have to be reconstructed from a broad range of sources composed for quite different and usually much more mundane reasons. This is especially true of the history of the common people. Their conditions and opinions became the subject of systematic social surveys only during the nineteenth century. Until then, the picture that we form of them is inevitably dominated by those activities that brought down on them the attention of the authorities: destitution, litigation, sedition and – most of all – common crime and offences against Church discipline. At times of popular discontent this attention was particularly intrusive, and whole areas of society which normally remain 'invisible' may be illuminated by legal and police records. The riots that periodically broke out in eighteenth-century London are a case in point.[14] Equally, fear of revolution may intensify official surveillance of lower-class activities, as in England during the Napoleonic Wars: 'but for spies, narks and letter-copiers, the history of the English working class would be unknown', wrote E.P. Thompson, with only a little overstatement.[15] Such opportunities are all the more precious because at other times information about the common people is usually much thinner. Court records are still useful, but in more settled conditions judicial activity was less intense, and it is therefore much more difficult to build up the profile of a local community. Before any generalization can be made with confidence, a vast number of court records has to be sifted, usually in conjunction with other local sources such as manorial records, tax registers, wills and the records of charitable institutions.

Church and state are the oldest record-keeping institutions in Western society. But from the fifteenth century onwards the historian can supplement them with an ever-increasing volume of records generated by private corporations and associations – guilds, universities, trade unions, political parties and pressure groups. Of particular interest are the records of businesses and firms. Their beginnings are shrouded in obscurity. The only major documentary archive of a medieval English trading firm which has come down to us is the papers of the Cely family, who were prominent in the export of wool to the Low Countries in the 1470s and 1480s.[16] By the eighteenth century, commercial records become really plentiful, and they are an essential source for historians of the Industrial Revolution. For example, the papers of the Stockport textile manufacturer Samuel Oldknow were discovered quite by chance in a disused mill in 1921; covering the period 1782–1812, they provide vivid documentation of the transition from the domestic to the factory system of production.[17] Many companies today have cash-books, inventories and ledgers dating back to the same period or earlier; the historian of England's brewing industry recalls:

> The family continuity in the industry has been such that in most cases I found myself working on the letters and the accounts of the ancestors of the present owners and managers of the concerns, reading their records on the same site where they had brewed in the eighteenth century.[18]

The records he examined included those of such well-known names as Whitbread, Charrington and Truman.

IV

Private papers

As a general rule, those activities which leave most evidence behind are *organized* activities, and especially those controlled by bodies that have a life-span beyond the careers of the individuals who happen to staff them at any one time – whether they be governments, religious bodies or businesses. For the greater part of recorded history, literate people have probably done most of their writing in the course of their professional or official duties. Nevertheless, there survives a vast mass of written material that has been set down by men and women as private individuals, outside the office or the counting house. Much the largest proportion is accounted for by private correspondence, and from the seventeenth century this becomes available in considerable quantities. For example, the Verneys were Buckinghamshire gentry who wrote copiously and were careful to preserve their correspondence. For the period between the 1630s and the mid-eighteenth century more than 30,000 letters survive. Through such letters, says Susan Whyman,

> We can see how individuals coped in a society based upon lineage, custom and manners. We can uncover a family's social code, and note whether they accepted or evaded its norms. ... We can see how people brought stability to their lives by constructing networks, maintaining friendships and communicating with absent loved ones. Through letters we can watch how people dealt with anxiety, illness and isolation.[19]

Nor should it be supposed that the gentry had a monopoly on letter-writing. Working-class people wrote fewer letters and preserved fewer still. But the letters of far-flung family members were sometimes kept, and they survive in considerable numbers from the nineteenth century. Irish emigrants to Australia treasured letters from home as 'oceans of consolation'; David Fitzpatrick has reconstituted the narratives of fourteen such families, drawing on a total of 111 surviving letters.[20] Such material gives a human face to a story more often presented in dry statistics.

There are no other sources that bring to life so clearly the family and social relationships of people in the past. Without private correspondence the biographer must be content with the public or business life – which indeed is all that medieval biographies can usually attain. One of the main reasons why it is possible to give a relatively full account of the private lives of the Victorians is that an efficient and frequent postal service enabled them to conduct a voluminous correspondence: an upper-class woman whose marriage took her away from her own family might write more than 400 letters in a single year.[21] This pattern remained common until the spread of the telephone after the First World War. But private letters are an essential source for historians of politics as well. This is because government records are more concerned with decisions and their implementation than with the motives of the people who made them. The private correspondence of public figures reveals much that is scarcely hinted at in the official record. The nineteenth and early twentieth centuries were the great age of personal correspondence, when close colleagues in public life wrote to each other daily. Much of this correspondence by-passed official channels and was intended to be seen by none but the recipient. Some politicians confided to a remarkable degree in friends who were without any formal position in politics at all. For three of the years (1912–15) during which he was Prime Minister, **H.H. Asquith** wrote once or twice a day to a young lady called Venetia Stanley. In these letters he could frankly express all his political anxieties and frustrations (as well as many more trivial reflections), confident that his remarks would go no further. Here, in a letter of March 1915, is his assessment of Winston Churchill, then First Lord of the Admiralty:

> As you know, like you, I am really fond of him; but I regard his future with many misgivings. ... He will never get to the top in English politics, with all his wonderful gifts; to speak with the tongue of men & angels, and to spend laborious days & nights in administration, is no good, if a man does not inspire trust.[22]

H.H. Asquith (1852–1928)
Liberal Prime Minister before and during the First World War, 1908–16.

Diaries

Private letters are associated with another source that is in some ways even more revealing of personality and opinion – the diary. Diary-keeping began in the sixteenth century and soon became a common literary accomplishment among the educated, especially in England, which in **John Evelyn** and **Samuel Pepys** produced two of the greatest masters of the art. Unlike chroniclers or annalists, diarists are as much preoccupied with their own subjective response as with the external events that they have witnessed. The considerations that induce someone to devote several hours each week to keeping up a diary are anything but frivolous. For creative writers, the diary satisfies the compulsion to observe and reflect, free of the constraints imposed by the formal requirements of the novel, poem or play. Of politicians it is sometimes assumed that a diary serves as little more than an *aide-mémoire* to be drawn on when the time comes to compose an autobiography. But for most political diarists this is a secondary consideration compared with the release from the intense pressures of life in the public eye that a diary affords. The diary that **Gladstone** kept from 1825 to 1896 has almost the character of a confessional: the record of daily engagements and political commentaries is broken up by long passages of painful self-analysis, an unremitting quest for purity of soul.[23] No historian who has not read the diary can hope to understand the personality of this giant among Victorian statesmen. In the case of the Labour politician, **Hugh Dalton**, diary-writing seems to have filled a psychological need directly related to his political performance. As Ben Pimlott explains, the diary, which spans the years 1916 to 1960, acted both as a 'sounding board for ideas' and as a safety valve for Dalton's 'very strong instinct towards political self-destructiveness', being fullest for those times when he was consumed by feelings of resentment or irritation against his closest political associates.[24]

For the historian of twentieth-century politics, letters and diaries are of particular significance, despite the almost limitless volume of official records. In the course of the last two generations, ministers and civil servants have tended to become more discreet in their official correspondence. During the nineteenth century, such correspondence was occasionally published by authority, for example in the **Blue Books** laid by British ministers before Parliament; but this was usually done almost immediately, for pressing propaganda reasons, and the published dispatches had in some cases been composed with that express purpose. In the 1920s, however, the select publication of official records grew out of all proportion, as governments strove to excuse themselves, and blame others, for responsibility for the First World War, often with scant regard for the reputation of individual officials twenty or thirty years earlier. Ministers and civil servants, especially those concerned with foreign policy, became much more inhibited in their official correspondence; hence what they wrote to each other privately, or recorded in their diaries, therefore gains in interest. Moreover, much that politicians *do* say in the course of their ministerial duties does not find its way into the official record. The civil servants who compile Cabinet minutes, for

John Evelyn (1620–1706)
Although active in politics after the Restoration, Evelyn is best known for his diary.

Samuel Pepys (1633–1703)
As well as keeping his celebrated diary, which includes an account of the Fire of London, Pepys was also, as Secretary to the Admiralty, a central figure in the development of British naval power.

Gladstone (1809–98)
William Ewart Gladstone was a towering figure in Victorian politics, serving as Prime Minister four times. His diary is a detailed account of his daily engagements, including, obscured behind a special code, his sexual practices.

Hugh Dalton (1887–1962)
Labour politician. As Chancellor of the Exchequer in Clement Attlee's 1945 government, Dalton played a central role in the post-war nationalization of heavy industry.

Blue Books
Reports of Victorian parliamentary committees and commissions were published – often selling surprisingly well – and were known as Blue Books after the colour of their covers.

example, are primarily concerned with the decisions reached; the heated political arguments, which are what interest the historian most about Cabinet meetings, go largely unrecorded. **Richard Crossman**, who served as a Cabinet minister under Harold Wilson from 1964 to 1970, kept a weekly diary which was intended, as he put it, to do something towards 'lighting up the secret places of British politics', among which the Cabinet featured prominently.[25] Crossman's diary is unusual in that, almost from the outset, he envisaged its publication within a few years. By contrast, the vast majority of the diaries and letters available to the historian were written without thought of a wider readership. Of all sources they are the most spontaneous and unvarnished, revealing both the calculated stratagems and the unconscious assumptions of public figures.

V

Why do sources survive?

From this discussion it will be apparent that a variety of factors have contributed to the survival of so much documentation from the past. Private letters and diaries have owed their survival to the writer's desire for posthumous fame, or the family piety of the heirs, or perhaps their inertia in leaving trunks and drawers undisturbed. In the case of public records the reasons are more straightforward and more compelling: they arise from the central role of written precedent in law and administration since the High Middle Ages. To put it bluntly, governments needed an accurate record of what was due to them in taxes, dues and services, while the king's subjects cherished evidence of privileges and exemptions that had been granted to them in the past. As the royal bureaucracy grew more unwieldy, it became increasingly necessary for officials to have a record of what their predecessors had done. As the practice of diplomacy became more formalized from the fifteenth century onwards, ministers could review the earlier relations of their governments with foreign powers and be briefed on their obligations and entitlements under foreign treaties. What was true of governments applied *mutatis mutandis* to other corporate bodies such as the Church, or the great trading companies and financial houses. The only way in which institutions with this sort of permanence could have a 'memory' was if a careful record of their transactions was preserved.

But practical motives are not everything. Written documents are also fragile, and the fact that they have weathered the hazards of fire, flood and sheer neglect in such profusion also requires explanation. Continuity of government and of basic law and order are vital. Throughout most of Europe, the fabric of literate civilization has endured without a break since the early Middle

Ages. Within Europe, the distribution of the surviving documentation is largely explained by the incidence of warfare and revolutionary upheaval. It is because England has had little of either that English medieval public records are so plentiful. Last but not least, the growth of historical consciousness itself has had important consequences in minimizing the destruction of documents once they have ceased to be of practical use. Here the Renaissance was the turning point. Curiosity about classical antiquity bred an antiquarian mentality which valued the relics of the past for their own sake – hence the beginning of both archaeology and the systematic conservation of manuscripts and books. It is the combination of these factors that accounts for the uniquely rich documentation of the history of Western society and distinguishes it from the other great literate cultures of China, India and the Muslim world, where the survival of written sources has been much more patchy.

Conservation and publication

Only relatively recently, however, has it become a reasonably simple matter to locate the sources and secure access to them. Without the coming of age of historical studies in the mid-nineteenth century and the growing political awareness of the need to preserve the raw materials of a national past, historians today would face a much more daunting prospect. Their task is easiest in the case of published sources. In England there is a good chance that the researcher, assisted by bibliographies and catalogues, will find what he or she wants in one of the great **'copyright' libraries**, which by Act of Parliament are entitled to a free copy of every book and pamphlet published in the United Kingdom; the most complete is the British Library (until 1973 the British Museum), whose entitlement dates back to 1757 and has been rigorously enforced since the 1840s. The copyright entitlement is a feature of other national libraries, notably the Library of Congress in Washington.

But what of the unpublished sources? The conservation of public and private documents, many of them written with no thought for the requirements of storage and reference, presents a considerable challenge. In some cases the problems have been partially solved by publication. An immense effort was devoted to this task during the nineteenth century, when the historical value of records gained common acceptance for the first time. The pattern was set by the *Monumenta Germaniae Historica* series, which began publication with government support in 1826 under the direction of the best historians of the day; by the 1860s most of the raw materials for medieval German history were in print.[26] Other countries quickly followed suit, including Britain, where the equivalent Rolls Series began to appear in 1858. The original promoters of these projects intended to publish *all* the extant primary sources. Even for the

'copyright' libraries
Other copyright libraries, in addition to the British Library, are Cambridge University Library, the Bodleian Library, Oxford, the National Libraries of Wales and Scotland and the Library of Trinity College, Dublin.

medieval period this was an ambitious goal; for later, more lavishly documented periods it was an obvious impossibility. In the late nineteenth century, therefore, attention was increasingly switched to the publication of 'calendars', or full summaries of the records. Calendars are an immense help to the researcher, but only because they indicate which documents are relevant to his or her purpose; they are no substitute for perusal of the documents in full.

Archives

In most countries, the historian's task is greatly eased by an elaborate archive service. But this is a relatively recent development, and the survival of documents from the remote past has often owed more to luck than good management. Many archival collections have perished by accident: the Whitehall fire of 1619 destroyed many of the Privy Council papers, and the fire that swept the Palace of Westminster in 1834 took with it most of the records belonging to the House of Commons. Other holdings have been deliberately destroyed for political reasons: a prominent feature of the agrarian revolts which broke out in the French countryside in July 1789 was the burning of manorial archives that authorized the exaction of heavy dues from the peasantry.[27] In Africa during the 1960s, departing colonial officials sometimes destroyed their files for fear that sensitive material would fall into the hands of their African successors.

In England, as elsewhere in Europe, the conservation of archives by the state dates back to the twelfth century. But until the nineteenth century each department of government retained its own archives. They were housed all over London in a variety of buildings, many of them highly unsuitable. Throughout the seventeenth and eighteenth centuries, the Chancery records in the Tower were kept above the Ordnance Board's gunpowder stores,[28] while other repositories were exposed to the ravages of damp and rodents. These conditions not only frustrated private litigants (and the occasional historian) wishing to track down precedents, but were also an embarrassment to the government itself: it was not unknown for the original of an important treaty to elude the most diligent search.[29]

The chaos of archival practice in the early modern era not only inconvenienced governments, it also frustrated historical research. The close link which is now assumed between archives and historians only became a reality during the nineteenth century. The French Revolution proclaimed the principle of free access, but it was many years before this became a reality. In Britain the Public Record Office was set up by Act of Parliament in 1838 (it was renamed the National Archives in 2003); within twenty years it had gained custody of all the main classes of government record, housed in a purpose-built archive in central London. Without that reorganization the immense progress made in the study of English medieval history in the late nineteenth and early twentieth centuries would scarcely have been possible. Today, the National Archives in Britain is the largest archive in the world (with over 100 miles of shelving) and offers some of the most up-to-date facilities to be found anywhere. A national archive has become a defining attribute of the modern nation state. When the new states of Asia and Africa became independent between the 1940s and 1970s, the consolidation of the records of colonial administration into a national archive was one of their first tasks in pursuit of

Figure 4.3 When the French Revolution broke out in 1789, many villagers took the opportunity to attack the châteaux of their local landowners and destroy all documents recording the feudal taxes and services they owed. Many other documents went up in smoke at the same time, a major blow to future historians of French history. © Mary Evans Picture Library.

a properly documented national past. The United States had also once been a new state, but in this case the setting up of a national archive was delayed until a decision by President Roosevelt in 1934. Individual states of the union had developed and conserved their archives for some time, but the records of the Federal Government had been neglected.

As the interests of historians have been enlarged to cover social and economic themes (see Chapter 3), the conservation and organization of local records have been increasingly taken in hand. This has been a formidable undertaking which has won scant public recognition. Under legislation passed in 1963, every county in England and Wales is required to maintain a county record office, whose job is to gather together the different categories of local record – quarter sessions, parish, borough and manorial records, etc. Many of the record offices originated in local initiatives taken before the Second World War, and they have extended their search well beyond the semi-official categories to include the records of businesses, estates and associations. Today the holdings of all the county record offices almost certainly exceed those of the National Archives. Local and regional studies have become a practicable proposition for professional historians for the first time.

Restrictions on access

Nowhere, however, have historians been granted complete freedom of access to public records. If historians were allowed to inspect files as soon as they had ceased to be in current use, they would be reading material that was only a few years old. All governments, whatever their political complexion, depend on a measure of confidentiality. Civil servants expect to be reasonably secure in the knowledge that what they set down officially shall not be publicly discussed in the foreseeable future. In Britain the 'closed period' laid down for public records varied considerably according to the department of origin until it was standardized at fifty years in 1958. Nine years later, after a vigorous campaign by historians, this period was reduced to thirty years (since 2013 the closed period has been reduced to twenty years). France followed suit in 1970, but in some countries, for example Italy, fifty years is still the rule. In the United States the Freedom of Information Act of 1975 allows both historians and the general public much wider access, but elsewhere the reduction of the closed period to thirty years is probably as far as the liberalization of access to public records is likely to go. Clearly this has major implications for the study of contemporary history, where historians are forced to rely much more than they would like on what was made public at the time, or what has been disclosed retrospectively in memoirs and diaries.

Yet, however galling these restrictions may seem, in Britain government archives are at least centralized and accessible. The same broadly applies to local public records. The case is entirely different with records in private hands. These are widely dispersed and subject to varying – and sometimes perverse – conditions of access; and while governments have usually acknowledged the need for some kind of archive conservation, however rudimentary, family and business records, which may serve no practical function, have often been completely neglected. Nor can the historian whose interest is confined to official documents afford to ignore these private collections. Until the Cabinet Secretariat laid down firm guidelines after 1916, it was common for retiring ministers and officials to keep official papers in their possession; from the sixteenth century onwards, a steady flow of State Papers passed out of public custody in this way,[30] and to this day most of the State Papers dating from **Robert Cecil**'s tenure of office (1596–1612) are at Hatfield House.

In most Western countries one of the functions of the national libraries set up during the nineteenth century was to secure possession of the most valuable private manuscript collections. Britain's national library dates back to the foundation of the British Museum in 1753. Of its foundation manuscript collections, the most important from the historian's point of view is that of Sir Robert Cotton, the early seventeenth-century collector and antiquarian; this numbered among its treasures a great many State Papers, one version of the Anglo-Saxon Chronicle, and two of the four surviving 'exemplifications' of Magna Carta (i.e. copies made at the time of the agreement between King John and the barons in 1215). Purchases and bequests since then have made the British Library far and away the largest repository of historical manuscripts in Britain outside the National Archives. Even so, the number of important documents held elsewhere is incalculable. Many private collections have been given or loaned indefinitely to public libraries, or to the county record offices. But many more remain in the hands of private individuals, companies and associations. For over a hundred years the Historical Manuscripts Commission promoted the care of manuscripts privately held in Britain (it was absorbed into the National Archives in 2003). Yet there is still scope for the historian with a nose for detective work. Several of the collections of private papers on which Namier relied for his studies in eighteenth-century English politics were discovered during what he called his 'cross-country paper-chases'.[31]

Robert Cecil (1563–1612)
Son of Queen Elizabeth I's minister, Sir William Cecil, Robert Cecil served as Secretary of State under both Elizabeth and James I. Hatfield House is the Cecil family home.

Unearthing source material

The position is worst in the case of the personal and ephemeral materials in the hands of ordinary people – the account books of small businesses, the minute books of local clubs, everyday personal correspondence and the like. Neither the local record offices nor the National Archives cast their net as widely as this, yet the recovery of everyday documentation is important if historians are ever to make good their oft-stated aspiration to treat the masses and not just their masters. This is a task for historians with a local focus everywhere, and exciting finds are sometime made by apprentice researchers. Since people are usually unaware that they hold material that might be historically significant, historians cannot wait for documents to be brought forward; they need to engage in propaganda and go out in search of them.

VI

Primary sources online

Given the distribution of archives and libraries, historians have often led peripatetic lives when tracking down their sources. But mobility is no longer quite the requirement it once was. Today, primary sources are increasingly accessed online and at the researcher's desk. The scale of the digitization enterprise makes it the most significant enlargement of access to primary sources since the establishment of state archives in the nineteenth century. It is also a comparatively recent change, dating back to the rapid dissemination of the World Wide Web in the late 1990s. One of the most ambitious early initiatives was the American Memory website, launched by the Library of Congress in 1994. There are now over nine million items, arranged in over 100 thematic collections. They include both published sources and manuscripts like the complete papers of George Washington and selective records of the Federal Government.[32] In Britain, as in other countries, digital sources are being rapidly expanded by a range of agencies. The National Archives have digitized the records of the 1901 and 1911 censuses, making the original enumerators' books available at a stroke.[33] The British Library has placed on line its vast holding of nineteenth-century British newspapers.[34] Digitization initiatives are not, however, confined to large institutions. Academics have secured funding to place on line sources with a high use-value for specialist research. A major instance is Old Bailey Online (launched in 2003), a digital record of nearly 200,000 criminal trials from 1674 to 1913 which gives the researcher access to indictments, evidence, verdict and sentence.[35] For Anglo-Saxon England it has proved possible to put together a website consisting of structured information about all the known individuals in that period; the range of possible searches means that researchers can, as the website states, 'move rapidly from the known to the unknown'.[36] There are also very extensive postings by amateurs of material relating to genealogy, local history and other leisure-related interests.

The headlong expansion of the Internet has not only transformed access to historical records, it also places no limit on how much may be stored in the future. In retrospect we may appear to be at no more than the threshold of the digital age. A big advantage of digitized records is that specified proper names, place names or concepts (i.e. keywords) can be quickly identified in very large bodies of material which would otherwise defy investigation. Many digitization schemes have also transformed the documentary base for the study of the poor and obscure. The editors of the Old Bailey website are almost certainly correct in describing it as 'the largest body of texts detailing the lives of non-elite people ever published'.[37] At the same time, although the Internet is sometimes spoken of as 'infinite', it is not comprehensive. Untold documentary resources lie outside its reach, from the letters of the poor to the estate records of the wealthy (like those sought by Namier). And if there is any reason to question the accuracy or authenticity of the digitized version, the originals must be tracked down.

They must also be experienced directly for a less tangible reason. Something is lost if the historian has not handled the originals, since they are the closest that he or she can get to the past. Arlette Farge has evoked the experience of archival research more vividly than anyone else; she maintains that mechanical modes of reproduction can drain the life out of the material, and she places a high value on 'the tactile and direct approach to the material, the feeling of touching the traces of the past'.[38] In the last analysis digitization does not dissolve the direct link which the historian prizes between the text, the person who composed it and the place in which it was written. The archive has not lost its allure. Knowing the sources in their original form is the surest foundation for making a critical evaluation, which is the subject of the next chapter.

Further reading

J.J. Bagley, *Historical Interpretation*, vol. I: *Sources of English Medieval History, 1066–1540*, Penguin, 1965.

J.J. Bagley, *Historical Interpretation*, vol. II: *Sources of English History, 1540 to the Present Day*, Penguin, 1971.

Miriam Dobson and Benjamin Ziemann (eds), *Reading Primary Sources*, Routledge, 2008.

Rebecca Earle (ed.), *Epistolary Selves: Letters and Letter-Writers, 1600–1945*, Ashgate, 1999.

David Knowles, *Great Historical Enterprises*, Nelson, 1963.

Andrew McDonald, 'Public records and the modern historian', *Twentieth-Century British History*, I, 1990.

Michael Moss, 'Archives, the historian and the future', in Michael Bentley (ed.), *Companion to Historiography*, Routledge, 1997.

Toni Weller (ed.), *History in the Digital Age*, Routledge, 2013.

Notes

1 Louis Gottschalk, *Understanding History: A Primer of Historical Method*, Knopf, 1950, pp. 53–5.
2 Marc Bloch, *The Historian's Craft*, Manchester University Press, 1954, p. 61.
3 Extract from Gerald of Wales, *Expugnatio Hibernica*, translated from the Latin in D.C. Douglas and G.W. Greenaway (eds), *English Historical Documents, 1042–1189*, Eyre & Spottiswoode, 1953, p. 386.
4 The best example is the autobiography of Pope Pius II, composed in the late 1460s. See Leona C. Gabel (ed.), *Memoirs of a Renaissance Pope: The Commentaries of Pius II*, Allen & Unwin, 1960.
5 David Reynolds, *In Command of History: Churchill Fighting and Writing the Second World War*, Allen Lane, 2004.
6 Quoted in David Vincent, *Bread, Knowledge and Freedom: A Study of Nineteenth-Century Working-Class Autobiography*, Methuen, 1981, p. 26.
7 See Kellow Chesney, *Crimean War Reader*, Severn House, 1975.
8 E.P. Thompson and Eileen Yeo (eds), *The Unknown Mayhew: Selections from the Morning Chronicle, 1849–50*, Penguin, 1973.
9 Peter Gay, *The Bourgeois Experience: Victoria to Freud*, vol. II: *The Tender Passion*, Oxford University Press, 1986; John Tosh, *A Man's Place: Masculinity and the Middle-Class Home in Victorian England*, Yale University Press, 1999, ch. 3.
10 V.H. Galbraith, *An Introduction to the Use of the Public Records*, Oxford University Press, 1934, pp. 54–5.
11 Thomas Cromwell to John Harding, 8 July 1536, quoted in G.R. Elton, *Policy and Police*, Cambridge University Press, 1972, pp. 342–3.
12 Garrett Mattingly, *Renaissance Diplomacy*, Cape, 1962, pp. 110, 306.
13 See, for example, Laura Gowing, *Domestic Dangers: Women's Words and Sex in Early Modern London*, Oxford University Press, 1996.
14 See, for example, George Rudé, *Paris and London in the Eighteenth Century: Studies in Popular Protest*, Fontana, 1970. For a critical review, see Joanna Innes and John Styles, 'The crime wave: recent writing on crime and criminal justice in eighteenth-century England', *Journal of British Studies*, XXV, 1986, pp. 380–435.
15 E.P. Thompson, *Writing by Candlelight*, Merlin Press, 1980, p. 126.
16 Alison Hanham (ed.), *The Cely Letters 1472–1488*, Oxford University Press, 1975.
17 George Unwin, *Samuel Oldknow and the Arkwrights*, Manchester University Press, 1924.
18 Peter Matthias, *The Brewing Industry in England, 1700–1830*, Cambridge University Press, 1959, p. xii.
19 Susan Whyman, '"Paper visits": the post-Restoration letter as seen through the Verney family archive', in Rebecca Earle (ed.), *Epistolary Selves: Letters and Letter-Writers, 1600–1945*, Ashgate, 1999, p. 25.
20 David Fitzpatrick, *Oceans of Consolation: Personal Accounts of Irish Migration to Australia*, Cornell University Press, 1994.
21 Pat Jalland, *Women, Marriage and Politics, 1860–1914*, Oxford University Press, 1988, pp. 3–4.
22 H.H. Asquith, *Letters to Venetia Stanley*, ed. M. and E. Brock, Oxford University Press, 1982, p. 508.
23 M.R.D. Foot and H.C.G. Matthew (eds), *The Gladstone Diaries*, 14 vols, Oxford University Press, 1968–94.
24 Ben Pimlott, 'Hugh Dalton's diaries', *The Listener*, 17 July 1980. An edited version of the diaries was published by LSE in association with Jonathan Cape in two volumes in 1986.

25 Richard Crossman, *The Diaries of a Cabinet Minister*, vol. I, Hamish Hamilton and Cape, 1975, p. 12.

26 David Knowles, *Great Historical Enterprises*, Nelson, 1963, pp. 65–97.

27 Georges Lefebvre, *The Great Fear of 1789*, New Left Books, 1973, pp. 100–21.

28 Elizabeth M. Hallam and Michael Roper, 'The capital and the records of the nation: seven centuries of housing the public records in London', *The London Journal*, IV, 1978, pp. 74–5.

29 R.B. Wernham, 'The public records in the sixteenth and seventeenth centuries', in Levi Fox (ed.), *English Historical Scholarship in the Sixteenth and Seventeenth Centuries*, Oxford University Press, 1956, pp. 21–2.

30 Ibid., pp. 20–3.

31 Julia Namier, *Lewis Namier: A Biography*, Oxford University Press, 1971, p. 282.

32 memory.loc.gov/ammem/index.html

33 www.1901censusonline.com; www.1911census.co.uk

34 http://infotrac.galegroup.com/itweb/britlibtr

35 www.oldbaileyonline.org

36 Prosopography of Anglo-Saxon England. www.pase.ac.uk/index.html.

37 www.oldbaileyonline.org

38 Arlette Farge, *The Allure of the Archives*, trans. Thomas Scott-Railton, Yale University Press, 2013, p. 15.

5   Using the sources

Having tracked the source material down, how should the historian set about using it? This chapter looks at different approaches that historians adopt: some start out with a specific set of questions, some follow whatever line of enquiry the sources themselves throw up. The chapter draws a distinction between the source critic, who analyses source material in great detail, and the historian, who does this too but puts the sources in the context of a wider knowledge of the period to which they relate. Sources have to be analysed for forgery, the author's bias has to be detected and taken account of, and historians need to know how to spot when material has been removed from the record or covered up. Digitized material is not exempt from these procedures. The archive itself – traditionally regarded as authoritative – is increasingly scrutinized for ideological distortion.

If the historian's business is to construct interpretations of the past from its surviving remains, then the implications of the vast and varied array of documentary sources described in the previous chapter are daunting. Who can hope to become an authority on even one country during a narrowly defined time-span when so much spadework has to be done before the task of synthesis can be attempted? If by 'authority' we mean total mastery of the sources, the short answer is: only the historian of remote and thinly documented **epochs**. It is, for example, not beyond the capacity of a dedicated scholar to master all the written materials that survive from the early Norman period in England. The **vicissitudes** of time have drastically reduced their number, and those that survive – especially record sources – tend towards the terse and economical. For any later period, however, the ideal is unattainable. From the **High Middle Ages** onwards, more and more was committed to paper or parchment, with ever-increasing prospects of survival to our own day. Since the beginning of the twentieth century the rate of increase has surged ahead at breakneck speed. Between 1913 and 1938, the number of dispatches and papers received annually by the British Foreign Office increased from some 68,000 to 224,000.[1] Additions to the National Archives at

epochs
Periods, eras.

vicissitudes
Changes in fortune.

High Middle Ages
Term usually applied to the eleventh and twelfth centuries, often taken to mark the climax of medieval society and culture.

present fill approximately 1 mile of shelving per year. Amid this documentary surfeit, where does the historian begin?

I

Different approaches to using source material

Ultimately the principles governing the direction of original research can be reduced to two. According to the first, the historian takes one source or group of sources that falls within his or her general area of interest – say the records of a particular court or a body of diplomatic correspondence – and extracts whatever is of value, allowing the content of the source to determine the nature of the enquiry. Recalling his first experience of the French Revolutionary archives, Richard Cobb describes the delights offered by a source-oriented approach:

> More and more I enjoyed the excitement of research and the acquisition of material, often on quite peripheral subjects, as ends in themselves. I allowed myself to be deflected down unexpected channels, by the chance discovery of a bulky *dossier* – it might be the love letters of a **guillotiné**, or intercepted correspondence from London, or the account-books and samples of a commercial traveller in cotton, or the fate of the English colony in Paris, or eyewitness accounts of the September Massacres or of one of the *journées*.[2]

guillotiné
Someone who was executed by guillotine during the French Revolution.

journées
Literally 'days'. The term was applied to moments of particular drama during the French Revolution.

The second, or problem-oriented, approach is the exact opposite. A specific historical question is formulated, usually prompted by a reading of the secondary authorities, and the relevant primary sources are then studied; the bearing that these sources may have on other issues is ignored, the researcher proceeding as directly as possible to the point where conclusions can be advanced. Each method encounters snags. The source-oriented approach, although appropriate for a newly discovered source, may yield only an incoherent jumble of data, or in the case of the Internet a compilation of keywords. The problem-oriented approach sounds like common sense and probably corresponds to most people's idea of research. But it is often difficult to tell in advance which sources *are* relevant. As will be shown later, the most improbable sources are sometimes found to be illuminating, while the obvious ones may lead the historian into too close an identification with the concerns of the organization that produced them. Moreover, for any topic in Western nineteenth- or twentieth-century history, however circumscribed by time or place, the sources are so unwieldy that further selection can hardly be avoided, and with it the risk of leaving vital evidence untouched.

In practice neither of these approaches is usually pursued to the complete exclusion of the other, but the balance struck between them varies a good deal. Some historians begin their careers with a narrowly defined project based on a limited range of sources; others are let loose on a major archive with only the vaguest of briefs. The former is on the whole the more common, because of the pressure to produce quick results that is imposed by the **Ph.D.** degree – the formal apprenticeship served by most academic historians. A great deal of research – probably the larger part – consists not in ferreting out new sources but in turning to well-known materials with new questions in mind. Yet too single-minded a preoccupation with a narrow set of issues may lead to evidence being taken out of context and misinterpreted – 'source-mining' as one acerbic critic put it.[3] It is vital, therefore, that the relationship between the historian and his or her sources is one of give and take. Many historians have had the experience of setting out with one set of questions, only to find that the sources which they had supposed would furnish the answers instead directed their research on to quite a different path. Emmanuel Le Roy Ladurie first turned to the land-tax registers of rural Languedoc with a view to documenting the birth of capitalism in that region; he found himself instead investigating its social structure in the broadest sense, and in particular the impact of **demographic** change:

> Mine was the classic misadventure; I had wanted to master a source in order to confirm my youthful convictions, but it was finally the source that mastered me by imposing its own rhythms, its own chronology, and its own particular truth.[4]

At the very least there must be a readiness to modify the original objective in the light of the questions that arise directly from the sources. Without this flexibility historians risk imposing on their evidence and failing to tap its full potential. The true master of the craft is someone whose sense of what questions can profitably be asked has been sharpened by a lifetime's exposure to the sources in all their variety. Mastery of all the sources remains the ideal, however improbable its complete accomplishment may be.

Analysing sources

The reason why the ideal remains for the most part unattainable is not only that the sources are so numerous but also that so many of them require careful appraisal. For the primary sources are not an open book, offering instant answers. They may not be what they seem to be; they may signify very much more than is immediately apparent; they may be couched in obscure and antiquated forms that are meaningless to the untutored eye. Before the historian can properly assess the significance of a document, he or she needs to

Ph.D.
Doctor of Philosophy. This is usually obtained after three years of detailed archival study resulting in the production of a thesis – a carefully argued case presented in the form of a short book.

demographic
Concerning changes in population.

find out how, when and why it came into being. This requires the application of both supporting knowledge and sceptical intelligence. 'Records', it has been said, 'like the little children of long ago, only speak when they are spoken to, and they will not talk to strangers.'[5] Nor, it might be added, will they be very forthcoming to anyone in a tearing hurry. Even for the experienced historian with green fingers, research in the primary sources is time-consuming; for the novice it can be painfully slow.

Historians have long been aware of the value of primary sources – and not merely the more accessible sources of a narrative kind. A surprising number of medieval chroniclers showed a keen interest in the great state documents of the day and reproduced them in their writings. William Camden, the leading English historian in Shakespeare's generation, was granted access to the State Papers in order to write a history of Elizabeth I's reign. But scholarly source criticism is a much more recent development. It was largely beyond the historians of the Renaissance, for all their sophistication. Camden, for example, regarded his record sources as 'infallible testimonies'.[6] Many of the technical advances that underpin modern source criticism were made during the seventeenth century – notably by the great **Benedictine** scholar Jean Mabillon. But their

Benedictine
Of the monastic Order of St Benedict.

Figure 5.1 The English historian Edward Gibbon (1737–94) said that the idea for writing his famous account of the *Decline and Fall of the Roman Empire* came to him while sitting one evening in the ruins of the forum in Rome. Gibbon started with one major question – what caused such a mighty empire to collapse? – and he embarked on his reading of the historical records with that question always in view. His conclusion, that it was due in large part to the debilitating effects of Christianity, was in line with the radical thinking of the Enlightenment but created a storm of public controversy. © Bridgeman Art Library/Private collection.

application was at first confined to monastic history and the lives of the saints, and historians continued to live in a different world from that of the source critic (*érudit*). Edward Gibbon, the greatest historian of the eighteenth century, drew heavily on the findings of the *érudits* in his *Decline and Fall of the Roman Empire* (1776–88), but he did not emulate their methods.

The introduction of a critical approach to the sources into mainstream history writing was Ranke's most important achievement. He owed his early fame and promotion to a merciless exposé of Guicciardini's faults as a scholar. His appetite for archival research was truly prodigious. And through his seminar at the University of Berlin, he brought into being a new breed of academic historians trained in the critical evaluation of primary sources – and especially the many archival sources that were being opened to research for the first time during the nineteenth century. It was with pardonable exaggeration that **Lord Acton** saluted Ranke as 'the real originator of the heroic study of records'.[7] Ranke won acceptance for the idea that the evaluation of sources and the writing of history must be kept in the same hands. The spread of Rankean method to Britain came comparatively late; it was primarily due to William Stubbs, whose reputation rested not only on his studies of English constitutional history but also on his scrupulous editing of medieval historical texts. To this day, what Marc Bloch called 'the struggle with documents' is one of the things that distinguishes the professional historian from the amateur.[8]

**Lord Acton
(1834–1902)**
British historian, Regius (i.e. royal) Professor of Modern History at Cambridge. Acton was formidably learned, and an obsessive note-taker. He edited the multi-volume *Cambridge Modern History* but never got round to writing a major work of history. It was he who wrote in a letter that 'power tends to corrupt and absolute power corrupts absolutely'.

II

Is it authentic?

The first step in evaluating a document is to test its authenticity; this is sometimes known as *external* criticism. Are the author, the place and the date of writing what they purport to be? These questions are particularly relevant in the case of legal documents such as charters, wills and contracts, on which a great deal could depend in terms of wealth, status and privilege. During the Middle Ages many royal and ecclesiastical charters were forged, either to replace genuine ones that had been lost, or to lay claim to rights and privileges never in fact granted. The Donation of Constantine, an eighth-century document that purported to confer temporal power over Italy on Pope Sylvester I and his successors, was one of the most famous of these forgeries. Documents of this kind might be termed 'historical forgeries', and detecting them may tell us a great deal about the society that produced them. But there is also the modern forgery to be considered. Any recently discovered document of great moment is open to the suspicion that it was forged by somebody who intended to make a great deal of money or to run rings round the most eminent scholars of the day.

The Hitler diaries did just that. Extracts of what purported to be the Führer's journal were published in a West German magazine in 1983. Although they appeared to add little of significance to our understanding of the Third Reich, being mostly taken up by lists of official engagements and announcements, the diaries aroused intense public interest. They were pronounced genuine by three scholars, including the eminent British historian Hugh Trevor-Roper, only to be exposed shortly afterwards as a forgery: forensic tests revealed that both the paper and the ink were modern. It later transpired that the forger, who specialized in Nazi memorabilia, had produced sixty-two volumes of the 'diary' in five years.[9]

Once suspicions are aroused, the historian will pose a number of key questions. First, there is the issue of provenance; can the document be traced back to the office or person who is supposed to have produced it, or could it have been planted? In the case of great finds that suddenly materialize from nowhere, this is a particularly significant question. Second, the content of the document needs to be examined for consistency with known facts. Given our knowledge of the period, do the claims made in the document or the sentiments uttered seem at all likely? If the document contradicts what can be substantiated by other primary evidence of unimpeachable authenticity, then forgery is strongly indicated. Third, the form of the document may yield vital clues. The historian who deals mostly in handwritten documents needs to be something of a **palaeographer** in order to decide whether the script is right for the period and place specified, and something of a **philologist** to evaluate the style and language of a suspect text. (It was philological tests that clinched Lorenzo Valla's case against the Donation of Constantine as early as 1439.) More specifically, official documents usually conform to a particular ordering of subject matter and a set of stereotyped verbal formulae, the hallmarks of the institution that issued them. *Diplomatics* is the name given to the study of these technicalities of form. Lastly, historians can call on the help of technical specialists to examine the materials used in the production of the document. For example, chemical testing can determine the age of parchment, paper and ink.

It would be misleading, however, to suggest that historians are constantly uncovering forgeries, or that they methodically test the authenticity of every document that comes their way. This procedure is certainly appropriate to certain branches of medieval history, where much may depend on a single charter of uncertain provenance. But for most historians – and especially the modern historian – there is little prospect of a brilliant detective coup. Their time is more likely to be spent perusing an extended sequence of letters or memoranda, recording humdrum day-to-day transactions, which would scarcely be in anyone's interest to forge. And in the case of public records under proper archival care, the possibility of forgery is remote.

palaeographer
One who studies ancient writings.

philologist
One who studies the development of language.

For the medievalist some of these skills of detection have another application – to help in preparing an authentic edition out of the several corrupt variants that survive today. Before the invention of printing in the fifteenth century, the only means whereby books could be circulated was by frequent copying by hand; during most of the Middle Ages the *scriptoria* of the monasteries and cathedrals were the main centres of book production. Inevitably errors crept into the copying, and they increased as each copy was used as the basis of another. Where the original (or 'autograph') does not survive, which is frequently the case with important medieval texts, the historian is often confronted by alarming discrepancies among the available versions. This is the unsatisfactory form in which some of the major chroniclers of the medieval period have come down to us. However, close comparison of the texts – especially their scripts and the discrepancies of wording – enables the historian to establish the relationship between the surviving versions and to reconstruct a much closer approximation to the wording of the original. The preparation of a correct text is an important part of a medievalist's work, requiring a command of palaeography and philology. This process is made easier now that the texts, which may be held by widely scattered libraries, can be photographed and examined alongside each other.

scriptoria **(sing.** *scriptorium***)**
(Latin) The writing rooms of a monastery, where documents were written and copied out.

III

Understanding the text

The authentication of a document and – where applicable – cleansing the text of corruptions are only preliminaries. The second and usually much more demanding stage is *internal* criticism, that is, the interpretation of the document's content. Granted that author, date and place of writing are as they seem, what do we make of the words in front of us? At one level this is a question of meaning. This involves more than simply translating from a foreign or archaic language, difficult though that may be for the novice trying to make sense of medieval Latin in abbreviated form. The historian requires not merely linguistic fluency but a command of the historical context that will show what the words actually refer to. Domesday Book is a classic example of the difficulties that can arise here. It is a record of land use and wealth distribution in the English shires in 1086, before the institutions of the Anglo-Saxons (and the Danes) had been much altered by Norman rule; but it was compiled by clerks from Normandy whose everyday language was French and who described what they had seen and heard in Latin. 'Translation' is an understatement for the process of interpretation needed in such a case; for example, scholars remain uncertain to what form of land tenure the term *manerium* (usually 'manor') refers.[10] Nor are our problems solved if we stick to documents written in English. For language itself is a product of history. Old words, especially the more technical ones, pass out of currency, while others acquire a new significance. We have to be on our guard against reading modern meanings into the past. In the case of the more culturally sophisticated sources, such as contemporary histories or treatises on political theory, different levels of meaning may have been embedded in the same text, and this becomes a major task of interpretation. In coming to terms with the instability of language, historians have been influenced by recent developments in literary studies, especially the Postmodernist preoccupation with theories of language (see Chapter 7).

Is it reliable?

Once historians have become immersed in the sources of their period and have mastered its characteristic turns of phrase and the appropriate technical vocabulary, questions of meaning tend to worry them less often. But the content of a document prompts a further, much more insistent question: is it reliable? No source can be used for historical reconstruction until some estimate of its standing as historical evidence has been made. This question is beyond the scope of any **ancillary** technique such as palaeography or diplomatics. Answering it calls instead for a knowledge of historical context and an insight into human nature. Here historians come into their own.

ancillary
Subsidiary, giving help to.

Figure 5.2 The National Archives at Kew house all government records since the Norman Conquest. They were moved from a central London location in the 1970s. Until 2003 the archives were known as the Public Record Office. © Matt Mindham/Photographers Direct.

episcopate
The rank of bishop.

Henry III (1207–72)
King Henry III inherited problems with the English barons from his father, King John. Opposition to Henry was led by Simon de Montfort and Stephen Langton, Archbishop of Canterbury, and led eventually to the summoning in 1265 of the earliest Parliament in English history.

corporate privileges
The privileges of particular groups, especially the barons.

heresy
Deviation from orthodox religious belief, as opposed to infidels (the unfaithful), who hold to a different religious belief entirely. Heresy was punishable by death in medieval Church courts.

Ashanti
A West African kingdom in modern-day Ghana. It was a major power in the region until the arrival of the British in the late nineteenth century. Britain annexed the Ashanti kingdom in 1901.

polygamy
The system whereby one man is allowed more than one wife. Although clearly in evidence in the Old Testament, it has always been severely condemned by the mainstream Christian churches.

Where a document takes the form of a report of what has been seen, heard or said, we need to ask whether the writer was in a position to give a faithful account. Was he or she actually present, and in a tranquil and attentive frame of mind? If the information was learned at second hand, was it anything more than gossip? The reliability of a medieval monastic chronicler largely depended on how often his cloister was frequented by men of rank and power.[11] Did the writer put pen to paper immediately, or after the sharpness of his or her memory had blurred? (A point worth bearing in mind when reading a diary.) In reports of oral proceedings, a great deal may turn on the exact form of words used, yet prior to the spread of shorthand in the seventeenth century there was no means of making a verbatim transcript; the earliest mechanical means of recording speech – the phonograph – was not invented until 1877. It is extraordinarily difficult to know exactly what a statesman said in a given speech: if he wrote it out in advance he may well have departed from his text; and press reporters, usually armed with only a pencil and note-pad, are inevitably selective and inaccurate, as can be seen by comparing the reports given by different newspapers of the same speech. In the case of speeches in Parliament a reliable verbatim record can be read, but even this dates back only to the reform of *Hansard* in 1909.

What influenced the author?

What most affects the reliability of a source, however, is the intention and prejudices of the writer. Narratives intended for posterity, on which a general impression of the period tends to be based, are particularly suspect. The distortions to which auto-biography is subject in this respect are too obvious for comment. Medieval chroniclers were often extremely partisan between one ruler and another, or between Church and state: Gerald of Wales's increasing antipathy towards Henry II was due to the king's repeated veto on his promotion to the **episcopate**; Matthew Paris's treatment of the disputes between **Henry III** and the English barons was slanted by his identification with virtually all forms of **corporate privileges** in their dealings with king or pope.[12] Chroniclers were often influenced too by the prejudices character-istic of educated people of their time – a revulsion against **heresy**, or a distaste for lawyers and money-lenders. Culture-bound assump-tions and stereotypes shared by virtually all literate people of the day call for particularly careful appraisal. For the historian of pre-literate societies, such as those of tropical Africa in the nineteenth century, the contemporary accounts of European travellers are a source of major importance, but nearly all of them were coloured by racism and sensationalism: judicial execution (as in **Ashanti**) appeared as 'human sacrifice', and **polygamy** was presented as a licence for sexual excess. Nor does creative literature have a special dispensation in this respect. Novelists, playwrights and poets have as many prejudices as anyone else, and these have to be allowed for when citing their work as historical evidence. E.M. Forster's *A Passage to India* (1924) is, among other things, a marvellously convincing and very unflattering portrayal of the **British Raj** at district level, but some account must surely be taken of Forster's own alienation from the kind of **stiff-upper-lip** public school man who controlled the administration in India.

The attraction of record sources – of 'witnesses in spite of themselves' (see p. 75) – on the other hand, is that through them the historian can observe or infer the sequence of day-to-day events, free from the controlling purpose of a narrator. But this is merely to eliminate one of the more obvious kinds of distortion. For however spontaneous or authoritative the source, very few forms of writing arise solely from a desire to convey the unvarnished truth. Even in the case of a diary composed without thought of publication, the writer may be bolstering his or her self-esteem and rationalizing motives. A document that appears to be a straightforward report of something seen, heard or said may well be slanted – either unconsciously, as an expression of deep-seated prejudice, or deliberately, from a wish to please or influence the recipient. Ambassadors in their dispatches home may convey a greater impression of bustle and initiative on their own part than is actually the case; and they may censor their impressions of the government to which they are **accredited** in order to fit them to the policies and preconceptions of their superiors. Historians today are much more sceptical than they used to be about the claims to objectivity of the great Victorian enquirers into the 'social problem': they recognize that the selection of evidence was often distorted to fit middle-class stereotypes about the poor and to promote the implementation of pet remedies.

British Raj
British imperial rule in India, lasting from the eighteenth century until 1947.

stiff-upper-lip
The attitude of stoicism and formality which was traditionally inculcated at British public schools in order to teach boys to hide their emotions, especially in the face of pain or adversity.

accredited
Ambassadors are sent by the government of their own country and accredited – attached – to the government of another.

The uses of bias

Once bias has been detected, however, the offending document need not be consigned to the scrap-heap. The bias itself is likely to be historically significant. In the case of a public figure it may account for a consistent misreading of certain people or situations, with disastrous effects on policy. In published documents with a wide circulation, bias may explain an important shift in public opinion. The reports of nineteenth-century Royal Commissions are a case in point. Newspapers provide other examples: the war reports of the many British dailies that were opposed to Asquith's government in 1915–16 are not a reliable guide to what was happening on the front, but they certainly help to explain why the Prime Minister's reputation at home declined so severely.[13] Autobiographies are notorious for their errors of recall and their special pleading. But in their very subjectivity often lies their greatest value, since the pattern that the writer makes of his or her own life is a cultural as much as a personal construct, and it also illuminates the frame of mind in which not only the book was written but the life itself was led. Even the most tainted sources can assist in the reconstruction of the past.

Reading sources in their context

As described so far, the evaluation of historical evidence may seem to be not unlike the cross-examination of witnesses in a court of law: in both cases the point is to test the reliability of the testimony. But the court-room analogy is misleading if it suggests that primary sources are always evaluated in this way. Public records have most often been studied from one of two standpoints. First, how did the institution that generated the records evolve over time, and what was its function in the body politic? And second, how were specific policies formulated and executed? In this context, reliability is hardly the issue, for the records are studied not as *reports* (i.e. testimonies of events 'out there'), but as parts of a *process* (be it administrative, judicial or policy making) which is itself the subject of enquiry. They are as much the creation of an institution as an individual, and therefore need to be examined in the context of that institution – its vested interests, its administrative routine and its record-keeping procedures. Considered apart from the series to which they belong, the records of long-vanished public institutions are almost certain to be mis-interpreted.[14] To understand the full significance of these records, the historian must if possible study them in their original groupings (a principle on the whole respected in the National Archives) rather than in the rearrangement of some tidy-minded archivist. And ideally they should be studied in their entirety. That means examining together incoming and outgoing correspondence. Before modern methods of reproduction, considerable effort was required to make copies of outgoing letters, and the result is that in many important collections they are completely absent; it is therefore difficult to be sure how policies were executed, or what pressures contributed to their genesis. Governments in England did not get on top of this problem until the late seventeenth century.

Sometimes it makes sense to treat a specific source not as a witness, but as a historical event in its own right. In the case of a major public document like Domesday Book, we need to understand how it came into being and what impact it had – by means of textual analysis, related documents from the same source, contemporary comment and so on.[15] More recent documents like the Second Reform Act (1867) or the Balfour Declaration on the future of Palestine (1917) invite a comparable approach. This is in effect the procedure now adopted by historians of ideas. Traditionally their subject was studied to reveal the pedigree of key concepts, such as parliamentary sovereignty or the freedom of the individual, through a canon of great theorists down the ages. This had the unfortunate effect of implying that the great texts were addressing 'our' issues, and thus obscured the contemporary significance of the sources themselves. But the first task of the historian is to treat these works like any other document of the time and to read them, as far as possible, in the specific intellectual and social contexts in which they were written. This means having regard to both the specific genre – or *discourse* – to which the work belonged, and its relation to other genres with which readers of the time would have been familiar. Scholars such as Quentin Skinner and J.G.A. Pocock have pointed out that what contemporaries made of, say, *Leviathan* (1651) almost certainly differed from what Thomas Hobbes himself meant to convey.[16] Context is at least as important as text in coming to terms with an original thinker in the past.

Officially published records

It is important that these collections should not be accorded special weight just because they are so accessible. They nearly always represent a selection, whose publication was intended to further some practical end, usually of a short-term political nature. The well-known series of *State Trials* was for a long time accepted as a reliable record of some of the major English criminal proceedings since the sixteenth century. But the first four volumes were promoted in 1719 by a group of propagandists in the Whig cause; as a source for the great political trials of the Stuart period they are therefore distinctly suspect.[17] During the nineteenth century the publication – often on a massive scale – of a politician's correspondence was often considered by his family and followers to be a fitting memorial, but there was usually an element of censorship so that the less savoury episodes were suppressed and the reputation of living persons protected or enhanced. Governments of the same period regarded the publication of select diplomatic correspondence (for example in the British Blue Books) as a legitimate means of building up public support for their policies; some of the 'dispatches' were composed for this very purpose. In all these cases the historian will obviously prefer to go to the originals. If these are not available, the published versions must be scrutinized carefully, and as much as possible must be found out from other sources about the circumstances in which they were compiled.

IV

Weighing sources against each other

It will be clear, then, that historical research is not a matter of identifying *the* authoritative source and then exploiting it for all it is worth, for the majority of sources are in some way inaccurate, incomplete or tainted by prejudice and self-interest. The procedure is rather to amass as many pieces of evidence as possible from a wide range of sources – preferably from *all* the sources that have a bearing on the problem in hand. In this way the inaccuracies and distortions of particular sources are more likely to be revealed, and the inferences drawn by the historian can be corroborated. Each type of source possesses certain strengths and weaknesses; considered together, and compared one against the other, there is at least a chance that they will convey an accurate reflection of the past.

This is why mastery of a variety of sources is one of the hallmarks of historical scholarship – an exacting one which is by no means always attained. One of the reasons why biography is often disparaged by academic historians is that too many biographers have studied only the private papers left by their subject, instead of weighing these against the papers of colleagues and acquaintances and (where relevant) the public records for the period. Ranke himself was criticized for relying too heavily on the dispatches of the Venetian ambassadors in some of his writings on the sixteenth century. Observant and conscientious as most of them were, the ambassadors saw matters very much from the point of view of the governing elite. They were also foreigners, free from local political loyalties, it is true, but lacking a real feel for the culture of the country to which they were accredited.[18] The need for primary evidence from 'insiders' as well as 'outsiders' is an important guideline for historical research, with wide ramifications. The failings of Western writers on African history before the 1960s could be summed up by saying that they relied on the testimony of the European explorer, missionary and administrator, without seeking out African sources.[19] Carroll Smith-Rosenberg recalls that when she started out in nineteenth-century American women's history, she found herself portraying women as victims because she had stuck to the well-thumbed educational and theological works that men wrote for and about women; her angle of vision was transformed when she uncovered the letters and diaries of ordinary women which documented the active consciousness of the 'insider'.[20]

Tough standards now tend to be expected of historians regarding the range of sources they use. In the history of international relations, for example, it is a golden rule that both sides of a diplomatic conversation must be studied before one can be certain which side put its case more effectively; this is why the inaccessibility of the Soviet archives prior to the **Gorbachev era** was so frustrating for Western historians of the origins of the Second World War. For historians of government policy in twentieth-century Britain, the temptation may be to confine research to the public records, because these survive in such profusion, and their number is increased every year as more records become available for the first

Gorbachev era
Under communist rule, access to state archives in the Soviet Union was virtually impossible. Under Mikhail Gorbachev, archives were opened to scholars as part of his policy of *glasnost* (openness).

time under the thirty-year rule (see p. 92). But this method is hardly conducive to a balanced interpretation. The public records tend to give too much prominence to administrative considerations (thus reflecting the principal interest of the civil servants who composed them) and to reveal much less about the political pressures to which ministers responded; hence the importance of extending the search to the press and *Hansard*, private letters and diaries, political memoirs and – for recent history – to first-hand oral evidence.[21]

Hidden traces in the records

The examples just discussed – international relations and government policy – are topics for which there exists primary source material in abundance. In each case there is a well-defined body of documents in public custody, with numerous ancillary sources to corroborate and amplify the evidence. But there are many historical topics that are much less well served, either because little evidence has survived, or because what interests us today did not interest contemporaries and was therefore not recorded. If historians are to go beyond the immediate concerns of those who created their sources, they have to learn how to interpret the sources more obliquely. First, many sources are valued for information that the writers were scarcely aware they were setting down and which was incidental to the purpose of their testimony. This is because people unconsciously convey on paper clues about their attitudes, assumptions and manner of life which may be intensely interesting to historians. A given document may therefore be useful in a variety of ways, depending on the questions asked of it – sometimes questions that would never have occurred to the writer or to people of the time. This, of course, is one reason why beginning research with clearly defined questions rather than simply going where the documents lead can be so rewarding: it may reveal evidence where none was thought to exist. From this point of view, the word 'source' is somewhat inapposite: if the metaphor is interpreted literally, a 'source' can contribute evidence to only one 'stream' of knowledge. (There is something to be said for abandoning 'source' in favour of 'trace' or 'track', though that suggestion has not been widely adopted.[22])

Unwitting evidence

This flair for turning evidence to new uses is one of the distinctive contributions of recent historical method. It has been most fully displayed by historians who have moved beyond the well-lit paths of mainstream political history to fields such as social and cultural history, for which explicit source material is more difficult to come by. A case in point is the religious beliefs of ordinary people in Reformation England. Although the switches of doctrinal allegiance among the elite are relatively well recorded, evidence is

dedicatory clause
The opening section of a will, which dedicates the testator's soul to the care of Almighty God.

mediation of Christ
Catholic theology teaches that the believer needs the agency of the Church in order to go to heaven after death. Protestants believe that the death of Jesus Christ on the cross provides all the mediation between God and mankind that is needed, and that a believer need only believe in Christ in order to enter into heaven.

Inquisition
Officially known as the Holy Office, this was the Catholic Church's legal department charged with investigating accusations of heresy.

Cathar
A form of religious heresy that spread rapidly in south-western France in the thirteenth century. It is also known as Albigensianism, from its centre in the town of Albi. It held that, since humans' true home is in heaven, the world must be evil. It was seen as a major doctrinal and political threat both by the papacy and by the kings of France, and was finally crushed by the Inquisition and by a ruthless military campaign known as the Albigensian Crusade.

Maigret
The painstaking fictional detective created by the Belgian crime writer Georges Simenon (1903–89).

very sparse for the rest of the population. But Margaret Spufford in her study of three Cambridgeshire villages used the unlikely evidence of wills to show how religious affiliation changed. Every will began with a **dedicatory clause**, which allows some inference to be drawn concerning the doctrinal preference of the testator or the scribe. From a study of these clauses, Spufford showed how by the early seventeenth century personal faith in the **mediation of Christ** – the hallmark of Protestant belief – had made deep inroads among the local people.[23] It was, of course, no part of the testators' intentions to furnish evidence of their religious beliefs; they were concerned only to ensure that their worldly goods were disposed of in accordance with their wishes. But historians alert to the unwitting testimony of the sources can go beyond the intentions of those who created them.

Legal history arouses relatively little interest among historians at present, but court records are probably the single most important source we have for the social history of the medieval and early modern periods, when the vast majority of the population was illiterate. This was how Emmanuel Le Roy Ladurie was able to write his micro-history of Montaillou (see above, p. 000). The bishop who carried out the **Inquisition** there intended to root out the **Cathar** heresy. But, as 'a sort of compulsive **Maigret**',[24] his meticulous recording of witnesses resulted in a detailed and salacious record of village life. As Le Roy Ladurie puts it, the high concentration of Cathar heretics in Montaillou 'provides an opportunity for the study not of Catharism itself – that is not my subject – but of the mental outlook of the country people'.[25] When historians distance themselves from the contemporary significance of a document in this way, its reliability may be of only marginal significance: what counts is the incidental detail. In eighteenth-century France it was the practice for unmarried pregnant women to make statements to the magistrate in order to pin responsibility on their seducers and salvage something of their reputations. Richard Cobb carried out a study of fifty-four such statements made at Lyon in 1790–2, and as he points out, the identity of the seducers is a trivial issue compared with the light that is shed on the sexual mores of the urban poor, their conditions of work and leisure and the popular morality of the day.[26] It is studies such as these that demonstrate the full force of Marc Bloch's injunction to his fellow historians to study 'the evidence of witnesses in spite of themselves' (see p. 67).

V

The analysis of statistical evidence

Nothing has been said until now about quantitative data. Does the precision of numbers not rescue us from the manifold problems of

Figure 5.3 When the Cathar heresy took hold in southern France in the thirteenth century, the Church
sent the Inquisition to stamp it out. Centuries later the French historian Emmanuel Le Roy
Ladurie used the Inquisitors' records to build up a remarkably detailed picture of the
intimate lives of the inhabitants of the little mountain village of Montaillou. Le Roy
Ladurie was reading the records with very different priorities from those of the men who
originally compiled them. © Paul Shawcross.

interpretation raised by textual sources? It is sometimes imagined
that the application of quantitative methods displaces the traditional
skills of the historian and calls for an entirely new breed of scholar.
Nothing could be further from the truth. Statistical know-how can
only be effective if it is subject to the normal controls of historical
method. Given the special authority that figures carry in our
numerate society, the obligation to subject quantitative data to tests
of reliability is at least as great as in the case of literary sources.
And once the figures have been verified, their interpretation and
their application to the solution of specific historical problems
require the same qualities of judgement and flair as any other
kind of evidence.

Unreliable statistical evidence

A historian is saved an immense amount of work if he or she is
lucky enough to find a set of ready-made statistics – say a table of
imports and exports or a sequence of census reports. Yet the reliability of such sources must never be taken for granted. We need to
know exactly how the figures were put together. Were the returns
made by the man-on-the-spot distorted by his own self-interest –
like the tax-collector who understated his takings and pocketed

Figure 5.4 Regular ten-year censuses in Britain started in 1801, during the Napoleonic Wars. They constitute a key resource for economic, social, local and even family historians; when the National Archives put the 1901 census returns on the web, demand for access was so great that the system immediately crashed. But how accurate are census returns? Were respondents telling the truth? Did census enumerators make mistakes? Quantitative methods cannot tell us. © CORBIS/Hulton Archive.

the difference? Were the figures conjured out of thin air by a desk-bound official, or totted up by a subordinate who was not competent in arithmetic? Both these possibilities arise in the case of impressive-looking statistics published by British colonial administrations in Africa, which were often based on returns made by poorly educated and underpaid chiefs. How much scope was there for errors of copying as the figures were passed on from one level of the bureaucracy to the next? Could the same item have been counted twice by different officials? Where statistics were compiled from questionnaires, as in social surveys or the census, we need to know the form in which the questions were put in order to determine the scope for confusion on the part of the respondents, and we have to consider whether the questions – on income or age, for example – were likely to elicit frank answers. Only an investigation of the circumstances of compilation can provide the answer to these questions.

Often what interests historians is less a single set of figures than a sequence over time which enables them to plot a trend. The figures must accordingly be tested not only for their reliability but for their *comparability*. However accurate the individual totals in such a sequence may be, they can only be regarded as a statistical sequence if they are strictly comparable – if, that is, they are measuring the same variable. It needs only a slight discrepancy in the basis of assessment to render comparisons null and void. A classification that seems clear and consistent on paper may be applied differently over time, or between one place and another, which is one reason why even today comparative criminal statistics have to be treated so cautiously. In the case of the English census, the increasing refinement of the **occupational schedule** in every count since 1841 means that it is difficult to quantify the growth and decline of specific occupations. Even the most seemingly straightforward statistical sequences may conceal pitfalls of this kind. Consider, for example, the official cost-of-living index, which measures the cost of a typical 'shopping-bag' against the current wage-rate. In Britain the index, begun in 1914, ought to provide a reliable picture of the declining standard of living during the Depression of the 1930s. But during the inter-war period the price side of the index continued to be based on the same 'shopping-bag', even though changing patterns of consumption meant that the weighting given to the various items (fresh vegetables, meat, clothing, etc.) in 1914 no longer corresponded with the actual make-up of the average family budget.[27]

occupational schedule
The list of recognized occupations in the census. The given occupation of individuals enumerated in the census had to conform to the schedule. The schedule was defined differently from one census to the next.

Compiling the statistics

Most quantitative history, however, is not based on ready-made statistics. It was only in the late seventeenth century that the advantages of a statistical approach to public issues began to be canvassed, only during the nineteenth century that the state acquired the resources of manpower and money to undertake such work and only in the twentieth century that statistical information was gathered in a really comprehensive way by both government and private bodies. For most of the questions that interest historians, the likelihood is that the figures will have to be laboriously constructed from the relevant surviving materials. To construct quantitative data in such a way that valid statistical inferences can be drawn from them is no easy matter. The issues of reliability and comparability will be posed, not once, but many times over, as the historian seeks out data from varied and scattered source materials.

For the historian of periods earlier than the nineteenth century, the problem of selection is likely to have been partly or wholly solved by the ravages of time. But the residue that survives is still a sample of the original range of records, and it is important to recognize that it is often anything but a random sample. Some types of record are more likely to survive than others because their owners had a greater interest in their survival or better facilities for preserving them, for reasons that may introduce a manifest distortion into the sample. Thus surviving business records are nearly always weighted in favour of the successful long-lasting firm, at the expense of smaller businesses that were unable to weather a crisis. Lawrence Stone was dogged by a problem of this kind in his study of the English aristocracy between 1558 and 1641. Although he had some information on all the 382 individuals who held titles at that period, the proportion of noble families whose private papers survive in abundance never rose above one-third, and these families were mostly those of wealthy earls rather than minor barons whose estates were more subject to disintegration or dispersal. Stone was accordingly obliged to make allowances for the fact that many of his findings were drawn from an unrepresentative sample.[28] This is just one of the pitfalls that lie in wait for the historian seeking clarity in quantification.

VI

Critiquing the digital record

Critical evaluation is equally necessary in the case of material downloaded from the Internet. Digitization may represent a revolution in the procedures of historical research (see pp. 94–5), but it does not render redundant the traditional skills of the documentary historian. In aggregate, the digital record is always a selection of the written record. The available online resources represent a series of editorial or commissioning choices. How do we deal with the fact that less than 5% of the British Library's stock is available in this way? What does the distribution of topics made available on the Internet say about themes which are not included? Are they technically problematic, or are they neglected because they lie outside the limits of current fashion (a point worth bearing in mind in the face of the massive coverage of genealogy and family history)? The identity of the editorial intermediary who has selected the material may be concealed. This means that it is often difficult to establish the standing of the digitized record, or its relation to comparable material. As one medievalist has put it, the researcher 'enters the undefined and blurred world of digital resources, where research essays, original records, reference material and edited texts co-exist without the canonical order of a print publication'.[29]

Keyword searches are perhaps the most commonly used means of exploiting digitized records, but they are not conducive to good practice. It is all too easy to skip from one instance to another without taking stock of the contexts in which each was used, which may subtly (but significantly) modify the meaning of the keyword. Modern scanning techniques do not always faithfully reproduce pre-nineteenth-century print, let alone handwriting, leading to a corrupt text.[30] This is a serious problem if digitization is accompanied by the destruction of the originals in the interests of saving storage space. Manuscript sources also sometimes convey an extra dimension of meaning through the weight and smell of the paper on which they were written. Nothing on the Internet is wholly original, though it is often treated as though it was.

Critiquing the archive

The last refuge of the historian seeking authentic survivals of the past must surely be the archive: created at the time to which it refers, handwritten by the historical protagonists (until the late nineteenth century), and the confidential repository of recording and policy-making. Certainly it was viewed in that spirit by the first historians to base all their research on the state records of European countries during the nineteenth century. For Ranke, the archive was the living and breathing embodiment of the past.[31] For Michelet, reading the documents and inhaling their dust raised up the dead before him; 'resurrection' – his preferred metaphor – presumed that the archive could yield a faithful representation.[32]

Today historians may still sometimes be affected by the allure and excitement of the archive, but such reactions are usually tempered by a more critical perspective. Partly this is because, as shown already, there can be many reasons why particular documents arouse suspicion. But the critique goes further, to encompass the nature of the archive as an institution. Archives were not created for the convenience of historians; they were established to assist the task of government. Hence what the researcher is able to read may be distorted by political concerns. In the State Papers, for example, almost all the letters to and from **Lord Chancellor Jeffreys** for the reign of James II are missing. Since Jeffreys himself died in the Tower in 1689 after the Revolution, it has been surmised that the papers were removed by some person who had changed sides at the critical moment and stood to gain by suppressing his connection with the infamous judge of the 'Bloody Assizes'.[33]

In Britain today it is still possible for the responsible official to ensure that a sensitive document never leaves the department in which it was produced. Since total preservation is manifestly impracticable, there is a recognized procedure for destroying ephemeral material judged to be of no historical interest, and this is open to abuse. Even if sensitive documents are not destroyed,

Lord Chancellor Jeffreys (1648–89)
George Jeffreys was a zealous and deeply unpopular judge under Charles II and James II. He became notorious for the 'Bloody Assizes' in the West Country, when he sentenced 300 people to death for taking part in the Duke of Monmouth's failed rebellion of 1685.

they can be mothballed so effectively as to be placed out of mind. It took a high-profile court case to reveal the existence of official files confirming the complicity of British colonial officials in the use of torture during counter-insurgency measures in Kenya during the 1950s. It then became clear that these files were the tip of the iceberg. In 2013 it was revealed that the Foreign Office had retained in a secret deposit some 1.2 million files, covering British foreign and colonial policy since the mid-nineteenth century. Dozens of historians have studied the 'official mind' of British policy-making, unaware of the volume of material which they were barred from reading. At the time of writing it is still not clear what proportion of these 'special collections' will be transferred to the National Archives, where they legally belong.[34]

The archive is thus a documentary resource marred by excisions and exclusions. But it is more than that. The archive is not just a record of government; it is an *instrument* of government. The priorities and prejudices in the written record are evidence of the kind of rule handed down to subjects or citizens. The unwary researcher may be led by the hand, taking on board the political perspective and professional concerns of those who wrote the records. One of the reasons why women's history was little studied until recently was because societies which excluded women from the public sphere were not likely to provide rich documentation of women, leading to the erroneous belief that women were 'outside history'. As Carolyn Hamilton has put it, 'archives are ... monuments to particular configurations of power'.[35] If so they should be studied as aspects of 'governmentality', instead of being taken for granted as mere repositories. This is increasingly the case, particularly in colonial societies, where the gulf between rulers and ruled was most pronounced. Ann Laura Stoler's study of the archives of the Dutch East Indies (modern Indonesia) conveys a contradictory but convincing picture: on the one hand, the imposition through the record of strictly delineated social categories was intended to lock the population into a colonial structure of authority and deference; on the other hand, the records betray on the part of officials a pervasive apprehension and uncertainty which called into question the stability of the colonial order.[36]

VII

Methodology and instinct

In approaching the sources, the historian is anything but a passive observer. The relevant evidence has to be sought after in fairly out-of-the-way and improbable places. The archives in which that evidence is found have to be scrutinized for political or ideological distortion. Ingenuity and flair are required to grasp the full range of uses to which a single source may be put. Of each type of evidence the historian has to ask how and why it came into being, and what its real import is. Divergent sources have to be weighed against each other, forgeries and gaps explained. No document, however authoritative, is beyond question; the evidence must, in E.P. Thompson's telling phrase, 'be interrogated by minds trained in a discipline of attentive disbelief'.[37] Perhaps these precepts hardly merit the name of method, if that suggests the deliberate application of a set sequence of scientific procedures for verifying the evidence. Innumerable handbooks of historical method have, it is true, been written for the guidance of research students since Ranke's time, and in mainland Europe and the United States formal instruction in research techniques has long been part of the postgraduate historian's training.[38] Britain, on the other hand, has until recently been the home of the 'green fingers' approach to source criticism. G.M. Young, an eminent historian of the inter-war period, declared that his aim was to read in a period until he could hear its people speak. He was later echoed by Richard Cobb:

> The most gifted researchers show a willingness to *listen* to the wording of the document, to be governed by its every phrase and murmur ... so as to *hear* what is actually being said, in what accent and with what tone.[39]

This suggests not so much a method as an attitude of mind – an instinct almost – which can only be acquired by trial and error.

But to argue further, as Cobb did, that the principles of historical enquiry defy definition altogether is a mystification.[40] In practice, unfavourable notice of a secondary work often turns on the author's failure to apply this or that test to the evidence. Admittedly, the rules cannot be reduced to a formula, and the exact procedures vary according to the type of evidence; but much of what the experienced scholar does almost without thinking can be described in terms that are comprehensible to the uninitiated. When spelt out in this way, historical method may seem to amount to little more than the obvious lessons of common sense. But it is common sense applied very much more systematically and sceptically than is usually the case in everyday life, supported by a secure grasp of historical context and, in many instances, a high degree of technical knowledge. It is by these taxing standards that historical research demands to be judged.

Further reading

Marc Bloch, *The Historian's Craft*, Manchester University Press, 1954.

G. Kitson Clark, *The Critical Historian*, Heinemann, 1967.

G.R. Elton, *The Practice of History*, Sydney University Press, 1967.

Jacques Barzun and Henry F. Graff, *The Modern Researcher*, 3rd edn, Harcourt Brace Jovanovich, 1977.

John Fines, *Reading Historical Documents: A Manual for Students*, Blackwell, 1988.

V.H. Galbraith, *An Introduction to the Study of History*, Watts, 1964.

Jacques Le Goff and Pierre Nora (eds), *Constructing the Past: Essays in Historical Methodology*, Cambridge University Press, 1985.

Edward Higgs, *A Clearer Sense of the Census: The Victorian Census and Historical Research*, PRO, 1996.

Arlette Farge, *The Allure of the Archives*, Yale University Press, 2013.

Carolyn Hamilton et al. (eds), *Refiguring the Archive*, Kluwer (Cape Town), 2002.

Notes

1 Anthony P. Adamthwaite, *The Making of the Second World War*, Allen & Unwin, 1977, p. 20.
2 Richard Cobb, *A Second Identity: Essays on France and French History*, Oxford University Press, 1969, p. 15.
3 J.H. Hexter, *On Historians*, Allen Lane, 1979, p. 241. The label is rather unfairly pinned on Christopher Hill.
4 Emmanuel Le Roy Ladurie, *The Peasants of Languedoc*, Illinois University Press, 1974, p. 4.
5 C.R. Cheney, *Medieval Texts and Studies*, Oxford University Press, 1973, p. 8.
6 William Camden, Preface to *Britannia* (1586), as quoted in J.R. Hale (ed.), *The Evolution of British Historiography*, Macmillan, 1967, p. 15.
7 Lord Acton, *Lectures on Modern History*, Fontana, 1960 (first published in 1906), p. 22.
8 Marc Bloch, *The Historian's Craft*, Manchester University Press, 1954, p. 86.
9 Robert Harris, *Selling Hitler: The Story of the Hitler Diaries*, Arrow, 1996.
10 Bloch, *The Historian's Craft*, p. 165; J.J. Bagley, *Historical Interpretation*, vol. I: *Sources of English Medieval History, 1066–1540*, Penguin, 1965, pp. 24, 29–30.
11 See, for example, the impressive list of informants and contacts in Richard Vaughan, *Matthew Paris*, Cambridge University Press, 1958, pp. 11–18.
12 Antonia Gransden, *Historical Writing in England, c.550 to c.1307*, Routledge & Kegan Paul, 1974, pp. 242–5, 367–72.
13 Stephen Koss, *Asquith*, Allen Lane, 1976, pp. 181–2, 217.
14 Andrew McDonald, 'Public records and the modern historian', *Twentieth-Century British History*, I, 1990, pp. 341–52.
15 V.H. Galbraith, *The Making of Domesday Book*, Oxford University Press, 1964. This approach is commended in T.G. Ashplant and Adrian Wilson, 'Present-centred history and the problem of historical knowledge', *Historical Journal*, XXXI, 1988, pp. 253–74.
16 Quentin Skinner, 'Meaning and understanding in the history of ideas', *History and Theory*, VIII, 1969, pp. 3–53, and J.G.A. Pocock, *Politics, Language and Time*, Methuen, 1972, especially ch. 1.

17 G. Kitson Clark, *The Critical Historian*, Heinemann, 1967, pp. 92–6, 109–14.

18 Herbert Butterfield, *Man on His Past*, Cambridge University Press, 1955, p. 90.

19 J.D. Fage (ed.), *Africa Discovers Her Past*, Oxford University Press, 1970.

20 Carroll Smith-Rosenberg, *Disorderly Conduct: Visions of Gender in Victorian America*, Oxford University Press, 1986, pp. 25–7.

21 For a fuller discussion, with examples, see Alan Booth and Sean Glynn, 'The public records and recent British economic historiography', *Economic History Review*, 2nd series, XXXII, 1979, pp. 303–15.

22 G.J. Renier, *History: Its Purpose and Method*, Allen & Unwin, 1950, pp. 96–105.

23 Margaret Spufford, *Contrasting Communities: English Villagers in the Sixteenth and Seventeenth Centuries*, Cambridge University Press, 1974, pp. 320–44.

24 Emmanuel Le Roy Ladurie, *Montaillou: Cathars and Catholics in a French Village, 1294–1324*, Penguin, 1980, p. xiii.

25 Ibid., p. 231.

26 Richard Cobb, 'A view on the street', in his *A Sense of Place*, Duckworth, 1975, pp. 79–135.

27 B.R. Mitchell and Phyllis Deane, *Abstract of British Historical Statistics*, Cambridge University Press, 1962, p. 466. For an account of the problems raised by cost-of-living indexes, see Roderick Floud, *An Introduction to Quantitative Methods for Historians*, 2nd edn, Methuen, 1979, pp. 125–9.

28 Lawrence Stone, *The Crisis of the Aristocracy, 1558–1641*, Oxford University Press, 1965, p. 130.

29 Arianna Ciula and Tamara Lopez, 'Reflecting on a dual publication: Henry III Fine Rolls print and web', *Literary and Linguistic Computing*, XXIV, 2009, p. 131.

30 Tim Hitchcock, 'Confronting the digital, or how academic history writing lost the plot', *Cultural and Social History*, X, 2013, pp. 9–23.

31 Bonnie Smith, *The Gender of History*, Harvard University Press, pp. 116, 119.

32 Steedman, *Dust*, Manchester University Press, pp. 26–7.

33 G.W. Keeton, *Lord Chancellor Jeffreys and the Stuart Cause*, Macdonald, 1965, p. 23.

34 *The Guardian*, 19 Oct. 2013, 28 Oct. 2013, 14 Jan. 2014.

35 Carolyn Hamilton, ed., *Refiguring the Archive*, Cape Town, p. 9.

36 Ann Laura Stoler, *Along the Archival Grain*, Princeton University Press, 2009.

37 E.P. Thompson, *The Poverty of Theory*, Merlin Press, 1978, pp. 220–1.

38 The classic work is C.V. Langlois and C. Seignobos, *Introduction to the Study of History*, Greenwood, 1979, first published in 1898. Louis Gottschalk, *Understanding History: A Primer of Historical Method*, Knopf, 1950, and Jacques Barzun and Henry F. Graff, *The Modern Researcher*, Harcourt Brace Jovanovich, 3rd edn, 1977, are more recent statements.

39 Richard Cobb, *Modern French History in Britain*, Oxford University Press, 1974, p. 14.

40 Richard Cobb, 'Becoming a historian', in his *A Sense of Place*, pp. 47–8. See also Jacques Barzun, *Clio and the Doctors*, Chicago University Press, 1974, p. 90.

6 Writing and interpretation

Most students' experience of historical writing is limited to produ-cing essays or assignments, or addressing questions and problems set by others for assessment purposes. Historians, however, are usually able to set their own questions of the material they have unearthed, and can plan and design their work as they choose. How, then, does the historian turn research into historical writing? And what role does the historian's interpretation play in the process?

The application of critical method to the primary sources along the lines described in the previous chapter generally results in the validation of a large number of facts about the past with a bear-ing on one particular issue, or a group of related issues, but the significance of this material can only be fully grasped when the individual items are related to each other in a coherent exposi-tion. There is nothing obvious or predetermined about the way in which the pieces fit together, and the feat is usually accomplished only as a result of much trial and error. Many historians who have a flair for working on primary sources find the process of composition excruciatingly laborious and frustrating. The temptation is to continue amassing material so that the time of reckoning can be put off indefinitely.

I

Do historians need to write history?

One school of opinion maintains that historical writing is of no real significance anyway. The intense excitement that such his-torians experience in contemplating the original documents has led them to the position that the only historical education worth the name is the study of primary sources – preferably in their original state, but failing that in reliable editions. One of the most austere proponents of this view was V.H. Galbraith, a distinguished medievalist who was **Regius Professor** at Oxford in the 1950s. Almost all his published work was devoted to elucidating particular documents and placing them in their historical context – notably **Domesday Book** and the chronicles of St Albans Abbey; he never wrote the broad interpretative work on fourteenth-century England for which he was uniquely qualified. As he put it:

> What really matters in the long run is not so much what we write about history now, or what others have written, as the original sources themselves. … The power of unlimited inspiration to successive generations lies in the original sources.[1]

There is a certain logic about this purist position. It will evoke a sympathetic response in all those historians whose research is source-oriented rather than problem-oriented (see p. 99), many of whom find it extraordinarily difficult to determine when, if ever, the time for synthesis has arrived. In history, more than most other disciplines, undirected immersion in the raw materials has an intellectual justification. Exposure to original sources ought to feature in any programme of historical study, and it is entirely proper that scholarly reputations should continue to be founded on the editing of these materials. But as a general prescription, Galbraith's rejection of conventional historical writing is completely misplaced. It would of course entail an abdication from all history's claims to social relevance, which require that historians communicate what they have learned to a wider audience. But it would be hardly less disastrous even supposing that these claims to relevance could be refuted. For it is in the act of writing that historians make sense of their research experience and bring into focus whatever insights into the past they have gained. Much scientific writing takes the form of a report expressing findings that are entirely clear in the scientist's mind before he or she puts pen to paper. It is highly doubtful whether any historical writing proceeds in the same way. The reality of any historical conjuncture as revealed in the sources is so complex, and sometimes so contradictory, that only the discipline of seeking to express it in continuous prose with a beginning and an end enables the researcher to grasp the connections between one area of historical experience and another. Many historians have remarked on this creative aspect of historical writing, which is what can make it no less exhilarating than the detective work in the archives.[2] Historical writing is essential to historical understanding, and those who shrink from undertaking it are something less than historians.

Regius Professor
A 'royal' professor appointed by the Crown. Regius professorships were introduced in the eighteenth century as a means of extending government control into the universities of Oxford and Cambridge.

Domesday Book
The famous survey of land tenure in England undertaken on the orders of King William I in 1086.

II

The forms of historical writing

Historical writing is characterized by a wide range of literary forms. The three basic techniques of description, narrative and analysis can be combined in many different ways, and every project poses afresh the problem of how they should be deployed. This lack of clear guidelines is partly a reflection of the great diversity of the historian's subject matter: there could not possibly be one literary form suited to the presentation of every aspect of the human past. But it is much more the result of the different and sometimes contradictory purposes behind historical writing, and above all of the tension that lies at the heart of all historical enquiry between the desire to *recreate* the past and the urge to *interpret* it. A rough and ready explanation for the variety of historical writing is that narrative and description address the first requirement, while analysis attempts to grapple with the second.

History as description

That the recreation of the past – 'the reconstruction of the historical moment in all its fullness, concreteness and complexity'[3] – is more than a purely intellectual task is plain to see from its most characteristic literary form: *description*. Here historians are striving to create in their readers the illusion of direct experience, by evoking an atmosphere or setting a scene. A great many run-of-the-mill historical works testify to the fact that this effect is not achieved by mastery of the sources alone. It requires imaginative powers and an eye for detail not unlike those of the novelist or poet. This analogy would have been taken for granted by the great nineteenth-century masters of historical description such as Macaulay and Carlyle, who were much influenced by contemporary creative writers and took immense pains with their style. Modern historians are less self-consciously 'literary', but they too are capable of remarkably evocative descriptive writing – witness Fernand Braudel's great panorama of the Mediterranean environment in the sixteenth century.[4] Whatever else they may be, such historians are artists, and there are too few of them.

History as narrative

Braudel's work is unusual today for the prominence that it accords to description. For effective – indeed indispensable – as such writing is, it cannot express the historian's primary concern with the passage of time. Its role has therefore always been subordinated to the main technique of the recreative historian:

narrative. In most European languages the word for 'history' is the same as that used for 'story' (French, *histoire*; Italian, *storia*; German, *Geschichte*). Narrative too is a form the historian shares with the creative writer – especially the novelist and the epic poet – and it explains much of the appeal that history has traditionally enjoyed with the reading public. Like other forms of story-telling, historical narrative can entertain through its ability to create suspense and arouse powerful emotions. But narrative is also the historian's basic technique for conveying what it felt like to observe or participate in past events. The forms of narrative that achieve the effect of recreation most successfully are those that approximate most nearly to the sense of time that we experience in our own lives: whether from hour to hour, as in an account of a battle, or from day to day, as in an account of a political crisis, or over a natural life span, as in a biography. The great exponents of recreative history have always been masters of dramatic and vividly evocative narrative. To mark the bicentenary of the French Revolution **Simon Schama** published an accomplished narrative history called *Citizens* (1989), appropriately subtitled *A Chronicle of the French Revolution*. Other historians have represented the great upheavals of the past by means of multiple narratives, seeing great events through the experience of many individuals. This technique is employed by Diane Purkiss in her account of the English Civil War, and by Orlando Figes in his history of the Russian Revolution: 'a human event of complicated individual tragedies', as he puts it.[5] In works of this kind we can see the virtues of historical narrative fully exemplified: exact chronology, the role of chance and contingency, the play of irony, and perhaps most of all the true complexity of events in which the participants so often foundered.

Simon Schama (1945–)
A pupil of the Cambridge historian J.H. Plumb, Schama wrote acclaimed works on The Netherlands in the seventeenth and eighteenth centuries before coming to general attention with *Citizens*, a highly readable but critical narrative account of the French Revolution written for the bicentennial celebrations in 1989. Schama went on to present a hugely popular *History of Britain* for BBC Television.

III

Historical causes and consequences

But the historian is of course engaged in very much more than an exercise in resurrection. It would be entirely consistent with this objective to treat events in the past as isolated and arbitrary, but the historian does not in fact treat them in this way. Historical writing is based on the presupposition that particular events are connected with what happened before, with contemporary developments in other fields, and with what came afterwards; they are conceived, in short, as part of a historical process. Those events which in retrospect appear to have been phases in a continuing sequence are deemed specially significant by the historian. The questions 'What happened?' and 'What were conditions like at such-and-such a time?' are preliminary – if indispensable – to asking 'Why did it happen?' and 'What were its results?' Historical writing based on these priorities may be said to have begun with the 'philosophic' historians of the Enlightenment. During the nineteenth century it drew further impetus from the great historical sociologists – de Tocqueville, Marx and **Weber** – who sought to explain the origins of the economic and political transformations of their own day.

Weber (1864–1920)
Max Weber, German political philosopher. Although, like Marx, Weber stressed the importance of class in determining the development of society, he put forward a much more complex and sophisticated analysis of what social class actually consists of. In particular he stressed the importance of social status, which might not equate to strict class categories and can change over time.

Asking the question 'Why?' may simply mean asking why an individual took a particular decision. Historians have always given close attention to the study of motive, both because of the traditional prominence of biography in historical studies and because the motives of the great are at least partially reflected in their surviving papers. Diplomatic history is particularly prone to dwelling on the intentions and tactics of ministers and diplomats. But even in this limited setting, the question 'Why?' is less simple than it looks. However honest and coherent statements of intention may be, they are unlikely to tell the whole story. Every culture and every social grouping has its unspoken assumptions – those nostrums and values that 'go without saying' and yet may deeply affect behaviour. In order to take account of this dimension, the historian must be well versed in the intellectual and cultural context of the period studied, and quick to pick up tell-tale hints of this context in the documents. With regard to the origins of the First World War, for instance, James Joll has called attention to the morbid fear of revolution and the fashionable doctrine of the survival of the fittest as underlying features of the European political mind; and he points out that in moments of crisis such as July 1914 policy-makers were most likely to fall back on their unspoken assumptions, acting in too great a panic to make a considered appraisal of their predicament.[6]

Beyond human motivation: latent causes, long-term consequences

However, the really significant questions in history do not turn on the conduct of individuals but concern major events and collective transitions that cannot possibly be explained by the sum total of human intentions. This is because underneath the *manifest* history of stated intention and conscious (if unspoken) preoccupation there lies a *latent* history of processes that contemporaries were only dimly aware of, such as changes in demography, economic structure or deep values.[7] The Victorians saw in the abolition of slavery in the 1830s a famous victory for humanitarianism, as exemplified in the campaigning zeal of men such as William Wilberforce. In retrospect we can see how the legislation of 1833 was also brought about by the declining fortunes of the Caribbean slave economy and the shift towards an industrialized society in Britain itself.[8] Because historians can look at a society in motion through time, they can register the influence of such factors. But the historical actors themselves could not possibly have a full grasp of all the structural constraints under which they were operating.

Nor could they anticipate the *outcome* of their actions. Like causes, consequences cannot simply be read off from the stated motives of the protagonists, for the simple reason that latent or structural factors so often come between intention and outcome. As E.H. Carr pointed out, our notion of the facts of history must be broad enough to include 'the social forces which produce from the actions of individuals results often at variance with, and sometimes opposite to, the results which they themselves intended'.[9] To revert to the issue of slavery, the intention of British abolitionists was certainly to confer liberty on the slaves and to improve their material conditions. But the extent of the improvement in practice varied greatly from one part of the Caribbean to another, in ways that the humanitarians had not foreseen. Moreover, other consequences unfolded that lay beyond their terms of reference altogether, notably the impact of the anti-slavery crusade on the propaganda techniques of other moral campaigns, such as those for temperance and social purity.[10] There is a sense in which, from the viewpoint of posterity, consequences are *more* significant than causes, since they usually determine the importance we accord to a given event. It is a curious fact that vastly more has been written on the causes of the English Revolution, for instance, than on its consequences: the extent to which it established a new political culture, or paved the way for more efficient forms of capitalism, is far less widely known than, say, the rise of **Puritanism** or the financial crises of the early Stuart monarchy.

Multi-layered analysis

The treatment of cause and consequence makes just as heavy demands on the skill of the writer as historical recreation does, but of a rather different kind. To convey the immediacy of lived experience calls for intricate narrative and evocative description on several different levels. To approximate to an adequate explanation of past events, on the other hand, requires analytical complexity. Causation in particular is always multiple and many-layered, owing to the manner in which different areas of human experience constantly obtrude on one another. At the very least, some distinction needs to be made between background causes and direct causes: the former operate over the long term and place the event in question on the agenda of history, so to speak; the latter put the outcome into effect, often in a distinctive shape that

Puritanism
A radical form of seventeenth-century Protestantism which sought to 'purify' the Church of England of its 'Catholic' features. Puritanism was also associated with political radicalism during the English Civil Wars.

no one could have foreseen. Lawrence Stone provided an effective example of a slightly more sophisticated version of this model. In his hundred-page essay, 'The causes of the English Revolution', he considered in turn the 'preconditions' that came into being in the century before 1629, the 'precipitants' (1629–39) and the 'triggers' (1640–2), and thus showed the interaction of long-term factors, such as the spread of Puritanism and the Crown's failure to acquire the instruments of autocracy, with the role of individual personalities and fortuitous events.[11]

Another way of understanding the task of historical explanation is to see any given conjuncture in the past as lying in a field where two planes intersect. One plane is vertical (or diachronic), comprising a sequence through time of earlier manifestations of this activity: in the case of the abolition of slavery this plane would be represented by the fifty years of campaigning for abolition before 1833, and by the ebb and flow of plantation profits over the same period. The other plane is the horizontal (or synchronic): that is, the impinging of quite different features of the contemporary world on the matter in hand. In the present example these might include the political momentum for reform around 1830 and the new **nostrums** of political economy. Carl Schorske likens the historian to a weaver whose craft is to produce a strong fabric of interpretation out of the warp of sequence and the woof of contemporaneity.[12]

nostrum
An idea, particularly one promoted zealously as a remedy for a problem.

The limitations of historical narrative

This analytical complexity means that narrative is most unlikely to be the best vehicle for historical explanation. It was certainly the characteristic mode of Ranke and the great academic historians of the nineteenth century, who in practice were interested in much more than 'how things actually were'. And one of the most widely read (and readable) professional historians in Britain – A.J.P. Taylor – hardly wrote anything else. But this traditional literary technique in fact imposes severe limitations on any systematic attempt at historical explanation. The placing of events in their correct temporal sequence does not settle the relationship between them. As Tawney put it:

> Time, and the order of occurrences in time, is a clue, but no more; part of the historian's business is to substitute more significant connections for those of chronology.[13]

post hoc propter hoc
(Latin) Literally 'after this therefore because of this'. In other words the false assumption that because two events happen in sequence there must necessarily be a causal connection between them.

The problem is two-fold: first, narrative can take the reader up a blind alley. Because B came after A does not mean that A *caused* B, but the flow of the narrative may easily convey the impression that it did. (Logicians call this the *post hoc propter hoc* fallacy.)

Figure 6.1 A.J.P. Taylor (1906–90) became a well-known figure through his historical writings for the popular press and his television lectures. His popularity and deliberately provocative analysis infuriated historians, who did not share his attachment to narrative history as a format for historical explanation. © Topfoto/Topham/Picturepoint.

Second, and much more importantly, narrative imposes a drastic simplification on the treatment of cause. The historical under-standing of a particular occurrence proceeds by enlarging the inventory of causes, while at the same time trying to place them in some sort of pecking order. Narrative is entirely inimical to this pattern of enquiry. It can keep no more than two or three threads going at once, so that only a few causes or results will be made apparent. Moreover, these are not likely to be the most significant ones, being associated with the sequence of day-to-day events rather than long-term structural factors. That can have a markedly impoverishing effect on our understanding of major structural changes in history. Reflecting on his book *Citizens*, Schama acknowledged,

> The drastic social changes imputed to the [French] Revolution seem less clear-cut or actually not apparent at all. ... Nor does the Revolution seem any longer to conform to a grand historical design, preordained by inexorable forces of social change. Instead it seems a thing of contingencies and unforeseen circumstances.[14]

The logic of narrative is no less clear in the history of war. Writing about the First World War, Taylor took a characteristically extreme view. 'It is the fashion nowadays', he wrote in 1969,

> to seek profound causes for great events. But perhaps the war which broke out in 1914 had no profound causes. For thirty years past, international diplomacy, the balance of power, the alliances and the accumulation of armed might produced peace. Suddenly the situation was turned round, and the very forces which had produced the long peace now produced a great war. In much the same way, a motorist who for thirty years has been doing the right thing to avoid accidents makes a mistake one day and has a crash. In July 1914 things went wrong. The only safe explanation is that things happen because they happen.[15]

In putting forward what might be termed the minimalist position, Taylor doubtless intended to provoke, but his outlook is more prevalent than one might suppose. It is implicated in any attempt to encompass any of the great transformations in history by narrative means. Neither **C.V. Wedgwood** nor Simon Schama, for instance, were much interested in the structural factors predisposing England or France to revolution; they wanted to place the role of human agency and the flux of events in the foreground. Both of them were reacting against the Marxist approach to revolution, and traditional narrative suited a perspective that was fully formed before they embarked on their books. The choice of narrative must be recognized for what it is: an interpretative act, rather than an innocent attempt at story-telling.

The limitations of narrative apply still more to institutional and economic change, where there may be no identifiable protagonists whose actions and reflections can be treated as a story. No one has succeeded in representing the causes of the Industrial Revolution in narrative form. The problems are clearest of all in the case of the 'silent changes' in history[16] – those gradual transformations in mental and social experience which were reflected on the surface of events in only the most oblique manner. As the scope of historical studies has broadened in the twentieth century to include these topics, so the hold of narrative on historical writing has weakened. Few intellectual rallying cries have proved more effective than the attack by the *Annales* school on *l'histoire événementielle*.

The strengths and weaknesses of analytical history

The result is that historical writing is now very much more analytical than it was a hundred years ago. In historical analysis,

C.V. Wedgwood (1910–97)
Dame Veronica Wedgwood, a popular historian of the English Civil Wars. Her *The King's Peace* and *The King's War* are vivid narratives, written from a viewpoint sympathetic to, if not always condoning, King Charles I.

l'histoire événementielle
(French) Events-led, as opposed to analytical or descriptive, history.

the main outline of events tends to be taken for granted; what is at issue is their significance and their relationship with each other. The multiple nature of causation in history demands that the narrative should be suspended and that each of the relevant factors be weighed in turn, without losing sight of their connectedness and the likelihood that the configuration of each factor shifted over time.

This is certainly not the only function of analytical writing. Analysis can serve to **elucidate** the connectedness of events and processes occurring at the same time, and especially to lay bare the workings of an institution or a specific area of historical experience. In British historiography, the classic instance is Namier's *Structure of Politics at the Accession of George III* (1929), a sequence of analytical essays on the various influences that determined the composition and working of the House of Commons around 1760. Structural studies of this kind are most prevalent in social and economic history, where some grasp of the totality of the social or economic system is required if the significance of particular changes is to be fairly assessed. Then there is the critical evaluation of the evidence itself, which may require a discussion about textual authenticity and the validity of factual inference, as well as a weighing up of the pros and cons of alternative interpretations. It has been said of Ranke that his careful evaluation of contemporary records was seldom allowed to ruffle the surface of his stately narrative;[17] few historians would be allowed to get away with that kind of reticence today. But it is in the handling of the big explanatory issues in history that analysis most comes into its own. As historical writing becomes more geared to problem solving, so the emphasis on analysis has increased, as a glance at any of the academic journals will show.

However, this does not mean that narrative is completely at a discount. For undiluted analytical writing raises its own problems. What it gains in intellectual clarity, it loses in historical immediacy. There is an inescapably static quality about historical analysis as if, in E.P. Thompson's much-cited metaphor, the time machine has been stopped in order to allow a more searching inspection of the engine room.[18] Namier's studies of eighteenth-century politics lay themselves open to criticism for this very reason.[19] Furthermore, explanations that seem convincing at an analytical level may prove unworkable when measured against the flux of events. The truth is that historians need to write in ways that do justice to both the manifest and the latent, both profound forces and surface events. And in practice this requires a flexible use of both analytical and narrative modes: sometimes in alternating sections, sometimes more completely fused throughout the text. This in fact is the way in which most academic historical writing is carried out today.

elucidate
To explain something complex.

Narrative and the social historian

For all the intellectual appeal of analysis, history without narrative is a non-starter. It is narrative that gives shape and direction to what would otherwise be a formless incoherent mess, thus allowing what Daniel Snowman calls 'the comfort of closure'.[20] Not surprisingly, then, today's historians are learning new ways of deploying narrative. Whereas in the nineteenth century it was often treated, without much reflection, as *the* mode of historical exposition, narrative is now the subject of critical scrutiny by scholars *au fait* with literary studies. **Hayden White**, for example, has emphasized the **rhetorical** choices made by every historian who resorts to narrative, and has identified some of the principal rhetorical stratagems found in their work (see p. 168).[21] Historians tend to be much more self-conscious and critical in their use of narrative than they used to be. In particular, the traditional association with political events is now much less evident. Social historians, in a reversal of their practice a generation ago, now favour narrative as a means of conveying how the social structures, life cycles and cultural values that they analyse in abstract terms were experienced by actual people. But instead of constructing a narrative for society as a whole, they compose exemplary or illustrative stories, perhaps best termed 'micro-narratives'.[22] Richard J. Evans has written a study of crime and punishment in nineteenth-century Germany in which each chapter begins with an individual story as a way into the theme that follows; appropriately he calls his book *Tales from the German Underworld* (1998). In a classic of this new genre, Natalie Zemon Davis recounts the tale of a peasant in the French Basque country who lived as the husband of an abandoned wife for three years during the 1550s, until the real husband turned up and the impostor was exposed and executed. *The Return of Martin Guerre* (1983) is an absorbing story, also made into a film, but for Davis the case 'leads us into the hidden world of peasant sentiment and aspiration', shedding light for example on whether people 'cared as much about truth as about property'.[23] Lawrence Stone was somewhat premature when he spoke in 1979 of a 'revival of narrative', but the last three decades have confirmed that historians are indeed breathing new life into the most traditional form of historical writing.[24]

Hayden White (1928–)
American literary theorist. His views on the artificiality of constructed narrative build heavily on the work of Jacques Derrida (1930–2004) and the deconstructionist school, which held that text and language itself is replete with the hidden assumptions and prejudices of the author and of his or her cultural background.

rhetorical
Rhetoric is the art of speaking or writing in order to persuade. It relies on skilful use of devices, such as 'rhetorical questions' (whose answers are deemed so obvious that they do not need to be stated), at least as much as on the actual qualities of the argument itself.

IV

Writing up research: the academic monograph

These problems of choice of form are usually confronted for the first time by the practising historian in the form of the monograph – that is, the writing up of a piece of original research, initially as a thesis for a higher degree and then as a book or an article in one of the learned journals. In this kind of writing, the complexities of the evidence are likely to be displayed in the text, and the statements made there validated by meticulous footnote references to the appropriate documents. Many monographs are highly technical and are hardly accessible to anyone but fellow specialists. And, since the essence of the monograph is that it is based on primary rather than secondary sources, its scope is likely to be very restricted. This is particularly so in the case of a young scholar presenting the results of three or four years' Ph.D. research. Although in a technical sense such works are 'an original contribution to knowledge' (as required under the regulations for higher degrees), their significance is often slight. The pressure to complete an acceptable thesis within a few years in order to secure an academic job often causes the researcher to play safe by focusing on a well-defined body of sources never previously studied – or at any rate not with the same historical problem in mind. Lucien Febvre caustically observed the tendency for most historical works to be written by people who 'simply set out to show that they know and respect the rules of their profession'.[25] That is doubtless an unavoidable consequence of the professionalization of history. At the same time, arresting results do from time to time emerge from postgraduate research: Michael Anderson's *Family Structure in Nineteenth-Century Lancashire* is still regarded as an important source of demographic information on the working class, even though it was published nearly forty years ago. Part of the explanation is that in 1971 the history of the family was a new field. The apprentice historian stands a much better chance of making a major contribution where existing interpretations are thin on the ground. At the very least, the Ph.D. provides a training in the conduct of research and the writing of monographs, and it is by these means that the stock of properly validated historical knowledge is extended.

Taking the broader view

Yet if historians confined their writings to those topics for which they have mastered the primary sources, historical knowledge would be so fragmented as to be meaningless. Making sense of the past means explaining those events and processes that appear significant with the passage of time and that are inevitably defined in terms which are broader than any researcher can encompass by his or her own unaided efforts: the origins of the English Civil War rather than the policies of **Archbishop Laud**, the social consequences of the Industrial Revolution rather than the decline of the handloom weavers of the West Riding, the Scramble for

Archbishop Laud (1573–1645) William Laud, Archbishop of Canterbury under King Charles I. Laud was a controversial choice, suspected of wanting to reintroduce Catholic practices into the Church of England and, even more controversially, into the Scottish Kirk. Scottish resistance to Laud's religious policies precipitated the crisis that developed into the English Civil War. Laud was arrested and impeached in 1641, and finally executed by order of Parliament.

Fashoda Crisis
A diplomatic crisis
between Britain and
France in 1898 over
control of the southern
Sudan, which for a time
threatened to push the
two countries into war.
A British military
expedition which had
conquered the northern
Sudan encountered a
much smaller French
exploratory mission,
which tried
unsuccessfully to claim
the country for France.

Africa rather than the **Fashoda Crisis**. It must be obvious that an understanding of topics of this complexity is not attained by the mere accumulation of detailed researches. In Marc Bloch's words, 'The microscope is a marvellous instrument for research; but a heap of microscopic slides does not constitute a work of art'.[26] When historians step back to take an overview of one of these topics, they face much more acute problems of interpretation – of combining many strands into a coherent account, of determining the weight of this factor or that. And even after a lifetime of research in the relevant primary sources, which may allow them to be discriminating in the use they make of other scholars, they will still have to take much of their work on trust.

The grand sweep of history

These difficulties are compounded when the historian steps still further away from the moorings of his or her first-hand research and attempts a comprehensive survey of an entire epoch. If a monograph is a secondary source, the survey can fairly be described as a 'tertiary' source, since the writer is inevitably placed in the position of making emphatic statements about topics based on no more than a reading of the standard secondary authorities. Nitpicking criticism by the specialists whose fields have been trespassed upon is the inevitable result. Works of this kind will be much more vulnerable to the vagaries of fashion, and their judgements will be overtaken by new research much more quickly than those of the narrowly conceived monograph. The academic standing of the synthesis by a single hand is further compromised by the sad truth that many are not true syntheses at all, but textbooks which for ease of reference summarize the state of knowledge in a rigidly compartmentalized and mechanical fashion. Some historians, conscious that their claims to professional expertise are most convincingly demonstrated in the evaluation of primary sources, feel instinctively that this is no work for 'real scholars'.[27] Others have sought to meet the demand for surveys by participating in collaborative histories. The prototype was the *Cambridge Modern History*, planned under the supervision of Lord Acton in 1896 and covering European history since the mid-fifteenth century in twelve volumes, each composed of national and thematic chapters by the leading authorities. Since then collaborative histories have proliferated. Yet, invaluable though they may be as concise statements of specialist knowledge, such compilations evade the issue. However like-minded the contributors and however forceful the editor, a consistency of approach cannot be attained, and the themes that cut across the specialist concerns of the contributors are completely omitted.

The wide-ranging survey by a single historian fulfils several vital functions. First, it is at its best a fertile source of new questions.

Unremitting primary research, with its necessary but obsessive attention to detail, can lead to a certain intellectual blinkering: 'the dust of archives blots out ideas', as Acton rather unkindly put it.[28] The historian who takes time off from the records to survey an extended period is much more likely to detect new patterns and new correlations which can later be tested in detailed research. E.J. Hobsbawm's *Age of Revolution* (1962), still unsurpassed as a survey of Europe from 1789 to 1848 under the twin impact of the French Revolution and the Industrial Revolution, positively bristles with arresting juxtapositions which no historian confined to a single country could have entertained. By selecting the period 1870–1914 for her survey of English social history, Jose Harris was able to show how many of the late twentieth century's preoccupations originated in her chosen period (the labour movement, feminism and religious doubt being just some of the themes she covers).[29] In a new field where major issues of interpretation have scarcely been formulated, this kind of stock-taking can yield rich dividends, particularly when there is a tendency to proceed initially by the accumulation of case studies. This has been notably true of the history of mentalities and the history of the colonial impact on Africa, to take just two examples. The dangers of fragmentation are obvious. There must come a point when the historian considers the individual cases together, so that a new landscape of continuity, change and contradiction can be discerned and a new agenda laid out.

Second, the grand survey is the principal means by which historians fulfil their obligations to the wider public. Popular interest in the writings of academic historians is by no means confined to survey works – witness the success of Emmanuel Le Roy Ladurie's *Montaillou* (1976). But the appeal of this book is primarily of a recreative kind. If historians are to succeed in communicating their understanding of historical change and of the connectedness of past and present, then it is through the ambitious overview that they will do it. Many historians, intent on preserving their academic standing at all costs, are unduly oppressed by the dangers of superficiality and outright error, and there is much snobbish disparagement of those who write for the general reader. But it is not impossible to combine sound scholarship with a lay appeal. *Haute vulgarisation*, as Hobsbawm describes his own highly distinguished ventures in this field,[30] is a necessary skill of the historian.

The march of history

Lastly, the large-scale synthesis raises questions of historical explanation which are profoundly important in their own right and which are beyond the scope of anything less ambitious. History is a 'progressive' subject in the sense that few people contemplating the past with the benefit of hindsight can fail to ask themselves in

Haute vulgarisation
(French) Making popular from on high. A play on the association of *haute* (high) with such exclusive pursuits as *haute cuisine* or *haute couture*.

what direction events were moving. This question is not a matter of metaphysical speculation but rather a recognition that fundamental areas of human experience are subject to cumulative change over time. The issue may be evaded in studies confined to a short time span, but it is central to any attempt to make sense of a whole era: can one detect increasing occupational specialization, or enlargement of social scale, or an expansion in the scope of government, or greater freedom of belief and expression – or any of these trends in reverse? Alternatively, to adopt a less incremental view of the historical process, a given period may be seen rather in terms of discontinuity and disjuncture, where new circumstances force a break with the inherited tendencies of the past. That is the implication, for example, of using the label 'the **New Imperialism**' to refer to European expansion towards the end of the nineteenth century.[31] Consideration of an extended period raises problems of historical interpretation of a different – and surely more significant – order than those that crop up in the study of a well-defined episode.

New Imperialism
Historians have seen the drive for European overseas expansion in the late nineteenth century as marking a distinctively assertive phase in the development of empire, different from the slower and more piecemeal expansion of previous decades. The 1880s and 1890s have therefore been termed the period of 'New Imperialism'.

Historical synthesis

One consequence of the immense expansion in the scope of historical enquiry that has taken place in the past hundred years is that our definition of a 'comprehensive' survey is much more demanding than that of the great nineteenth-century masters: it includes both the giddy passage of 'events' and the material and mental conditions of life which in many periods – and certainly in the pre-industrial world – changed very slowly if at all, and yet constrained what people could do or think. G.R. Elton's affirmation that 'history deals in events, not states; it investigates things that happen and not things that are'[32] is a questionable half-truth. How surface and background – or events and 'structure' – are related is central to any understanding of historical process, as we have seen already. The large body of writing inspired by the Marxist tradition can be interpreted as one manifestation of this concern (see Chapter 8), but it is the *Annales* school that has confronted the problem most directly, and Braudel more than anyone else. 'Is it possible', he asks,

> somehow to convey simultaneously both that conspicuous history which holds our attention by its continual and dramatic changes – and that other, submerged history, almost silent and always discreet, virtually unsuspected either by its observers or its participants, which is little touched by the obstinate erosion of time?[33]

The plurality of social time

For Braudel the root of the difficulty lies in the conventional historian's idea of unilinear time – that is, a single time-scale characterized by continuity of historical development. Because of the historian's emphasis on the documents and the aspiration to get inside the minds of those who wrote them, this time-scale can hardly be other than a short-term one which registers the sequence of events to the exclusion of structure. Braudel's solution is to jettison unilinear time altogether and to introduce instead the 'plurality of social time'[34] – the notion that history moves on different planes or registers, which can for practical purposes be reduced to three: the long term (*la longue durée*), which reveals the fundamental conditions of material life, states of mind and above all the impact of the natural environment; the medium term, in which the forms of social, economic and political organization have their life span; and the short term, the time of the individual and of *l'histoire événementielle*. The problem, which Braudel himself did not solve in *The Mediterranean*, is how to convey the co-existence of these different levels in a single moment of historical time – how to elucidate their interaction in a coherent exposition which incorporates different levels of narrative, description and analysis. This is an issue about which contemporary historians are much more keenly aware than their predecessors; it is perhaps the most fundamental that they face.

V

Comparative history

Problems of time-scale and time-depth are most often explored by scholars working on a single society. But historical explanation and historical exposition also have to come to terms with the fact that the experience of a given society in the past was never entirely distinctive: it shared features with other societies of similar type. Lurking behind the statements we make about, say, **feudal relations** in twelfth-century England, or **plantation slavery** in the nineteenth-century United States, is an implied comparison – in the first case with the feudal societies of Western Europe, in the second case with the slave societies of the Caribbean and Brazil. Such comparisons can have an important bearing on historical understanding. If, for example, slavery is viewed as an essentially uniform institution reflecting both a common culture of racism and a particular stage in the development of capitalist relations of production, then the version which prevailed in the United States will seem much less of a 'peculiar institution', and the contingencies of the American scene will have much less explanatory significance.

This explains the appeal of *comparative history*. It can be defined as the systematic comparison of selected features in two or more past societies that are normally considered apart. It requires mastery of at least two national contexts: bringing together a number of free-standing national studies into the covers of an

feudal relations
The system in medieval England whereby social position was determined by a person's relationship to the land. Land was always 'held' (hence 'tenure') from someone else, usually – though not always – a social superior. Ultimately all land was held from the Crown.

plantation slavery
The predominant crops grown in the southern states of the nineteenth-century United States were tobacco and cotton. The most economically efficient way to farm them was in large plantations worked by African slave labour, hence 'plantation slavery'.

edited volume does not qualify. The merits of comparative history have most often been demonstrated by closely focused comparisons over a short time span. For example Susan Grayzel has sought to understand the impact of the First World War on understandings of gender by comparing Britain and France; her conclusion is that the implications for women of involvement in the war were essentially the same in both countries, despite their divergent national cultures. By contrast, the welfare historian Susan Pedersen's Anglo-French perspective brings to light quite different public strategies for supporting families during the war and in the inter-war period.[35] Closely defined by period and topic, it is usually expected that such studies should be based on primary sources in both societies. In the case of well-documented nations like Britain and France that is no small commitment.

But the ambitions of comparative history go further. Comparison is no less illuminating when applied to trajectories of national development or social change over an extended period. The difference is that it is even harder to accomplish, and the number of successful large-scale comparative histories is therefore small. A recent *tour de force* is J.H. Elliott's study of the British and Spanish empires in the Americas over their entire history of three centuries. Britain's North American colonies and the Spanish dependencies in Central and South America have generally been viewed as very different enterprises. Elliott's research uncovered further differences. He likens doing comparative history to playing the accordion:

> The two societies under comparison are pushed together, but only to be pulled apart again. Resemblances prove after all not as close as they look at first sight; differences are discovered which at first sight lay concealed.[36]

Part thematic comparison, part parallel narrative, part all-encompassing synthesis: history of this complexity makes heavy demands on both the research skills and the powers of composition of the writer. The comprehensive primary research that would be expected of the conventional monograph is not feasible; Elliott makes extensive use of quotations from published primary sources such as travel literature and diaries, but his interpretation rests primarily on a phenomenal range of secondary works. The comparative approach is sometimes applied in a mechanical compartmentalized fashion. Elliott's treatment is freer, 'constantly comparing, juxtaposing and interweaving the two stories'.[37]

Comparative history remains a minority pursuit among historians, but it is an essential means of deepening our understanding of the past. To always work within the boundaries of a single society is to deprive oneself of a critical angle of vision. Local developments can be mistakenly treated as unique, and the significance of variations from the norm can be overlooked; as Elliott himself has remarked, 'the besetting sin of the national historian is exceptionalism'.[38] Transnational history (discussed on p. 64) tackles the problem head-on, by insisting that the distinctiveness so often claimed by historians of one nation be measured against the experience of other nations. At the very least, comparative history offers a corrective to blinkered parochialism. In some cases it opens up the possibility of a new line of analysis. Space, as well as time, defines the nature of historical enquiry.

VI

Historical controversy

Probably no aspect of the discipline of history mystifies outsiders more than its propensity for debate and dispute. They seem to arise in relation to almost every topic worth investigating. 'Revisionism' is frequently invoked, either as a call to arms or as a badge to be pinned on the other side. Many historians relish combat in print. Yet historians are supposed to be endowed with 'authority', and they enjoy the advantage of examining a past which is dead and buried. Why then are they so contentious? The answer lies in the convergence of two variables: the indeterminacy of the subject matter and the intellectual formation of the historian.

Historians sometimes fall out over the interpretation of narrowly conceived points, but the major controversies concern large-scale events or tendencies: the origins of the First World War, or the impact of the frontier on American national development. Everyone is agreed that a wide range of factors must be considered; where they disagree is how wide the net should be cast and the respective weight to be accorded to one factor over another. In the case of profound changes (like those just mentioned), living through the events is no guarantee of wisdom: contemporaries had only a partial view, based on incomplete or misleading evidence. Given that history goes on 'over our heads', it falls to the historian to make an interpretation after the event. The professional ideal is, in Bernard Bailyn's words, to 'embrace the whole of the event, see it from all sides', something which those alive at the time could not do.[39] But this is seldom possible: the historian too is handicapped by weaknesses in the sources and by a lack of agreed procedure for knitting together the relevant factors.

Revolutions illustrate these problems well. The term is usually taken to denote a dramatic upheaval resulting in a change of regime. But the revolutions which attract most study are those which not only overturned the existing rulers but launched society on a fresh trajectory, like the revolutions in England (1640), America (1776), Russia (1917) or China (1949). It then becomes critical to determine the connection between the revolutionaries and the long-term changes which became visible after the event.

Was the outcome produced by unforeseeable contingencies, or was it planned and executed by the revolutionaries? Was the old regime abreast of the new directions, but dilatory in pushing them forward? In tackling such questions historians are conditioned by the direction of their preparatory studies, by the emphasis of their primary research, and by their political values.

Debating revolution

Thus, to take the key event in early modern English political history, the revolution of the 1640s has long been seen as a crucial transition towards a capitalist society, in which trade and finance increasingly prevailed over landed wealth. (Some, but by no means all, of these historians were Marxists.) Particular attention was paid to the class composition of the opposition to the king, both in the House of Commons and the country. But the published sources for the period also give ample evidence of a ferment of radical political ideas, suggesting an intellectual reaction against the powers of the monarchy. Yet neither of these interpretations is so evident to scholars who have studied the day-to-day sequence of events leading up to the outbreak of war in 1642. For them, the crisis is more readily explained as the result of political rivalries within the elite, and a limited jockeying for position between Crown and Parliament. Indeed once the Revolution was examined through the manoeuvres of the elite, it ceased to look like a revolution at all. How to establish the respective weight of these different approaches is beyond the reach of primary research. It is determined by the judgement of the historian. That judgement will be informed by the individual scholar's sense of where the Revolution is placed in the broad sequence of English history, and that in turn is likely to be influenced by political inclination. The debates are not always a dialogue of the deaf. They also serve to refine interpretation and to identify ways in which the different positions converge. In short, something would be seriously amiss if there was academic consensus on this topic.[40]

The English Revolution is perhaps too easy a demonstration of the controversial nature of history. What about a more limited topic where politics and ideology do not obtrude to the same degree? One example is the reduction in English family size in the late Victorian and Edwardian period – from an average of six children to couples married in the 1860s, to under three children born to couples married on the eve of the war. This is obviously an important topic in social history, with significant knock-on consequences. On the other hand, demography is a technical subject associated with statistical measures – not, one might think, the stuff of intense historical debate. Two conclusions are accepted by most scholars regarding the *means* by which the reduction was achieved: first, a later age of marriage reduced the period of fertility; secondly, births were spaced by means of sexual abstinence or withdrawal, since contraception was not widely available until after the First World War, and it was widely condemned, not least by feminists in the name of 'social purity'.[41]

But about *motive* there is no such agreement. The effect of recent research has been to bring into play an ever-widening range of factors bearing on this question. Class is relevant, since family limitation in the working class lagged well behind the middle class (especially professional people). The power dynamic of marriage is at the heart of the issue. Were wives the dominant voice, dreading further pregnancies, and perhaps repelled by intercourse? Did the husband plan the family in the light of his financial resources? Or did spouses have an open discussion? Because family planning decisions are largely impenetrable, it is hard to see how these questions can be resolved. Attitudes towards children are not quite so obscure. A lower value was placed on working-class children now that their earning potential was curtailed by compulsory school attendance. At the same time the decline in child mortality may have shifted the calculation of how many births were required to achieve the desired family size.[42] Here the debates among historians are driven by the very uneven evidence and the highly diverse range of potentially relevant factors.

Is disagreement of this kind a liability? One way to answer that question is to consider what history would be like without controversy. History is an intellectually invigorating subject *because* it provokes so much disagreement. Argument about the respective merits of different interpretations sharpens our understanding of each of them, while discrediting some of the less well-founded statements. Disagreement and debate lie at the heart of current discussion about politics, society, culture and individual reputation, so why should we suppose that the record of the past is any different? Provoking controversy is part of the territory. It is not so much a liability as the lifeblood of the discipline (see also Chapter 7).

The qualities of a historian

What qualities does the successful practice of history call for? Outside observers have often taken an unflattering view. Probably the most famous put-down of the profession ever written was **Dr Johnson**'s:

> Great abilities are not requisite for an Historian; for in historical composition, all the greatest powers of the human mind are quiescent. He has the facts ready to hand so there is no exercise of invention. Imagination is not required in any high degree; only about as much as is used in the lower forms of poetry.[43]

This was hardly fair comment even in Johnson's day, and in the light of the development of the profession since the eighteenth

Dr Johnson (1709–84) Samuel Johnson, English writer and lexicographer, best known for having produced the world's first dictionary of the English language. Johnson was given to pithy comments, which still lend themselves to quotation. He was the subject of an extensive biography by his friend James Boswell.

century it seems even less apt. For the truth is that the facts do *not* lie ready to hand. New facts continue to be added to the body of historical knowledge, while at the same time the credentials of established facts are subject to constant reassessment; and, as Chapters 4 and 5 showed, the defective condition of the sources renders this dual enterprise far more difficult than might appear at first sight. The training of academic historians instituted in the nineteenth century was – and still is – primarily intended to disabuse them of any notion that the facts can be apprehended without effort. The qualities most emphasized in manuals of historical method are accordingly mastery of the primary sources and critical acumen in evaluating them.

But these skills can only take the historian one stage along the road. The process of interpretation and composition suggests a number of other equally essential qualities. First, the historian has to be able to perceive the relatedness of events and to abstract from the mountains of detail those patterns that make best sense of the past: patterns of cause and effect, patterns of periodization that justify such labels as 'Renaissance' or 'medieval', and patterns of grouping that make it meaningful to speak of a *petit bourgeoisie* in nineteenth-century France or 'rising gentry' in early seventeenth-century England. The more ambitious the scope of the enquiry, the greater the powers of abstraction and conceptualization required. The small number of really satisfying syntheses on the grand scale is a measure of how rare a generous endowment of these intellectual qualities is.

Imagination

As well as an intellectual cutting edge, the historian also requires imagination. This term can easily lead to confusion in the context of historical writing. It is not intended to convey the idea of sustained creative invention, though it was evidently against this yardstick that Dr Johnson found historians wanting. The point is rather that any attempt to reconstruct the past presupposes an exercise of imagination, because the past is never completely captured in the documents which it left behind. Again and again historians encounter gaps in the record which they can fill only by being so thoroughly exposed to the surviving sources that they have a 'feel' or instinct for what might have happened. Matters of motive and mentality frequently fall into this category, and the more alien and remote the culture, the greater is the imaginative leap required to understand it. Those books condemned as 'dry as dust' are usually the ones in which the accumulation of detail has not been brought to life by the play of the writer's imagination.

How is the historical imagination nurtured? It helps, of course, to keep your eyes and ears (and nostrils) open to the world around you. As Richard Cobb found:

petit bourgeoisie
Bourgeois simply means 'of the town' and is therefore applied to those, principally the 'middle' classes, whose sphere of operation is urban rather than rural. However, since this ranges from the wealthy merchant and professional classes down to small shopkeepers, the term needs to be qualified. *Bourgeoisie* is usually reserved for substantial businessmen and those in the professions, while *petit bourgeoisie* (i.e. the 'little' bourgeoisie, sometimes rendered as 'petty bourgeois' in English) refers to shopkeepers and small businessmen.

A great deal of Paris eighteenth-century history, of Lyon nineteenth-century history can be walked, seen, and above all heard, in small restaurants, on the platform at the back of a bus, in cafés or on the park bench.[44]

The historian's knowledge of life

The ability to empathize with people in the past presupposes a certain self-awareness, and some historians have suggested that psychoanalysis might form part of the apprentice's training.[45] Breadth of experience, however, is a much more promising foundation. In the days when history writing was largely confined to political narrative, experience of public life was widely regarded as the best training for historians; as Gibbon said of his short career as an MP: 'The eight sessions that I sat in parliament were a school of civil prudence, the first and most essential virtue of an historian.'[46] Wartime service probably deepened the insights of many twentieth-century historians of politics, diplomacy and war. But it is *variety* of experience that really tells – experience of different countries, classes and temperaments – so that the range of imaginative possibilities in the historian's mind bears some relation to the range of conditions and mentalities in the past. Unfortunately the usual career pattern of academic historians nowadays makes little allowance for this requirement. A suggestion some years ago that the best training for a historian is a trip round the world and several jobs in different walks of life may have been impracticable, but it was not meant to be flippant.[47]

It is one thing, however, to have an imaginative insight into the past, and quite another to be able to convey this to the reader. Verbal or literary skills are of considerable importance to the historian. At any time prior to the nineteenth century this would have been taken for granted. Since classical times the profession of historian had been considered by its leading exponents to be above all a literary accomplishment. History had its presiding **muse** (Clio), a secure place in the culture of the reading public and a range of rhetorical and stylistic conventions which it was the principal task of the aspirant historian to master. All this changed with the rise of academic history. The problems that exercised the professional historians who followed in Ranke's footsteps were those of method rather than presentation. Command of the sources or 'scholarship' has often been counterposed to 'writing', to the detriment of the latter; 'Clio, once a Muse, is now more commonly seen, with a reader's ticket, verifying her references at the Public Record Office.'[48] As a result a great deal of unreadable history has been written in the last hundred years.

But good writing is more than an optional extra or a lucky bonus. It is central to the recreative aspect of history. The insights derived from the exercise of historical imagination cannot be

muse

In Greek mythology, the muses were the daughters of Zeus and Mnemosyne, the goddess of memory. Each presided over a particular branch of knowledge and the arts, such as music, poetry, comedy and mime. The muse of history was Clio.

shared at all without a good deal of literary flair – an eye for detail, the power to evoke mood, temperament and ambience, and an illusion of suspense – qualities that are most fully developed in creative writing. History of the explanatory kind does not share so much common ground with creative literature, which may be one reason why those historians who set most store by the literary claims of their discipline – G.M. Trevelyan or C.V. Wedgwood, for example – have contributed relatively little to this sphere. Close argument and the need to hedge so many statements with qualifications and caveats are not conducive to 'literary' expression. Nevertheless, the problem of combining narrative with analysis, which attends any venture in historical explanation, is essentially a problem of literary form. Its solution is hardly ever dictated by the material.

Set out in this way, it may be that none of the qualities or skills required of the historian seems particularly demanding. But it is rare to find all of them combined in sufficient measure in the same

Figure 6.2 In classical mythology, Clio was the muse who inspired historians, just as other muses inspired poets and musicians, etc. When Clio is invoked today, the implication is that history is one of the literary arts and should be judged by aesthetic standards. © akg-images, London.

person. Very few historians are equally endowed in the technical, intellectual, imaginative and stylistic spheres, and despite the immense expansion of professional scholarship in recent decades, the number of fully satisfying historical works in any branch of study remains small. At the same time, the varied nature of the historian's equipment serves to reiterate another point – that history is essentially a *hybrid* discipline, combining the technical and analytical procedures of a science with the imaginative and stylistic qualities of an art.

Further reading

G.R. Elton, *The Practice of History*, Fontana, 1969.

William Lamont (ed.), *Historical Controversies and Historians*, UCL Press, 1998.

Peter Burke (ed.), *New Perspectives on Historical Writing*, Polity Press, 1991.

L.P. Curtis (ed.), *The Historian's Workshop*, Knopf, 1970.

Bernard Bailyn, 'The challenge of modern historiography', *American Historical Review*, LXXXVII, 1982.

W.H. Walsh, 'Colligatory concepts in history', in Patrick Gardiner (ed.), *The Philosophy of History*, Oxford University Press, 1974.

Alun Munslow, *Deconstructing History*, Routledge, 1997.

Hayden White, *Metahistory: The Historical Imagination in Nineteenth-Century Europe*, Johns Hopkins University Press, 1973.

Notes

1 V.H. Galbraith, *An Introduction to the Study of History*, C. Watts, 1964, p. 80.

2 See, for example, E.H. Carr, *What is History?*, Penguin, 1964, pp. 28–9, and J.G.A. Pocock, 'Working on ideas in time', in L.P. Curtis (ed.), *The Historian's Workshop*, Knopf, 1970, pp. 161, 175.

3 H. Butterfield, *History and Human Relations*, Collins, 1951, p. 237.

4 Fernand Braudel, *The Mediterranean and the Mediterranean World in the Age of Philip II*, 2 vols, Collins, 1972.

5 Diane Purkiss, *The English Civil War: A People's History*, Harper, 2006; Orlando Figes, *A People's Tragedy: The Russian Revolution, 1891–1924*, Jonathan Cape, 1996, p. xix.

6 James Joll, 'The unspoken assumptions', in H.W. Koch (ed.), *The Origins of the First World War*, Macmillan, 1972.

7 For an excellent discussion of this notion, see Bernard Bailyn, 'The challenge of modern historiography', *American Historical Review*, LXXXVII, 1982, pp. 1–24.

8 The classic statement of this viewpoint is Eric Williams, *Capitalism and Slavery*, University of North Carolina Press, 1944.

9 Carr, *What is History?*, p. 52.

10 Christine Bolt and Seymour Drescher (eds), *Anti-Slavery, Religion and Reform*, Dawson, 1980 (especially the essay by Brian Harrison).

11 Lawrence Stone, *The Causes of the English Revolution 1529–1642*, Routledge & Kegan Paul, 1972, ch. 3.

12 Carl E. Schorske, *Fin-de-Siècle Vienna: Politics and Culture*, Weidenfeld & Nicolson, 1980, p. xxii.

13 R.H. Tawney, *History and Society*, Routledge & Kegan Paul, 1978, p. 54.

14 Simon Schama, *Citizens: A Chronicle of the French Revolution*, Penguin, 1989, p. xiv.

15 A.J.P. Taylor, *War by Timetable: How the First World War Began*, Macdonald, 1969, p. 45.

16 R.W. Southern, *The Making of the Middle Ages*, Hutchinson, 1953, pp. 14–15.

17 Agatha Ramm, 'Leopold von Ranke', in John Cannon (ed.), *The Historian at Work*, Allen & Unwin, 1980, p. 37.

18 E.P. Thompson, *The Poverty of Theory*, Merlin Press, 1978, p. 85.

19 H. Butterfield, *George III and the Historians*, Collins, 1957.

20 Daniel Snowman, *Histories*, Palgrave, 2007, pp. 10–11.

21 Hayden White, *Metahistory*, Johns Hopkins University Press, 1973.

22 Peter Burke, 'History of events and the revival of narrative', in P. Burke (ed.), *New Perspectives on Historical Writing*, Polity Press, 1991, p. 241.

23 Natalie Zemon Davis, *The Return of Martin Guerre*, Penguin, 1985, pp. 4, viii.

24 Lawrence Stone, 'The revival of narrative', 1979, reprinted in his *The Past and the Present Revisited*, Routledge & Kegan Paul, 1987.

25 Lucien Febvre, 'A new kind of history', 1949, translated in Peter Burke (ed.), *A New Kind of History*, Routledge & Kegan Paul, 1973, p. 38.

26 Marc Bloch in *Annales*, 1932, quoted in R.R. Davies, 'Marc Bloch', *History*, LII, 1967, p. 273.

27 See, for example, F.M. Powicke, *Modern Historians and the Study of History*, Odhams, 1955, p. 202.

28 Quoted in H. Butterfield, *Man on His Past*, Cambridge University Press, 1955, p. 91.

29 Jose Harris, *Private Lives, Public Spirit: Britain, 1870–1914*, Penguin, 1994.

30 E.J. Hobsbawm, *The Age of Revolution: Europe 1789–1848*, Cardinal, [1962] 1973, p. 11.

31 See, for example, C.C. Eldridge (ed.), *British Imperialism in the Nineteenth Century*, Macmillan, 1984.

32 G.R. Elton, *The Practice of History*, Fontana, 1969, p. 22.

33 Braudel, *The Mediterranean*, vol. I, p. 16.

34 Fernand Braudel, 'History and the social sciences: *la longue durée*', 1958, reprinted in his *On History*, Weidenfeld & Nicolson, 1980, p. 26.

35 Susan R. Grayzel, *Women's Identities at War: Gender, Motherhood and Politics in Britain and France During the First World War*, University of North Carolina Press, 1999; Susan Pedersen, *Family, Dependence and the Origins of the Welfare State*, Cambridge University Press, 1993.

36 J.H. Elliott, *Empires of the Atlantic World: Britain and Spain in America, 1492–1830*, Yale University Press, 2006, p. xvii.

37 Ibid., p. xviii.

38 J.H. Elliott, *Times Literary Supplement*, 23 June 1989, p. 699.

39 Bernard Bailyn, quoted in Colin Brooks, 'Bernard Bailyn and the scope of American history', in William Lamont (ed.), *Historical Controversies and Historians*, UCL Press, 1998, pp. 170–71.

40 The vast historiography on this topic is lucidly analysed in Norah Carlin, *The Causes of the English Civil War*, Blackwell, 1999.

41 Simon Szreter, *Fertility, Class and Gender in Britain, 1860–1940*, Cambridge University Press, 1996.

42 Wally Seccombe, 'Starting to stop: working-class fertility decline', *Past & Present*, CXXVI, 1990; Hera Cook, *The Long Sexual Revolution: English Women, Sex, and Contraception, 1800–1975*, Oxford University Press, 2004.

43 R.W. Chapman (ed.), *Boswell's Life of Johnson*, Oxford University Press, 1953, p. 304.

44 Richard Cobb, *A Second Identity*, Oxford University Press, 1969, pp. 19–20.

45 H. Stuart Hughes, *History as Art and as Science*, Chicago University Press, 1964, pp. 65–6.

46 M.M. Reese (ed.), *Gibbon's Autobiography*, Routledge & Kegan Paul, 1970, p. 99.

47 Theodore Zeldin, 'After Braudel', *The Listener*, 5 November 1981, p. 542.

48 Galbraith, *Introduction*, p. 4.

7 The limits of historical knowledge

Historians make many claims for their subject, but can any historical account amount to anything more than its author's personal take on the past? This chapter looks at the debate surrounding the essential nature of historical work and therefore, to some extent, its value. The positivist position sees history as a form of science, in which historians amass facts from hard evidence and draw valid conclusions; the idealists on the other hand stress that the incomplete and imperfect nature of the historical record obliges the historian to employ a considerable degree of human intuition and imagination. Challenging both positions are the Postmodernists, who point to the highly subjective values and assumptions latent not just in the historical record but in the very language that historians use to express their ideas. Does this mean that objective historical accounts are an impossibility, and if so, what is the student to make of a philosophy that questions history's very existence as a subject?

The earlier chapters of this book were essentially descriptive. They were intended to show how historians go about their work – their guiding assumptions, their handling of the evidence and their presentation of conclusions. The point has now been reached where some fundamental questions about the nature of historical enquiry can be posed: how securely based is our knowledge of the past? Can the facts of history be taken as given? What authority should be attached to attempts at historical explanation? Can historians be objective? Answers to these questions have taken widely divergent forms and have occasioned intense debate, much of it fuelled by criticisms from outside the ranks of historians. The profession is deeply divided about the status of its findings. At one extreme there are those who maintain, as Elton did, that humility in the face of the evidence and training in the technicalities of research have steadily enlarged the stock of certain historical knowledge; notwithstanding the arguments which the professionals take such delight in, history is a cumulative discipline.[1] At the other extreme, Theodore Zeldin holds that all he (or any historian) can offer his readers is his

Figure 7.1 History publishing is a huge business, with thousands of new titles appearing every year. Does this mean that we are closer to the truth about the past, or does it just mean that there are as many histories as there are people prepared to write them? © James Leynse/ CORBIS.

personal vision of the past, and the materials out of which they in turn can fashion a personal vision that corresponds to their own aspirations and sympathies: 'everyone has the right to find his own perspective'.[2] Although the weight of opinion among academic historians inclines towards Elton's position, every viewpoint between the two extremes finds adherents within the profession. Historians are in a state of confusion about what exactly they are up to – a confusion not usually apparent in the confident manner with which they often pronounce on major problems of interpretation.

I

Is history a science?

To ask such questions about history or any other branch of learning is to enter the terrain of philosophy, since what is at issue is the nature of knowledge itself; and the status of historical knowledge has been hotly contested among philosophers since the Renaissance. Most working historians – even those disposed to reflect on the nature of their craft – take little account of these debates, believing with some justification that they often obscure rather than clarify the issues.[3] But the intense disagreement that divides historians reflects a tradition of keen debate among philosophers. During the nineteenth century, two sharply opposed positions crystallized around the question of whether or not history was a science; as recently as the 1960s, when E.H. Carr created such a stir, this was still the key **epistemological** issue in history. In our own day, the ground of debate has shifted to the nature of language and the extent of its bearing on the real world, past and present. Both these debates – the scientific and the linguistic – will now be examined in turn.

epistemological
Relating to the theory of knowledge, how we know things.

The central question in the debate about history and science has always been whether humankind should be studied in the same way as other natural phenomena. Those who answer this question in the affirmative are committed to the methodological unity of all forms of disciplined enquiry into the human and natural order. They argue that history employs the same procedures as the natural sciences and that its findings should be judged by scientific standards. They may differ as to how far history has in fact fulfilled these requirements, but they are agreed that historical knowledge is valid only in so far as it conforms to scientific method. During the twentieth century, conceptions of the nature of science were radically modified, but the nineteenth-century view was straightforward enough. The basis of all scientific knowledge was the meticulous observation of reality by the **disinterested**, 'passive' observer, and the outcome of repeated observations of the same phenomenon was a generalization or 'law' that fitted all the known facts and explained the regularity observed. The assumption of this, the 'inductive' or 'empirical' method, was that generalizations flowed logically from the data, and that scientists approached their task without preconceptions and without moral involvement.

disinterested
Neutral, objective. Not to be confused with 'uninterested'.

Positivism: induction from facts

As a result of its immense strides in both pure and applied work, science enjoyed unrivalled prestige during the nineteenth century. If its methods unlocked the secrets of the natural world, might they not prove the key to understanding society and culture? *Positivism* is the name given to the philosophy of knowledge that expresses this approach in its classic, nineteenth-century form. Its implications for the practice of history are clear. The historian's first duty is to accumulate factual knowledge about the past – facts that are verified by applying critical method to the primary sources; those facts will in turn determine how the past should be explained or interpreted. In this process the beliefs and values of historians are irrelevant; their sole concern is with the facts and the generalizations to which they logically lead. Auguste Comte, the most influential positivist philosopher of the nineteenth century, believed that historians would in due course uncover the 'laws' of historical development. Full-blown professions of positivist faith are still made occasionally,[4] but nowadays a watered-down version is preferred. Latter-day positivists maintain that the study of history cannot generate its own laws; rather, the essence of historical explanation lies in the correct application of generalizations derived from other disciplines supposedly based on scientific method, such as economics, sociology and psychology.

Idealism: intuition and empathy

The second position, which corresponds to the school of philosophy known as *idealism*, rejects the fundamental assumption of positivism. According to this view, human events must be carefully distinguished from natural events because the identity between the enquirer and his or her subject matter opens the way to a fuller understanding than anything that the natural scientist can aspire to. Whereas natural events can only be understood from the outside, human events have an essential 'inside' dimension composed of the intentions, feelings and mentality of the actors. Once the enquirer strays into this realm the inductive method is of limited use. The reality of past events must instead be apprehended by an imaginative identification with the people of the past, which depends on intuition and empathy – qualities that have no place in the classical view of scientific method. According to idealists, therefore, historical knowledge is inherently subjective, and the truths that it uncovers are more akin to truth in the artist's sense than the scientist's. Furthermore, historians are concerned with the individual, unique event. The generalizations of the social sciences are not applicable to the study of the past, nor does history yield any generalizations or laws of its own.

   This outlook came naturally to the nineteenth-century proponents of historicism (see Chapter 1) with their demand that every age be understood in its own terms, and their practical emphasis on political narrative made up of the actions and intentions of 'great men'. Ranke's fame as the champion of rigorous source criticism has sometimes been allowed to obscure the emphasis that he laid on contemplation and imagination: 'after the labour of criticism', he insisted, 'intuition is required'.[5] In the English-speaking world the most original and sophisticated exponent of the idealist position was the philosopher and historian R.G. Collingwood. In his posthumously published *The Idea of History* (1946), he maintained that all history is essentially the history of thought, and that the historian's task is to re-enact in his or her own mind the thoughts and intentions of individuals in the past. Collingwood's influence is evident in the case of present-day opponents of 'scientific' theory such as Zeldin, who deplores the tendency for history to become 'a coffee-house in which to discuss the findings of other disciplines in time perspective' and pleads for a history concerned with individuals and their emotions.[6] Conversely, history's scientific pretensions tend to be taken much more seriously by historians of collective behaviour – voting or consumption for example – because in these spheres regularities are evident that can sometimes form the basis of firm generalizations.

But the implications of the unresolved clash between positivism and idealism go much further than the distinction between traditional political history and the more recent fields of economic and social history. They help to explain why there is so much disagreement among historians about the nature of virtually every aspect of their work, from primary source evaluation through to the finished work of interpretation.

II

An incomplete and tainted record

Much of the professional self-esteem of the new breed of academic historians in the nineteenth century was based on the rigorous techniques that they had perfected for the location and criticism of primary sources. The canons they established have governed the practice of historians ever since, so that the whole edifice of modern historical knowledge is founded on the pains-taking evaluation of original documents. But the injunction 'Be true to your sources' is less straightforward than it looks, and sceptics have seized on a number of problem areas. First, the primary sources available to the historian are an *incomplete* record, not only because so much has perished by accident or design, but in a more fundamental sense because a great deal that happened left no material trace whatever. This is particularly true of mental processes, both conscious and unconscious. No histor-ical character, however prominent and articulate, has ever set down more than a tiny proportion of his or her thoughts and assumptions, and often some of the most influential beliefs are those that are taken for granted and therefore are not discussed in the documents.

Second, the sources are *tainted* by the less than pure intentions of their authors and – more insidiously – by their confinement within the assumptions of men and women in that time and place. 'The so-called "sources" of history record only such facts as appeared sufficiently interesting to record';[7] or, more polemically, the historical record is forever rigged in favour of the ruling class, which at all times has created the vast majority of the surviving sources. This point is particularly worth bearing in mind with regard to archives. As explained in Chapter 5, the archive is not just a record of government; it is an *instrument* of government, and the accuracy of its records is skewed by administrative priorities and prejudices.

There is an element of truth in both these criticisms, but those who push them to extremes betray an ignorance of how historians actually work. What a researcher can learn from a set of documents is not confined to its explicit meaning. When properly applied, the critical method enables the historian to make allowances for both deliberate distortion and the unthinking reflexes of the writer – to extract meaning 'against the grain of the documentation', in Raphael Samuel's useful phrase.[8] Much of the criticism directed against historical method rests on the common misconception that primary sources are the testimonies of witnesses – who like all witnesses are fallible but in this instance are not available for cross-examination. Yet, as was shown in Chapter 5, a great deal of the historian's documentation is made up of record sources which themselves constitute the event or process under investigation: historians interested, say, in the character of Gladstone or the administrative machinery of the medieval Chancery are not dependent on contemporary reports and impressions (interesting though these may be); they can base their accounts on the private correspondence and diaries of Gladstone himself, or on the records generated in the course of the Chancery's day-to-day business. Moreover, much of the importance attached to primary sources derives not from the intentions of the writer but from information that was incidental to his or her purpose and yet may provide a flash of insight into an otherwise inaccessible aspect of the past. The historian, in short, is not confined by the categories of thought in which the documents were composed.[9]

A *surfeit of records*

But there is a third and more formidable difficulty in the notion that historians simply follow where the documents lead, and this turns on the *profusion* of the available sources. These sources may, it is true, represent a very incomplete record; yet for all but very remote periods and places they survive in completely unmanageable quantities. This is a problem that was confronted only during the twentieth century. Nineteenth-century historians, especially those of a positivist turn of mind such as Lord Acton, believed that finality in historical writing would be attained when primary research had brought to light a complete assemblage of the facts; many of these facts might seem obscure and trivial, but they would all tell in the end. These writers were blinded to the limitations of their method by the very narrow way in which they conceived both the content of history and a primary source: when Acton wrote 'nearly all the evidence that will ever appear is accessible now',[10] he was referring only to the great collections of state records. Since Acton's day the subject matter of history has been vastly enlarged, and the significance of whole bodies of source material whose existence nineteenth-century historians were scarcely aware of has been established. Faced with the virtually limitless content that history could in theory embrace, modern historians have been compelled to subject the notion of historical 'fact' to severe scrutiny.

What are facts?

Objection is sometimes made to the idea of 'facts' in history on the grounds that they rest on inadequate standards of proof: most of what pass for the 'facts' of history actually depend on inference. Historians read between the lines, or they work out what really happened from several contradictory indications, or they may do no more than establish that the writer was probably telling the truth. But in none of these cases can the historian observe the facts in the way that a physicist can. Historians generally have little time for this kind of critique. Formal proof may be beyond their reach; what matters is the validity of the inferences. In practice historians spend a good deal of time disputing and refining the inferences that can be legitimately drawn from the sources, and the facts of history can be said to rest on inferences whose validity is widely accepted by expert opinion. Who, they ask with some justice, could reasonably ask for more?

Historians are much more troubled by the implications of the apparently limitless number of facts about the past that can be verified in this way. If the entire past of humankind falls within the historian's scope, then every fact about that past may be said to have some claim on our attention. But historians do not proceed on this assumption – not even the specialist in some limited aspect of a well-defined period. There is in practice no limit to the number of facts that have a bearing on the problem in hand, and the historian who resolved to be guided solely by the facts would never reach any conclusion. The common-sense idea (and the central tenet of positivism) that historians efface themselves in front of the facts 'out there' is therefore an illusion. The facts are not given, they are selected. Despite appearances, they are never left to speak for themselves. However detailed a historical narrative may be, and however committed its author to the recreation of the past, it never springs from the sources ready-made; many events are omitted as trivial, and those that do find a place in the narrative tend to be seen through the eyes of one particular participant or a small group. Analytical history, in which the writer's intention is to abstract the factors with greatest explanatory power, is more obviously selective. Historical writing of all kinds is determined as much by what it leaves out as by what it puts in. That is why it makes sense to distinguish with E.H. Carr between the facts of the past and the facts of history. The former are limitless and in their entirety unknowable; the latter represent a selection made by successive historians for the purpose of historical reconstruction and explanation: 'The facts of history cannot be purely objective, since they become facts of history only in virtue of the significance attached to them by the historian.'[11]

The selection and rejection of facts

If historical facts are selected, it is important to identify the criteria employed in selecting them. Are there commonly shared principles, or is it a matter of personal whim? One answer, much favoured since Ranke's day, is that historians reveal the essence of the events under consideration. Namier expressed this idea metaphorically:

> The function of the historian is akin to that of the painter and not of the photographic camera; to discover and set forth, to single out and stress that which is of the nature of the thing, and not to reproduce indiscriminately all that meets the eye.[12]

But this amounts to little more than a restatement of the original question, for how is the 'nature of the thing' to be determined? It makes for less confusion if it is admitted outright that the standards of significance applied by the historian are defined by the nature of the historical problem that he or she is seeking to solve. As M.M. Postan put it:

> The facts of history, even those which in historical parlance figure as 'hard and fast', are no more than relevances: **facets** of past phenomena which happen to relate to the preoccupations of historical inquirers at the time of their inquiries.

facets
Features, characteristics.

As new historical facts are accepted into the canon, so old ones pass out of currency except, as Postan mischievously remarks, in textbooks that are full of 'ex-facts'.[13]

There is an element of rhetorical exaggeration about this view. Historical knowledge abounds in facts, such as the Great Fire of London or the execution of Charles I, whose status is for all practical purposes unassailable, and critics such as Elton have seized on this point to discredit the distinction between the facts of the past and the facts of history, which they feel introduces a dangerous element of subjectivity.[14] But, as anyone who has sampled the work of professional historians knows, historical writing is never composed entirely, or even principally, of these unassailable facts. The decision whether to include this set of facts rather than that is closely affected by the purpose that informs the historian's work.

Clearly, then, much depends on the kind of questions that the historian has in mind at the outset of research. As was discussed in Chapter 5, there is something to be said for selecting a rich and previously untapped vein of source material and being guided by whatever questions it throws up (see p. 99). The difficulty with this method is that nobody actually approaches the sources with a completely open mind – the grounding in the standard secondary literature which precedes any research will see to that. Even if no specific questions have been formulated, the researcher will study the sources with certain assumptions that are only too likely to be an unthinking reflection of current orthodoxy, and the result will be merely a clarification of detail or a modification of emphasis within the prevailing framework of interpretation.

Historical hypotheses

Significant advances in historical understanding are more likely to be achieved when a historian puts forward a clearly formulated hypothesis that can be tested against the evidence. The answers may not correspond to the hypothesis, which must then be discarded or modified, but merely to ask new questions has the important effect of alerting historians to unfamiliar aspects of familiar problems and to unsuspected data in well-worked sources. The origins of the English Civil War (discussed in Chapter 6) illustrates the point. Nineteenth-century historians approached this as a problem of competing political and religious ideologies, and they selected accordingly from the great mass of surviving information about early seventeenth-century England. From the 1930s onwards an increasing number of scholars sought to test a Marxist approach to the conflict, and as a result new material which related to the economic fortunes of the gentry, the aristocracy and the urban bourgeoisie became critically important. From the 1970s onwards, several historians employed a 'Namierite' approach in which the constitutional and military conflicts were seen as the expression of rivalry between political factions: hence the networks of patronage and the intrigues at court are now coming more into play. The point is not that the Marxist or Namierite position amounts to a rounded explanation of the war but rather that each hypothesis has brought into focus certain previously neglected factors which will have a bearing on any future interpretation. Marc Bloch, whose own work proceeded on the basis of hypotheses, put the issue clearly:

> Every historical research supposes that the inquiry has a direction at the very first step. In the beginning, there must be the guiding spirit. Mere passive observation, even supposing such a thing were possible, has never contributed anything productive to any science.[15]

The scientific paradigm

Significantly, scientists today would themselves mostly agree. The positivist theory still dominates the lay person's view of science, but it no longer carries much conviction among the scientific community. Inductive thought and passive observation have ceased to be regarded as the hallmarks of scientific method. Rather, all observation, whether of the natural or the human world, is selective and therefore presupposes a hypothesis or theory, however incoherent it may be. In **Karl Popper**'s influential view, scientific knowledge consists not of laws but of the best available hypotheses; it is provisional rather than certain knowledge. Our understanding advances through the formulation of new hypotheses that go beyond the evidence currently available and must be tested against further observation, which will either refute or corroborate the hypothesis. And because hypotheses go beyond the evidence, they necessarily involve a flash of insight or an imaginative leap, often the bolder the better. Scientific method, then, is a dialogue between hypothesis and attempted refutation, or between creative and critical thought.[16] To historians this is a much more congenial definition of science than the one it has replaced.

Karl Popper (1902–94) British scientist and philosopher. Popper rejected induction as a basis for science and argued that the proper role of scientific observation was to refute existing theories rather than to try to confirm them.

The importance of imagination

But although history and the natural sciences may converge in some of their fundamental methodological assumptions, important differences remain. First, far greater play is allowed to the imagination in history. It is by no means confined to the formulation of hypotheses but permeates the historian's thinking. Historians are not, after all, only concerned to explain the past; they also seek to reconstruct or recreate it – to show how life was experienced as well as how it may be understood – and this requires an imaginative engagement with the mentality and atmosphere of the past. As Joseph C. Miller puts it:

> History turns data into evidence not by pursuing the technical attributes of data but by substituting a distinctively intuitive, humanistic, holistic strategy for the experimental method of science.[17]

In maintaining that all history is the history of thought, Collingwood unduly confined the scope of the subject. But it is certainly true that the evaluation of documentary sources depends on a reconstruction of the thought behind them; before anything else can be achieved, the historian must first try to enter the mental world of those who created the sources.

Furthermore, although idealists from Ranke to Collingwood placed an exaggerated emphasis on 'unique' events, individuals are certainly a legitimate and necessary object of historical study, and the variety and unpredictability of individual behaviour (as opposed to the regularities of mass behaviour) demand qualities of empathy and intuition in the enquirer as well as logical and critical skills. And whereas scientists can often create their own data by experiment, historians are time and again confronted by gaps in the evidence which they can make good only by developing a sensitivity as to what *might* have happened, derived from an imagined picture that has taken shape in the course of becoming immersed in the surviving documentation. In all these ways imagination is vital to the historian. It not only generates fruitful hypotheses, it is also deployed in the reconstruction of past events and situations by which those hypotheses are tested.

The impossibility of consensus

The second and even more critical distinction to be made between history and the natural sciences is that the standing of explanations put forward by historians is very much inferior to that of scientific explanation. It may be that scientific explanations are no more than provisional hypotheses, but they are for the most part hypotheses on which all people qualified to judge are in agreement; they may be superseded one day, but for the time being they represent the nearest possible approximation to the truth and are commonly recognized as such. In matters of historical explanation, on the other hand, a scholarly consensus scarcely exists. The known facts may not be in doubt, but how to interpret or explain them is a matter of endless debate, as the example of the English Civil War illustrated. The 'faction hypothesis' has not superseded the 'class-conflict hypothesis' or the 'ideology hypothesis'; all are very much alive and receive varying emphases from different historians.

The reason for this diversity of opinion lies in the complex texture of historical change. We saw in Chapter 6 how both individual and collective behaviour are influenced by an immense range of contrasting factors. What needs stressing here is that each historical situation is unique in the sense that the exact configuration of causal factors is unrepeatable. It might be argued, for instance, that the reasons why the European powers withdrew from most of their African colonies during the 1950s and 1960s were common to some thirty-odd different territories. But this would be valid only as a very broad-brush statement. The respective strength of the colonial power and the nationalist movement varied from one country to another according to its value to the metropolis, its experience of social change, the size of the resident European community and so on.[18] In practice, therefore, each situation has to be investigated afresh, with the strong possibility of different findings, and as a result the basis for a comprehensive theory of historical causation simply does not exist.

A multiplicity of hypotheses

Perhaps this would not matter if certainty was attainable in explaining *particular* events. But this more modest objective eludes historians as well. The problem here is that the evidence is never sufficiently full and unambiguous to place a causal interpretation beyond doubt. This is true of even the best-documented events. In a case like the origins of the First World War, the sources provide ample evidence of the motives of the protagonists, the sequence of diplomatic moves, the state of public opinion, the upward spiral of the arms race, the relative economic strength of all the nations involved and so on. But what the evidence alone cannot do is tell us the *relative* importance of all these varied factors, or present a comprehensive picture of how they interacted with each other.[19] In many instances the sources do not directly address the central issues of historical explanation at all. Some of the influences on human conduct, such as the natural environment or the neurotic and irrational, are apprehended subconsciously; others may be experienced directly but not disclosed in the sources. Questions of historical explanation cannot, therefore, be resolved solely by reference to the evidence. Historians are also guided by their intuitive sense of what was possible in a given historical context, by their reading of human nature and by the claims of intellectual coherence. In each of these areas they are unlikely to concur. As a result, several different hypotheses can hold the field at any one time. Jakob **Burckhardt** frankly acknowledged the problem in the Preface to his *Civilization of the Renaissance in Italy* (1860):

> In the wide ocean upon which we venture, the possible ways and directions are many; and the same studies which have served for this work might easily, in other hands, not only receive a wholly different treatment and application, but lead also to essentially different conclusions.[20]

Burckhardt (1818–97)
Jakob Burckhardt, Swiss historian. He is credited with having coined the term 'Renaissance' (French: 'rebirth') to describe the cultural changes and revival of classical form in fifteenth-century Italy.

The area of knowledge beyond dispute is both smaller and much less significant in history than it is in the natural sciences. This is a crucial limitation that is not properly confronted by present-day champions of 'objectivity' in history.[21]

III

The historian as selector

This comparison between history and natural sciences is perhaps somewhat contrived, given that the assumptions most people make about the standing of scientific knowledge are an outdated residue of nineteenth-century positivism; scientific knowledge is in reality less certain and less objective than is commonly supposed. But what the comparison does bring out is the extent to which our knowledge of the past depends on choices freely exercised by the historian. The common-sense notion that the business of historians is simply to uncover the past and display what they have found will not stand up. The essence of historical enquiry is *selection* – of 'relevant' sources, of 'historical' facts and of 'significant' interpretations. At every stage, both the direction and the destination of the enquiry are determined as much by the enquirer as by the data. Clearly, the rigid segregation of fact and value demanded by the positivists is unworkable in history. In this sense, historical knowledge is not, and cannot be, 'objective' (that is, **empirically** derived in its entirety from the object of the enquiry). This does not mean, as sceptics might suppose, that it is therefore arbitrary or illusory. But it does follow that the assumptions and attitudes of historians themselves have to be carefully assessed before we can come to any conclusion about the status of historical knowledge.

empiricism
Reasoning from experiment and experience, rather than from theoretical principles. Although strict scientific experimentation is a form of empiricism, so too is deduction based on ill-defined 'common sense', which can lend empiricism an ambiguous intellectual status.

The historian in context

Up to a point those standards can be seen as the property of the individual historian. The experience of research is a personal and often very private one, and no two historians will share the same imaginative response to their material. As Richard Cobb put it, 'the writing of history is one of the fullest and most rewarding expressions of an individual personality'.[22] But however rarefied the atmosphere that historians breathe, they are, like everyone else, affected by the assumptions and values of their own society. It is more illuminating to see historical interpretation as moulded by social rather than individual experience. And because social values change, it follows that historical interpretation is subject to constant revision. What one age finds worthy of note in the past may well be different from what previous ages found worthy. This principle can be illustrated many times over within the relatively short span of time since the emergence of the academic profession of history. For Ranke and his contemporaries, the sovereign nation states that dominated the Europe of their day seemed the climax of the historical process; the state was the principal agent of historical change, and human destiny was largely determined by the shifting balance of power between states. This world view was seriously eroded by the First World War. After 1919 a much more jaundiced view was taken of the nation state. There was a countervailing growth of interest in both the history of internationalism, and the history of ordinary people as expressed in social history.

More recently, the way in which historians study the world beyond Europe and the United States has been transformed in the light of the changes they have lived through. Fifty years ago, the history of Africa was still treated as an aspect of the expansion of Europe, in which the indigenous peoples scarcely featured except as the object of white policies and attitudes. Today the perspective is very different. African history exists in its own right, embracing both the pre-colonial past and the African experience of – and response to – colonial rule, and stressing the continuities of African historical development, which had previously been completely obscured by the stress on the European occupation. And those continuities have already been reassessed: whereas in the 1960s historians of Africa were mainly concerned with placing African nationalism in a historical perspective of pre-colonial state formation and resistance to colonial rule, they are now, after forty years' disillusionment with the fruits of independence, preoccupied with the historical antecedents of Africa's deepening poverty. Twice in the course of a single lifetime the standards of significance applied by historians to the African past have been substantially revised (see Chapter 10).

However, to say that history is rewritten by each generation (or decade) is only part of the truth – and positively misleading if it suggests the replacement of one consensus by another. In the case of history written during the High Middle Ages or the Renaissance it might be appropriate to speak of a scholarly consensus, since historians and their audience were drawn from a very restricted sector of society, and at this distance in time the differences between historians seem much less significant than the values they held in common. But the attainment of universal literacy and the extension of education in Western society in the twentieth century mean that historical writing now reflects a much wider range of values and assumptions. The towering political personalities of the past such as Oliver Cromwell or Napoleon Bonaparte are interpreted in widely divergent ways by professional historians as well as lay people, partly according to their own political values.[23] Liberal or conservative historians such as **Peter Laslett** tend to conceive of social relations in pre-industrial England as reciprocal, while radically inclined historians like E.P. Thompson see them as exploitative.[24] **Michael Howard** has made public confession of a bias that is widely shared – a bias in favour of a liberal political order in which alone the historian has been permitted to work without censorship.[25] Many other historians, however, would set a higher value on material progress or equality in social relations than on freedom of thought and expression. Historical interpretation is a matter of value judgements, moulded to a greater or lesser degree by moral and political attitudes. At the beginning of the twentieth century, Acton's successor at Cambridge, J.B. Bury, looked forward to the dawn of scientific history with these words: 'Though there be many schools of political philosophy, there will no longer be divers schools of history.'[26] It would be nearer the truth to say that for as long as there are many schools of political philosophy there will be divers schools of history. Paradoxically there is an element of present-mindedness about all historical enquiry.

Peter Laslett (1915–2001)
British historian. He pioneered the study of the history of the English family. His ground-breaking work of social history *The World We Have Lost* (1965) overturned many common assumptions about everyday life in early modern England.

Sir Michael Howard (1922–)
British military historian, Regius Professor of Modern History at Oxford 1980–9.

The search for origins

The problem, of course, is to determine at what point present-mindedness conflicts with the historian's aspiration to be true to the past. The conflict is clearest in the case of those writers who ransack the past for material to fuel a particular ideology, or who falsify it in support of a political programme, as Nazi historians did under the Third Reich and supporters of Holocaust denial do today. Such works are propaganda, not history, and it is usually clear to the professional – and sometimes the lay person – that evidence has been suppressed or manufactured. Among historians themselves, present-mindedness commonly takes two forms. The first is an interest in the historical origins of the modern world, or some particularly salient feature of it – say the nuclear family household or parliamentary democracy. In itself, this is a positive response to the claims of social relevance, and it has the merit of providing a clear principle of selection leading to an intelligible picture of the past. But it also carries risks of superficiality and distortion. The problem with seeking the historical antecedents of some characteristically 'modern' feature is that the outcome can so easily seem to be pre-determined, instead of being the result of complex historical processes. Abstracting one strand of development to be traced back to its origins too often means an indifference to historical context; the further back the enquiry proceeds, the more likely will a stress on linear descent obscure the contemporary significance of the institution or convention in question. Thus the Whig historians of the nineteenth century completely misunderstood the structure of medieval English government because of their obsessive interest in the origins of Parliament. As Butterfield put it in *The Whig Interpretation of History* (1931) – probably the most influential polemic ever written against present-minded history – 'the study of the past with one eye, so to speak, upon the present is the source of all sins and sophistries in history, starting with the simplest of them, the anachronism'.[27] 'Whig' history exhibits a tendency to underestimate the differences between past and present – to project modern ways of thought backwards in time and to discount those aspects of past experience that are alien to modern ideas. In this way it reduces history's social value, which derives largely from its being a storehouse of past experiences contrasted to our own.

A voice for the oppressed

Today a second variant of present-minded history (or 'presentism') is much more prevalent. This is the history written out of political commitment to a social group that has previously been marginalized by the prevalent historiography. As explained in Chapter 1, effective political action in the present requires an articulate social memory, and to supply this has been one of the main objectives of black historians and women's historians in Britain and the United States, uncovering what was previously 'hidden from history'.[28] As will be shown in Chapter 10, there is an abundance of distinguished work in these fields, but where ethnic particularism or gender loyalty is allowed full rein, differences between 'then' and 'now' may be downplayed in the cause of forging a pre-determined identity which spans the ages. Thus the complicity of West African societies in the transatlantic slave trade might be omitted, or the sexual conservatism of much nineteenth-century feminism, while no serious effort may be made to understand the experience of other groups with a part in the story. Such distortions make for poor history; they have the additional consequence of prompting from conservative historians a more hard-nosed defence of the established order than that which existed before.

'Everyman his own historian'

If the outcome of historical enquiry is so heavily conditioned by the preferences of the enquirer and can so easily be altered by the intervention of another enquirer, how can it merit any credibility as a serious contribution to knowledge? If fact and value are inextricably tied together, how can a distinction be drawn between sound and unsound history? Between the two World Wars it was the fashion in some quarters to concede most, if not all, of the sceptics' case. Historical interpretation, these historians averred, should be considered true only in relation to the needs of the age in which it was written. With the phrase 'everyman his own historian',[29] the American scholar Carl M. Becker renounced the aspirations to definitive history that had characterized the profession since Ranke. A more recent and more temperate view was put forward by Gordon Connell-Smith and Howell Lloyd:

> History is not 'the past', nor yet the surviving past. It is a reconstruction of certain parts of the past (from surviving evidence) which in some way have had relevance for the present circumstances of the historian who reconstructed them.[30]

The unattainability of the past

The implications of this position are disturbing. Not surprisingly historians are reluctant to allow their discipline's claim to academic respectability to be so lightly abandoned. Over the past fifty years the orthodox response to relativism has been to make what is essentially a restatement of historicism. Historians, the argument goes, must renounce any standards or priorities

G.R. Elton (1921–94)
Sir Geoffrey Elton first
made his name with a
detailed study, based
on his Ph.D. thesis, of
what he called *The
Tudor Revolution in
Government.* He held
that Thomas Cromwell
had instituted such a
strikingly modern
system of bureaucracy
at Henry VIII's court that
it amounted in effect to
an administrative
revolution. However,
Elton was sometimes
accused of seeing
everything in Tudor
England as if it related
to bureaucratic
administration.

external to the age they are studying. Their aim is to understand the past in its own terms, or in **Elton**'s words 'to understand a given problem from the inside'.[31] Historians should be steeped in the values of the age and should attempt to see events from the standpoint of those who participated in them. Only then will they be true to their material and their vocation.

But this claim to speak with the voice of the past will not bear inspection. On the face of it, historians may appear to be strikingly successful in assimilating the values of those they write about: diplomatic historians usually accept the ethics of *raison d'état* which have governed the conduct of international relations in Europe since the Renaissance, and the historian of a political movement may well be able to achieve an empathy with the outlook and aspirations of its members. However, as soon as historians cast their net more widely to embrace an entire society, 'the standards of the age' becomes a question-begging phrase. Whose standards should be adopted – those of the rich or the poor, the colonized or the colonizers, Protestant or Catholic? It is a fallacy to suppose that historians who renounce all claim to 'relevance' thereby ensure the objectivity of their work. In practice their writing is exposed to two dangers. On the one hand they may find themselves confined by the priorities and assumptions of those who created the sources; on the other, the end-product is quite likely to be influenced – if only unconsciously – by their own values, which are difficult to make allowances for because they are undeclared. Elton's work illustrates both these tendencies: his Tudor England is seen through the spectacles of the authoritarian paternalist bureaucracy whose records Elton knew so intimately and whose outlook was evidently congenial to his own conservative convictions.[32] Recreative history is a legitimate pursuit, but it is a mistake to suppose that it can ever be completely realized, or that it carries the promise of objective knowledge about the past.

History and hindsight

There is another serious difficulty encountered by the strictly historicist approach. We can never recapture the authentic flavour of a historical moment as it was experienced by people at the time because we, unlike them, know what happened next; and the significance which we accord to a particular incident is inescapably conditioned by that knowledge. This is one of the most telling objections that can be made against Collingwood's idea that historians re-enact the thought of individuals in the past. Like it or not, the historian approaches the past with a superior vision conferred by hindsight. Some historians do their best to renounce this superior vision by confining their research to a few years or even months of history, for which they can give a blow-by-blow account with a minimum of selection or interpretation, but the total divestment of hindsight is not intellectually possible. Besides, should not hindsight be viewed as an asset to be exploited rather than a disability to be overcome? It is precisely our position in time relative to the subject of our enquiry that enables us to make sense of the past – to identify conditioning factors of which the historical participants were unaware, and to see consequences for what they were rather than what they were intended to be. Strictly interpreted, 'history for its own sake' would entail surrendering most of what makes the subject worth pursuing at all, without achieving the desired goal of complete detachment. The problems of historical objectivity cannot be evaded by a retreat into the past for the past's sake.

IV

The challenge of Postmodernism

So far this evaluation of historical enquiry has implied a hierarchy of approaches in which positivist science stands as the ultimate yardstick of intellectual rigour. Scientific method is here viewed as the only means of gaining direct knowledge of reality, past or present. The procedures of historicism offer a scarcely tenable defence, and to the extent that they fall short of scientific method must be deemed inferior. This debate has been running for as long as history has been seriously studied, and it shows no sign of being resolved. However, in the past three decades the hand of the sceptics has been strengthened by a major intellectual shift within the humanities which has rejected historicism as the basis for history and all other text-based disciplines. This is Postmodernism. Its hallmark is the prioritization of language over experience, leading to outright scepticism as to the human capacity to observe and interpret the external world, and especially the *human* world. The implications of Postmodernism for the standing of historical work are potentially serious and must be addressed with some care.

The tyranny of language

Modern theories of language stand in a tradition first laid out by Ferdinand de Saussure at the beginning of the twentieth century. Saussure declared that, far from being a neutral and passive medium of expression, language is governed by its own internal structure. The relationship between a word and the object or idea it denotes – or between 'signifier' and 'signified' in Saussure's terminology – is in the last resort arbitrary. No two languages have an identical match between words and things; certain patterns of thought or observation that are possible in one language are beyond the resources of another. From this, Saussure drew the conclusion that language is non-referential – in other words that speech and writing should be understood as a linguistic structure governed by its own laws, not as a reflection of reality: language is not a window on the world but a structure that determines our perception of the world. This way of understanding language has the immediate effect of downgrading the status of the writer: if the structure of the language is so constraining, the meaning of a text will have as much to do with the formal properties of the language as with the intentions of the writer, and perhaps more. Any notion that writers can accurately convey 'their' meaning to their readers falls to the ground. In a much-quoted phrase, Roland Barthes spoke of 'the death of the author'.[33] One might equally speak of the death of the textual critic in the traditional sense, since those who interpret texts have as little autonomy as those who wrote them. There can be no objective historical method standing outside the text, only an interpretative point of address fashioned from the linguistic resources available to the interpreter. The historian (or literary critic) does not speak from a privileged vantage point.

However, it is simplistic to speak of the 'language' of any society in the singular, if by this we mean a common structure and uniform conventions. Any language is a complex system of meanings – a multiple code in which words often signify different meanings to different audiences; indeed the power of language partly resides in the unintended layers of meaning it conveys. The kind of textual analysis in which the immediate or 'surface' meaning is set aside in favour of the less obvious is called in Postmodern circles '**deconstruction**' (though the term dates back to Jacques Derrida). Deconstruction covers a bewildering mass of daring and dissonant readings. The creative approach to interpreting texts – playful, ironic and subversive by turns – is a hallmark of Postmodern scholarship.[34]

deconstructionists
Also known as constructionists; the literary forebears of historical Postmodernists. Inspired by the French literary scholar Jacques Derrida, they stressed the importance of analysing not just the wording of a text but the hidden assumptions and social or moral values within its vocabulary, even questioning whether text actually denotes what its words theoretically mean.

Intertextuality: text and context

For most exponents of the linguistic turn, however, some limit is placed on the freedom with which we can 'read' texts by the constraints of 'intertextuality'. According to this perspective, the texts of the past should not be viewed in isolation, because no text has ever been composed in isolation. All writers employ a language that has already served purposes similar to their own, and their audience may interpret what they write with reference to yet other conventions of language use. At any given time the world of texts is composed of diverse forms of production, each with its own cultural rationale, conceptual categories and patterns of usage. Each text belongs, in short, to a 'discourse' or body of language practice. Today the term 'discourse' is best known in the distinctive twist given to it by French philosopher **Michel Foucault**. For him 'discourse' meant not just a pattern of language use but a form of 'power/knowledge', pointing to the way in which people are confined within the regulatory scope of specific discourses. He showed how new, more restrictive discourses of madness, punishment and sexuality became established in Western Europe between 1750 and 1850, challenging the conventional interpretation of this period as one of social and intellectual progress.[35] Foucault was unusual among the founding fathers of Postmodernism in conveying a strong sense of period. But as used by most literary scholars, 'discourse' and 'intertextuality' have a tendency to float free of any anchorage in the 'real' world, thus bearing out Derrida's celebrated aphorism, 'there is nothing outside the text'.[36]

Michel Foucault (1926–84)
French philosopher and social historian. Foucault's studies of restrictive or oppressive institutions, such as nineteenth-century hospitals, prisons and mental asylums, have led to a new understanding of the power relationship between the individual and the state.

Relativism: nothing is certain

Analysing discourse, like all the critical procedures associated with modern linguistics, is founded on relativism. Its champions dismiss the idea that language reflects reality as the representational fallacy. Language, they assert, is inherently unstable, variable in its meanings over time and contested in its own time. If accepted at face value, that indeterminacy is fatal to traditional notions of historical enquiry. It becomes meaningless to attempt a distinction between the events of the past and the discourse in which they are represented; as Raphael Samuel put it in a neat summary of Roland Barthes, history becomes 'a parade of signifiers masquerading as a collection of facts'.[37] As we saw in Chapter 5, historians certainly do not regard their primary sources as infallible, and they are accustomed to reading them against the grain for implicit meanings. But underlying their scholarly practice is the belief that the sources can yield up some, at least, of the meaning they held for those who wrote and read them originally. That is **anathema** to the deconstructionist, for whom no amount of technical expertise can remove the subjectivity and indeterminacy inherent in the reading of texts. Deconstructionists offer us instead the pleasure of finding any meanings we like, provided we do not claim authority for any of them. No amount of scholarship can give us a privileged vantage point. All that is available to us is a free interaction between reader and text, in which there are no approved procedures and no court of appeal. To claim any more is naïvety or – in the more intemperate Postmodernist statements – a deception practised on the innocent reader.

anathema
Completely unacceptable. The term comes from the Roman Catholic Church, where it is used to denote ideas and beliefs that are entirely incompatible with Catholic doctrine.

The negation of history

Because historians claim vastly more than this, every aspect of their practice is open to challenge by Postmodernism. Once the validity of the historical method of interpreting texts is undermined, all the procedures erected on that foundation are called into question. The Rankean project of recreating the past collapses, because it depends on a privileged, 'authentic' reading of the primary sources. In place of historical explanation, Postmodernist history can only offer intertextuality, which deals in discursive relations between texts, not causal relations between events; historical explanation is dismissed as no more than a chimera to comfort those who cannot face a world without meaning.[38] The conventional actors of history fare no better. If the author is dead, so too is the unified historical subject, whether conceived of as an individual or as a collectivity (such as class or nation): according to the Postmodernist view, identity is constructed by language – fractured and unstable because it is the focus of competing discourses. Perhaps most important of all, deconstructing the individuals and groups who have been the traditional actors in history means that history no longer has a big story to tell. The nation, the working class, even the idea of progress, all dissolve into discursive constructions. Continuity and evolution are rejected in favour of discontinuity, as for example in Foucault's conception of four unconnected historical epochs (or 'epistemes') since the sixteenth century.[39] Postmodernists are generally scathing about the 'grand narratives' or 'meta-narratives' of historians – such as the rise of capitalism or the growth of free thought and toleration. The most they will concede is that the past can be arranged into a multiplicity of stories, just as individual texts are open to a plurality of readings.

A reappraisal as radical as this has major implications for how we understand the activity of being a historian. Postmodernists have brought two important perspectives to bear on this. First, they emphasize that historical writing is a form of literary production which, like any other genre, operates within certain rhetorical conventions. In his very influential *Metahistory* (1973), Hayden White analyses these conventions in aesthetic terms and classifies historical writing according to twelve stylistic permutations and four underlying '**tropes**'. The specifics of this elaborate analysis are less important than White's theoretical conclusion, that the character of any work of history is determined not so much by the author's scholarship or ideology as by the **aesthetic** choices that he or she makes (usually unconsciously) at the outset of the enquiry and that inform the discursive strategies of the text. With its privileging of the aesthetic over the ideological, this is a somewhat purist position. Postmodernism is currently more strongly identified with a second perspective, in which the historian is seen as the vector of a range of political positions rooted in the here and now. Because the documentary residue of the past is open to so many readings, and because historians employ language that is ideologically tainted, history writing is never

trope
A metaphor or figure of speech.

aesthetic
Artistic or relating to art or beauty.

innocent. There being no shape to history, historians cannot reconstruct and delineate it from outside. The stories they tell, and the human subjects they write about, are merely subjective preference, drawn from an infinity of possible strategies. Historians are embedded in the messy reality they seek to represent, and hence always bear its ideological imprint. They may do no more than replicate the dominant or '**hegemonic**' ideology; alternatively, they may identify with one of a number of radical or subversive ideologies; but all are equally rooted in the politics of today.

hegemonic
Dominant, exercising power over a region or domain.

From this angle all versions of history are 'presentist', not just the politically committed ones. In Keith Jenkins's phrase, history becomes 'a discursive practice that enables present-minded people(s) to go to the past, there to delve around and reorganise it appropriately to their needs'.[40] Since those needs are diverse, and even mutually exclusive, there can be no community of historians and no dialogue between those who hold to different perspectives. Fifty years ago, E.H. Carr represented the limits of scepticism in the historical profession when he acknowledged the dialogue between present and past that animates any work of history. Postmodernists take a big step closer to relativism by accepting – even celebrating – a plurality of concurrent interpretations, all equally valid (or invalid). 'One must face the fact', writes Hayden White, 'that, when it comes to the historical record, there are no grounds to be found in the record itself for preferring one way of construing its meaning rather than another.'[41] Historians, it is said, do not uncover the past; they invent it. And the time-honoured distinction between fact and fiction is blurred.

V

Postmodernism in context

How should historians respond to this onslaught? One task for which they are well equipped is to place Postmodernism itself in historical context. This means recognizing that it is located in a particular cultural moment. As the name implies, Postmodernism is a reactive phenomenon. 'Modernism' denotes the core beliefs that underpinned the evolution of modern industrial societies from the mid-nineteenth to the mid-twentieth century, especially the belief in progress and faith in the efficacy of disciplined, rational enquiry. In throwing them over, Postmodernists signal their desire for the new and for their emancipation from the previous generation. But the appeal of Postmodernism is best explained by its resonance with some of the defining tendencies in contemporary thought. For some time now, the view that much that the West has traditionally stood for has come to a dead end has gained currency: its global supremacy is in decline, its technological flair has become a liability (as in the arms race) and its much-vaunted monopoly of reason is held to be irrelevant to an increasing range of human problems, from the understanding of the psyche to the care of the environment. The Holocaust, instead of being treated as an aberration, is now taken to be a grimly ironical commentary on the conventional equation of progress with Western civilization. There is widespread disillusion with the previously uncontested virtues of scientific method. Postmodernism is the theoretical stance that best illustrates these tendencies. By calling into question the possibility of objective enquiry, it undermines the authority of science. By denying shape and purpose to history, it distances us from all that we find hardest to face in our past – as well as that in which we used to take pride. If, as Postmodernism asserts, history really has no meaning, it follows that we must become fully responsible for finding meaning in our own lives, bleak and demanding though the task may be. History as traditionally conceived becomes not only impractical but irrelevant.

The precursors of Postmodernism

This is not the first time that the credentials of history as a serious discipline have been called into question. The emphasis placed by Postmodernists on the indeterminacy of language and the pervading tone of cultural pessimism are very contemporary, but their denial of historical truth has a very familiar ring about it. In the era of religious wars in Europe in the sixteenth and seventeenth centuries, historians were dismissed by philosophers as credulous impostors, and their much-vaunted sources written off as unreliable. The nineteenth-century historicists, despite their more rigorous standards of scholarship, were soon being attacked by relativists who argued that absolute historical truth was a chimera. In fact there have been sceptics for as long as history has been written. Doubts about the status of the 'real', and our ability to apprehend it in the past or the present, have been part of the Western philosophical tradition since the ancient Greeks. Historians themselves have participated in these debates. Postmodernism is less of a novelty than its proponents sometimes claim.

History adapts

Nor is the relationship between history and Postmodernism quite so antagonistic as this account so far implies. It may be, as some Postmodernists argue, that the Rankean documentary ideal is finished and that history as we know it is destined for the scrap-heap.[42] But what this gloomy prognosis overlooks is that historians are already in the process of assimilating aspects of the Postmodernist perspective. As has so often been the case in the past, root-and-branch critiques of the discipline have a tendency to attack a **straw man**. Historians have always shown a capacity to engage with critics of the truth claims of their discipline and to take on board some of their arguments. They are not nearly so committed to the unified historical subject as some critics have supposed; it is now rare for scholarly writers to structure a book around 'the nation' or 'the working class' without carefully analysing the changing and contested significance of these labels.[43] Equally, many of the 'grand narratives' of Western history – such as the Whig interpretation of English history or the Industrial Revolution – have been subjected to much more devastating attack by empirically minded historians than they have by Postmodernists.[44]

straw man
An old term for an idea or body that is not as strong as it looks.

Historical writing has also been directly influenced by the linguistic turn in the humanities. Recognizing the structural constraints that language may impose on its users has proved a particularly helpful insight. Gareth Stedman Jones proved as much in his reassessment of Chartism in *Languages of Class* (1983). The failure of the Chartists to sustain a mass campaign for popular democratic rights after the middle-class agenda had been met in the **Reform Act** of 1832 had been explained in various ways by historians. Stedman Jones concluded that the movement essentially failed because its politics was constituted by a discourse inherited from the past, which was inappropriate to a rapidly changing political landscape. It is a powerful (though not undisputed) case for 'an analysis of Chartism which assigns some autonomous weight to the language within which it was conceived'.[45] Historians are also sympathetic to the notion that texts embody more than one level of meaning, and that the implicit or unconscious meaning may be what gives the text its power. In late nineteenth-century Britain, for example, the popular language of the New Imperialism was obviously about nationalism and racism; but with its stress on 'manliness' and 'character' it also carried a heavy charge of masculine insecurity, which arose from changes in women's position in the family and the workplace. When politicians used that language, they both reflected and intensified an uncertain sense of manhood, almost certainly without meaning to.[46] Determining the discourse to which a particular text belongs, and its relation to other relevant discourses, is a task that goes beyond the procedures of source criticism as traditionally understood. As a result, historians now tend to be more sensitive to the counter-currents of meaning in their sources, pushing Marc Bloch's well-known aphorism about 'witnesses in spite of themselves' in a new and rewarding direction.

Reform Act
The pioneering measure of parliamentary reform, which was finally passed into law in 1832. Historians point out that its provisions were relatively modest but that its symbolic importance was immense.

Language and cultural hegemony

Equally, the Postmodern critique of historical writing has met with some positive responses among historians. In particular,

Hayden White's dissection of the literary conventions embedded in historical narrative has resulted in a renewed awareness of historical writing as a literary form and a greater readiness to experiment.[47] Even more promising, the Postmodern deconstruction of discourse as a form of cultural power has made it harder to ignore the fact that history writing itself can be an expression of cultural hegemony, and this in turn has opened up opportunities for radical contestation by groups previously excluded from the record. Edward Said's interest in how language is formed and how a subject is constituted has gone hand in hand with his investigation of the Arab and the Palestinian in Western discourse; his path-breaking *Orientalism* (1976) proved to be a turning point in the emergence of a postcolonial or multicultural history (see Chapter 10). Feminists, in their ambition to penetrate the limitations of 'man-made language', have acknowledged a comparable debt to the linguistic turn.[48] These instances go some way to support the Postmodernists' contention that their perspective holds out the prospect of democratic empowerment. When to that is added the pervasive influence of language-led theory on the development of cultural history in recent years (as discussed in Chapter 9), it is clear that the encounter between Postmodernism and more traditional theories of history has been quite fruitful.

VI

The limitations of Postmodernism

However, there is a limit beyond which most historians will not go in embracing Postmodernism. Many welcome a greater sophistication in interpreting texts and a heightened awareness of the cultural significance of historical writing. But few are prepared to join in a rejection of the truth claims of history as usually practised. Confronted by the full force of the deconstructionist critique, historians tend to be confirmed in their preference for experience and observation over first principles. In theory, an impeccable case can be made for the proposition that all human language is self-referential rather than representational. But daily life tells us that language works extremely well in many situations where meaning is clearly articulated and correctly inferred. On any other assumption human interaction would break down completely. If language demonstrably serves these practical functions in the present, there is no reason why it should not be understood in a similar spirit when preserved in documents dating from the past. Of course there is an *element* of indeterminacy about all language; the lapse of time serves to increase it, and a 300-year-old text straddling two or three discourses may be very difficult to pin down. Historians frequently acknowledge that they cannot fathom all the levels of meaning contained in their documents. But to maintain that *no* text from the past can be read as an accurate reflection of something outside itself flies in the face of common experience. In a set of trade figures or a census return the relation between text and reality is palpable (which is not to say that it is necessarily accurate). A carefully considered literary production such as an autobiography or a **political tract** disguised as a sermon presents much more complex problems, but it is still important to recognize that their authors were attempting a real engagement with their readers, and to get as close as we can to the spirit of that engagement.

It is at this point that historians invoke the discipline of historical context. The meanings that link words and things are not arbitrary but follow conventions created by real culture and real social relations. The task of scholarship is to identify these conventions in their historical specificity and to take full account of them in interpreting the sources. Whereas exponents of the linguistic approach treat 'context' as meaning *other texts* only, with the further complication that they too invite a variety of readings, historians insist that texts should be set in the full context of their time. That means taking seriously not just the resources of language but the identity and background of the author, the conditions of production of texts, the intended readership, the cultural attitudes of the time and the social relations that enveloped writer and readers. Every text is socially situated in specific historical conditions; in the useful phrase of Gabrielle Spiegel, there is a 'social logic of the text' which is open to demonstration by historical enquiry.[49] So, for example, my reading of the language of late nineteenth-century imperialism can be taken seriously because the strains in gender relations at that time are very well documented, and because the cultural identification of empire with masculinity bore some relation to imperial realities. No doubt deconstruction could yield other interpretations, more elegant and intriguing than this; but unless they have a firm anchorage in historical context, they amount to an imposition by the critic on the text. Respect for the historicity of the sources is fundamental to the historical project; the point at which it is breached is where historians part company with the deconstructionists. Historians do not claim that in all cases their method can uncover every dimension of textual meaning; in order for historical work to be done, it is sufficient to demonstrate that *some* of the original meaning can be reclaimed. The verification of historical events and the discipline of historical context mean that historians can distinguish between what happened in history and the discourse in which it is represented.

The need for historical explanation

Historians are no more willing to jettison the truth claims of the accounts that they themselves construct. It is one thing to

political tract
A tract is a small booklet, larger than a pamphlet but smaller than a book, which puts across an argued case. Tracts were widely used in the nineteenth century by church and religious reform groups, but there were plenty of political tracts as well.

acknowledge the rhetorical aspects of historical writing but quite another to treat it as only – or largely – rhetoric. Historical narratives are certainly moulded by the historian's aesthetic sense, but they are not inventions: some, like the major revolutionary upheavals, arise partly from the consciousness of those who lived through them; others fall into shape through the benefit of historical hindsight. The stories we tell ourselves about the past may not be completely coherent or completely convincing, but they are rooted in the fact that human beings not only believe them but *enact* them on the assumption that social action is a continuum through past, present and future. The task of historical explanation is similarly one that cannot be shirked. It represents not an escape from the real world, as the bleaker versions of Postmodernism insist, but an application of reason, based on patterns of cause and consequence which go beyond the confined domain of intertextuality. As for the **emancipatory** potential of competing narratives, this amounts to little if the ambitions of each identity group are confined to producing a history that is 'true' only for its own members. Real empowerment comes from writing history that carries conviction beyond one's own community, and this means conforming to the scholarly procedures that historians of all communities respect. That, rather than the consolation prize of a permissive relativism, has been the objective of most 'multicultural' historians. Despite the pessimism of some conservative commentators,[50] pluralism does not necessarily mean **relativism**.

The nub of the Postmodernist critique is that historicism is dead and should be abandoned as a serious intellectual endeavour. In fending off this attack, historians point out not only that the weaknesses of historical enquiry have been grossly exaggerated but that a broadly historicist stance towards the past is culturally indispensable. It is a precondition of critical social thought about the present and the future. As Joyce Appleby, Lynn Hunt and Margaret Jacob put it, 'Rejecting all meta-narratives cannot make sense, because narratives and meta-narratives are the kinds of stories that make action in the world possible.'[51] A consciousness of the past as 'other', a set of coherent narratives linking past and present, and an explanatory mode of historical writing are all practical necessities. If the ambition to know the past is completely surrendered, we shall never be able to determine how the present came to be. The social function of history is not to be so lightly abandoned.

emancipatory
Liberating.

relativism
The idea that all codes of values or ethics are equivalent and exist in relation to their context; it is therefore not possible to say that any one of them is in any sense 'better' than any other.

VII

Theoretical objections, practical answers

In questioning the credentials of historical knowledge, Postmodernism has breathed fresh life into a strand of scepticism that stretches back to the Renaissance. The fallibility (or 'indeterminacy') of the sources, the gap between validated facts and the explanations that endow them with meaning, and the personal and political investment that historians bring to their work have long been hostages to fortune. Positivism condemned them as damning departures from scientific rigour; Postmodernism subsumes them in a larger refutation of rational enquiry. Whether viewed from a positivist or a Postmodern standpoint, the epistemological credentials of history do not look impressive. Primarily this is because abstract theories are best tested in carefully controlled conditions, whereas history is a hybrid discipline that defies simple pigeon-holing. The divergent and sometimes contradictory objectives that historians pursue are what gives the subject its distinctive character, but they also expose it to theoretical attack.

Though some historians still seek refuge in an untenable empiricism,[52] the more thoughtful defenders of the discipline concede that it is open to major theoretical objections. Commentators such as Appleby, Hunt and Jacob, or Richard J. Evans, know that historical knowledge always involves an encounter between present and past in which the present may weigh too heavily on the past. They know that the sources do not 'speak' directly, that facts are selected, not given, that historical explanation depends on the application of hindsight, and that every historical account is in some sense moulded by the aesthetic and political preferences of the writer. Their defence rests on the contention that, while *in theory* these features may invalidate historical work, *in practice* they can be – and are – confined to manageable proportions. History is neither an exemplar of realism nor a victim to relativism. It occupies a middle ground in which scholarly procedures are upheld in order to keep the avenues of enquiry as close to the 'real' and as far removed from the 'relative' as possible.[53] Historians are members of a profession, one of whose principal functions is to enforce standards of scholarship and to restrain waywardness of interpretation. Peer-group scrutiny operates as a powerful mechanism for ensuring that within the area of enquiry they find significant, historians are as true as they can be to the surviving evidence of the past.

The historian's safeguards: self-awareness and peer review

Three requirements stand out in this respect. First, the historian should scrutinize his or her own assumptions and values in order to see how they relate to the enquiry in hand. One of the attractions of E.P. Thompson is that he made no secret of his sympathies – even acknowledging that one chapter in *The Making of the English Working Class* was **polemic**.[54] This kind of awareness is particularly important in the case of those historians who have no particular axe to grind but can all too easily be the

polemic
An angry and impassioned argument.

unconscious vector of values taken for granted by people of their own background. That is one reason why, as emphasized by Zeldin, self-knowledge is a desirable trait among historians (see p. 143) – and also why the confessional mode of historical writing should be welcomed, at least in the author's preface or introduction. Second, the risk of assimilating findings to expectations is reduced if the direction imparted to the enquiry is cast in the form of an explicit hypothesis, to be accepted, rejected or modified in the light of the evidence – with the author always the first to try to pick holes in his or her interpretation. The appropriate conduct for historians is not to avoid social relevance but to be fully aware of why they are attracted to their particular slice of history and to show as much respect for contrary as for supporting evidence. It is sometimes forgotten by non-practising critics that much of the excitement of historical research comes from finding results that were *not* anticipated and pushing one's thesis into a new direction in mid-stream. Third and above all, historians must submit their work to the discipline of historical context. In different ways both 'presentism' and deconstructionism remove events and personalities from their real time and place, forcing them into a conceptual framework that would have meant nothing to the age in question. In fact, historians have much less excuse for falling into this trap than they used to. The enlargement of the scope of historical studies during the past fifty years, and the way in which the best historical syntheses reflect this enlargement, means that historians today should have a much better-developed sense of context than their predecessors did; **peer review** operates particularly effectively in this area.

peer review
Academic work is usually scrutinized in detail by other academics in a process known as peer review.

Respect for these three injunctions does much to limit the amount of distortion in historical writing. It does not, however, put an end to debate and disagreement. It would be wrong to suppose that if all historians could only attain a high degree of self-awareness, make their working hypotheses explicit and maintain a scrupulous respect for historical context they would then concur in their historical judgements. Nobody can become completely dispassionate about his or her own assumptions or those of earlier ages; the evidence can usually be read in support of conflicting hypotheses; and, since the sources never recapture a past situation in its entirety, the sense of historical context depends also on an imaginative flair that will vary according to the insight and experience of the individual scholar. The nature of historical enquiry is such that, however rigorously professional the approach, there will always be a plurality of interpretation. That should be counted as a strength rather than a weakness. For advances in historical knowledge arise as much from the play of debate between rival interpretations as from the efforts of the individual scholar. And the same debates that enliven the historical profession are intimately connected with the alternative visions we hold of our society in the present and the future. If history was uncontested it would fail to provide the materials for critical debate on the social issues of the day. Plurality of historical interpretation is an essential – if underestimated – prerequisite for a mature democratic politics. The past will never be placed beyond controversy; nor should it be.

Further reading

Richard J. Evans, *In Defence of History*, Granta, 1997.

E.H. Carr, *What is History?*, Penguin, 1961.

G.R. Elton, *The Practice of History*, Fontana, 1969.

W.H. Walsh, *An Introduction to Philosophy of History*, 3rd edn, Hutchinson, 1967.

R.G. Collingwood, *The Idea of History*, Oxford University Press, 1946.

Keith Jenkins, *On 'What is History?'*, Routledge, 1995.

Alun Munslow, *Deconstructing History*, Routledge, 1997.

Hayden White, *The Content of the Form*, Johns Hopkins University Press, 1987.

Joyce Appleby, Lynn Hunt and Margaret Jacob, *Telling the Truth about History*, Norton, 1997.

Notes

1 G.R. Elton, *The Practice of History*, Fontana, 1969.

2 Theodore Zeldin, 'Ourselves as we see us', *Times Literary Supplement*, 31 December 1982. See also his article, 'After Braudel', *The Listener*, 5 November 1981.

3 See, for example, Elton, *The Practice of History*, pp. vii–viii.

4 Lee Benson, *Toward the Scientific Study of History*, Lippincott, 1972.

5 L. von Ranke, quoted in Peter Novick, *That Noble Dream: The 'Objectivity Question' and the American Historical Profession*, Cambridge University Press, 1988, p. 28.

6 Zeldin, 'After Braudel'. See also his article, 'Social and total history', *Journal of Social History*, X, 1976, pp. 237–45.

7 K.R. Popper, *The Open Society and its Enemies*, vol. II, 5th edn, Routledge & Kegan Paul, 1966, p. 265.

8 Raphael Samuel (ed.), *People's History and Socialist Theory*, Routledge & Kegan Paul, 1981, editor's introduction, p. xlv.

9 E.H. Carr, *What is History?*, Penguin, 1964, p. 16, rather surprisingly falls into this error.

10 Lord Acton, letter to the contributors to the *Cambridge Modern History*, 1896, reprinted in Fritz Stern (ed.), *Varieties of History*, 2nd edn, Macmillan, 1970, p. 247.

11 Carr, *What is History?*, p. 120.

12 L.B. Namier, *Avenues of History*, Hamish Hamilton, 1952, p. 8.

13 M.M. Postan, *Fact and Relevance*, Cambridge University Press, 1970, p. 51.

14 Elton, *Practice of History*, pp. 74–82.

15 Marc Bloch, *The Historian's Craft*, Manchester University Press, 1954, p. 65.

16 Popper's views are lucidly expounded in Bryan Magee, *Popper*, Fontana, 1973.

17 Joseph C. Miller, 'History and Africa/Africa and History', *American Historical Review*, CIV, 1999, p. 27.

18 R.F. Holland, *European Decolonization 1918–81*, Macmillan, 1985.

19 Christopher Clark, *The Sleepwalkers: How Europe Went to War in 1914*, Allen Lane, 2012; James Joll, *The Origins of the First World War*, Longman, 1984.

20 Jakob Burckhardt, *The Civilization of the Renaissance in Italy*, Phaidon, [1860] 1960, p. 1.

21 This is particularly true of Elton, *Practice of History*.

22 Richard Cobb, *A Second Identity*, Oxford University Press, 1969, p. 47. See also Zeldin's comments in the same vein in *France 1848–1945*, vol. I, Oxford University Press, 1973, p. 7.

23 See, for example, Pieter Geyl, *Napoleon: For and Against*, 2nd edn, Cape, 1964.

24 Compare, for example, Peter Laslett, *The World We Have Lost*, 2nd edn, Methuen, 1971, with E.P. Thompson, *Whigs and Hunters*, Penguin, 1977.

25 Michael Howard, *The Lessons of History*, Oxford University Press, 1981, p. 21.

26 J.B. Bury, 'The science of history', 1902, reprinted in Stern, *Varieties of History*, p. 215.

27 H. Butterfield, *The Whig Interpretation of History*, Penguin, [1931] 1973, p. 30.

28 Cf. Sheila Rowbotham, *Hidden from History*, Pluto Press, 1973.

29 Cited in J.H. Hexter, *On Historians*, Collins, 1979, p. 15.

30 Gordon Connell-Smith and Howell A. Lloyd, *The Relevance of History*, Heinemann, 1972, p. 41.

31 Elton, *Practice of History*, p. 31.

32 Elton's conservative convictions are most clearly set out in his two inaugural lectures, 'The future of the past' (1968) and 'The history of England' (1984), reprinted in his *Return to Essentials*, Cambridge University Press, 1991.

33 Roland Barthes, *Image, Music, Text*, Fontana, 1977, pp. 42–8.

34 The textual theories that have grown up in the wake of Saussure are usefully set out in Raman Selden, Peter Widdowson and Peter Brookes, *A Reader's Guide to Contemporary Literary Theory*, 4th edn, Prentice Hall, 1997.

35 For a good introduction, see P. Rabinow (ed.), *The Foucault Reader*, Penguin, 1991.

36 Jacques Derrida, *Of Grammatology*, Johns Hopkins University Press, 1976, p. 158.

37 Raphael Samuel, 'Reading the signs', *History Workshop Journal*, XXXII, 1991, p. 93.

38 Hayden White, *The Content of the Form*, Johns Hopkins University Press, 1987, p. 72.

39 Michel Foucault, *The Archaeology of Knowledge*, Tavistock, 1972.

40 Keith Jenkins, *Re-Thinking History*, Routledge, 1991, p. 68.

41 Hayden White, quoted in Novick, *That Noble Dream*, p. 601.

42 See, for example, Alun Munslow, *Deconstructing History*, Routledge, 1997; Keith Jenkins, *On 'What is History?'*, Routledge, 1995.

43 Linda Colley, *Britons: Forging the Nation, 1707–1837*, Yale University Press, 1992, is a good example of a highly critical analysis uninfluenced by Postmodernism.

44 For attacks on the Whig interpretation of history, see J.C.D. Clark, *English Society 1688–1832: Ideology, Social Structure and Political*

Practice during the Ancien Régime, Cambridge University Press, 1985, and Conrad Russell, *The Causes of the English Civil War*, Oxford University Press, 1990. For attacks on the concept of the Industrial Revolution, see R. Floud and D. McCloskey (eds), *The Economic History of Britain since 1700*, 2 vols, Cambridge University Press, 1981.

45 Gareth Stedman Jones, *Languages of Class: Studies in English Working Class History 1832–1982*, Cambridge University Press, 1983, p. 107.

46 H. John Field, *Toward a Programme of Imperial Life*, Clio Press, 1982; John Tosh, 'What should historians do with masculinity? Reflections on nineteenth-century Britain', *History Workshop Journal*, XXXVIII, 1994, pp. 179–202.

47 For a review of these trends, see Peter Burke (ed.), *New Perspectives on Historical Writing*, Polity Press, 1991.

48 See, for example, Joan Scott, *Gender and the Politics of History*, Columbia University Press, 1988.

49 Gabrielle M. Spiegel, 'History, historicism, and the social logic of the text', *Speculum*, LXV (1990), pp. 59–86.

50 Gertrude Himmelfarb, *On Looking Into the Abyss*, Knopf, 1994.

51 Joyce Appleby, Lynn Hunt and Margaret Jacob, *Telling the Truth About History*, Norton, 1994, p. 236.

52 Elton, *Return to Essentials*; Arthur Marwick, 'Two approaches to historical study: the metaphysical (including "Postmodernism") and the historical', *Journal of Contemporary History*, XXX, 1995, pp. 5–35.

53 Appleby, Hunt and Jacob, *Telling the Truth About History*; Richard J. Evans, *In Defence of History*, Granta, 1997.

54 E.P. Thompson, *The Making of the English Working Class*, revised edn, Penguin, 1968, p. 916.

8 History and social theory

What role should theory play in the work of a historian? Some approach history from a Marxist point of view and find that the application of social theory helps to make sense of a past that might otherwise defy analysis. However, others see such theorizing as dangerous, twisting the facts to fit the theory. This chapter considers the relationship between history and different social theories. It suggests that Marxism in particular might have rather more to offer the historian than its detractors have allowed for.

It was suggested in the previous chapter that one of the ways in which historians can guard against unconsciously assimilating their interpretations of the past to their own bias is by formulating hypotheses to be tested against the available evidence. Such a hypothesis may be no more than a provisional explanation suggested to the historian by a reading of the relevant secondary authorities and exclusive to the historical problem in hand. But a closer inspection often reveals a more elevated parentage. A hypothesis is not just a preliminary assessment of a particular historical conjuncture in its own terms; it usually reflects certain assumptions about the nature of society and the nature of culture; in other words, historical hypotheses amount to an application of *theory*. In many disciplines 'theory' represents the abstracting of generalizations (sometimes laws) from an accumulation of research findings. Historians hardly ever use the term in this sense. Theory for them usually means the framework of interpretation that gives impetus to an enquiry and influences its outcome. Historians sharply differ about the legitimacy of this procedure. Some are strongly committed to a particular theoretical orientation; some acknowledge the stimulus that a theoretical point of departure can offer, while resisting any imposition of theory on the historical evidence; others regard any use of theory as an insidious encroachment on the autonomy of history as a discipline.

The current practice of history is strongly influenced by two quite distinct bodies of theory. The more recent of these addresses the problem of meaning and representation. Traditionally historians have relied on their techniques of source criticism in order to capture the meanings that people in the past have given to their experience. Yet the more remote and alienating the experience, the more inadequate that methodology becomes. As the scope of cultural history has broadened, historians have increasingly acknowledged the insights of other disciplines – psychoanalysis, literary theory and above all **cultural anthropology**. Chapter 9 will examine more fully the problems of interpreting cultural meaning and the debt that many historians now acknowledge towards these disciplines. The second body of theory seeks to understand whole societies: how they hold together, and how they change over time (or not, as the case may be). It comprises an extraordinarily rich intellectual tradition, going back at least to the Enlightenment. In practice no historian seeking to understand the major changes in the pre-modern and modern world can afford to ignore social theory. That is the main reason why Marxism has been so influential, and why it continues to be so despite its collapse as a political programme. In this chapter, the general debate about the merits and demerits of social theory is first reviewed; then Marxism and its application is examined in some detail.

cultural anthropology
The study of the cultural meanings by which people live in society (usually small-scale societies).

I

The need for abstract theory

Broadly speaking, social theories arise from the problems presented by three aspects of historical explanation. There is first the difficulty of grasping the inter-relatedness of every dimension of human experience at a given time. For most historians up to the end of the nineteenth century this was not in practice a major problem, since their interest tended to be confined to political and constitutional history; accordingly some notion of the body politic was all the conceptual equipment they required. But during the twentieth century, the enlargement in the scope of historical enquiry, together with the pressures towards thematic specialization, demanded an ever greater capacity to think in terms of abstractions. We saw in Chapter 3 how easily historians fall into the trap of seeing the past as compartmentalized into 'political', 'economic', 'intellectual' and 'social' history, and how the idea of 'total history' arose as a corrective (see p. 68). But total history is unattainable without some concept of how the component aspects of human experience are linked together to form a whole – some theory of the structure of human society in its widest sense. Most concepts of this kind depend heavily on analogies with the physical world. Society has been variously conceived as an organism, a mechanism and a structure. Each of these metaphors is an attempt to go beyond the crude notion that any one sphere determines the rest, and to express the reciprocal or mutually reinforcing relationship between the main categories of human action and thought.

Identifying the motor of historical change

The second problem that invites the application of theory is that of historical change. Historians spend most of their time explaining change – or its absence. This dominant preoccupation inevitably raises the question of whether the major transitions in history display common characteristics. Is historical change driven by a motor, and if so what does the motor consist of? More specifically, does industrialization require adherence to one particular path of economic development? Can one identify in history the essential components of a revolutionary situation? In framing their hypotheses in particular instances, historians are often influenced by this kind of theory – for example the idea that **demography** holds the key[1] or that the most durable changes in society arise from the **gradualist** reforms conceded by **paternalistic** ruling classes rather than from revolutionary demands articulated from below.[2]

demography
The study of the growth and development of population.

gradualist
Proceeding slowly, making very gradual progress.

paternalistic
Instituting changes and reforms from 'on high', i.e. carried out by those in authority for those below them, rather than introduced by the beneficiaries themselves.

Seeking the meaning of history

Third, and most ambitiously, there are the theories that seek to explain not merely *how* historical change takes place but the direction in which all change is moving; these theories are concerned to interpret human destiny by ascribing a meaning to history. Medieval writers conceived history as a linear transition from the Creation to the Last Judgement, controlled by Divine Providence. By the eighteenth century that view had been secularized as the idea of progress: history was interpreted as a story of material and intellectual improvement whose outcome in the future would be the triumph of reason and human happiness. Modified versions of that outlook continued to have a powerful hold in the nineteenth century: on the European continent history meant the rise of national identities and their political expression in the nation state; for the Whig historians of England it meant the growth of constitutional liberties. Full-blown professions of faith in progress may be rare today,[3] given the trail of destruction that marked the history of the twentieth century; but theories of progressive change still underpin many historical interpretations in the economic and social sphere, as is shown by the frequency with which historians reach for such words as 'industrialization' and 'modernization'.

The rejection of theory

Although these three types of historical theory are analytically distinct, they all share an interest in moving from the particular to the general in an effort to make sense of the subject as a whole. It might be supposed that this is a natural progression, shared by all branches of knowledge. A great many historians, however, reject the use of theory completely. They see two possible grounds for doing so. The first argument concedes that there may be patterns and regularities in history but maintains that they are not accessible to disciplined enquiry. It is hard enough to provide an entirely convincing explanation of any one event in history, but to link them in a series or within an overarching category places the enquirer at an intolerable distance from the verifiable facts. As Peter Mathias (here acting as **devil's advocate**) concedes:

> The bounty of the past provides individual instances in plenty to support virtually any general proposition. It is only too easy to beat history over the head with the blunt instrument of a hypothesis and leave an impression.[4]

devil's advocate
One who deliberately sets out to put the opposite case for the purposes of debate. The term comes from the process whereby the Vatican used to decide on proposals for creating a new saint, where the devil's advocate presented the case against the candidate.

On this view, theoretical history is speculative history and should be left to philosophers and prophets.[5]

The possibility that theory will 'take over' from the facts is certainly not to be made light of. The gaps in the surviving historical record, and especially the lack of clinching evidence in matters of causation, leave a great deal of scope for mere supposition and wishful thinking. At the same time, the range of evidence bearing on many historical problems is so large that selection is unavoidable – and the principles governing that selection may prejudice the result of the enquiry. The record of recent centuries is so voluminous and varied that contradictory results can be obtained simply by asking different questions. In the context of American history, Aileen Kraditor puts this point as follows:

> If one historian asks, 'Do the sources provide evidence of militant struggles among workers and slaves?' the sources will reply, 'Certainly'. And if another asks, 'Do the sources provide evidence of widespread **acquiescence** in the established order among the American population throughout the past two centuries?' the sources will reply, 'Of course'.[6]

acquiescence
Acceptance.

Almost any theory can be 'proved' by marshalling an impressive collection of individual instances to fit the desired pattern.

Safeguards against excessive theorizing

Theory-oriented history is certainly prone to these dangers – but so too, it must be recognized, is the work of many historians who reject theory and remain blissfully unaware of the assumptions and values that inform their own selection and interpretation of evidence. The way forward is not to retreat into an untenable empiricism but to apply much higher standards to the testing of theory. Wishful thinking is more likely to be controlled by historians who approach their enquiries with explicit hypotheses than by those who try to follow where the sources lead. When selection of the evidence cannot be avoided, it must be a representative selection which will reveal both contrary and supporting indicators. A given theory may account for *part* of the evidence relating to the problem in hand, but that is not enough; it must be compatible with the weight of the evidence overall. In Kraditor's words, 'the data omitted must not be essential to the understanding of the data included'.[7] All this assumes a certain detachment on the part of historians towards their theories, and a readiness to change tack because of the lack of evidence. But where these controls are neglected, the profession as a whole is vigilant in their defence. Historians are seldom happier than when citing contrary evidence and alternative interpretations to cast doubt on the work of their colleagues – especially those who seem to have a bee in their bonnet. Moreover, a great deal of historical synthesis consists of comparing the merits of competing theories in order to determine which, if any, illuminates the problem under discussion. The speculative tendencies in theoretical history do not go unchecked for long.

II

Is theory relevant to historical enquiry?

The second and more challenging line of attack questions the legitimacy of theory-making in history on the grounds that it denies the very essence of the discipline. Human culture, the argument goes, is so richly diverse that we can only understand man in specific epochs and locations: 'he remains an irreducible subject, the one non-object in the world'.[8] Models of human behaviour are therefore a delusion. The business of the historian is to reconstruct events and situations in their unique individuality, and on their own terms; their interpretations apply only to particular sets of circumstances. Nothing is to be gained from comparing historical situations separated by time or space – indeed a great deal will be lost, since the result can only be to obscure the essentials of each. In David Thomson's words, 'the historical attitude, by definition, is hostile to system-making'.[9] This view has a distinguished pedigree. It captures the essence of historicism as expounded in the nineteenth century. Ranke's injunction that historians should study the past 'to show how things actually were' was intended primarily as an antidote to the great evolutionary schemes of the Enlightenment historians and the followers of Hegel. Ranke's narrative style was hostile to abstraction and generalization and well suited to conveying the particularity of events. The classical historicist position is inimical both to comprehensive theories of social structure and to theories of social change, while its demand that every age should be evaluated in its own terms is difficult to reconcile with any view of history as progress towards a desirable goal.

The dangers of determinism

These grounds for rejecting theories of history are closely related to another argument which has often been given heavy emphasis: that theory denies not only the 'uniqueness' of events but also the dignity of the individual and the power of human agency. Traditional narrative shorn of any explanatory framework gives maximum scope to the play of personality, whereas a concern with recurrent or typical aspects of social structure and social change elevates abstraction at the expense of real living individuals. Worst of all from this viewpoint are theories of the third kind, whose insidious effect is to confer an inevitability on the historical process which individuals are powerless to change, now or in the future. All theories of history, the argument goes, have determinist elements, and determinism is a denial of human freedom.[10] The polar opposite of determinism is the rejection of any meaning in history beyond the play of the contingent and the unforeseen – a view held by many historians in the mainstream of the discipline. A.J.P. Taylor delighted in informing his readers that the only lesson taught by the study of the past is the incoherence and unpredictability of human affairs: history is a chapter of accidents and blunders.[11]

Lastly, the traditionalists recoil from one of the main practical consequences of writing theory-oriented history, which is to place history in a dependent relationship with the social sciences. Theory-minded historians, they maintain, do not develop their own models but apply the theoretical findings of sociology, social anthropology and economics – disciplines whose focus is on the present not the past, and who are interested in history only as a testing ground for their own theories. Theoretical historians simply play into their hands and undermine the autonomy of their own discipline. Historians ought to be vigilant about threats to the distinctiveness of their calling, whether from within or without.[12]

The conservatism of historians

The views of the traditionalists – sometimes expressed intemperately – suggests one explanation as to why the historical profession has been so strongly averse to theory, and that is its conservatism.[13] The study of history has attracted more than its fair share of conservatives concerned to invoke the sanction of the past in defence of institutions threatened by radical reform, or

Utopian
Unrealistically idealistic.
The term comes from
Sir Thomas More's
book *Utopia*, which
imagines a perfect but
unattainable society.
'Utopia', derived from
the Greek *u-topos*,
means 'no such place'.

minutiae
Very small details.

quite simply to find a mental escape from the disorienting impact of rapid social change around them. The true conservative, lacking a vision of progress, distrusts theories of the meaning of history as the rhetoric of the **Utopian** Left and is alarmed by the notion of a general model of social change which might be employed to push through undesirable projects of social engineering in the future. But the research methods of historians themselves have also acted as a strong antidote to theory. As M.M. Postan put it,

> the critical attitude to **minutiae** has become in the end a powerful agent of selection. It now attracts to history persons of a cautious and painstaking disposition, not necessarily endowed with any aptitude for theoretical synthesis.[14]

In fact a great deal of the opposition to theory is born of prejudice. The negative tendencies that the traditionalists have identified are certainly there, and if allowed free rein would lead to the damaging consequences that alarm them so much; but as any examination of the better examples of theoretical history will show, these tendencies do not go unchecked, and the outcome is an enrichment rather than an impoverishment of historical understanding.

The need to generalize

Consider, first of all, the contention that theory detracts from the uniqueness of historical events. Historians have in fact never written of events as though they were entirely unique, because it is impossible to do so. The very language that historians employ imposes a classification on their material and implies comparisons beyond their immediate field of interest. The only reason why scholars can use the phrase 'feudal tenure' of a particular relationship between lord and tenant, or the word 'revolution' of a major political upheaval, is because they share with their readers a common notion of what those words mean, based on a recognition that the world would be incomprehensible if we did not all the time subsume particular instances into general categories. The point was clearly made by E.E. Evans-Pritchard, a major figure in British social anthropology, who advocated a cordial relationship between history and the social sciences:

> Events lose much, even all, of their meaning if they are not seen as having some degree of regularity and constancy, as belonging to a certain type of event, all instances of which have many features in common. King John's struggle with his barons is meaningful only when the relations of the barons to Henry I, Stephen, Henry II and Richard are also known; and also when the relations between the kings and barons in other countries with feudal institutions are known; in other

words, where the struggle is seen as a phenomenon typical of, or common to, societies of a certain kind.[15]

But if the use of generalizing concepts alerts us to regularities in the material, it also exposes those aspects that resist categorization and which give the event or situation its unique qualities. The contention of the theoretical historian is that if these comparisons are implicit in any historical analysis worth the name, then there is everything to be gained in clarity of thought by making them explicit – by constructing, for example, a model of feudal society or of revolutionary change.

Is *history concerned with individuals?*

Equally, the claim that history is the rightful province of the individual looks dangerously misleading on closer inspection. Historians are compelled at every turn to classify people into groups, whether by nationality, religion, occupation or class. This is because it is these larger identities that confer significance on them as social beings. And what these groups have in common is a tendency to think and act in certain ways, to the point where their response can be predicted. No two individuals are ever entirely alike, but how they behave in certain roles (e.g. as consumers of foodstuffs or as adherents of a particular creed) may follow a highly regular pattern. The emphasis that historians place on group activity is not, therefore, a denial of human individuality but simply a recognition that what the individual does in common with others usually has far greater impact, historically, than anything else he or she does.

Furthermore, the cumulative effect of the actions that a particular group takes in pursuit of its objectives is to *institutionalize* that behaviour – that is, to entrench it in such a way that the options open to individuals thereafter are constrained or (to use a useful sociological term) *structured*. This is not the same as saying that people's actions are determined: certain patterns of behaviour may be strongly indicated, but they can be rejected or modified by the resolve of a new generation to break out of the mould. No one has expressed the tension between human agency and social structuring more lucidly than Philip Abrams, who significantly combined the professions of historian and sociologist:

> When we refer to the two-sidedness of society we are referring to the ways in which, in time, actions become institutions and institutions are in turn changed by action. Taking and selling prisoners becomes the institution of slavery. Offering one's services to a soldier in return for his protection becomes feudalism. Organizing the control of an enlarged labour force on the basis of standardized rules becomes bureaucracy. And

slavery, feudalism and bureaucracy become the fixed, external settings in which struggles for prosperity or survival or freedom are then pursued.[16]

The best theories – and I will argue shortly that Marxism is one of these – owe their appeal precisely to the fact that they seek to elucidate the reciprocal relationship of action and structure. Theory does not devalue the individual; it seeks rather to explain the constraints that limit people's freedom and frustrate their intentions, and in doing so it uncovers patterns in history. By contrast, the historian who maintains an exclusive focus on the thoughts and actions of individuals (as diplomatic historians all too often do) is likely to find no shape and to see instead only a chaotic sequence of accident and blunder.

Lessons from social science

As for the threatened submergence of history by the social sciences, there are strong reasons why historians should – in the first instance at least – avail themselves of imported theory. The social sciences are by definition concerned with what people do in aggregates rather than as individuals; and since their range embraces entire societies, social scientists have from the outset needed theory in order to engage with their subject matter at all. Economists since **Adam Smith** in the late eighteenth century and sociologists since **Auguste Comte** in the mid-nineteenth century have regarded explicit theory as a prerequisite for interpreting their data, and as a result a body of sophisticated theoretical knowledge has been built up in both disciplines, and latterly in social anthropology too. The use made by historians of these theories is simply an acknowledgement that the social sciences have a head start. In fact history has always been influenced by theorists from without, Smith and Comte being cases in point. But it is only in the past fifty years that historians have begun to take the measure of the full range and versatility of social science theory.

There are two real problems here. One is that much social science theory, especially in economics, is intended to explain quite restricted fields of activity, often in a somewhat artificially detached way, and the result of applying this theory to historical work may be to intensify the 'tunnel vision' to which historians specializing in a particular branch are anyway so prone. An extreme case was the use of statistical economic models in economic history. Known as 'Cliometrics', high hopes were expressed for this approach in the United States during the 1960s and 1970s. Cliometrics was based on the belief that a national economy is a closed system, entirely explicable in terms of statistical models, and that the same laws that appear to explain economic change in the present applied in the past also. The main drawback to this

Adam Smith (1723–90)
Scottish economist. Smith is the most important member of the eighteenth-century neo-classical school of economic theory; his 1776 work *The Wealth of Nations* is generally credited with having invented the modern study of economics. Smith held that economies are governed by a 'hidden hand' of market forces and therefore thrive best when government regulation and interference are kept to a minimum.

Auguste Comte (1798–1857)
French political philosopher and founder of the positivist school. Positivism aims to integrate the different branches of knowledge into a coherent whole.

approach was that it started from the premise that human beings in seeking to fulfil their material needs are governed by motives of a 'rational' profit-maximizing, cost-cutting kind. Yet often this is exactly what needs to be demonstrated, not assumed, since economic activity may be influenced by non-economic factors. The limitations of Cliometrics were sharply exposed when it was applied to the slave system of the American South in R.W. Fogel and S.L. Engerman's *Time on the Cross* (1974).[17] A theory that explains human behaviour in 'ideal' conditions is unlikely to do so when confronted by the social and cultural factors that operate in a historically specific situation, and historians who insist on using such a theory on the grounds that they are interested in purely technical problems are afflicted by a particularly disabling form of 'tunnel vision'.

The other problem concerns the alleged indifference to history of the social sciences. This charge is not without foundation. Many theories, for example that of the free market economy, are based on the premise of equilibrium, which strikes historians as a profoundly **ahistorical** way of conceiving society – a denial of the trajectories of change and adjustment that are present in every case; and other theories (such as the modernization theory so

ahistorical
In breach of the rules of the historical discipline, e.g. by dealing with historical events out of context, or even in the wrong context.

JOHN LILBURNE ON THE PILLORY.

Figure 8.1 John Lilburne, political agitator and English leader of the Levellers in the 1640s. Here, he appeals to a crowd as he stands at a pillory. © Mary Evans Picture Library.

prevalent in American sociology) which purport to embrace a historical dimension are based on a naïve antithesis between 'traditional' and 'modern', which is at odds with any sense of process in history. Certainly much of the borrowing by historians from the social sciences has been shallow and uncritical, and it has too readily assumed that theory is somehow value-free and objective, whereas it is the subject of sharp ideological differences among social scientists themselves.[18]

Neither of these objections is a reason for avoiding theory; they suggest only that historians should be discriminating about what they take on board. In fact, the theories whose influence on recent historians has been particularly pervasive are those that seek to encompass social structure or social change as a whole, and of these theories the most influential are derived from the great social thinkers of the nineteenth century, who had a profound sense of history – Max Weber and above all Karl Marx. But the real answer to the traditionalists' fear of absorption by the social sciences is that these theories are not tablets from heaven to be inscribed on the historical record. They should be seen rather as a point of departure. The result of historical work will be to modify them, probably quite drastically, and to erect in their place theories that represent a genuine cross-fertilization between history and social science. Both sides can only benefit from that outcome.

III

The case against Marxist history

The way is now open for a discussion in which the Marxist interpretation of history can be assessed in the context of the dangers and opportunities that attend any venture in theoretical history. The dangers in this case are familiar enough: Marx's detractors have made such play with some of the less attractive tendencies in his thought that, to all except the fairly restricted number of people who have read Marx himself or academic commentaries on his writings, he is associated with a bleak determinism and an utter cynicism about human nature. On this reading, the central tenets of Marxism go something like this. 'History is subject to the inexorable control of economic forces, which move all human societies along the road to socialism through the same stages, capitalism being the stage currently occupied by most of humankind. At all times, material self-interest has been the mainspring of human behaviour, regardless of the motives people have actually professed. Classes represent the collective expression of this self-interest, and all history is therefore nothing more than the history of class conflict. Ideology, art and culture are merely a mirror of this fundamental identification, having no historical dynamic of their own. The individual is the product of his or her own age and class, and however talented and forceful is powerless to affect the course of history; it is the masses who make history, but even they only do so according to a predetermined pattern.' At one time or another in the hundred years or so that have elapsed since Marx's death, each of these propositions has been subscribed to by Marxists, but all of them represent a crude simplification of what he actually wrote. Marx's thought was developed over some thirty years of research and reflection, and the resulting corpus of theory is far more complex and subtle than the **shibboleths** of 'vulgar' Marxism allow.

shibboleth
(Hebrew) A derogatory term for a slogan or catchphrase.

The basis of Marxist theory

Marx began with the fundamental premise that what distinguishes people from animals is their ability to produce their means of subsistence. In the struggle to satisfy their physiological and material needs, men and women have developed progressively more efficient means of exploiting their environment (or mastering nature, as Marx would have put it). To the question 'What is history about?' Marx answered that it is about the growth of human productive power, and he looked forward to the time when the basic needs of all people would be amply satisfied: only then would humanity find self-fulfilment and achieve its potential in every sphere. In maintaining that the only true, objective view of the historical process was rooted in the material conditions of life, Marx sharply distinguished himself from the main currents of nineteenth-century historiography with their choice of nationalism, freedom or religion as the defining themes of history. It is entirely appropriate that Marx's view should be referred to as 'historical materialism', a term coined by his lifelong collaborator and intellectual heir, Friedrich Engels. From this basic perspective, first sketched in *The German Ideology* (1846), Marx never wavered. For the rest of his life, much of his effort was devoted to working out its implications for the interpretation of social structure, the stages of social evolution and the nature of social change.

Marx's analysis of society

Marx conceived of society as comprising three constituent levels. Underlying all else are the *forces of production* (or productive forces): that is, the tools, techniques and raw materials together with the labour power that realizes their productive potential. The forces of production have certain implications for the *relations of production* (or productive relations), by which Marx meant the division of labour and the forms of cooperation and subordination required to sustain production – in other words the economic structure of society. This structure in turn forms a base or foundation on which is built the *superstructure*, composed of legal and political institutions and their supporting ideology. The most succinct summary of Marx's view of social structure appears in the preface to his *A Contribution to the Critique of Political Economy* (1859):

> In the social production of their existence, men inevitably enter into definite relations, which are independent of their will, namely relations of production appropriate to a given stage in the development of their material forces of production. The totality of these relations of production constitutes the economic structure of society, the real foundation, on which arises a legal and political superstructure and to which correspond definite forms of social consciousness. The mode of production of material life conditions the general process of social, political and intellectual life. It is not the consciousness of men that determines their existence, but their social existence that determines their consciousness.[19]

A determinist model?

However, this is not the crudely deterministic model that it has so often been taken to be. First, the forces of production are by no means confined to the instruments of production and the brawn of the workers. Technical ingenuity and scientific knowledge (on which the further development of the forces of production so clearly depended by Marx's day) are also included: full allowance is made for human creativity, without which we would remain slaves of the natural world around us. Second, although it clearly follows from Marx's view that politics and ideology – the traditional preoccupations of the historian – can only be understood in relation to the economic base, Marx also allowed for influences in the reverse direction. For example, no system of economic relations can become established without a prior framework of property rights and legal obligations; that is to say, the superstructure does not just reflect the relations of production but has an enabling function as well. The three-tier model thus allows for reciprocal influences.[20] And third, Marx did not suggest that all non-economic activities were determined by the base. It is arguable whether artistic creation should be included in the superstructure at all. But even those spheres that belong unequivocally to the superstructure are not *exclusively* determined by the base. Both political institutions and religion have their own dynamic, as Marx and Engels acknowledged in their own historical writings, and in the short term especially economic factors may be of subsidiary importance in accounting for events; as Braudel observes, Marx was essentially a theorist of *la longue durée* (see p. 137).[21]

It is probably closer to the spirit of Marx's thought to see the economic structure as setting limiting conditions rather than determining the elements of the superstructure in all their particularity. Engels was most emphatic on this point. As he wrote to a correspondent some years after Marx's death:

> According to the materialistic conception of history, the *ultimately* determining element in history is the production and reproduction of real life.
>
> More than this neither Marx nor I has ever asserted. Hence if somebody twists this into saying that the economic element is the *only* determining one he transforms that proposition into a meaningless, abstract, senseless phrase. The economic situation is the basis, but the various elements of the superstructure ... also exercise their influence upon the course of the historical struggles and in many cases preponderate in determining their *form*.[22]

Clearly the base/superstructure metaphor lends itself to a deterministic interpretation, and several of Marx's utterances can be so interpreted, but his *oeuvre* as a whole does not suggest that he saw it in such stark terms.

oeuvre
(French) An author's complete works.

Marx's analysis of history

One of the best-known features of Marx's thought is his periodization of history. He distinguished three historical epochs down to his own day, each moulded by a progressively more advanced mode of production. These were Ancient Society (Greece and Rome), Feudal Society, which emerged after the fall of the Roman Empire, and Capitalist (or 'modern bourgeois') Society, which had first come into being in England in the seventeenth century and had since triumphed elsewhere in Europe, particularly as a consequence of the French Revolution. What gave political edge to the periodization was Marx's conviction that Capitalist Society must in due course give way to Socialist Society and the complete self-fulfilment of humankind; indeed, when he first sketched the scheme in 1846 he believed the advent of socialism to be imminent. Marx maintained that his periodization was the outcome of his historical enquiries rather than of dogmatic theorizing, and that is borne out by the changes and qualifications he made in the light of fuller research. He later posited an additional mode of production in the form of Germanic Society, contemporaneous with Ancient Society and one of the sources of Feudal Society.[23] Marx reproved those critics who

> must metamorphose my historical sketch of the genesis of capitalism in Western Europe into a historic-philosophic theory of the general path every people is fated to tread, whatever the historical circumstances in which it finds itself.[24]

In short, Marx did not lay down a single evolutionary path which all human societies are predetermined to follow exactly.

Dialectic in production as the motor of social change

Such a rigid periodization would have ill consorted with Marx's view of social change, the richest and most suggestive part of his theory of history. Marx summed up his interpretation in the passage that immediately follows the extract from the 1859 preface quoted earlier:

> At a certain stage of development, the material productive forces of society come into conflict with the existing relations of production or – this merely expresses the same thing in legal terms – with the property relations within the framework of which they have operated hitherto. From forms of development of the productive forces these relations turn into their fetters. Then begins an era of social revolution. The changes in the economic foundation lead sooner or later to the transformation of the whole immense superstructure.[25]

Marx believed that the contradiction or *dialectic* between the forces of production and the relations of production was the principal determinant of long-term historical change: each mode of production contains within it the seeds of its successor. Thus, to take an example on which he held emphatic views, the English Revolution of the seventeenth century occurred because the forces of production characteristic of capitalism had reached the point where their further development was held back by the feudal property relations sanctioned by the early Stuart monarchy; the outcome of the Revolution was a remodelling of the relations of production, which cleared the way for the Industrial Revolution a hundred years later.

Class conflict

This rather abstract conception of historical change is made visible in the form of *class conflict*. Marx identified classes not according to wealth, status or education – the usual criteria employed in his day – but quite specifically in terms of their role in the productive process. The division of labour that has characterized every mode of production since Ancient Society results in the creation of classes whose true interests are mutually antagonistic. Each successive stage has had its dominant class and has also harboured the class destined to overthrow it. Thus Marx ascribed the English Revolution to the urban bourgeoisie, who were developing the new capitalist forces of production, just as he expected socialism to be achieved in his own day by the new factory **proletariat** spawned by industrial capitalism. It is class conflict expressing the contradictions within society that drives history in a forward direction. This is not to say that the masses are the makers of history. Although Marx believed that humanity's prospects for a better future lay in the hands of the proletariat, his interpretation confined the masses to an **ancillary** role in earlier history; he was only too well aware that the world in which he lived was essentially the creation of the bourgeoisie, whom Marx both admired and reviled for what they had achieved.

Marx's conception of class is the point at which his view of the role of human agency in history can be assessed. Class is defined in structural terms according to its relation to the means of production, but Marx knew that for a class to be effective politically requires a *consciousness* of their class in its members. The long-term trajectory of change may be determined by the dialectic between the forces and relations of production, but the timing and the precise form of the transition from one stage to the next depend on the awareness and capacity for action of real human beings. Indeed, Marx's entire career was devoted to equipping the proletariat of his time with an understanding of the material forces at work in their own society so that they would know when and how to act against the capitalist system. People are the victims of material forces, but in the right conditions they have the opportunity to be agents of historical change. That paradox lies at the centre of Marx's view of history. As he wrote in his finest piece of contemporary history, 'The eighteenth Brumaire of Louis Bonaparte' (1852):

> Men make their own history, but they do not make it just as they please; they do not make it under circumstances chosen by themselves, but under circumstances directly encountered, given, and transmitted from the past.[26]

proletariat
The industrial working class. The term passed into general use after it was popularized in the writings of Karl Marx.

ancillary
Secondary, subordinate.

IV

Marx's critique of historians

What were the implications of Marx's theories for the actual writing of history? As we have seen, these theories lend themselves to a simplified rigid schema, and this was the form in which they were expounded by many of the first Marxists, whose primary interest was in the political struggle and who were content with an unequivocal determinism which pointed towards a proletarian revolution in the near future. But Marx himself was emphatic that his theory was a guide to study, not a substitute for it:

> Viewed apart from real history, these abstractions have in themselves no value whatsoever. They can only serve to

facilitate the arrangement of historical material, to indicate the sequence of its separate strata. But they by no means afford a recipe or schema, as does philosophy, for neatly trimming the epochs of history. On the contrary, our difficulties begin only when we set about the observation and the arrangement – the real depiction – of our historical material, whether of a past epoch or of the present.[27]

What Marx rejected was not historical study as such, but the method employed by the leading historians of his day. Their error, he maintained, lay in taking at face value what the historical actors said about their motives and aspirations; in so doing, Ranke and his imitators imprisoned themselves within the dominant ideology of the age in question, which was merely a cloak for the real material interests of the dominant class. 'Objective' history – that is, the dialectic of forces and relations of production – was accessible through research into the economic structure of past societies without reference to the subjective utterances of historical personalities. At the same time, Marx never developed a clear methodology of history. His own historical writings veered from the compelling political narrative of 'The eighteenth Brumaire' (1852) to the abstract economic analysis of the first volume of *Capital* (1867). And there remain ambiguities in his conception of both the forces and the relations of production, as well as the connection between base and superstructure. So historians working within the Marxist tradition have had plenty of interpretative work to do.

The impact of Marxism

During the generation after Marx's death in 1883, historical materialism began to have a pervasive though somewhat blurred effect on the climate of intellectual opinion, as his major writings were translated into other European languages and socialist parties of a Marxist persuasion sprang up. Marxism was certainly one of the main currents contributing to the emergence of economic history as a distinct field of enquiry. As J.H. Clapham – no friend of socialism – conceded in 1929, 'Marxism, by attraction and repulsion, has perhaps done more to make men think about economic history and inquire into it than any other teaching.'[28] But the content and method of the Marxist interpretation took longer to make an impact. It first affected the practice of professional historians on a significant scale in the Soviet Union, where, from the Bolshevik takeover until Stalin's clampdown in 1931–2, historical research and debate within a Marxist framework were very lively.[29] The subjection of historical work to a strict party line in Russia coincided with the emergence of Marxism as a powerful intellectual stimulus in the West. This was prompted by

Capital
Marx's major work of economic analysis, first published in 1867. It was originally intended to be a three-part work, but only the first part was ever published in full. It contains Marx's analysis of the development of capitalism out of the feudal and primitive economies that had preceded it, and his argument that capitalism, as an inherently exploitative system, would inevitably implode, leading to the establishment of a socialist system.

the obvious crisis in capitalism as a result of the **Great Crash of 1929** and the apparent bankruptcy of liberal democracy in the face of Fascism. But although important pioneer work in Marxist history was done in Britain and elsewhere during the 1930s, it was mostly achieved by active members of the Communist Party, who were viewed with suspicion by most historians and received little academic preferment. From the 1950s, however, Marxist approaches to history were much more widely influential – and with historians who had no connection with the Communist Party and in many cases were not politically active at all. Many of the acknowledged leaders of the profession, such as Christopher Hill and E.J. Hobsbawm, wrote from a Marxist perspective.

Why is it that a historical interpretation that originated as a revolutionary critique of contemporary society and which is open to dogmatic abuse commands so much attention among scholars? The reason can hardly be any longer the central role accorded by Marxism to economic history, since the majority of economic historians (particularly in Britain and the United States) are non-Marxist. Nor can the appeal of Marxism be attributed to the attractions of an 'underdog' view of history: although the Marxist approach gives great weight to the role of the masses at certain historical conjunctures, it does not offer a worm's-eye view of history, nor is it concerned to celebrate the heroism of earlier generations of proletarians. The real reason for Marxism's strong appeal is that it answers so well to the historian's need for theory – and in all three of the areas with which this chapter began.

Great Crash of 1929
The disastrous fall in prices on the New York Stock Exchange on 24 October 1929, which ended the prosperity of the 1920s and ushered in the worldwide economic depression of the 1930s. Also known as the Wall Street Crash.

The usefulness of Marxist social analysis

Through the base/superstructure model Marxism offers a particularly useful way of conceiving the totality of social relations in any given society. It is not just that the political, social, economic and technological all have their place; in a full-scale Marxist analysis these familiar distinctions lose their force. Social and economic history become inseparable, and the study of politics is saved from becoming the minute reconstruction of the antics of professional politicians in their own arena. The appeal of 'total history' as practised by the *Annales* school also rests on its opposition to compartmentalization, but Braudel and his followers have conspicuously failed to develop a satisfactory model for integrating political history with the environmental and demographic studies that provide the backbone of their work. In this respect at least, it must be counted as inferior to Marxist history with its emphasis on the reciprocal interaction between the productive forces, the relations of production and the superstructure. It is no accident that Hobsbawm, one of the finest writers of the broad historical survey today, was a Marxist with a profound grasp of the master's own writings.[30]

It is the same reciprocal interaction that saves Marxism from the ahistorical error so common in other theories, of regarding social equilibrium as the norm. Marxist historians hold as a fundamental premise that all societies contain both stabilizing elements and disruptive elements (or contradictions), and that historical change occurs when the latter burst out of the existing social framework and through a process of struggle achieve a new order. Historians have found the notion of the dialectic to be an invaluable tool in analysing social change of varying intensity, from the barely perceptible movement within a stable social formation to periods of revolutionary ferment.

Divisions within Marxism: culturalism vs. economism

Response to the strong pull exerted by Marxism's theoretical range does not, however, mean that historians practising in the Marxist tradition are confined within an orthodoxy. What is striking about the growth of Marxist historiography during the past fifty years is its diversity. As familiarity with Marx's writing has spread, so historians have responded to the different and quite contradictory strands in his *oeuvre*, reflected in a major divide in recent Marxist scholarship between what insiders call 'culturalism' and 'economism'. This divide is best illustrated by reaction to the most widely read work of Marxist history ever written in Britain – E.P. Thompson's *The Making of the English Working Class* (see p. 59). The central theme of the book is how, in reaction to proletarianization and political repression, the English labouring classes developed a new consciousness so that by 1830 they had achieved a collective identity as a working class and the capacity for collective political action: that consciousness was not the automatic by-product of the factory system, but was the outcome of reflection on experience in the light of a vigorous native radical tradition. The book is thus 'a study in an active process, which owes as much to agency as to conditioning'.[31] Thompson himself maintained that his book was true to Marx's recognition that men do, in some measure, 'make their own history'. His critics argued that Thompson underestimated the force of the qualification added by Marx to that statement. They pointed out that in omitting any detailed discussion of the transition from one mode of production to another, Thompson failed to acknowledge the rootedness of class in economic relations and therefore exaggerated the role of collective agency; because Thompson was lax in his theory, he became trapped within the subjective experience of his protagonists.[32] Thompson was unrepentant; he reaffirmed the need to hold theory and experience in some kind of balance and to interpret Marxism as an evolving and flexible tradition rather than a closed system.[33]

The working class and Marxist theory

The Making of the English Working Class expresses another marked tendency within British Marxist historiography, and that is its interest in the history of popular movements, almost regardless of their efficacy. One of the criticisms that can be made of Marxism, as of other goal-oriented interpretations of history, is that it distorts our understanding of the past by concentrating unduly on those people and movements that were on the side of 'progress'. But Thompson's emphasis falls less on the new factory workforce, which was the nucleus of the organized working class of the future, than on the casualties of the Industrial Revolution – people such as the **handloom weavers**, whose means of livelihood was destroyed by the factory system. At the same time, it would be a mistake to assume from this 'underdog' perspective that Marxist history is merely 'history from below'. Struggles between classes are ultimately resolved at the political level, and it is through control of the state that new dispositions of class power are sustained. In fact it can be argued, though it is not very fashionable to do so, that 'history from above' is just as important a perspective for Marxist historians.

V

Marxism and the fall of communism

The extended treatment that has been given to the Marxist theory of history may seem to some readers like a self-indulgent surrender to an outmoded radicalism. Has not Marxism now been placed on the scrap-heap with the reduction of the world's Marxist governments to a tiny rump and the collapse of international communism since 1989? Are not Marxist historians now trapped in a time-warp? Like other scholars, historians would not be human if they were unaffected by the political atmosphere in which they work. The circumstances in which a Marxist scholar can work today are far less propitious than they were forty years ago. For that reason alone, there are many fewer historians who accept the label. Most of the towering achievements of Marxist history were made between the 1960s and 1980s – by Thompson, Hobsbawm and Hill in Britain, as well as a galaxy of foreign scholars which included Georges Lefebvre in France and Eugene Genovese in the United States. Marxist history is unlikely to enjoy such a high profile in the future.

But for as long as historians recognize the need for a theoretical orientation which addresses both social structure and social change, Marxism will be relevant. They may not be Marxists in the sense of working within Marx's system of thought, but they will draw on the concepts and categories of the Marxist tradition.

handloom weavers
Those who wove cloth on individual looms usually operated within the worker's home under the old 'domestic' system of textile production, which preceded the introduction of factory production. Handloom weavers were eventually forced out of the market by competition from factories, so they are often used by historians as an indication of the impact of the new methods of production in the early nineteenth century.

Figure 8.2 After the fall of the Berlin Wall in November 1989, popular insurrection overturned communist governments across Eastern Europe. Some held that Marxism itself had been discredited; graffiti on this statue of Marx and Engels in Dresden, in East Germany, has them declaring 'we are not guilty', a view shared by many who saw the Soviet dictatorship as a perversion of Marxism. Not everyone agreed, however, and many statues of Marx and Engels, like those of Lenin, were overturned and smashed. © Alamy/ICP.

Medieval English history is a case in point. To argue that the relation between lords and peasants was one of class conflict, and that this tension was the main driver of social change in the Middle Ages, is clearly a Marxist position. It was closely associated with Rodney Hilton, a prominent member of the Communist Party Historians' Group. Yet this interpretation remains very much in contention, as a commemorative conference on Hilton's work established. In Chris Wickham's words, 'far from Marxist ideas being dead or moribund, they are everywhere. But they have been normalized.'[34] The same can be said of modern history. Peter Clarke, a distinguished political historian who admits to being a 'wishy-washy Cambridge liberal', concedes that 'Marxism as history [as distinct from prediction] can still be made to yield insights for us'.[35] Marxist history has come into its own in the highly stratified societies of the Third World. In South Africa, for example, it was critical in showing how segregation and apartheid – often dismissed as an irrational aberration – in fact served the interests of capitalism by guaranteeing a supply of cheap labour to the white economy.[36] Marxism can certainly not be written off as a museum-piece.

Objection might also be made to the priority accorded to Marxism in a chapter on historians and social theory. Marxism was surely not the only theoretical game in town, and is not its decline testimony to the superior attractions of other bodies of theory? It is true that even in its heyday Marxism faced competition, particularly in the United States where liberal modernization theory was much used as a means of accounting for the transition from traditional to modern industrial society with more benign effects than are allowed within Marxism. More recently, feminists have developed theories of gender that explain social structure in comparatively novel terms of sexual difference, the divide between public and private spheres and patriarchal power (see Chapter 10). On top of that, when historians issue calls to embrace theory – as they increasingly do – what they usually have in mind is not social theory at all, but cultural theories which tackle questions of meaning and representation (see Chapter 9). This most recent trend exposes one of the principal weaknesses of Marxism, namely its tendency to see culture as secondary: neither nationality nor religion receive their due. During the 1990s, theories that treat culture as an autonomous dimension of society had all the excitement of novelty, against which Marxism inevitably seemed staid and dated. The conflict between social and cultural approaches was played out in the journals (notably *Social History* between 1992 and 1996), and Marxism was generally reckoned to have lost out.

Yet, as this chapter has demonstrated, Marxist theory has had a unique place in the explanatory resources of history. No other theory offers such a comprehensive model of social structure, or such a dynamic theory of social and political change. That Marxism has been a living theoretical tradition for more than 150 years is only partly due to its origins as a political weapon. It is also because historians and social theorists have recognized its capacity for continuing development. There are already signs that the cultural tide may be retreating. As it does, the merits of a theoretical approach that is rooted in the material realities of human life, which recognizes the centrality of productive relations and which highlights the tension between collective agency and social determination, will once more be recognized.

Social theory and the 'big questions' of history

As we have seen, academic opinion is divided about the merits of theory. But all historians, unless they are diehard traditionalists, concede that theory has been very productive in stimulating hypotheses. Its value, they claim, lies not in its explanatory power but in its capacity to raise interesting questions and to alert scholars to fresh source material – in a word, it has merit as a **heuristic** device. Historical research usually demonstrates that a given theory does not hold when confronted by the richness of actual experience, but in the process a new area of historical enquiry may be opened up. From this angle Marxist theory has a

heuristic
Learning from discovery and experiment.

very good track record as a source of 'fertile error':[37] whatever its failings it has generated a great deal of historical knowledge about the connections between political process and the socio-economic structure.

This might be termed the minimalist justification of the use of theory by historians. What it overlooks is that historical knowledge consists of more than specific conjunctures and processes in the past. Historians with their professional commitment to primary research all too easily forget that there are large-scale problems of historical interpretation which cry out for treatment: how to explain long-term processes such as the growth of industrialization or bureaucracy, and the recurrence of institutions such as feudalism or plantation slavery in widely separated societies. The broader the scope of the enquiry, the greater the need for theory that does not simply alert the historian to fresh evidence, but which actually attempts to *explain* the process or pattern in question. Marxist historiography, if it has done nothing else, has at least brought some of the 'big questions' of history more insistently to the centre of the scholarly arena, and has served to expose to scrutiny the unconscious models that so often inform the work of historians most vehement in their rejection of theory.

reductionism
The prior selection of one level of reality as fundamental, and the interpretation of everything else in terms of that one level.

The conscious application of social theory by historians to these broad questions has given rise to a great deal of **reductionist** history by second-rate scholars anxious to prove their theoretical credentials. But in the hands of the best historians – and it is by their efforts that the enterprise should surely be judged – the awareness of context and the command of the sources ensure a proper relationship between theory and evidence. As Thompson put it, historical understanding advances by means of 'a delicate equilibrium between the synthesizing and the empiric modes, a quarrel between the model and the actuality'.[38] It is to be expected that, submitted to this discipline, social theories should be tried and found wanting, but that is no reason for renouncing their use. The business of historians is to apply theory, to refine it and to develop new theory, always in the light of the evidence most broadly conceived. And they do so not in pursuit of the ultimate theory or 'law' which will 'solve' this or that problem of explanation, but because without theory they cannot come to grips with the really significant questions in history.

Further reading

Mary Fulbrook, *Historical Theory*, Routledge, 2002.
Peter Burke, *History and Social Theory*, Polity Press, 1995.
L.S. Feuer (ed.), *Karl Marx and Friedrich Engels: Basic Writings on Politics and Philosophy*, Fontana, 1969.
John Seed, *Marx: a Guide for the Perplexed*, Continuum, 2010.
Matt Perry, *Marxism and History*, Palgrave, 2002.

Eric Hobsbawm, *On History*, Abacus, 1997.

Harvey J. Kaye, *The British Marxist Historians*, Polity Press, 1984.

S.H. Rigby, *Marxism and History: A Critical Introduction*, Manchester University Press, 1987.

Notes

1 See Emmanuel Le Roy Ladurie, *The Mind and the Method of the Historian*, Harvester, 1981, ch. 1.

2 Some such theory evidently underlies much of G.R. Elton's work, and also the 'high politics' school of historiography, discussed above, pp. 50–51.

3 A major exception is E.H. Carr, *What is History?*, Penguin, 1961.

4 Peter Mathias, 'Living with the neighbours: the role of economic history', 1970, reprinted in N.B. Harte (ed.), *The Study of Economic History*, Cass, 1971, p. 380.

5 For this view, see Jacques Barzun, *Clio and the Doctors*, Chicago University Press, 1974.

6 Aileen S. Kraditor, 'American radical historians on their heritage', *Past and Present*, LVI, 1972, p. 137.

7 Ibid., p. 137.

8 Paul K. Conkin, 'Intellectual history', in Charles F. Delzell (ed.), *The Future of History*, Vanderbilt University Press, 1977, pp. 129–30.

9 David Thomson, *The Aims of History*, Thames & Hudson, 1969, p. 105.

10 Isaiah Berlin, 'Historical inevitability', 1954, reprinted in Patrick Gardiner (ed.), *The Philosophy of History*, Oxford University Press, 1974.

11 Comments in this vein recur in A.J.P. Taylor's *Bismarck*, Hamish Hamilton, 1955, and in his *The Origins of the Second World War*, Penguin, 1964.

12 G.R. Elton, *The Practice of History*, Fontana, 1969, pp. 55–6.

13 G.R. Elton, *Return to Essentials* (Cambridge University Press, 1991), pp. 13–15, 27; Arthur Marwick, '"A fetishism of documents?" The salience of source-based history', in Henry Kozicki (ed.), *Developments in Modern Historiography*, Macmillan, 1993, pp. 110–11.

14 M.M. Postan, *Fact and Relevance*, Cambridge University Press, 1971, p. 16.

15 E.E. Evans-Pritchard, 'Anthropology and history', 1961, reprinted in his *Essays in Social Anthropology*, Faber, 1962, p. 49.

16 Philip Abrams, *Historical Sociology*, Open Books, 1982, pp. 2–3.

17 For critical responses to *Time on the Cross*, see Paul David et al., *Reckoning with Slavery*, Oxford University Press, 1976.

18 See the criticism of Gareth Stedman Jones, 'From historical sociology to theoretical history', *British Journal of Sociology*, XXVII, 1976, pp. 295–305, and Tony Judt, 'A clown in regal purple: social history and the historians', *History Workshop Journal*, VII, 1979, pp. 66–94.

19 Karl Marx, *A Contribution to the Critique of Political Economy*, Lawrence & Wishart, 1971, pp. 20–1.

20 This interpretation is convincingly argued in Melvin Rader, *Marx's Interpretation of History*, Oxford University Press, 1979. For a contrary view, see G.A. Cohen, *Karl Marx's Theory of History: A Defence*, Oxford University Press, 1978.

21 Fernand Braudel, 'History and the social sciences: *la longue durée*', 1958, reprinted in his *On History*, Weidenfeld & Nicolson, 1980, p. 51.

22 Engels to J. Bloch, 21 September 1860, reprinted in Karl Marx and Friedrich Engels, *Basic Writings on Politics and Philosophy*, ed. L.S. Feuer, Fontana, 1969, pp. 436–7.

23 Karl Marx, *Pre-Capitalist Economic Formations*, Lawrence & Wishart, 1964, especially Introduction by E.J. Hobsbawm.

24 Marx to the editorial board of *Otechestvennive Zapiski*, November 1877, reprinted in Marx and Engels, *Basic Writings*, p. 478.

25 Marx, *A Contribution*, p. 21.

26 Marx, 'The eighteenth Brumaire of Louis Bonaparte', 1852, reprinted in Marx and Engels, *Basic Writings*, p. 360.

27 Marx and Engels, 'The German ideology', 1846, in *Basic Writings*, p. 289.

28 J.H. Clapham, 'The study of economic history', 1929, reprinted in Harte, *Study of Economic History*, pp. 64–5.

29 John Barber, *Soviet Historians in Crisis, 1928–30*, Macmillan, 1981.

30 See his *Age of Revolution*, Weidenfeld & Nicolson, 1962, and his *Age of Capital*, Weidenfeld & Nicolson, 1976.

31 E.P. Thompson, *The Making of the English Working Class*, Penguin, 1968, p. 9.

32 See Richard Johnson, 'Thompson, Genovese and socialist-humanist history', *History Workshop Journal*, VI, 1978, pp. 79–100, and Perry Anderson, *Arguments within English Marxism*, Verso, 1980.

33 E.P. Thompson, *The Poverty of Theory*, Merlin Press, 1978, especially pp. 110–19.

34 Christopher Dyer et al. (eds), *Rodney Hilton's Middle Ages*, Oxford University Press, 2007; Chris Wickham, 'Memories of underdevelopment: what has Marxism done for Medieval history, and what can it still do?', in C. Wickham (ed.), *Marxist History-Writing in the Twenty-first Century*, Oxford University Press, 2007, p. 35.

35 Peter Clarke, 'The century of the hedgehog: the demise of political ideologies in the twentieth century', in Peter Martland (ed.), *The Future of the Past: Big Questions in History*, Pimlico, 2002, p. 125.

36 Shula Marks and Richard Rathbone (eds), *Industrialisation and Social Change in South Africa*, Longman, 1982.

37 H.R. Trevor-Roper, 'History: professional and lay' (1957), reprinted in H.L. Lloyd-Jones, V. Pearl and B. Worden (eds), *History and Imagination*, Duckworth, 1981, p. 13.

38 Thompson, *The Poverty of Theory*, p. 78.

9 Cultural evidence and the cultural turn

Whereas the social theories discussed in the previous chapter focus on structure, change and agency, cultural theory attends to meaning and representation. Its influence is evident today in the very high profile enjoyed by cultural history. To some extent cultural history draws on the well-established field of art history (and also the history of film). But its approach to questions of meaning is much more strongly influenced by literary theory and by anthropology. The chapter ends with an assessment of the present state of history in the light of what has come to be called the cultural turn.

In present-day historical scholarship, no concept is more frequently invoked than 'culture'. It serves as an indicator not just of the content of a given study but the theoretical orientation taken by the author. What makes 'culture' so baffling to the novice is that its meaning takes quite varied forms. Thus we speak not only of visual culture, literary culture and material culture, but also the culture of violence and a culture of fear – the implication being that these very different areas are conceptually related in some way. To speak of 'cultural history' or 'the cultural turn' registers a significant shift in the priorities of historians, but it takes some persistence to fathom what kind of culture is being referred to. Thirty years ago the great cultural critic Raymond Williams remarked, 'culture is one of the two or three most complicated words in the English language'.[1] That is no less true today.

Much of this complication arises from the fact that culture has one set of meanings in common parlance, and another in academic discourse. Still the most familiar referent of culture is those artistic and literary activities – sometimes referred to as 'high' culture – whose appreciation depends on education, taste and the necessary leisure to develop that taste; a 'cultured' person might be expected to be widely read in 'great' literature, and to regularly frequent art galleries and concert halls. Culture in this sense has a long and absorbing history, going back to the earliest efforts to represent human experience or observation before writing had been invented. The academic study that has examined high culture most closely is art history. Cultural historians share many concerns with historians of art. While in theory covering all of visual culture, the history of art is largely concerned with art as a self-conscious elite experience, particularly with reference to painting and sculpture. More recently, the assumption that culture is the preserve of an elite has been refuted in the name of popular culture. This is the second dimension of culture. The ordinary population may have been largely excluded from 'high' art, but other cultural forms reflected or constructed their outlook on the world – from the popular religious images of the Middle Ages, through the chapbooks of the seventeenth century, to the mass culture of the popular press and best-selling novels in the twentieth century. Unlike elite culture, the history of popular culture has not generated a separate academic discipline, and historians are much more to the fore in researching it.

Both the history of art and the history of popular culture are object-oriented: in each case the point of departure is a body of artefacts or texts which manifestly had a cultural purpose. In recent years, however, a much broader definition of culture has become prevalent in academia. In the usage of historians, culture has lost its association with specific cultural forms. It is understood not as 'high' or 'low' culture, but as the web of meanings that characterize a society and hold its members together. How, in any given society in the past, did people apprehend their daily experience? What were their attitudes to time and space, the natural world, pain and death, family relationships and religious observance? What were their common values? Peter Burke has defined culture as 'a system of shared meanings, attitudes and values, and the symbolic forms (performances, artefacts) in which they are expressed or embodied'.[2] Note that meanings and values come before the forms in which they were expressed. Cultural history in this sense amounts to nothing less than the reconstruction of the mental, emotional and conceptual world of the past.

Finally, historians today talk much of 'the cultural turn'. By this they mean not just the arrival of a new sub-discipline but a reorientation in the priorities of historians. If culture is very broadly defined – along the lines of Burke's 'system of shared meanings' – there is no limit to the scope of cultural history; it can be applied to political conflicts, the divide between rich and poor, the position of women and so on. From this it is a short step to the insistence that culture is the most important dimension of historical experience. In some versions of the cultural turn it is the *only* dimension of the past that is deemed accessible to historical enquiry: culture has become, in the words of one critic, 'the bottom line, the real historical reality'.[3] This point of view has negative implications for other perspectives on the past. The challenge has been most keenly felt in social history – the dominant branch of study in the 1970s and 1980s, but now sometimes condemned as wedded to an outdated Marxism and a naïve methodology. The tension between social and cultural approaches has run through the historical profession for at least the past ten years. In this chapter I describe each of the above branches of cultural history, as well as evaluating the more imperial pretensions of the cultural turn.

I

Art history

All surviving material from the past is grist to the historian's mill. If that precept holds, it must apply to visual no less than textual sources, in which case the historian should be as quick to draw conclusions from paintings, sculpture and material objects as from deeds and diaries. Yet that is not the impression one is likely to get from perusing the work of historians. Most historians do not make detailed analysis of the art of their chosen period; art is seldom treated as evidence in a systematic way; and illustrations in works of history are usually just that – included for their decorative appeal rather than for close reading. To understand why this is so we must take account of the practice of those most expert in visual sources – the art historians. The first art historians were connoisseurs: they prided themselves on their skill in dating works of art, identifying the artist and grouping works of art into 'styles'. Nowadays that is regarded as a narrow and outmoded approach. But the tradition of connoisseurship nevertheless underpins the claim that works of art are fundamentally different from written sources, because understanding them depends on very specific technical skills, and because they reflect different conventions of representation. Their language is veiled and multi-layered – in fact so elusive that only an exclusive expertise can do justice to them.

Two strands in art history take approaches that are rather more congenial to historians. First is an emphasis on the intellectual and literary content of paintings. In the 1930s, a highly influential school of German art historians led by **Erwin Panofsky** developed the idea of 'iconography': the reading of art in relation to the intellectual world in which it was commissioned and created. This worked particularly well in the case of artists like those of the Italian Renaissance, who were employed by highly accomplished patrons and delivered works with philosophical or mythological themes.[4] More recently, a group of socialist scholars has reacted sharply against the tendency in traditional art history to abstract works of art from the society that produced them. According to T.J. Clark, the ideological nexus binding artists to the dominant structures of society is crucial to understanding their work. Painting and sculpture are not intrinsically different

Erwin Panofsky (1892–1968)
One of an extraordinary generation of gifted Jewish art historians who began their careers in Germany between the wars, but were obliged to flee the Nazis. Panofsky left for America. Others, notably Aby Warburg and Ernst Gombrich, settled in England, where they transformed the profession of art history.

from any other kind of work: they require certain conditions of production, and they feed off a certain kind of audience or consumer. The task of the art historian is to bring to light the links between a given work of art and the social structures and historical processes in which it was created. It follows that, as Clark puts it, 'there can be no art history apart from other kinds of history'.[5]

Art history for historians

Where do historians fit into the world of art history? Some of the purists' case must be conceded. The extended research sometimes required to elucidate a single painting is not likely to appeal to a historian for whom the work in question is part of a much bigger picture. Thus an intellectual historian of **neo-Platonist** philosophy in the Renaissance could hardly be unaware of its impact on painters like Botticelli and Raphael who represented it in **allegory**; but engaging directly in research on the iconography of particular paintings could probably only be pursued at the cost of the overall project. In such cases there is a demarcation of focus between the historian and the art historian.

However, that is only one kind of art, and one kind of interpretative strategy. What about art as direct representation? The art of the past depicts a vast range of everyday detail – clothing, implements, buildings – that are incidental to the artist's purpose but included in the interests of verisimilitude or 'background'. Such material should be seen as yet another instance of Marc Bloch's 'witnesses in spite of themselves' (see p. 75). Among art history theorists, it is not uncommon to dismiss this kind of evidence. According to Stephen Bann, the visual image proves nothing, 'or whatever it does prove is too trivial to count as a component in historical analysis'.[6] But historians like Peter Burke rightly question this point of view.[7] Their argument is most convincing in the case of images of a documentary kind. Thus the appearance of the City of London – including Old St Paul's, its proudest monument – before the Great Fire of 1666 is not a trivial matter, which is why historians pay close attention to the highly detailed topographical engravings made by Wenceslaus Hollar in the 1640s. Art provides equally valuable evidence for the design of weapons, furniture and tableware. It is also worth bearing in mind that in recent years the objects themselves – where they have survived – have become a focus of study under the label 'material culture'.[8]

Another category of great interest to historians is art in the service of the state or its opponents. Our understanding of the Nazi regime has been deepened by the study of official propaganda, which combined crude slogans with highly effective

Neo-Platonism
An intellectual movement in Renaissance Italy that sought to revive the philosophy of Plato. It was much favoured among the ruling elites, especially in Florence. Neo-Platonism reflects the readiness of Renaissance thinkers to find inspiration outside the Christian revelation.

allegory
A story of representation to be understood symbolically rather than literally.

Figure 9.1 Old St Paul's Cathedral, London, *c.*1640, by Wenceslaus Hollar. Hollar was a gifted Czech engraver who provided an invaluable record of London before the Great Fire of 1666. This image is the more striking because the style of the old cathedral is utterly different from the one that Christopher Wren designed after the fire, and which survives to this day. © Bridgeman Art Library/Guildhall Library, City of London.

images; satirical attacks on the regime are no less useful for understanding the play of political forces in Germany during the 1930s. In England the political cartoon – highly critical and sometimes vitriolic – has a history extending back to the eighteenth century, and some of its leading exponents today acknowledge the influence of their distinguished predecessors. These examples suggest that for the historian 'bad' art is often more illuminating than great art – a view not shared by art historians, for whom aesthetic response counts much more.

Interpreting a medieval masterpiece

One further example illustrates the place of visual evidence in historical reconstruction. The most famous work of art produced in medieval England is probably the Bayeux Tapestry, depicting the Norman Conquest of England in 1066. The Tapestry is seventy metres long and comprises a succession of embroidered panels in narrative sequence, not unlike a strip cartoon. It was probably made in Canterbury between 1077 and 1082, by English craftsmen working to a Norman agenda. Most people who view the Tapestry are intrigued by the vividness with which artefacts are represented, particularly the weapons and armour used at the battle of Hastings.

However, the importance of the Bayeux Tapestry does not lie only in its accumulation of evidential detail. It was also an ambitious attempt to establish an official version of events, and it was probably commissioned for this purpose by William the Conqueror's half-brother, who had fought at Hastings. The early scenes, featuring William's claim to be the rightful successor of Edward the Confessor, were politically of the utmost importance. The concluding depiction of William's coronation in Westminster Abbey set the seal on the new king's legitimacy. 'One of the most powerful pieces of visual propaganda ever produced' is the verdict of one authority.[9] Interpreting its propaganda content is crucial, because the tapestry ranks alongside two written chronicles as one of the very small number of primary sources for the Norman Conquest. Not surprisingly, it has attracted intense scholarly effort from art historians, archaeologists and historians.

There are plenty of reasons, then, why historians should not hold the visual arts at arm's length. It is true that they are the province of a highly specialized academic discipline. Yet art historians are often concerned to extract the last ounce of hidden

Figure 9.2 The centrepiece of the Bayeux Tapestry was the battle of Hastings, during which King Harold was killed. Here that moment is signalled by the Latin text 'Rex Interfectus Est'. The entire tapestry is exhibited in the town of Bayeux (Normandy). © Getty Images/ Hulton Archive.

meaning from the works they study, rather than dwell on their more accessible message. Historians are less inclined to see painting as the product of a coterie or cabal; they are more interested in meanings that were transparent to all, and which were repeated in different works and different media. Above all, historians insist – along with T.J. Clark – that art, like all other survivals of the past, cannot be understood apart from its historical context, which means placing it in its economic, social and cultural milieu. That procedure has the effect of anchoring works of art in specific time and place, rather than viewing them as symptomatic of the 'spirit of the age' (*zeitgeist*), as nineteenth-century scholars tended to do.

II

Popular culture: pre-literate and modern

At first glance the distinction between 'high' culture and popular culture may seem invidious. It carries more than a hint of snobbish elitism. It also loses sight of the capacity of culture to transcend social divisions and speak to all people. This is particularly true of Christian art. During the Renaissance and the **Baroque**, some of the greatest paintings were displayed in churches, where they were intended to intensify the spiritual experience of ordinary worshippers. However, in both history and cultural studies, 'popular' culture holds a recognized place, and for good reasons. Fine art may sometimes have reached out to a popular audience, but very seldom has that been its sole objective; such works were heavily imbued by the aesthetic and symbolic concerns of the artist or the patron, or both. Popular consumption, on the other hand, demands that the cultural product be reasonably transparent, and that it be extensively disseminated. That requirement became much easier to fulfil with the invention of printing in the fifteenth century. Printing held out the possibility, not just of spreading the printed word, but of reaching illiterate people through images. This is a vital corrective to the older notion that illiterate societies are 'outside history' in the sense of being beyond the reach of historical reconstruction.

Reformation Germany provides a striking example. At one level the conflict between the Catholic Church and the followers of Martin Luther was played out within an elite composed of learned theologians and their powerful lay patrons. But grassroots support was also vital to the ambitions of the Reformers. As Luther himself said, images were 'for the sake of children and the simple folk who are more easily moved to recall sacred history by pictures and images than through mere words or doctrines'. R.W. Scribner documented the huge outpouring of cheap prints that lionized the reformers and satirized the Catholic Church in Germany. Most of them included text, but the real

Baroque
The style that prevailed in the visual arts in Europe in the seventeenth century. It was strongly associated with the Catholic Church. It tended to emphasize the dramatic, the emotional and the richly ornate.

meat was provided by images, which were often more complex than the captions accompanying them. This was a new kind of propaganda war, but Scribner pointed out that the association between religion and visual imagery was not new: the laity was encouraged to understand their faith in this way, and late medieval religion was intensely visual in its devotional practices. Inevitably there are limitations to this kind of analysis. We cannot tell whether the visual material brought to light by Scribner reflected popular attitudes to religion, or whether it was just a crude attempt to brainwash the multitude. Nor can we easily tell whether the propaganda modified people's beliefs and behaviour. Yet for an early modern society where literacy was skin-deep, the inventory of Lutheran images is a precious resource.[10]

In modern societies with mass literacy, popular culture requires different emphases. The period between the Reformation and the Industrial Revolution is reckoned to have witnessed a progressive withdrawal of European elites from popular culture, making the distinction between 'high' and 'low' much sharper.[11] By 1900, most Western societies were controlled by modernizing elites. Parliamentary institutions were part of this modernizing model, with a progressively higher proportion of the population entitled to vote. These were the circumstances in which literacy became nearly universal by the beginning of the twentieth century. The historian is presented with a mass of written evidence. Much of it bears on one of the key issues in the study of popular culture: how much of what the working class consumed was genuinely popular, and how much was an attempt by the political elite to impose its values? In late Victorian Britain the most widely read newspapers, like the *Daily Mail,* were owned by individual proprietors with pronounced political views, but circulation depended on addressing the concerns of the readership.

These issues lie at the heart of the controversy about popular attitudes towards imperialism during the Scramble for Africa and the years leading up to the First World War. The Conservative Party – in power for most of the period from 1885 to 1905 – not only supported imperial expansion but believed that it would make the party much more appealing to ordinary voters. The Conservative press therefore promoted an aggressive flag-waving triumphalism known to its critics as 'jingoism'. At the same time, commercial advertisers often used colonial imagery to sell items of domestic consumption (like Bovril and Pears Soap), suggesting a popular identification with the Empire. But cultural forms over which working-class people exercised more control tell a different story. Music hall was at its zenith during this period. Away from the more expensive venues in London's West End, music hall managements needed to be sensitive to the prejudices of their lower-class audience. Enthusiasm for the Empire was muted: there was support for the British soldier, but relative indifference

Figure 9.3 Bovril was invented in the 1880s as a strengthening beef tea. Its advertisements were famous for linking the product with imperialism. Here, British success in the Anglo-Boer War is attributed (in part) to the soldiers' consumption of the product. © Getty Images/ Hulton Archive.

towards the causes for which he was fighting. Another recurrent theme was the pain of saying goodbye to loved ones emigrating overseas. The Empire was woven into the fabric of British society, but the assumption that it was the object of wild popular enthusiasm needs to be treated with some care.[12]

III

Photography and film

For the twentieth century the study of popular culture is transformed by a new medium – photography and film. The photographic camera had been invented in the 1840s, but initially it was a rich person's hobby, and its application was restricted by technical limitations. Photography became more widely accessible in the 1880s with the arrival of cheaper cameras and faster shutter speeds. Photo journalism rapidly spread, while much of the texture of daily life was recorded by a plethora of amateur photographers. By 1905, one in ten of the British population had use of a camera.

How have historians made use of this resource? On any broad definition, photography and film are 'documents': like other primary sources, they provide evidence of the time in which they were created. The difference is that they bring the past before our eyes, apparently short-circuiting the laborious and often unreliable process of working from written sources. Newly discovered film can make a big difference to our sense of 'knowing' the past. In the most dramatic coup of its kind, more than 800 reels of film were found in a disused basement in Blackburn in 1994. Shot between 1901 and 1907 by the partnership of Mitchell and Kenyon, they document the daily life of the town, specializing in crowd scenes such as football matches, temperance parades and workers pouring through the factory gate. Most of the subjects were caught off guard; but others waved and smiled at the camera, knowing that later in the day they could pay to see themselves on screen (since Mitchell and Kenyon were running a thoroughly commercial operation). The films document the visual arrival of the working class – as both subject and audience.[13]

Documentary film became a recognized genre in the 1930s. Its impact on audiences was well understood, with the result that it was often loaded with a social or political message. In the United States the **New Deal** administration commissioned leading photographers to compile a visual record of ordinary people during the Depression. The results were compelling, but they were constrained by very specific guidelines. Smiling was discouraged; people in their Sunday best were told to change into everyday clothes; and only the 'worthy' poor were photographed.[14] Moving film was subject to comparable pressures. Newsreels shown in cinemas were perhaps the main sources of current affairs for British audiences between the World Wars. Yet their potential to critically inform viewers was inhibited by the belief that any hint of political controversy would drive away the audience. The acute social problems of the Depression were not allowed to undermine the upbeat tone of the newsreels. Robert Rosenstone asks 'What does the documentary document?'[15] The answer is that it documents the priorities of the film-maker as much as the slice of life appearing on screen.

Feature film offers much more than a documentary record. It is itself a cultural product, and a particularly powerful one. For three decades – from the invention of 'talkies' until the rise of television – feature films were the British public's principal source of entertainment; in 1946 one third of the entire population went to the cinema at least once a week.[16] The cultural importance of

New Deal
The new directions pursued in the United States by the administration of Franklin D. Roosevelt who took office in 1933 at the height of the Depression. The central plank of the New Deal was direct intervention by the state to stimulate the economy and create jobs.

films was recognized at the time. Film-makers studiously avoided content that could be criticized as too sexual or too political. During the Second World War they were nudged in the direction of propaganda by the government. Much of the routine film output could be described as 'escapist', yet the terms in which the 'good' life (or the lost life) was characterized said much about popular values. As Ross McKibbin points out, audience taste in Britain showed a decided preference for American films, particularly those that emphasized the differences of American from British culture: these were summed up as 'glamour'; but admiration also extended to the competitive individualism that dominated so many American films.[17] After 1945 the prominence given to war films points to a national mood preoccupied by memories of the 'good war' and by a yearning for an outmoded British masculinity.[18]

In 1927 the avant-garde photographer László Moholy-Nagy said, 'the illiteracy of the future will be ignorance of photography'.[19] The intervening years have seen the balance between the textual and the visual drastically shifted in favour of the latter. Yet historians have still not taken the full measure of Moholy-Nagy's statement. In the works of historians, photographs are more often encountered as illustrations, rather than treated as cultural productions requiring critical analysis. Not many scholars are fully informed about the techniques of film-making before the age of digitization – especially those like montage and interpellation, which come between the viewer and the supposed realism of film. The most one can say is that photography and film are taken more seriously than they used to be, both as uniquely revealing sources and as significant features of popular culture.

IV

Writing cultural history

As suggested above, 'culture' and 'cultural history' have come to mean something much broader and more ambitious than the study of visual sources. They stand for the whole spectrum of meaning in the life of society. Visual sources are not excluded, but they take their place alongside all the other forms of human behaviour that are endowed with meaning, which of course means most of them. One example will clarify what is involved in the shift to a cultural perspective. The history of the treatment of mental disorders is a well-established theme in social history; but only recently have historians tried to enter the mentality of the insane and of those who labelled them so – in recognition that the history of madness is, in Roy Porter's words, 'centrally about confrontations between alien thought worlds'.[20] There is all the difference between writing about those mental confrontations and describing the institutions to which the insane were committed:

the first is a cultural approach, the second is social history. Cultural history is a vast and absorbing field, embracing everything from formal belief through ritual and play to the unacknowledged logic of gesture and appearance.

Baldly stated, there is nothing new about this kind of cultural history. Curiosity about – and respect for – the cultural difference of the past is in keeping with the spirit of historicism. Ranke and his followers believed that technique and intuition would enable them to reach across the gulf of time and listen to the past on its own terms. But the emphasis today is rather different. For Ranke, the interpretation of meaning was a means to an end – the recreation of human action and the destiny of nations; the sources were central because they yielded authenticated detail out of which that story could be told. Present-day scholars increasingly study meaning as an end in itself, in the belief that how people interpreted their world and represented their experience is a matter of intrinsic interest. This means that they depart from Ranke's practice in another respect. Whereas he regarded textual meaning as the property of the individual (whose background and attitudes were accordingly central to the enquiry), it is the shared or collective meanings that historians value most today. For this purpose, instinct and empathy are manifestly inadequate. Uncovering collective meanings calls for theoretical sophistication. Cultural history is a contentious field, and one of the reasons is that it is pursued through competing bodies of theory. The three that have proved most illuminating are next described in turn: psychology, literary theory and anthropology.

The Annales *school: a historical psychology?*

The first historians who tried to investigate collective psychology in the past were those of the *Annales* school. The founders of *Annales*, especially Lucien Febvre, called for a *history of mentalities*. In Febvre's view, the worst kind of historical anachronism is psychological anachronism – the unthinking assumption that the mental framework with which people interpreted their experience in earlier periods was the same as our own. What, he asked, were the psychological implications of the differences between night and day and between winter and summer which were experienced much more harshly by medieval men and women than they are today? Febvre called for a 'historical psychology', developed by historians and psychologists working together.[21] Instead of looking at formally articulated principles and ideologies, the history of mentalities is concerned with the emotional, the instinctive and the implicit – areas of thought that have often found no direct expression at all. Robert Mandrou has probably come closest to fulfilling Febvre's programme. In

his *Introduction to Modern France, 1500–1640* (1961) he characterized the outlook of ordinary French people as 'the mentality of
the hunted':[22] helplessness in the face of a hostile environment
and chronic under-nutrition produced a morbid hypersensitivity,
in which people reacted to the least emotional shock by excessive
displays of grief, pity or cruelty.

Freud and 'psychohistory'

Historical psychology raises large theoretical issues, given that
human psychology is such a heavily theorized area of study. Febvre
himself was not especially drawn to theory, but since his day one
of the key questions for historians in this area is how far they
should make use of the findings of psychoanalysis. Freud claimed
that, as a result of his clinical work with neurotic patients, he had
arrived at a theory that placed our understanding of the human
mind on an entirely new and more scientific footing. His theory
turned on the concept of the unconscious – that part of the mind
imprinted by the experience of traumas in infancy (weaning,
toilet-training, Oedipal conflict, etc.) which determines the emotional response of the individual to the world in later life. For
Freud and the many followers who modified or extended his
theory, the primary use of psychoanalysis lay in the treatment of
psychiatric disorders. But Freud himself believed that his theory
also offered a key to the understanding of historical personalities,
and in a famous essay on **Leonardo da Vinci** (written in 1910) he
in effect carried out the first exercise in 'psychohistory'. From the
1950s onwards, this approach to biography enjoyed a considerable
following, especially in the United States, where psychoanalysis
was more widely accepted than in any other country. At its best,
psychohistory introduces a valuable element of psychological
realism into historical biography, as in Bruce Mazlish's controversial study of **James Mill** and **John Stuart Mill** – two lives in
which the intellectual is otherwise particularly likely to obliterate
the emotional.[23] With the benefit of hindsight it is all too easy to
bend the lives of people in the past to a satisfying shape that
emphasizes rationality and steadiness of purpose. Psychohistory,
by contrast, dwells on the complexity and inconsistency of human
behaviour; in Peter Gay's words, it depicts people as

> buffeted by conflicts, ambivalent in their emotions, intent on
> reducing tensions by defensive stratagems, and for the most
> part dimly, or perhaps not at all, aware why they feel and act
> as they do.[24]

In this way the inner drives can be restored to historical figures,
instead of confining their motives to the public sphere in which
their careers were played out.

**Leonardo da Vinci
(1452–1519)**
Italian artist and
engineer. His work was
based upon close
observation of the
natural world; his
notebooks are full of
anatomical sketches as
well as designs for
works of engineering,
although some of the
most apparently far-
seeing of these, such as
his design for a
helicopter, have been
shown to be later
forgeries.

**James Mill
(1773–1836)**
British philosopher and
follower of the utilitarian
ideas of Jeremy
Bentham, which
stressed the need for
modernizing social and
administrative reform in
order to ensure the
greatest happiness of
the greatest number.
His 1817 *History of
British India* criticized
the 'backwardness' of
native Indian culture. He
was the father of John
Stuart Mill.

**John Stuart Mill
(1806–73)**
British philosopher. His
1859 work *On Liberty*
argued the case for
individual freedom
within the growing hold
of the state. Mill was a
committed believer in
female emancipation
and in widening the
parliamentary franchise
into the working class.

The psychology of the collective

The insights of psychoanalysis are not confined to individual lives. Indeed, from the perspective of the cultural historian, the main contribution of psychoanalysis has been to direct attention to *cultural* patterns of parenting, nurture and identification, and to the play of the unconscious in collective mentality. In *The Protestant Temperament* (1977), one of the most wide-ranging applications of a psychoanalytical perspective, Philip Greven identified three patterns of child-rearing in colonial America: the 'evangelical' or authoritarian, the 'moderate' or authoritative, and the 'genteel' or affectionate. While these labels signal the directing influence of theology and social position, the impact of each pattern is traced through the characteristic psychic development of children raised in these ways. Greven described the ensuing personalities or 'temperaments' by reference to attitudes towards the self: hostility in the case of the evangelicals, control in the case of the moderates and indulgence in the case of the genteel. Within a common Freudian framework, Greven's approach made allowance for the cultural diversity of seventeenth- and eighteenth-century America without insisting that every American enacted one of the three models. The appeal of psychoanalytical categories is particularly strong in the case of those facets of the past that we consider irrational or pathological but which made compelling sense to those involved. Racism lends itself to this approach. Models of repression and projection have been used to excellent effect to explain white attitudes to other races during the heyday of colonial expansion – as for example in **Jacksonian America**.[25]

Objections to psychohistory

Of all the technical and methodological innovations made in the past fifty years, psychohistory has attracted the most curiosity outside the profession, but it is also open to quite serious objections, for two principal reasons. First, there is the problem of evidence. Whereas the therapist seeks to recover the infantile experience of the patient through the analysis of dreams, verbal slips and other material produced by the subject, the historian has only the documents, which are likely to contain very little, if any, material of this kind and very few direct observations about the subject's early infancy. Much personal material that we might consider highly relevant is completely unobtainable, yet this is the bricks and mortar without which a psychohistorical theory of personality cannot be devised. Second, there is no reason to assume that the propositions of psychoanalysis hold equally good for previous ages. Indeed, the assumption should rather be the reverse: Freud's picture of emotional development is very culture-bound,

Jacksonian America
The period 1828–37, covering the presidency of Andrew Jackson (1767–1845). Jackson, a successful general from North Carolina, adopted a robust approach to politics. He was a firm believer in keeping the powers of the federal authorities to a minimum; paradoxically, he enforced his view by using his presidential right of veto far more than his predecessors had done. He engaged in a long and generally popular battle against the Bank of the United States, believing it to be an example of centralized tyranny.

rooted in the child-bearing practice and mental attitudes (especially towards sex) of late nineteenth-century middle-class urban society. The application of Freud's insights (or those of any other contemporary school of psychoanalysis) to individuals living in any other period or society is anachronistic. For the structure of human personality over time is precisely what needs to be investigated, instead of being reduced to a formula. Even the notion of the self, which we (like Freud) may regard as a fundamental human attribute, was probably quite foreign to Western culture before the seventeenth or eighteenth century. As one particularly trenchant critic has put it, psychohistory can easily become a determinist form of 'cultural **parochialism**'.[26] Historians who draw on psychoanalytic theory have to be particularly careful to temper their interpretations with a respect for historical context.

parochialism
Narrow-minded concern with one's own immediate locality and concerns without regard to their wider context. 'Parochial' means literally 'referring to a parish'.

V

Literary theory

The second body of theory that bears on cultural history is drawn from literary studies. This is the critical stance towards texts variously known as deconstruction or discourse theory. We saw in Chapter 7 how literary theorists have rejected the notion of the authentic authorial voice, and instead view the text as open to a multiplicity of 'readings' in which different audiences find different meanings. That chapter dwelt on the exceedingly troubling implications that the indeterminacy of texts holds for the epistemological status of history. But it is important to recognize that, at a practical level, the new theories of the text open up the prospect of significant advances in the cultural reconstruction of the past. Traditionally, historians regarded their primary sources as a point of access to events or states of mind – to what had an 'objective' or demonstrable existence beyond the text. Literary theory teaches historians to focus on the text itself, since its value lies less in any reflection of reality than in revealing the categories through which reality was perceived. From this perspective, primary sources are essentially *cultural* evidence – of rhetorical strategies, codes of representation, social metaphors and so on. Literary theory gives historians the confidence to move beyond the letter of the text (the traditional focus of their scholarship) and listen to a wider range of voices that goes well beyond the scope of the injunction to treat the sources as 'witnesses in spite of themselves'. Close reading – or reading 'against the grain' – is even more time-consuming than the time-honoured procedures of historical method, and for this reason it tends to be applied to smaller bodies of source material of considerable textual richness.

Linguistic discourse and the language of politics

These ideas have had a marked impact on the history of political thought. For if language facilitates certain modes of thought while excluding others, and if there is a sense in which language determines consciousness (rather than the other way round, as common sense declares), then the political order must depend on linguistic as much as administrative structures: politics is constituted within a field of discourse, as well as within a particular territory or society. In modern polities there is usually a number of alternative and interlocking discourses jostling for ascendancy – expressing, for example, reverence for the state, class solidarity or ethnic exclusivity. A well-documented example is the English Revolution. Kevin Sharpe argued that prior to 1642, Crown and Parliament still shared many political values, and their disputes were framed by a common respect for the law and for precedent. What was truly revolutionary about the Civil War was that those who rebelled against the king were led to act in ways which their language could not as yet represent. By the end of the seventeenth century, as a result of the Glorious Revolution of 1688–9, the relationship between king and people had been redefined in terms of rights and contract. According to this interpretation, the shift in discourse was no less significant than the institutional and economic changes of the period.[27] A comparable case has been made for the French Revolution. Legitimized under the banner of *liberté*, *egalité*, *fraternité*, the Revolution was among other things 'the invention of a new form of discourse constituting new modes of political and social action'.[28] Language, then, is power. In taking on board this central perception of discourse theory, historians are redefining their understanding of political thought. They are demonstrating how the members of a **polity** experience, reflect and act politically within the conceptual boundaries of particular discourses, and how these discourses are themselves subject to contestation, adaptation and sometimes total rupture.

Discourse analysis also has much to contribute to the historical understanding of nationality – a category traditionally used by historians almost without much reflection. It was pointed out in Chapter 1 how national identity is never 'given', but arises from specific historical circumstances which change over time. If nations are forever being constructed anew or 'invented', much will depend on the elaboration of cultural symbols and on highly selective renderings of the national past. The dissemination of this material to a mass audience is fundamental to nationalism in the modern world. For this reason in *Imagined Communities* (1983) – one of the most influential analyses of nationalism – Benedict Anderson places great weight on 'print capitalism' as a prerequisite for the growth of nationalism since the sixteenth

Liberté, egalité, fraternité
'Liberty, equality, fraternity', the slogan often inscribed on buildings, documents and other forms of officialdom during the French Revolution. It attempted to sum up the essential spirit of the *Declaration of the Rights of Man*.

polity
A state or other entity run by some form of civil government.

century. More detailed work on the languages of patriotism shows how the content of particular nationalisms has changed over time. In England since the **Reformation**, it has had a shifting relation to the monarchy, popular liberties and foreigners – to name just three indicators of political hue. Because 'the nation' is more imaginary than real, the metaphors in which it is expressed have great potency, and their popular meaning – be it democratic or authoritarian – becomes a battleground between rival conceptions of the political order.[29]

The language-led approach to texts is also evident in the attention that some historians are now giving to the literary form – or genre – in which their sources are written. Here, the argument is that our interpretation of the ostensible content of a text may need to be considerably modified in the light of the genre to which it belonged – and which conditioned the understanding of its readers. When Natalie Zemon Davis studied the **letters of remission** submitted to the French courts in the sixteenth century by supplicants seeking a royal pardon, she soon realized that they could not be regarded simply as direct personal statements. They were drawn up by **notaries** in an avowedly literary way which reflected several contemporary genres, including fictional ones, each with its own conventions. 'I am after evidence of how sixteenth-century people told stories', she writes,

> ... what they thought a good story was, how they accounted for motive and how through narrative they made sense of the unexpected and built coherence into immediate experience.[30]

Davis calls her book *Fiction in the Archives*, not because she regards the letters of remission as fabrications, but to draw attention to the essentially literary issues that they pose. The question of whether the supplicants were guilty is here subordinated to questions of meaning and representation.

VI

Anthropology

But for recent historians the most fertile source of ideas in the area of collective mentality has been not textual theory but *cultural anthropology*. Although the relevance to history of the study of small-scale societies of the present day may not be readily apparent, there are good reasons why historians should be alert to the findings of anthropology. These reasons are most obvious in the case of those historians who are themselves specializing in some area of Third World history, but they apply also to their colleagues in more conventional fields. The findings of anthropology suggest something of the range of mentalities to be found

Reformation
In England, the process of religious change in the early sixteenth century in which the English Church first renounced the authority of the papacy in favour of that of the monarch and then established a form of Protestantism known as Anglicanism.

letters of remission
Official letters requesting a royal pardon or a reduction in the sentence imposed by a court.

notaries
Legal clerks with the authority to draw up legal documents.

blood feud
A bitter conflict, often involving the families and friends of the protagonists and stretching over more than one generation.

among people who are acutely vulnerable to the vagaries of climate and disease, who lack 'scientific' control of their environment and who are tied to their own localities – conditions that obtained in the West during most of the medieval and early modern periods. Certain long-lost features of our own society such as the **blood feud** or witchcraft accusations still persist in some parts of the world today; direct observation of the modern variant prompts a sounder grasp of the relevant questions to be asked about comparable features in our own past for which the direct evidence may be very sparse or uneven. The classic demonstration of this is Keith Thomas's *Religion and the Decline of Magic* (1971) which drew on the studies of Evans-Pritchard and other ethnographers to define a new agenda for the study of witchcraft in early modern England. For historians encountering a past society through the medium of documentary sources there is – or ought to be – the same sense of 'culture shock' that the modern field-worker experiences in a remote and 'exotic' community.

The anthropology of mentality

Since Thomas's path-breaking work the relevance of anthropology to the cultural historian has broadened to become one of method and theory, not just a source of suggestive analogies. The key issue is how anthropologists get to grips with the world-view of their subjects. Because they conduct their research by combining the roles of participant and observer, anthropologists can hardly fail to register the vastly different mental assumptions that operate in pre-literate, technologically simple societies. Indeed 'mentality' is at the heart of their specialist expertise, and the concept of 'culture' now most in vogue with historians is essentially an anthropological one. In fieldwork, anthropologists pay special attention to symbolic behaviour – such as a naming ceremony or a rain-making ritual – partly because the sense of strangeness is then most challenging, and partly because symbol and ritual are seldom one-dimensional but express a complex range of cultural values; the seemingly bizarre and irrational tend to reflect a coherence of thought and behaviour which in the last resort is what holds society together. The influential American anthropologist Clifford Geertz referred to his own cultural readings of very densely textured, concrete behaviour as 'thick description': one episode – in the best-known case a Balinese cock-fight – may provide a window on an entire culture, provided we do not impose on it a coherence that makes sense in our terms.[31] There is an interesting convergence with literary theory here: just as a text is open to many readings, so a ritual or symbol may yield a range of meanings. Geertz himself regarded culture as being like an assemblage of texts, and he explains the goal of cultural anthropology in terms of 'the text analogy'.[32]

Since descriptions of ritual provide some of our best evidence for pre-literate societies of the past, it is not surprising that historians have welcomed the insights of cultural anthropology. Natalie Zemon Davis is one of many historians who acknowledge the influence of Geertz. She invokes the 'text analogy' in describing her work on sixteenth-century French society:

> A journeyman's initiation rite, a village festive organization, an informal gathering of women for a **lying-in**, or of men and women for story-telling or a street disturbance could be 'read' as fruitfully as a diary, a political tract, a sermon or a body of laws.[33]

lying-in
Childbirth.

The mass in late medieval England, the carnival in early modern France and the rituals of monarchy are just some of the symbolic material that has attracted enquiry along these lines. In a bravura demonstration of the technique of 'thick description', Robert Darnton has analysed the trivial episode of a cat-killing by apprentice printers in Paris during the 1730s. By placing the reminiscences of one of the printers in the context of a varied range of contemporary cultural evidence, Darnton shows how the massacre of cats combined veiled elements of a witch-hunt, a workers' revolt and a rape – which is why the apprentices found it such a hugely amusing way of letting off steam. 'To get the joke in the case of something as unfunny as a ritual slaughter of cats is a first step towards "getting" the culture.'[34] In this kind of history, carefully observed detail really counts, often several times over.

The limitations of anthropology

Darnton's cat massacre demonstrates the excitement of this approach – but also its limitations. Whereas the anthropologist, as a participant-observer, is in a position to observe the ritual and generate additional contextual evidence, the historian has to accept the limits of the sources. The cat-killing is described in only one account, and a retrospective one at that. Darnton treats the cat-killing as a workers' revolt which prefigured the French Revolution. But, as Raphael Samuel points out, the story could just as well have served an analysis of adolescent culture or a study of social attitudes towards animals; a single source lends itself all too readily to 'symbolic overloading'.[35] Cultural historians are for the most part thrown back on oblique and ambiguous evidence of what went on in the minds of ordinary people, and it is appropriate to recognize these limitations before wholeheartedly embracing the interpretative procedures of cultural anthropology or textual theory. In fact, the value of the anthropological approach lies as much in its general orientation as in its handling of detail. It serves as a strong reminder that history is not just about trends and structures that can be observed from the outside, but also demands an informed respect for the culture of people in the past and a readiness to see the world through their eyes.

VII

The impact of the cultural turn

Twenty years ago most social history, and much political history also, was confidently written in terms of coherent collectivities such as class and nation. It made sense to write about 'the working class' or 'the French nation' because these groups were grounded in a shared existence from which they derived a common, defining consciousness, extending beyond the life span of the individuals who happened to constitute the group at any one time. This was most explicit in the case of the Marxists' handling of class and class consciousness, but liberal scholarship was little different in its treatment of political parties, religious denominations and nations as historical actors spanning the generations. In both liberal and Marxist writing, these social identities acquired an almost material reality, which served to drive forward 'grand narratives' of progress or revolutionary destiny. By the 1970s this social, material and progressive paradigm may not have taken over the mainstream, but it undoubtedly represented the cutting edge and was the focus of the most important historiographical debates.

That social paradigm has come under attack from two directions. First in the field were the *Annales* historians with their emphasis on collective mentalities. They had, from the beginning, asserted that no picture of the past could be complete without a reconstruction of its mental landscape. Braudel incorporated mentalities into his structural scheme by including them alongside geographical factors in his *longue durée*. By the 1980s, the leading *Annalistes* were claiming more than this, declaring that mentality was the fundamental level of historical experience, and culture its principal expression. As Georges Duby has put it:

> Men's [sic] behaviour is shaped not so much by their real condition as by their usually untruthful image of that condition, by behavioural models which are cultural productions bearing only a partial resemblance to material realities.[36]

By the 1990s, the main impetus for the attack on the social paradigm came from textual theory, with its assault on referential notions of representation. It proved to be a short step from rejecting authentic meaning in texts to fracturing accepted social identities, since what does identity depend on if not a shared language and shared symbols? Class, race and nation all lost their 'hard' objective character and became no more than unstable discourses. Social historians had appealed to 'experience', but the foundational status of experience was now questioned on the grounds that it had no existence prior to language.[37] Culture itself was seen as a construction, rather than a reflection of reality. The Postmodernist attack on 'grand narratives' completed the job of demolition, by discrediting the persistence of active social identities over time. What is left is the study of representation – of how meanings are constructed, not what people in the past did. Cultural history is the principal beneficiary of this shift in historical thinking because the priority it gives to language makes questions of meaning and representation more important than anything else. The consequences can be unsettling. For example, the dominant theme of Italian history in the nineteenth century is usually taken to be the Risorgimento – the movement to unite Italy under Italian rule (finally achieved in 1870). It has long been studied as a series of political and military initiatives, dominated by the charismatic figure of Garibaldi and his mobilization of popular support in many parts of Italy. The Risorgimento is no less studied today, but in recent books the focus has shifted away from the political and military drama. Italian national feeling is now viewed as an essentially cultural phenomenon (as in opera and novels), and Garibaldi is reproached as the maker of his own legend – an 'invented hero' rather than the great general of popular renown. Italian unity becomes a chimera.[38]

The benefits and limitations of the cultural agenda

If taken to extremes, it is clear that the cultural turn would undermine much of the traditional agenda of historians. The issue is starkly posed when representation is proposed as the *only* legitimate field of historical study. An article by Patrick Joyce advocating just this was provocatively titled 'The end of social history?'[39] By this he meant that the history of class and class relations in the mould of E.P. Thompson no longer has validity; in his own writing Joyce has, for example, analysed the subject of industrial work in cultural rather than economic terms, thus detaching it from labour history.[40] For all its rhetorical skill, Joyce's position has found little favour with other historians. It amounts to an acceptance of the Postmodernist charge-sheet against history as usually practised. Most of the profession is little inclined to see the scope of their work pared down to the indeterminate dimensions of discourse, and this goes for the majority of cultural historians too. Taking representation seriously does not necessarily mean disparaging everything else. Nor does a cultural agenda signal a minimalist position on the issue of historical truth. Most historians working in the field acknowledge the positive ways in which textual theory has enriched the subject, without taking on board its destructive epistemology.

Yet the difference of emphasis remains. The historian of class conflict is doing something different from one who analyses industrial relations as a ritual bound by the conventions of a game; writing a traditional political history produces different results from a focus on the cultural instability of national identity; and so on. This difference is crucially one of theory. For the first group of historians, the subject of their research usually holds interest because of its place in a social narrative, which in turn is interpreted by reference to a dynamic theory of social change (sometimes Marxist). The second group, on the other hand, is essentially interested in contextualizing – in making cultural connections within a single plane, as it were, often with scant attention to changes over time. Theories of the mind, of the text and of culture itself provide the conceptual underpinning for this work, and they too serve to enrich contextual understandings rather than illuminate historical process. Once again, as in Chapter 1, we see the tension in historical writing between the explanatory mode and the recreative mode. Social theory continues the agenda set in the Enlightenment of interpreting the direction of human history; events and processes are deemed significant in terms of the place they hold in a more extended narrative. Cultural theory takes up the historicists' emphasis on the inherent strangeness of the past, and the need for intellectual effort to interpret its meaning. This chapter and Chapter 8 have described two quite different kinds of history, and the conflict between them is very much of our time. But the tension they reflect is as old as the discipline itself.

Further reading

Simon Gunn, *History and Cultural Theory*, Longman, 2006.

Sarah Barber and Corinna M. Peniston-Bird (eds), *History Beyond the Text: A Student's Guide to Approaching Alternative Sources*, Routledge, 2009.

Peter Burke, *Eyewitnessing*, Reaktion, 2001.

Ludmilla Jordanova, *The Look of the Past: Visual and Material Evidence in Historical Practice,* Cambridge University Press, 2012.

Marnie Hughes-Warrington, *History Goes to the Movies: Studying History on Film*, Routledge, 2007.

Peter Gay, *Freud for Historians*, Oxford University Press, 1985.

Sally Alexander and Barbara Taylor (eds), *History and Psyche: Culture, Psychoanalysis and the Past*, Palgrave Macmillan, 2012.

Peter Burke, *What Is Cultural History?*, 2nd edn, Polity Press, 2008.

Karen Harvey (ed.), *History and Material Culture*, Routledge, 2009.

Lynn Hunt (ed.), *The New Cultural History*, California University Press, 1989.

Notes

1 Raymond Williams, *Keywords*, Fontana, 1983, p. 87.
2 Peter Burke, *Popular Culture in Early Modern Europe*, Temple Smith, 1978, p. 270.
3 Carolyn Steedman, 'Culture, cultural studies and the historians', in Lawrence Grossberg et al. (eds), *Cultural Studies*, Routledge, 1992, p. 617.
4 Erwin Panofsky, *Studies in Iconology*, Harper & Row, 1962, ch. 6.
5 T.J. Clark, *The Image of the People: Gustave Courbet and the 1848 Revolution*, Thames & Hudson, 1973.
6 Stephen Bann, *Under the Sign*, University of Michigan Press, 1994, p. 122.
7 Peter Burke, *Eyewitnessing*, Reaktion, 2001.
8 Karen Harvey (ed.), *History and Material Culture*, Routledge, 2009.
9 Suzanne Lewis, *The Rhetoric of Power in the Bayeux Tapestry*, Cambridge University Press, 1999, p. xiii.
10 R.W. Scribner, *For the Sake of Simple Folk*, 2nd edn, Oxford University Press, 1995. The quotation from Luther is on p. 244.
11 Burke, *Popular Culture in Early Modern Europe*.
12 John MacKenzie (ed.), *Propaganda and Empire*, Manchester University Press, 1986; Bernard Porter, *The Absent-Minded Imperialists*, Oxford University Press, 2004.
13 Vanessa Toulmin et al. (eds), *The Lost World of Mitchell and Kenyon: Edwardian Britain on Film*, BFI, 2004.
14 Abigail Solomon-Godeau, *Photography at the Dock*, Minnesota University Press, 1991, pp. 177–9.
15 Robert A. Rosenstone, *History on Film/Film on History*, Longman, 2006, p. 70.
16 Ross McKibbin, *Classes and Cultures in England, 1918–51*, Oxford University Press, 1998, p. 419.
17 Ibid., pp. 431–5.
18 John Ramsden, *The Dam Busters*, I.B. Tauris, 2002.
19 László Moholy-Nagy, quoted in Derak Sayer, 'The photograph: the still image', in Sarah Barber and Corinna M. Peniston-Bird (eds), *History Beyond the Text: A Student's Guide to Approaching Alternative Sources*, Routledge, 2009, p. 49.
20 Roy Porter, *Mind Forg'd Manacles: A History of Madness in England from the Restoration to the Regency*, Athlone, 1987, p. x.
21 Lucien Febvre, 'History and psychology', 1938, reprinted in Peter Burke (ed.), *A New Kind of History*, Routledge & Kegan Paul, 1973.
22 Robert Mandrou, *Introduction to Modern France, 1500–1640: An Essay in Historical Psychology*, Arnold, 1975 (French edition 1961), p. 26.
23 Bruce Mazlish, *James and John Stuart Mill: Father and Son in the Nineteenth Century*, Hutchinson, 1975.
24 Peter Gay, *Freud for Historians*, Oxford University Press, 1985, p. 75.
25 Michael P. Rogin, *Fathers and Children: Andrew Jackson and the Subjection of the American Indian*, Knopf, 1975.
26 David E. Stannard, *Shrinking History: On Freud and the Failure of Psychohistory*, Oxford University Press, 1980, p. 30.
27 Kevin Sharpe, *Politics and Ideas in Early Stuart England*, Frances Pinter, 1989, ch. 1.
28 Keith Baker, 'On the problem of the ideological origins of the French Revolution', in Dominick La Capra and Steven L. Kaplan (eds), *Modern European Intellectual History: Reappraisals and New Perspectives*, Cornell University Press, 1982, p. 204.
29 Raphael Samuel (ed.), *Patriotism: The Making and Unmaking of the British National Identity*, 3 vols, Routledge, 1989.

30 Natalie Zemon Davis, *Fiction in the Archives*, Polity Press, 1987, p. 4.

31 Clifford Geertz, *The Interpretation of Cultures*, Hutchinson, 1975, ch. 1.

32 Clifford Geertz, *Local Knowledge: Further Essays in Interpretive Anthropology*, Fontana, 1983.

33 Natalie Zemon Davis, *Society and Culture in Early Modern France*, Duckworth, 1975, pp. xvi–xvii.

34 Robert Darnton, *The Great Cat Massacre and Other Episodes in French Cultural History*, Allen Lane, 1984, p. 262.

35 Raphael Samuel, 'Reading the signs: II', *History Workshop Journal*, XXX, 1992, pp. 235–8, 243.

36 Georges Duby, 'Ideologies in social history', in Jacques Le Goff and Pierre Nora (eds), *Constructing the Past: Essays in Historical Methodology*, Cambridge University Press, 1985, p. 151.

37 Joan Scott, 'The evidence of experience', *Critical Inquiry*, XVII, 1991, pp. 773–97.

38 See for example Lucy Riall, *Garibaldi: Invention of a Hero*, Yale University Press, 2007.

39 Patrick Joyce, 'The end of social history?', *Social History*, XX, 1995, pp. 73–91.

40 Patrick Joyce (ed.), *The Historical Meaning of Work*, Cambridge University Press, 1987.

10 Gender history and postcolonial history

This chapter examines some of the most dramatic extensions of history's subject matter. Fifty years ago women were ignored, and Third World countries were treated in a narrowly Western perspective. Today, women's and gender history is regarded as central to the understanding of the past. Meanwhile postcolonial historians are not only developing histories of Africa and Asia 'from below', but are insisting that the history of the former colonial powers be reassessed from the perspective of the colonized.

Placing gender history and postcolonial history in the same chapter may seem an odd procedure – even a demeaning one if it suggests that women and Third World societies can be lumped together as marginal add-ons. My treatment of them should dispel any such impression. The reason for considering them together is that they raise comparable opportunities and problems for historians. Both aspire to give a voice to huge constituencies that previously had no place in the historical record; and in doing so, both have thrown up challenges to what historians do, critiquing their methods and even the validity of their practice. Women's history and postcolonial history not only represent an incremental enlargement of the range of historical study; they have the potential to modify the character of the discipline as a whole.

I

Women's history

That outcome seemed highly unlikely when women's history was first formulated during the 1970s. As described in Chapter 1, women's history emerged as a feature of Women's Liberation. It was part of a broad feminist strategy to contest the masculinist assumptions of academic knowledge. The pioneers of women's history were not only curious about the lives of women in the past; they understood that reclaiming those lives was essential to a fully formed women's consciousness in the present.

Owenism

Robert Owen
(1771–1858) was a Welsh
industrialist whose
experiments in running
his spinning mill at New
Lanark in Scotland along
humanitarian and
co-operative lines led him
to found the Grand
National Consolidated
Trades' Union to
represent the entire
skilled working class. The
union was killed off in
1834 when a group of
farm labourers at
Tolpuddle in Dorset was
transported to Australia
for swearing an oath of
loyalty to it. However,
Owen's ideals were
revived ten years later by
a group of trade unionists
in Rochdale, Lancashire,
who founded the first
co-operative movement,
in which all members
would sink their
subscription into a
central fund, which would
be used to maintain a
co-operative shop that
could sell goods to
members at lower prices
than elsewhere. Co-op
shops are still found on
the high street today.

Chartism

A working-class political
movement in the 1830s
and 1840s. It derived its
name from the People's
Charter, drawn up in
1838, which laid out a
comprehensive set of
proposals for the reform
of Parliament.

'angel mother'

The image, often found in
Victorian literature and
popular culture, of a
mother who is at once
beautiful, caring, dutiful
and obedient.

Part of the required political energy was generated by studies of women's daily lives that highlighted their subordination to men. History provided some of the most compelling evidence for the centuries-long existence of patriarchy, and awareness of the extent of patriarchy was central to consciousness-raising. The other source of political energy was the lives of those women who had taken action to resist the political and social oppression of their day. Explicitly feminist organizations, like the suffragists and suffragettes of Edwardian Britain, were an obvious focus. More surprising was the role found to have been played by women in organizations like **Owenism** and **Chartism**, which have gone down in history as masculine preserves.[1] The effect of such studies was to demonstrate that women had a history, not only in a separate strand, but as an integral element of 'mainstream' history.

In the course of assembling historical material supportive of feminist objectives, women's historians touched the concerns of several established branches of history. Initially their impact was least in the field of political history, since until the twentieth century women had no standing in political systems. The principal impact of women's history was on social history. This was an obvious consequence of the priority given by feminism to ordinary women's lives, and the existing social history was on particularly weak ground in justifying its prevalent male-centred perspective. One example of the social emphasis of women's history was its engagement with labour history. Accounting for the ebb and flow of women's employment since the Industrial Revolution proved to be an illuminating angle on the workings of capitalism – whether the focus was on female spinners and weavers in the early Lancashire cotton mills or the munitions workers who substituted for men at the front during the First World War.[2]

It is with regard to the family that the social impact of women's history has been greatest. Historians in the 1960s had conducted a rather narrow debate about household size and levels of fertility, mostly using quantitative analyses.[3] Other scholars had studied the family through the lens of didactic literature – the homilies that have been written in every generation to advise couples how to behave towards each other and how to raise their children. The new focus on women drew attention to the internal dynamics of the family in terms of power, nurture and dependence. A variety of qualitative sources – court records, diaries, letters – were scoured for evidence, not of the statistical norm, but of life as it was actually experienced in specific families. But this was not straightforward reclamation. The consequence was the undermining of some unexamined assumptions. For example, the ornamental **'angel mother'** of Victorian family piety turned out to be more independent, more given to philanthropic work outside the home and more likely to be in conflict with her

Figure 10.1 In the late 1960s and early 1970s, the Women's Liberation movement led to the development of a feminist approach to history, which sought to bring out the contribution of women and the many ways in which they were held down by the male-dominated societies of the past. © Corbis/Bettmann.

husband than the popular stereotype suggests.[4] As a result of this and other work, the whole realm of the private – as distinct from the public world of conventional history – is being brought within the scope of historical understanding.

Particularly during its early years in the 70s and 80s, women's history identified more readily with women's studies than with the discipline of history. Key articles were often published in *Signs* (USA) or *The Feminist Review* (Britain). Because of this alignment, readers sometimes expect to find a consistent political line. In fact, feminism is no less divided than other ideologies, and this was reflected in debates within women's history from the start. Thus in the 1970s and 1980s the reassessment of the 'angel mother' was a conflicted process, particularly in America. Much depended on how the notion of 'separate spheres' was interpreted in practice. One group of historians emphasized the controlling power of patriarchy and the corresponding victimhood of women in the early nineteenth century. Another group put a more positive spin on the domestic confinement of women: subservience to men, it was said, did not stop them from developing an autonomous women's culture (or 'sisterhood') which later made possible a growth in feminist awareness.[5] Women's roles in trade, in religion and in modern warfare have been the subject of other historical controversies, confirming the intellectual vitality of women's history.

An early modern case-study

The book that best sums up this phase of women's history is Olwen Hufton's *The Prospect Before Her* (1995), an extraordinarily wide-ranging and learned survey of women in Europe from 1500 to 1800. It is structured around the defining phases of women's life cycles, from girlhood through marriage and motherhood to widowhood. Special attention is given to those who stood outside the conventional life story – single women, nuns, sex workers and so on. Hufton's book is social history on a grand scale, in which large generalizations are combined with vivid incidents in individual lives. Viewed critically as a piece of women's history, the most important point about *The Prospect Before Her* is that the many historical contexts in which women lived during this period are fully mastered and deftly interwoven with the analysis. This is particularly true of religion: the Reformation and its profound consequences for all branches of Christianity are highlighted, in a way which for many readers brings home the historical distance between them and their Early Modern forebears.

Hufton's work also raises the question of audience. The first forays in women's history had been written for a readership that was not only female but feminist, in that it was looking for a politically relevant reading of the past. *The Prospect Before Her* is addressed more to the generality of historians. It not only contextualizes women's past experience, it makes that experience manifestly part of the more familiar themes of the period, such as poverty, domestic service and religious vocation. It is thus a major contribution to the social history of early modern Europe. In this respect Hufton was in tune with the younger generation of women's historians who were coming to the fore during the 1980s and 1990s. They were less interested in raising feminist consciousness than in changing the terms on which the study of history was pursued.

Moving on from 'women's history'

As a mature historical practice, women's history is today characterized by three principles which together open the way for its integration into mainstream history. First, 'woman' is no longer seen as a single undifferentiated social category. In America women's history faced a critical period of soul-searching when African-American historians took issue with the white middle-class focus of women's history to that point. In addition to race, class and sexual orientation have had an immense influence on how women are perceived – and also on how they perceive themselves – and most historical work now relates to specific groups rather than womanhood in general. This enhances the bearing of women's history on social history, where these distinctions are central. Second, just as the category of 'woman' has been disaggregated, so too has the notion of a uniform and constant oppression by men. The term 'patriarchy' has been criticized as implying that sexual difference is *the* fundamental principle of stratification in human society, present in all periods and thus 'outside' history; by claiming to explain everything, it explains nothing. 'Patriarchy' can still usefully be used to denote sexual hierarchy in the household, particularly where men control a form of domestic production, as they did in pre-industrial Europe. But the record of the past shows immense variety in the extent of oppression, resistance, accommodation and convergence in relations between men and women, and the task of the historian is to explain this variation rather than subsume it under a universal principle of sexual oppression.[6]

Third and most challenging of all, women's history has increasingly taken the history of men within its scope: not men in their traditional guise of genderless autonomous beings, but men in relation to the other half of humanity. This means that men are considered historically as sons and husbands, while in the public sphere, men's exclusion of women becomes a matter for investigation, instead of being taken for granted. As Jane Lewis has put it:

> our understanding of the sex/gender system can never hope to be complete until we have a deliberate attempt to understand the total fabric of men's worlds and the construction of masculinity.[7]

That last phrase stands for a very extensive historical agenda. History may have been a male monopoly for centuries, but understanding masculinity was not part of the project. As a result of work in this area, we now take for granted, for example, that the soldiers who manned the trenches in the First World War were motivated not just by the call of king and country, but by a code of masculinity instilled by school, juvenile literature and youth organizations.[8]

II

Gender history and relations between the sexes

These new directions in women's history entail a change of name: *gender history* signals the aspiration to move beyond an exclusively women's perspective to modify the writing of *all* history. It is by no means the only current within women's history, but it holds out the greatest promise for the discipline as a whole. In current usage, 'gender' means the social organization of sexual difference. It embodies the assumption that most of what passes for natural (or God-given) sexual difference is in fact socially and culturally constructed, and must therefore be understood as the outcome of historical process. (Of course it is that very confusion between nature and culture that has given stratification by gender such staying power, and has caused it to escape notice in much of the historical record.) The focus of gender history is less on the predicament of one sex than on the whole field of relations *between* the sexes. And this field includes not just the obvious points of contact such as marriage and sex, but all social relations and all political institutions which, on this view, are in varying degrees structured by gender: by the exclusion of women, by the polarization of masculine and feminine attributes, and so on. Men are no less constructed by gender than women are. Both men's social power and their 'masculine' qualities can only be apprehended as aspects of a gender system: neither 'natural' nor constant, but defined by a shifting relation to the feminine. This perspective underlies recent writing on the tortuous evolution of the term 'manliness' since the early modern period, and the best work on the history of the family.[9] Because both sexes can only be correctly understood in relational terms, the history of gender is conceptually equipped to attain a fully comprehensive social reach and to feature in any serious theory of social structure and social change.

Gender history and Marxist theory

Comparisons with Marxist history are illuminating. Gender history has experienced the same tension between the demands of historical explanation and the politics of emancipation as the history of class has done. With its potential for a comprehensive social analysis, gender history also promises at the very least to make good some of the deficiencies of Marxist theory. Marxist historians are second to none in analysing production, but their theory gives much less weight to reproduction – whether viewed as a biological event or a process of socialization. More broadly, gender history has the effect of collapsing the rigid distinction between the public and private spheres which has informed almost all historical writing. That this distinction may have obscured the true complexity of economic and social life in the past is strongly indicated by Leonore Davidoff and Catherine Hall's *Family Fortunes* (1987). Their central thesis is that in early nineteenth-century England one of the key objectives of the burgeoning business world was to support the family and domesticity – and conversely that the approved domestic traits of middle-class men (sobriety, sense of duty and so on) answered to the requirements of entrepreneurial and professional life. In work of this kind, the historical relationship of gender and class begins to be uncovered in all its intricate particularity.

III

Gender and the cultural history of meaning

Thus far, gender has been characterized as a tool for deepening our understanding of the social structures of the past. But gender is not only a structural question. It touches on subjectivity and identity in profound ways. These perspectives are best considered as the province of the cultural turn. They do not have the same political resonance as the classic feminist agenda of consciousness-raising, patriarchy and resistance. Indeed the popularity of cultural approaches to women's history reflects in many cases a disenchantment with political feminism – as having either gone far enough or being doomed to failure in attempting to achieve more. The cultural turn is also in tune with broader contemporary changes in gender and sexuality. Sexual difference is today seen less as a biological given, and increasingly as a matter of personal choice, mediated by culture. Once the traditional binary distinction between male and female is modified to take account of the gender diversity that actually exists, the articulation of masculinities and femininities becomes more and more a matter of psychology and culture. Last, the cultural turn bears on the vexed question of primary evidence – always a problem for historians bent on recovering a hidden past. The cultural turn makes a virtue of the paucity of documentation by reading the texts as 'discourse': not imprisoned within a single meaning, but open to diverse – and even subversive – readings.

The cultural creation of gender

In practical terms, this shift means two things. First, if gender difference is not principally a matter of nature or instinct, it must be instilled. Parents may experience this as an individual task, but it is essentially cultural in character, since those who are charged with childcare operate within certain cultural understandings of sexual difference and personality development. Gender, in short, is knowledge. Until the very recent past, sexual difference was naturalized (and simplified) into predetermined scripts which most people did not question. Those forms of knowledge took a variety of forms: explicit knowledge about the body, as in sex manuals such as *Aristotle's Masterpiece* (repeatedly reprinted in England throughout the eighteenth century and beyond); or heavily moralized teaching about sexual character, as in nineteenth-century writings about the proper lady; or again, the assumptions about sexual difference that pervade literature in both its elite and popular forms. Recent historians have given close attention to all this material, tracking the contradictions and subtle shifts of emphasis against the bedrock assumptions that remained firm for generations.[10]

The second dimension of the cultural approach to gender takes up the issue of difference. All social identities work partly by a process of exclusion. We are defined as much by what we are not, as by what we are. Often the negative stereotyping of those beyond the pale is just as powerful as the corresponding belief in what members have in common. In the case of sexual difference, defining the self in relation to 'the other' is particularly pronounced because the social consciousness of most young children is predicated on a fundamental distinction between male and female. All attributes can be mapped on to this binary opposition. Hence all gender definitions are relational, in the sense that they arise from interaction with the other sex and express assumptions about that sex: the enduring discourse of 'effeminacy' as a boundary for men's behaviour bears ample witness to that. Discourse is vital to this process of 'othering', partly because binary structures are deeply embedded in language (good vs. bad, black vs. white, etc.), and partly because language registers this opposition between male and female in an endless variety of culturally specific forms. In psychoanalysis, the tradition associated with **Jacques Lacan** also places prime emphasis on language as the means by which children acquire their sexed identities.[11]

One field in which the discourse approach has proved particularly fruitful is the history of sexuality. As defined in recent work, this is a broader theme than might be imagined. It can be studied through the prism of medical knowledge, or as a set of legal definitions and prohibitions, reflected in the social mores of the day.[12] The approach that has most resonance with contemporary sexual politics prioritizes the question of identity. At what point, for example, did men and women begin to categorize themselves – and each other – as 'heterosexual' and 'homosexual'? And were these exclusive categories? The answers given by historians have become more complicated since the pioneering studies in the 1970s. Matt Houlbrook shows that in the first half of the twentieth century 'queer London' did not comprise a single homosexual identity. He draws on a range of vivid personal evidence to distinguish three types: the effeminate self-dramatizing 'queen', the discreet middle-class homosexual, and the working-class man who had sex with both women and men and regarded himself as 'normal'. In the period covered by Houlbrook, all homosexual acts were still against the law. The story he tells is as much concerned with evasion and entrapment as with self-discovery – a reminder that homophobia has deep historical roots.[13]

Jacques Lacan (1901–81)
One of the most influential psychoanalysts of the twentieth century. A French Freudian, he developed a 'structural psychoanalysis' which explored the relationship between language, texts and the unconscious. He became a central theorist for the linguistic turn, and thus for an influential strand of cultural studies. Although Lacan had little to say about history, he has been drawn upon by psychoanalytical historians.

Gender and the new polarities of power

The fracturing of identity that is now found in gay history and other branches of gender history is a far cry from the earlier feminist emphasis on the common experience and common oppression summed up in 'sisterhood'. Once representation and discourse are given full play, 'identity' cannot be frozen at this macro-level; dissecting the complex web of meanings in which individuals situate themselves has the effect of breaking down these large categories by opening up fissures along lines of class, nation, ethnicity, region, age, sexuality and so on. The notion of women as a collectivity becomes hard to sustain. That does not mean, however, that gender has become drained of political content; instead gender history reflects a different kind of politics. Joan Scott argues strongly that a linguistic approach serves to expose the gender dimension of all power relations. Her argument hinges on two closely related propositions. First, gender is a structural (or 'constitutive') element of all social relationships, from the most intimate to the most impersonal, because there is always an assumption either of the exclusion of one sex, or of a carefully regulated (and usually unequal) relationship between the sexes. Second, gender is an important way in which relationships of power are signified in cultural terms.[14] To take a recurrent case, the uncompromisingly 'masculine' terms in which war is referred to have for a very long time served to legitimate the sacrifice of life that young men are called upon to endure. In the Victorian era the idea of state-funded welfare was damned as 'sentimentality' – a feminine attribute – by its enemies.[15] Many other comparable examples could be cited. Furthermore, these gendered meanings should not be seen as static or given, and an obvious task for politically informed analysis is to trace their reinterpretation and contestation in different contexts. Gender history of the cultural variety may be resistant to the solid collectivities of old, but it has much to contribute to an understanding of how power is articulated in personal and social relations.

This point can be illustrated with reference to the scholarly career of Judith Walkowitz. Her first book, published in 1980, analysed prostitution in Victorian society through the prism of class and gender: it documented the double sexual standard of the day, the material exploitation of the prostitutes and the political strategies of those who wished to repeal the **draconian** legislation that regulated the trade. Its political sympathies were plain – indeed the help of the Women's Liberation movement is explicitly acknowledged.[16] Twelve years later, Walkowitz followed this up with *City of Dreadful Delight* (1992), a study of sexual scandals and sexual discourses in London during the 1880s. Within the perspective of the earlier book, child prostitution and **Jack the Ripper** – the main subjects here – would have invited a materialist analysis of the vice trade and the power relations between procurers, prostitutes and clients. These matters are not ignored, but Walkowitz is now less interested in what happened than in what was *represented* as happening. The book's subtitle,

draconian
Excessively harsh.

Jack the Ripper
The nickname current at the time and since for the perpetrator of a series of extremely brutal murders of prostitutes in Whitechapel, in the East End of London, in 1888. Speculation about the identity of the murderer, which has led to accusations against, among others, a famous painter and a member of the royal family, has spawned a virtual industry of 'ripperologists'. The fascination the case continues to exert is as interesting to historians as the original murders themselves.

'*Narratives of Sexual Danger in Late-Victorian London*', accurately reflects her concern with which stories prevailed and why. But, as she emphasizes, this is a deeply political question, since popular notions of sexual character and sexual morality were contained within a regulatory discourse, of which the newspaper press was merely one element. *City of Dreadful Delight* may lack the political bite of the earlier book, but it is a fine study of the cultural processes that make some gender discourses hegemonic, while marginalizing others.

There can, then, be no simple answer to the question 'What has gender history contributed to the discipline as a whole?' Writing about gender has become integral to both social history and cultural history, as Walkowitz's trajectory suggests. It is no longer acceptable for historians to write about 'the people' or 'the working class' without dealing explicitly with women. And they

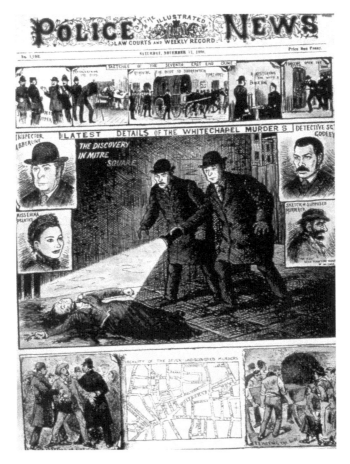

Figure 10.2 The notorious 'Jack the Ripper' murders of 1888 provide a case study not only of crime and prostitution in late Victorian London but also of the collective cultural mentality that found the murders so fascinating. © Topfoto/Topham/Picturepoint.

are unlikely to do so without closely qualifying the category of 'woman' according to the specific historical context. As Susan Pedersen has put it,

> If cultural history ... has accomplished anything, it has been to call into question the assumption that one can evaluate gender relations in different societies by a single standard.[17]

Equally, questions of cultural identity are complex and contentious; but gender is always part of the mix – not as a ready-made theory, but as an open-ended cluster of issues to do with the experience and representation of gendered lives. Last, as a metaphorical language gender has been taken up by political historians, thus enriching our understanding of political culture and its purchase on the political community.

IV

Postcolonialism: a new paradigm

Postcolonial history, like gender history, takes as its starting point the marginalization or dispossession of a large category of people in the past. But its scope is much wider. While global or comparative studies are not unknown in gender history, it has usually been conceptualized within national boundaries, and often at the level of the local community. Postcolonial history, on the other hand, is intrinsically global. Local studies abound, but they are premised on the salience of global relations: not in the anodyne sense so often conveyed by analysts of contemporary globalization, but in terms of the relations of power and subordination that account for the parlous condition of so many Third World societies. The 500-year-long colonial project of the West is seen to have impoverished and humiliated those societies. Rescuing their history from the patronizing stereotypes of Westerners is a precondition for their emancipation. But for postcolonial scholars a question-mark hangs over the academic discourse of history as the West has understood it, for historians were deeply implicated in the silencing of non-Western traditions. The outcome has been some disturbing critiques in which major doubts have been aired about the validity of history as a scholarly pursuit.

About the longstanding exclusion of colonized societies from the scope of historical study there can be no doubt. To go no further back than the emergence of the historical profession in the nineteenth century, Ranke confined his huge output of historical writing to the European sub-continent. His *Universal History*, on which he was working when he died in 1886, was a history of Europe from the last centuries of the Roman Empire. His successors and imitators worked within a national frame which sometimes included the empire builders of the past, but not the societies on which they preyed. Marx had broader interests. He wrote perceptive commentaries on events in India, but India itself he regarded as being outside history because its mode of production lacked an internal dynamic of change: in order to share the progressive development of Western societies, it needed to be conquered and administered by one of those societies, which is why Marx regarded British rule in India as broadly positive. At a theoretical level at least, it could not be denied that India and China had a history, since there was evidently some parallel between their sophisticated state structures and those of Europe. But Africa was denied even this qualification for historical study because it was wrongly assumed to have evolved no state structures at all.

The ending of formal colonial rule was one of the most striking features of world history in the twentieth century. Within the space of twenty years (1947–66), most of the countries of South Asia and Africa became independent. (The only precedent was the emancipation of the American colonies held by Britain, Spain and Portugal between 1776 and 1822.) However, independence brought equality in only the most formal sense: in many countries the dependence and impoverishment that had characterized colonial status intensified during the first decades of self-rule. At the same time, sovereign peoples could not be patronized in quite such a brutal fashion as they had been under colonial rule. Their leaders were in many cases highly educated and well versed in Western thought. One of the priorities of these states was the development of a modern education system, including entirely new institutions of higher education. Historical research was conducted in the universities of Third World countries in order to furnish the schools with a history curriculum appropriate to an independent nation: one very practical reason why the time was ripe for a reappraisal of the colonial relationship and its enduring legacy.

But the implications of that reappraisal are complex. At first glance 'postcolonial' is simply a convenient chronological marker, designating our age as one in which colonialism has been dismantled; it could even be taken to mean that the colonial era lies in the past and should remain there while we focus on the future. That is not how the label 'postcolonial' is interpreted by the scholars who have adopted it for themselves. Their contention is that colonialism used its control over the resources of learning and culture to establish forms of knowledge that not only gave Europeans a distorted picture of colonial societies, but were internalized by the colonized themselves. Those distortions persist, inhibiting the development of ex-colonies to this day. For this reason the superficial temporal reading of the term 'postcolonial' is rejected: colonialism has not really ended but

continues in less formal and more covert ways (sometimes referred to as 'neo-colonialism'). A still more radical strand of postcolonialism maintains that because Western learning served so
long as a means of subordinating colonial societies, its intellectual
standing – embracing the entire Enlightenment tradition – is
fatally compromised. At this point postcolonialism moves beyond
the colonial world and becomes – alongside Postmodernism – a
further strand in the negative critique of the Western intellectual
tradition.

Theorists from the Third World and the West

Postcolonialism sounds like the authentic voice of the Third
World, and in one sense it is. The leading lights – Edward Said,
Homi Bhabha and Gayatri Chakravorty Spivak – come or came
from the Middle East or South Asia. But – with the notable exception of Said – their writings are abstract and opaque (not least to
readers in their countries of origin). All three are (or were)
employed by American universities. Furthermore, despite the
rejection of European thought that is sometimes proclaimed by
postcolonial scholars, their theories are not home-grown, but are
derived from some of the most high-profile Western intellectuals.
But it is the rebels and the radicals who have inspired them,
rather than the liberals or even the Marxists. Much the most
important influence is Foucault. As explained in Chapter 7, Foucault regarded all discourses as forms of power/knowledge, which
served to confine people within specific ways of understanding the
world and their place in it. According to Foucault, language is not
just one variant of power; it is the most important kind of power.
Because the users of language are not aware of being constrained,
they mistakenly suppose that it expresses the world as it is.
Edward Said, the most influential postcolonial theorist, applied
Foucault's thinking to Western writing about the Arab world
during the nineteenth and twentieth centuries. Said was a literary
scholar rather than a historian, but his path-breaking *Orientalism*
(1978) is deeply versed in historical representations of the Middle
East. His analysis was based on the idea that when one culture
seeks to represent another, the power function of discourse is
intensified because it is attempting to pin down the Other – a
cultural construct perceived as a pathological opposite of one's
own culture. Repeated over many decades, the rendering of the
Arab Other hardened into a set of essentialist judgements which
Said called 'Orientalism'. It permeated the views of 'experts' on
the Arab world, administrators posted to colonial territories in
the Middle East, and – most insidiously – many Arabs educated
in the Western tradition who were encouraged to reject their own
culture. Orientalism gave imperialists the confidence to dominate,
and it undermined the cultural resources of the colonized. Said

Figure 10.3 Western portrayals of Oriental life emphasized its otherness by displaying women as sex objects and sex slaves. *The Women of Algiers* (1834) by Eugène Delacroix is a relatively restrained depiction of a harem. © Bridgeman Art Library/Louvre, Paris, France/Giraudon.

summed up Orientalism as a 'science of imperialism', his goal being to 'reduce the effects of imperialist shackles on thought and human relations'.[18]

V

Race and racism

One of those shackles was the concept of 'race'. During the colonial era, racist ideologies were developed to explain the supposed inferiority of 'native' peoples – both their indigenous culture and their inability to assimilate Western culture. 'Race' was treated as fixed and biologically determined, which logically meant that Western domination should last indefinitely; indeed some racist writers argued that white and black were on different evolutionary paths. Highly derogatory stereotypes of other races served in turn to sustain a flattering self-image of the British – or French or German – 'race'. The postcolonial reaction has taken two antithetical forms. Minorities with a strong ethnic identity have constructed what might be called a 'reverse discourse'; they embrace the concept of 'race' because the term brings biological descent and culture together in a powerful amalgam that maximizes group cohesion and emphasizes distance from other groups. Among black people in America and Britain there is considerable support for Afrocentrism – the belief in an absolute sense of ethnic difference and in the transmission of an authentic cultural tradition from Africa to black people of the modern diaspora. It is no accident that this way of thinking is strongest among people of African descent: it is an understandable reaction to centuries of enslavement which was an assault on their cultural identity as well as their human dignity. But Afrocentrism is based on ahistorical assumptions. It is as essentialist as the white forms of racism against which it is mobilized. Very few nations or racial groups have ever been ethnically homogeneous. The societies of the African diaspora have been in close – and sometimes intimate – contact with white communities for five centuries, and their character has been deeply influenced by that contact (as has that of white society). The formation of racial and national identities is never a once-and-for-all event, but an unfolding process.[19]

Instead of making a mirror-image out of colonial racism, a more radical approach is to dispute the premise of race altogether, and this is what the mainstream of postcolonial thinking sets out to do. Biology is deemed irrelevant, because the physical differences between races are either non-existent or superficial. What may appear to be 'racial' difference is the outcome of cultural adaptation, including contact with other cultures. The significant point about colonial discourse was that it seized on these specificities as evidence of an unbridgeable gulf between white and black. 'Race' itself became the centrepiece of colonial discourse, bolstering the self-confidence of the colonist and marginalizing the colonized. Demonstrating the social construction of race in this way is all the more important because colonial-style racism has not disappeared. It still mars relations between the West and Third World countries, as well as the white perception of black communities in the former colonial **metropole**s such as Britain.

One of the reasons why postcolonialism has proved a rich vein for historians is the different emphases within the theory. Much has been made of some of the contradictions in Said's work. There is something uncompromising – even rigid – about his rendering of the West's cultural dominance over the East. Orientalism is presented as an all-powerful fiction which eliminated other cultural responses on the part of Westerners. But as Homi Bhabha has pointed out, within a colonial relationship there was room for cultural adaptation, as each side was drawn to traits of the other through desire or ambition: for him hybridity is the key to the colonial encounter.[20] The boundaries of colony and metropole were porous, making for a single field. A related issue is how all-powerful colonial discourses should be taken to be. Said inscribes a binary distinction of powerful/powerless on

Metropole
'Metropole' used to mean the same as 'metropolis'. In academic writing it denotes an imperialist nation that has been at the centre of a global network of trade and exploitation (for example, Britain and the United States).

the colonizer and the colonized, allowing little scope for the latter to make responses that are not choreographed by the oppressor. Other writers recognize that the colonial subject could manipulate the discursive categories of the West, even turning them to account as tools of resistance, with the result that colonial rule was more precarious than it appeared.[21] Much here turns on how we see the indigenous elite who straddled traditional and Western culture: were they creatures of colonial discourse or potentially autonomous actors? At the same time, this debate tends to operate at a high level of abstraction. It is rare to find a postcolonial theorist who acknowledges a role for individual or even collective agency.

VI

Historians and postcolonialism

How then have historians made use of a body of theory that in some ways is quite antithetical to the habitual practice of their discipline? We can begin by looking at how historians responded more broadly to the ending of the colonial era. Africa is the prime example, since nowhere else had the colonial ignorance of the indigenous past been so profound. The 1960s and 1970s saw an impressive output of scholarly works of African history, written partly by African scholars trained in the West, and partly by young Western scholars who identified with the aspirations of African independence. They set themselves to confound the twin assumptions that Africa had no history apart from the activities of outsiders, and no historical evidence that might substantiate such a history. In fact the documentary resources proved much richer than anyone had supposed. The European trading companies and missionary societies, which had been in contact with Africa since the fifteenth century and by the nineteenth century had penetrated deep into the interior, were found to have extensive records; these included close observation of local chiefdoms on whose support the incomers depended, as well as descriptions of African culture and society. In the Islamic regions of the Sahel, the western Sudan and the East African coast, where the frontiers of literacy extended far into black Africa, there are local chronicles dating back in some cases to the sixteenth century, and even – in a few states such as the **Sokoto caliphate** of northern Nigeria – a nucleus of administrative records.

Most exciting of all was the development of a methodology for collecting and interpreting oral tradition. This was a universal feature of pre-literate societies, and conversely destined to wither away as literacy spread. The first generation of independence was therefore a privileged moment in capitalizing on 'the heritage of the ears' (see Chapter 11). Pre-colonial political entities like the

Sokoto caliphate
The most powerful Islamic state in West Africa in the nineteenth century, centred on what is now northern Nigeria. It expanded by means of *jihad* (holy war). Sokoto was brought under British rule at the beginning of the twentieth century, but its ruler retained considerable authority during the colonial era.

medieval states of **Ghana** and **Zimbabwe** now emerged into the light of history, and the early stages of incorporation of the African interior into the overseas commerce were reconstructed. The colonial period had been studied by historians, but from the perspective of the colonizers, as the story of development and of statesmanlike preparation for independence. Now it featured the theme of resistance – armed resistance to the initial colonial occupiers, and political mobilization against the colonial state during the approach to independence. But historians also focused on more accommodating responses, particularly peasant initiatives that were intended to support the beginnings of a consumer economy.[22]

This pioneer work in African history was largely innocent of theory. Its practitioners were for the most part confident that the well-tried methods of Western historiography would serve them well. Colonial records required nothing more than the habitual scepticism of the archival researcher. Even the novel resource of oral tradition attracted comparatively little theoretical analysis at this stage.[23]

Subaltern Studies

It was in India during the 1980s that postcolonial theory made a decided impact on historians for the first time. This was the achievement of the Subaltern Studies group, led by Ranajit Guha. Initially its point of reference was Marxist history, especially the 'history from below' associated with E.P. Thompson. The orientation of the group was defined by a profound rejection of the nationalist elite in India – men like **Nehru** and the leaders of the Indian National Congress who had channelled popular resistance to the British Raj and had then inherited control of the state apparatus in 1947. Ideologically, the Subaltern historians claimed there was little to choose between the nationalist politicians and the historians who chronicled their achievements. Both belonged to the 'bourgeois-nationalist elite', far removed from the interests and the attitudes of ordinary Indians. Hence the choice of the term 'subaltern': it was drawn from the Marxist thinker **Antonio Gramsci** to denote disempowered social groups. The task of radical historians was to shift the focus from the professional politician to the subaltern, and in particular to reveal the subaltern's place at the heart of popular nationalism. This aspiration was all the more convincing because the frequency of popular disturbances from 1919 in British India was undeniable: what was lacking was a historical account that went beyond elite response and elite manipulation.

Framed in this way, Subaltern Studies was a predictable 'people's history' reaction against nationalist historiography (though it is worth pointing out that in Africa the radical rejection of

Ghana
A West African state that flourished between the ninth and eleventh centuries. The basis of its prosperity was the trans-Saharan trade, particularly in gold. The medieval state lay well to the north of the present-day Ghana.

Zimbabwe
A Central African state that flourished between the eleventh and fourteenth centuries. It is famous for its technically accomplished dry-stone architecture, notably the ruins of Great Zimbabwe. The modern state of Zimbabwe takes its name from its medieval predecessor.

Jawaharlal Nehru (1889–1964)
India's first Prime Minister, in office from 1947 to 1962.

Antonio Gramsci (1891–1937)
A leading figure in the Italian Communist Party after the First World War, he was imprisoned by the Fascist regime of Mussolini and died in prison. His immense influence stems from his theoretical writings, in which he developed new ways of understanding popular political culture and the pre-conditions of revolution.

nationalism was much weaker). Very quickly, however, the Subaltern historians came under the influence of Said and other postcolonial theorists. The emphasis shifted from material to cultural power, as more and more attention was given to deconstructing what the colonial authorities had written in such profusion. Part of the reason for doing so was to demonstrate how much of what (even now) counts as objective knowledge represented a discursive imposition by the colonial regime: in India the classic instance is 'caste' (in Africa it is 'tribe'). But the main purpose of this close textual study was to make up for the silencing of the poor that had occurred throughout the colonial period and which (it was said) was replicated in the writings of the first generation of post-independence historians. Peasants and workers would be brought into the light of history despite the extent of popular illiteracy under the Raj: 'the voice of the subaltern' would be heard. Guha and his colleagues strove to overcome the paucity of subaltern writing by reading the voluminous government sources against the grain. Guha's own work on peasant insurgency in colonial India suggests that a partial restoration of the peasant voice is possible, based on official eavesdropping or 'intercepted discourse'. As he explains, government counter-insurgency compulsively recorded whatever might have a bearing on rebel activities – be it rumours in the bazaar, slogans shouted in the street or incidental detail in court evidence.[24]

VII

The postcolonial reappraisal of British history

Postcolonialism originated in a determination to change the conceptual map by which Third World cultures were studied. But colonialism was a two-sided relationship that also changed the culture and mentality of the colonizing society. In the past this theme received even less attention from historians than the colonial impact overseas. In the British case there is a long tradition of regarding the empire as 'out there' – a destination for British enterprise and conquest, but without a significant imprint on metropolitan life. Postcolonial theory subjects that assumption to critical scrutiny, based on the proposition that colony and metropole were parts of a single system, with influences flowing in both directions. As Antoinette Burton puts it, the empire was 'not just a phenomenon "out there", but a fundamental and constitutive part of English culture and national identity at home'.[25] It follows that the end of empire makes Britain – no less than its former dependencies – a postcolonial society.

So, far from being 'out there', the empire was integral to British life for 300 years, and became more obviously so as it neared its end. This was not just a matter of registering the proportion of pink on the world map (a universal experience for British schoolchildren). Edward Said maintained that the literary canon of nineteenth- and twentieth-century England was permeated by an imperial consciousness (most controversially in Jane Austen's novel, *Mansfield Park*). But the nub of the argument concerns the experiences that were shared by the British people as a whole. By 1900 most families had kin living in the colonies; virtually everyone consumed colonial products whose provenance was carefully labelled; adventure fiction and boys' stories were staged against a colonial backdrop. These were the constituents of an imperial culture. Indeed, the argument has been advanced that it was colonialism that made it possible for British people to think of themselves (as distinct from their English or Scottish selves) as a nation.[26] The converse of that proposition would be that Britishness is in radical need of redefining now that the empire is no more. It is hardly surprising, then, that debates around this issue feature not just in postcolonial history, but in polemic intended for a wider audience, notably in the work of Paul Gilroy.[27]

Said's work on Orientalism portrayed a unified West imposing a unified discourse on the East. Even at the cultural level (with which he was exclusively concerned) this now looks like an oversimplification. Without downplaying the violence and authoritarianism of empire, postcolonial historians emphasize the two-way flow of influences, not all of which ministered directly to power. As Catherine Hall has explained, the histories of 'metropolis' and 'peripheries' do not follow a simple binary model.[28] In her book *Civilising Subjects* (2002), she treats Jamaica and Birmingham as interlocking – and equally important – sites of empire in the mid-nineteenth century. Only with this double focus, Hall argues, can we understand both British popular attitudes towards the empire and the political culture of the ex-slaves in the Caribbean; and she gives special weight to the missionaries who were the main channel of communication between Jamaica and Birmingham. Colonial realities sometimes impinged on the metropolitan imagination in unexpected ways. In the 1790s, Mary Wollstonecraft bolstered the case for women's rights by drawing an analogy with plantation slavery (there were more than eighty references to slavery in her celebrated *Vindication of the Rights of Woman*).[29] In a less constructive way, colonial ideas of race were superimposed on social distinctions back home – as in the **'racialization' of the London poor** in the mid-Victorian period.[30] Most striking of all was the profound cultural adjustment made by all immigrant communities living in Britain, which suggests that Bhabha's notion of hybridity has even more purchase in metropolitan society than it does in the colonies.

The debate about the connections between Britishness and empire is complicated by the fact that different sectors of the British population had – and have – radically divergent memories

Mansfield Park
Novel by Jane Austen, published in 1814. Like all Austen's novels, the book concerns the marriage prospects of young ladies of the propertied class. It is not a novel about the empire. At the same time, it is made clear that the family wealth is based on slavery plantations in the West Indies, and Sir Thomas Bertram's prolonged absence from the family home is explained by the need to attend to his affairs in Antigua.

The **'racialization' of the London poor**
In the second half of the nineteenth century, educated people often compared the poor to the benighted heathen overseas. The implication was not only that the poor were culturally and morally inadequate, but that they belonged to a separate race.

Figure 10.4 West Indian immigrants aboard the *SS Empire Windrush* (1948), the first ship to bring a large group of West Indians to Britain. The new arrivals had high expectations of 'the mother country', which were rudely shattered by popular hostility towards them. © Getty Images/Popperfoto.

of empire. Partly this is a dimension of the 'three kingdoms' problematic: the Scots and Irish were ubiquitous in the colonies, while the levers of power lay in London with an English-dominated government. But the key issue concerns the colonial immigrants who settled in Britain. Large-scale black immigration only began in the 1950s, just as the empire was being dismantled, but people of African and Asian descent have been continuously present in Britain since at least the sixteenth century, not just as curiosities but in sufficient numbers to take their place in urban society, especially in London and the major ports. The fact that many of them were slaves introduced colonial relationships and colonial racial stereotypes into the metropole that have endured long after the ending of slavery. As the bicentenary of the abolition of the slave trade in 2007 showed, slavery still touches a raw nerve in Britain: for many white people it has been subsumed in a self-regarding narrative of national philanthropy, which addresses the end of slavery rather than its long history. For many black people, on the other hand, slavery and the slave trade should be treated as another Holocaust, with an implied duty of compensation (see Chapter 12). Seldom heard in this debate is the voice of black people in the past, for the familiar reason that they feature so little in the primary sources: few were literate, and fewer still had access to the public sphere (hence the intense attention given to the handful of eighteenth-century black propagandists against slavery).

VIII

Problems and obstacles

The difficulties inherent in finding a historical voice for the sub-altern are real enough. An important strand in postcolonialism has responded by questioning the validity of the academic dis-cipline that has framed their efforts hitherto: if historical research cannot yield the desired perspective, then 'history' itself must be found wanting. From a subaltern perspective the charge-sheet is compelling. An obvious point is that during the nineteenth and twentieth centuries many historians took part in the Orientalist project, and Said argued that in his own day there were influential historians whose Oriental expertise was placed in the service of Western (particularly American) imperialism. But there is a broader point to be made with regard to the structural imbalance between Western history and all other histories – what Dipesh Chakrabarty calls the problem of 'asymmetric ignorance'.[31] Historians in the Third World are expected to know European history, whereas most of their counterparts in Europe are ignor-ant of the history of Asia and Africa. The implication is that the 'grand narratives' of the Western experience – nationalism, democracy, capitalism and so on – are the benchmark against which other societies should be measured. No one makes the reverse evaluation.

There are also troubling questions to be asked about the colo-nial archive, which includes extensive documentation in the former colonies and also the national archives of the metropolitan countries. Not only did these archives reflect the prejudice and ignorance of colonial officials; as pointed out in Chapter 5 they were instruments of rule, intended to mould social reality to the designs of the colonial regime: no amount of 'reading against the grain' can take us into the world of the subaltern. In a challenging article, 'Can the subaltern speak?', Spivak drew on the well-stu-died Hindu practice of *sati*, which placed on widows the duty of throwing themselves on the funeral pyre of their husbands. His-torical research has documented in detail the debates within the British administration that led to the official proscription of *sati* in 1833, as well as the arguments mounted for its retention by patriarchal traditionalists, but the voice of the victims remains obdurately silent.[32]

At the root of the postcolonial critique lies the relationship between academic history and the nation state. Because historians have generally observed the boundaries of states, even when they have not been chronicling the history of the state itself, their work has had the effect of validating the nation state as the pre-eminent category of social organization and political identity. If critique along these lines is current in Britain, it is still more pertinent in a country like India, where the effect of a focus on 'the nation' is to exclude huge social categories from the agenda of history. As Chakrabarty has put it, history is complicit 'in assimilating to the projects of the modern state all other possibilities of human solidarity'.[33] The secularism of Western historiography is open to attack in comparable terms, as an ideological position that is manifestly unable to engage with the spirituality of Indian cultures. Some postcolonial scholars would go further still, dismissing the universal claims of the Enlightenment tradition as an apologia for the West against all its Others.[34] In theory at least, the way is open not only for authentically Third World histories, but for entirely new perspectives on the West – what Chakrabarty calls the 'provincializing of Europe'.

Acknowledging the cultural turn

To read Dipesh Chakrabarty on postcolonial history or Joan Scott on gender history is to doubt the future of the discipline of history as it is practised by most scholars today. These writers (and others like them) challenge the traditional academic ideals of scholarly detachment, authentic recreation and empirically grounded analysis, and they roundly attack those who subscribe to them. The tone is similar to that adopted by Postmodernists, and that is no accident. The more radical views of gender and postcoloniality that I have described are compatible with Post-modernism: indeed Joan Scott's theoretical writings are generally placed under that heading. However, it should not be assumed that these radical critiques will become the received wisdom of the profession in the future. Working historians for the most part shrink from the full implications of postcolonial or gender theory. The influence of gender and postcolonialism on historical scholarship is to be measured not in theoretical virtuosity, but in the way they have projected new and illuminating perspectives into the scholarly arena.

At the same time, recent developments in gender history and postcolonial history clearly demonstrate the costs that are incurred by embracing the cultural turn. There is little place here for the material basis of social stratification or for the collective agency of social groups pursuing their political ends. The fact that power – whether exercised over a colony or over a subordinate sex – has a cultural dimension does not mean that it is a cultural phenomenon *tout court*. Academics may be beguiled by the power of words and images, but for many of the groups they study, power was experienced in sharply material forms. That truth was more evident in the first generation of scholarship in these fields than it is now. A re-engagement with that tradition, without losing the insights of cultural analysis, would be timely.

Further reading

Laura Lee Downs, *Writing Gender History*, Hodder Arnold, 2004.

Joan W. Scott, *Gender and the Politics of History*, Columbia University Press, 1988.

Bonnie G. Smith, *The Gender of History: Men, Women and Historical Practice*, Harvard University Press, 1998.

John Tosh, *Manliness and Masculinities in Nineteenth-Century Britain*, Longman, 2005.

Barbara Bush, *Imperialism and Postcolonialism*, Longman, 2006.

Edward Said, *Orientalism*, 3rd edn, Penguin, 2003.

Catherine Hall and Sonya O. Rose (eds), *At Home with the Empire: Metropolitan Culture and the Imperial World*, Cambridge University Press, 2006.

Catherine Hall (ed.), *Cultures of Empire*, Manchester University Press, 2000.

Caroline Neale, *Writing 'Independent' History: African Historiography, 1960–1980*, Greenwood Press, 1985.

Notes

1 Jutta Schwarzkopf, *Women in the Chartist Movement*, Macmillan, 1991.
2 See, for example, Angela Woollacott, *On Her Their Lives Depend: Munitions Workers in the Great War,* University of California Press, 1994.
3 Peter Laslett and Richard Wall (eds), *Household and Family in Past Time*, Cambridge University Press, 1972.
4 Leonore Davidoff and Catherine Hall, *Family Fortunes: Men and Women of the English Middle Class, 1780–1850*, 2nd edn, Hutchinson, 2002.
5 Ellen Dubois et al., 'Politics and culture in women's history: a symposium', *Feminist Studies*, VI, 1980, pp. 26–64.
6 The classic airing of the pros and cons of patriarchy is in the short interventions of Sheila Rowbotham, Sally Alexander and Barbara Taylor in Raphael Samuel (ed.), *People's History and Socialist Theory*, Routledge & Kegan Paul, 1981, pp. 363–73.
7 Jane Lewis (ed.), *Labour and Love: Women's Experience of Home and Family 1850–1940*, Blackwell, 1986, editor's introduction, p. 4. See also John Tosh, 'What should historians do with masculinity? Reflections on nineteenth-century Britain', *History Workshop Journal*, XXXVIII, 1994, pp. 179–202.
8 George L. Mosse, *The Image of Men: The Creation of Modern Masculinity*, Oxford University Press, 1996, ch. 6.
9 Alexandra Shepard, *Meanings of Manhood in Early Modern England*, Oxford University Press, 2003; John Tosh, *Manliness and Masculinities in Nineteenth-Century Britain*, Longman, 2005; Davidoff and Hall, *Family Fortunes*.

10 Roy Porter and Lesley Hall, *The Facts of Life: The Creation of Sexual Knowledge in Britain, 1650–1950*, Yale University Press, 1995, ch. 2; John Tosh, *A Man's Place: Masculinity and the Middle-Class Home in Victorian England*, Yale University Press, 1999.

11 For a discussion of the implications of Lacan for gender historians, see Sally Alexander, *Becoming a Woman and Other Essays in 19th and 20th Century Feminist History*, Virago, 1994, pp. 105–10, 225–30.

12 The classic work in the medical category is Thomas Laqueur, *Making Sex: Body and Gender from the Greeks to Freud*, Harvard University Press, 1990. For the legal approach, see Harry Cocks, *Nameless Offences: Homosexual Desire in the 19th Century*, I.B. Tauris, 2003, and Sean Brady, *Masculinity and Male Homosexuality in Britain, 1861–1913*, Palgrave Macmillan, 2005, ch. 4.

13 Matt Houlbrook, *Queer London: Perils and Pleasures in the Sexual Metropolis, 1918–1957*, Chicago University Press, 2005.

14 Joan W. Scott, 'Gender: a useful category of historical analysis', *American Historical Review*, XCI, 1986, pp. 1053–75.

15 Stefan Collini, 'The idea of "character" in Victorian political thought', *Transactions of the Royal Historical Society*, 5th series, XXXV, 1985, pp. 29–50.

16 Judith R. Walkowitz, *Prostitution and Victorian Society*, Cambridge University Press, 1980, p. ix.

17 Susan Pedersen, 'Comparative history and women's history: explaining convergence and divergence', in Deborah Cohen and Maura O'Connor (eds), *Comparison and History: Europe in Cross-National Perspective*, Routledge, 2004, p. 95.

18 Edward Said, *Orientalism*, 2nd edn, Penguin, 1995, p. 354. Said's views have proved controversial. For a critique by a historian, see John M. MacKenzie, *Orientalism: History, Theory and the Arts*, Manchester University Press, 1995.

19 Stephen Howe, *Afrocentrism: Mythical Pasts and Imagined Homes*, Verso, 1998.

20 Homi K. Bhabha, *The Location of Culture*, Routledge, 1994.

21 Ibid.

22 Both these strands feature in a major work of the 1970s: John Iliffe, *The Modern History of Tanganyika*, Cambridge University Press, 1979.

23 The present writer must be numbered among these naïve fieldworkers. See John Tosh, *Clan Leaders and Colonial Chiefs in Lango*, Oxford University Press, 1978.

24 Ranajit Guha, *Elementary Aspects of Peasant Insurgency in Colonial India*, Oxford University Press, 1983, pp. 14–16.

25 Antoinette Burton (ed.), *After the Imperial Turn: Thinking With and Through the Nation*, Duke University Press, 2003, editor's introduction, p. 3.

26 Antoinette Burton, 'Who needs the nation? Interrogating "British" history', in Catherine Hall (ed.), *Cultures of Empire*, Manchester University Press, 2000.

27 Paul Gilroy, *After Empire: Melancholia or Convivial Culture?*, Routledge, 2004.

28 Catherine Hall, 'Histories, empires and the post-colonial moment', in Iain Chambers and Lidia Curti (eds), *The Post-Colonial Question*, Routledge, 1996, p. 70.

29 Moira Ferguson, *Colonialism and Gender Relations from Mary Wollstonecraft to James Kincaid*, Columbia University Press, 1993, pp. 8–33.

30 John Marriott, *The Other Empire: Metropolis, India and Progress in the Colonial Imagination*, Manchester University Press, 2003, ch. 6.

31 Dipesh Chakrabarty, 'Postcoloniality and the artifice of history: who speaks for "Indian" pasts?', *Representations*, XXXVII, 1992, pp. 1–3.

32 G.C. Spivak, 'Can the subaltern speak?', in Patrick Williams and Laura Chrisman (eds), *Colonial Discourse and Postcolonial Theory: A Reader*, Harvester Wheatsheaf, 1993, pp. 94–104.

33 Chakrabarty, 'Postcoloniality', p. 23.

34 Ashis Nandy, 'History's forgotten doubles', *History and Theory*, theme issue 34, 1995.

11 Memory and the spoken word

History is both a form of memory and a discipline that draws on memory as source material. Today some of the most productive discussions about the nature of history are pursued in this area. This chapter looks at the culture of commemoration before examining in more depth the practice of oral history, in which people are interviewed about their memories. Oral sources have had a major impact on social history, and on the pre-colonial history of Africa. Such material can give an exhilarating sense of touching the 'real' past, but it is as full of pitfalls and difficulties as any other sort of historical material. What questions should historians ask of oral material, and what role do they themselves play in its creation?

This book began with the relationship between history and memory. In Chapter 1 it was pointed out that academic history can be regarded as a form of memory, in that it provides society with the best available record of past experience. But that does not mean that no distinction should be made between history and other forms of memory. 'Social memory', or 'collective memory', refers to the stories and assumptions about the past that illustrate – or account for – key features of the society we know today. Out of the limitless stock of recoverable knowledge about the past, social memory prioritizes material that validates cultural values or political loyalties in the present, sometimes in the teeth of the available evidence about the past. Academic history, on the other hand, insists on two key principles; that the study of the past should not simply mirror our own preoccupations, but should pay special attention to what is different and remote from our experience; and that all historical interpretation should be rigorously tested against the evidence. In short, both the standards and the social role of the discipline of history depend on its standing apart from social memory.

However, these distinctions do not mean that other forms of memory are of no consequence to historians. Historians today are keenly interested in two forms of memory. Collective representations of the past as they circulate in popular culture are one focus of interest. The other is the memories of individuals about their own lifetime, often solicited by the historian. Each of these strikes a different balance between authentic recall and the remodelling of memory after the event. Each in different ways demonstrates the immense cultural significance of the remembered past.

I

Collective memory

How a community – whether national or local – visualizes its past conditions, its understanding of society and its political consciousness. All societies draw on memories that extend further back than the lifetimes of its present-day members. The more remote past is not confined to history books and archives; it is present also in popular consciousness, fed by a variety of com-memorative activities and recorded in a variety of media. These constitute the social or collective memory of the society. Here the relationship between past and present takes two complementary forms. First, social memory usually gives at least partial access to what happened in the past, and this historical knowledge condi-tions popular understanding of the present. At the same time, collective memory is also a mirror of the present, reflecting its concerns in time perspective, which means that it is subtly – and sometimes not so subtly – modified over time. Historians' study of social memory starts from the assumption that its content will diverge from their professional understanding of the past, but that that very divergence provides clues about the construction of popular memory. If written history represents a selection of the past thought worthy of recall, collective memory is an even more drastic simplification, designed to reinforce a cultural identity or a potential for agency in the present. As James Fentress and Chris Wickham put it, 'social memory is not stable as information; it is stable, rather, at the level of shared meanings and remembered images'.[1]

The contribution of collective memory to social integration is clearest in those pre-literate societies whose knowledge of the past is wholly dependent on spoken narratives handed down from one generation to the next. Although practically extinct in highly industrialized countries, *oral tradition* is still a living force in those countries where literacy has not yet displaced a pre-dominantly oral culture. Oral tradition conveys a strong aura of cultural authenticity. But its historical significance can only be fully grasped if it is treated as a secondary source, since there is no direct link between the testimony and the event or experience which it purports to recount.

In many African societies, ethnic identity, social status, claims to political office and rights in land are still validated by appeals to oral tradition; what in Western society would be formalized by written documents, in oral societies derives its authority from the memories of the living. In the 1950s in Africa, historians began to evaluate oral tradition for its historical content and to lay down procedures for its collection and interpretation. They collected detailed bodies of tradition which by genealogical reckoning extended back four or five centuries, complete with named individuals and their exploits – the very stuff of conventional historiography. Their faith in the reliability of the traditions was greatly strengthened by the discovery that in some of the more centralized chiefdoms the transmission of tradition was the business of trained specialists reciting fixed texts; in some societies, material relics such as royal tombs or regalia were used as **mnemonic** devices to ensure that the reigns of earlier rulers were recalled in correct sequence. It was maintained that the methods required to evaluate a formal oral tradition were in principle no different from those required by written documents.[2] Oral tradition, it appeared, gave direct access to a hitherto unknown past – and in an idiom untouched by Western literacy.

mnemonic
An aid to memory.

The role of oral tradition

Longer experience of oral tradition and reflection on the nature of oral society soon showed that the position was not nearly so straightforward. In particular, the analogy with written texts broke down on the element of performance that characterizes the transmission of oral tradition. Like story-tellers everywhere, the performers of a tradition are alert to the atmosphere among their audience and their sense of what is acceptable to them. Each retelling of the story is likely to diverge from the one before, as the content becomes subtly adjusted to social expectations. Traditions are not kept alive by story-tellers who, by some mysterious faculty beyond the grasp of literate people, are able to remember great epics and lists without effort; they are handed down because they hold meaning for the culture concerned.

Broadly speaking, oral traditions in Africa fulfil two social functions. First, they teach the values and beliefs that are integral to the culture – the proper relationship between humans and animals, for example, or the obligations of **kinship** and **affinity**. Second, they serve to validate the particular social and political arrangements that currently prevail – the distribution of land, the claims of one powerful lineage to the chiefship or the pattern of relations with a neighbouring people. By the time a tradition has been handed down over four or five generations, its social function is likely to have modified the content considerably, by suppressing detail that no longer seems relevant, and by elaborating the rhetorical or symbolic elements in the story. And this process can continue indefinitely, as changes in social or political

kinship
Ties of blood, as between parents and children, or brothers and sisters.

affinity
Relationships through marriage: thus one's in-laws can be referred to as 'affines'.

circumstances leave their imprint on the corpus of oral tradition. Sometimes these adjustments are made quite deliberately. Among the Kuba people of the Congo, a dynastic tradition could only be recounted after its content had been carefully vetted in private by a council of notables; as one of them put it, 'After a while, the truth of the old tales changed. What was true before, became false afterwards.'[3]

The sensitivity of oral tradition to the demands of its audience and the prestige of the written word was strikingly borne out when the black American writer Alex Haley went to the Gambia in 1966 in search of his slave-boy ancestor, Kunta Kinte. Although the oral traditions current in the region do not contain information about real people before the nineteenth century, Haley duly found an elder who recited a tradition about the boy's capture into slavery by 'the king's soldiers' in the mid-eighteenth century. Haley had made no secret of his story and what he was looking for, and there seems little doubt that the 'tradition' was concocted for him. Several years later, as a result of the publicity surrounding Haley's best-selling book *Roots* (1976), many more specialists in tradition were able to recite the story of Kunta Kinte with further lively embellishments.[4]

The interpretation of oral tradition

Using oral traditions for historical reconstruction therefore raises major problems. Not only are they mostly narratives intended for the edification of posterity – and thus rather low down in the historian's hierarchy of sources (see pp. 75–7), they have also been constantly reworked to relate their meaning more closely to the changing expectations of their audience. The result is that historians are now very cautious about accepting the veracity of oral tradition. On the other hand, the picture is by no means uniformly negative. Criticisms of oral tradition have most force when the researcher is confronted by a single body of tradition. But a cluster of related traditions opens the path to the kind of comparative evaluation that historians are well accustomed to practise in the case of written sources. When Jan Vansina tackled the pre-colonial history of **Rwanda** he found a well-established body of royal traditions which had been learned by heart in the royal court and later published as the definitive account. It was the recovery of a much wider cross-section of traditions that enabled him to critique the official version and to reconstruct the nineteenth-century history of the kingdom.[5] But the value of oral tradition to the historian is not limited to retrospective reconstruction. Its value is as much cultural as historical. In pre-literate communities the remembered past is placed at the service of the present. It resembles a canvas on which the political and social values of the community are symbolically and succinctly delineated.

Rwanda
The pre-colonial state of Rwanda formed the nucleus of the German colony founded in the 1890s, and transferred to Belgium in 1919. Since independence in 1962, the history of Rwanda has been marked by strife between the Hutu and the Tutsi – the legacy of divide-and-rule policies pursued by the Belgians.

II

National and local memory

Oral culture in Africa may seem a world away from historical consciousness in the West, but oral tradition has its place here too. The difference is that oral transmission has to contend with the authority and prevalence of both the written word and visual culture (such as film and television). Hence it has become customary to define 'collective memory' in a broader sense to include not only what is recounted in oral narratives, but the commonly accepted versions of the past, whatever their provenance. Consider, for example, the dominant collective memories of the two World Wars in Britain. The First World War is remembered as the 'bad war': an unrelieved tragedy in which a generation of young men was led to futile slaughter, unredeemed by principled motives. Conversely, the Second World War is cast as a heroic epic, symbolized by Britain's 'finest hour' in 1940 and Churchill's inspired leadership. While it is true that the stories told by veterans have a special prestige, what chiefly sustains these memories is the full resources of popular culture: the media, feature films, documentaries, museums, war memorials and commemorative parades (such as those on Remembrance Sunday). The cultural significance of these memories of war is no less clear. They express a view of not only what it meant to be British then, but what it should mean to be British now, and for that reason they are impervious to developments in historical scholarship. Thus no amount of revisionism seems able to rehabilitate the First World War as a struggle to preserve liberal democracy, or as a decisive victory for British arms. As regards the Second World War, Britain's contribution to the allied victory continues to be inflated, while the memory of Churchill remains untarnished by the mounting evidence of his erratic and sometimes disastrous military leadership. The fact that these views are so prevalent among the young and middle-aged who did not actually experience either of the wars demonstrates the moral power of collective memory. Its true function is to provide lessons in the national interest and the national character.[6]

At the same time, it should not be assumed that everyone subscribes to national memories of this kind. Class, locality and religion can each generate memories that are sharply at variance with the dominant public memory. In Catholic France at the beginning of the eighteenth century, the Protestant Camisards rebelled against the royal army, fighting a guerrilla war for two years. That experience dominates the oral culture of the region to this day, in re-tellings in family and village. The Camisard revolt is not only the key event of collective memory, but the standard that determines which subsequent events are worthy of recall.

Local tradition has little or nothing to say about the French Revolution or the First World War; on the other hand the Resistance during the Second World War was seen then as a reprise of Camisard heroism, and its place in recent memory confirms that link. In this instance, collective memory has taken an oppositional form, expressing the determination of a local group to retain its own identity vis-à-vis the national culture.[7]

Part of the reason why there is such an enduring and coherent tradition among the Camisards is that the Cevennes, where they live, is mountainous and inaccessible. Until recently there was comparatively free transmission between generations, and the region was thrown on its own cultural resources. In most parts of the Western world those conditions have long ceased to apply. Countries like Britain now experience high levels of spatial mobility and also the intrusive power of the commercialized media. Less authority is accorded to the elderly, and their renditions of the past are of less interest to the young. The place of oral tradition in collective memory has been steadily declining, and consequently it has become much less rewarding as a focus of research. Instead the emphasis in memory studies is tending to shift to other indicators of historical consciousness.

Anniversaries and collective memory

One aspect of this shift is commemorative ritual. Most countries celebrate a national day which falls on the anniversary of a formative or symbolic event in the nation's history. In France the celebration of 14 July (Bastille Day) sums up the process whereby the French Revolution has over the last century become central to the national self-image. In Serbia even greater weight is given to 28 June – the day on which the medieval empire of Serbia was crushed by the Ottoman Turks at Kosovo Polje in 1389. Symbolically that battle exemplifies the Serb self-image as a brave but beleaguered people; and because Kosovo lies to the south of the present Serbian heartland, the anniversary has the potential to stoke the fires of Serb territorial expansion, as happened during the wars that destroyed Yugoslavia during the 1990s.[8] 'Kosovo' is an article of faith, expressing a sacramental view of the past. Even without such a strong nationalist ideology, anniversaries starkly express the principles of political selection that underpin collective memory.

In this respect Britain is unusual. There is no national day, and none for England either (though there are days for Scotland and Wales). Anniversaries that were observed in the past, like the Glorious Revolution of 1688 or the accession of Queen Victoria, have withered away. The main one that survives has also shed its historical and ideological associations. Bonfire Night on 5 November commemorates the Gunpowder Plot of 1605, when the arrest of the Catholic conspirator, Guy Fawkes, delivered James I and his Parliament in the nick of time. Barely had the conspirators been tried and executed than Parliament ordained that the anniversary should be marked by church services in every parish. Popular participation was based on gratitude for the mercy of Divine Providence, and a consuming hatred for Catholics, whether at home or abroad. But by the mid-nineteenth century anti-Catholic prejudice was a shadow of its former self, and the statutory service of thanksgiving was dropped in 1859. Bonfire Night today lacks any historical referent at all, and no one any longer supposes that it is a national day. It has become symbolically impoverished, except perhaps in marking the onset of winter – though one might add that it also bears witness to the comparative indifference of the English to formal invocations of their national history.[9]

Figure 11.1 France's national day is 14 July. The parades held all over France commemorate the storming of the Bastille, which began the French Revolution in 1789. It has become a common symbol acceptable to all French people, except monarchists. © Getty Images/AFP.

Memories in stone

Public commemoration also takes the more material form of monuments and statues. Most capital cities feature many such reminders of the past, usually selected as a contribution to national pride. In London the most prominent examples are the Queen Victoria monument outside Buckingham Palace, and Trafalgar Square which is dedicated to military and naval heroes. Unlike oral tradition, these are 'frozen' memories, relatively resistant to reinterpretation. Statues and the like usually attract considerable public attention when they are unveiled, but they seldom convey much information. Continuing public recognition depends on the posthumous standing of the **honorand**. However, most monuments in stone are little more than prompters; their role is not so much to create memory as to remind the viewer of events or persons which he or she knows about already. Indeed, the point may be reached when neither the name nor the image registers with the public mind at all. Such was the fate of Sir Henry Havelock, the general lionized for his role in suppressing the Indian rebellion of 1857 and commemorated by a statue in Trafalgar Square (and by street names all over England). As part of a debate about re-planning the square in 2001, the Mayor of

honorand
Recipient of an honour or distinction (in this case commemoration).

Figure 11.2 Sir Henry Havelock's most celebrated exploit was the relief of the British community in Lucknow, during the Indian rebellion of 1857. He died of fever shortly afterwards. Havelock was acclaimed a hero on all sides, and was commemorated by a statue in Trafalgar Square. © Getty Images/Hulton Archive.

London, Ken Livingstone, declared Havelock to be a completely obscure individual who no longer merited a statue. Although removal of the statue was regarded as a somewhat draconian course, there is little doubt that Livingstone, in expressing his ignorance of Havelock, spoke for the overwhelming majority of Londoners. The same fate has overcome many other worthies who were names to conjure with in their own day.

But the prevalence of monuments not only raises questions about the after-life of those commemorated; it also throws into relief the commemorative impulse itself. The commissioning and siting of so many monuments suggests a society in which collective memory can no longer be taken for granted. As an integral aspect of culture it has been eroded or displaced, and it must now be artificially promoted if it is to survive at all. What has displaced memory is history itself: the critical, evidence-based study of the past, which is not tied to any political agenda. That at least is the influential thesis of Pierre Nora: history 'is how modern societies organize a past they are condemned to forget because they are driven by change'; history, he goes on, is deeply hostile to memory, which in its traditional form is 'all-powerful, sweeping, un-self-conscious, and inherently present-minded'.[10] Nora overplays the antithesis for rhetorical effect. More of a memory culture survives in modern societies than he allows, while historians are by no means innocent of selecting and moulding their work for political effect. Nevertheless Nora is right that memory in modern societies is not spontaneous, but managed: commemoration is focused on events or people that have either passed out of memory altogether, or are only dimly perceived. And Nora shows how his own country – France – has been subjected to relentless memorialization for over a hundred years: the contributors to his *magnum opus* analyse some 130 'sites of memory' (*lieux de mémoire*), expressing a variety of cultural and political goals, but all of them dedicated to an idea of France.[11]

In such societies collective memory cannot be regarded as part of the authentic culture of ordinary people. Elements of spontaneous oral transmission certainly survive, but they are inextricably combined with readings of the past that have been promoted for political ends, and with residues of the past that have been deliberately preserved. Yet, whether inwardly grown or absorbed from a hegemonic culture, popular historical consciousness is an important ingredient of political and cultural history. Much more research is needed to tease out the relations between these different elements. The signs are that the task will be pursued with some vigour; for, in prioritizing the study of representation and meaning, the study of collective memory is fully in tune with the cultural turn; indeed it is an integral part of it.

III

First-hand memories

In the study of collective memory, individual voices are often lost sight of, because the past is not the property of the individual but a community possession. The position is quite different with regard to first-hand reminiscence. Although hardly independent of cultural influences, personal testimony is centred on the experience and opinions of the individual informant, often recounted with vividness of detail and an emotional power.

The origins of oral history lie in the United States. During the 1930s, the Federal Writers' Programme carried out hundreds of interviews with ex-slaves, creating a priceless archive of African-American history. Somewhat later, historians of labour took up oral history too. By this time historians had begun to develop a methodology for recording and interpreting evidence about the past acquired from interview. Given the close association of historical scholarship with archival research, this was a significant novelty. For many historians, especially those on the Left, it was a breath of fresh air which enabled them to reconstruct the lives of ordinary people in their own words, instead of relying on the official record and the observations of elite writers. As the American labour historian Staughton Lynd said of his own interviewing, 'It's like history from the bottom up carried a step further, because it's people at the bottom doing their own history'.[12] The new technique became known as *oral history*. It is valued for two different reasons. First, it can bring the past vividly to life, providing authentic evidence of popular experience fifty or sixty years ago: for example, the discipline of the schoolroom or the impact of industrial strife on working-class communities. Here oral evidence is treated as a primary source analogous to the documentary record, enjoying the same privileged status. But closer examination often reveals that the testimony of informants – especially elderly informants – departs from the known record by omission or by the incorporation of extraneous elements. What they remember from several decades back is modified by the impact of subsequent experience and the recollections of other people. This is the second reason why oral material is now so closely studied. Like collective memory transmitted over the generations, it provides precious evidence of how the past continues to evolve in the minds of the living.

The pedigree of oral history

It is only very recently that professional historians have acquired any experience of collecting oral sources. Even today the mainstream of the historical profession remains sceptical and is often

Herodotus (c.485–425 BCE)
Generally regarded as 'the father of history'. He travelled widely throughout the Greek-speaking world and relied extensively on local informants.

Thucydides (c.460–400 BCE)
Athenian historian who wrote principally about the Peloponnesian War between Athens and Sparta. He, too, relied on informants. He is renowned for his dispassionate impartiality.

Herbert Morrison (1885–1965)
Labour politician. He was a major figure in the development of London between the wars, especially the capital's public transport network. He served in Ramsay MacDonald's 1929 Labour government, and as Home Secretary in Churchill's wartime coalition. He was Deputy Prime Minister in Clement Attlee's post-war Labour government and was in charge of steering the programme of nationalization through the House of Commons. He was the grandfather of the Blairite New Labour minister, Peter Mandelson.

not prepared to enter into discussion about the actual merits and drawbacks of oral research. Arthur Marwick gave it short shrift in *The New Nature of History* (2001). Yet oral sources provided the bulk of the evidence used by those who are now revered as the first historians – **Herodotus** and **Thucydides**. The chroniclers and historians of the Middle Ages were hardly less dependent on oral testimony; and although written sources grew rapidly in importance from the Renaissance onwards, the older techniques still survived as a valued adjunct to documentary research. It was only with the emergence of modern academic history in the nineteenth century that the use of oral sources was entirely abandoned. The energies of the new professional historians were taken up by the study of written documents, on which their claim to technical expertise was based, and their working lives were largely confined to the library and the archive. The French historian Jules Michelet was highly unusual in saluting the memories of the common people as 'living documents'.[13]

Ironically, many of the written sources cited by today's historians were themselves oral in origin. Social surveys and official commissions of enquiry, which loom so large in the primary sources for nineteenth-century social history, are full of summarized testimonies; historians routinely draw on them, often with little regard for the selection of witnesses or the circumstances in which they were interviewed. Yet the idea that historians might add to the volume of oral evidence by conducting interviews themselves continues to arouse misgivings. The reason is partly that historians are reluctant to see any compromise with the principle that contemporaneity is the prime requirement of historical sources – and oral sources have an inescapable element of hindsight about them. Perhaps too there is a reluctance to grapple with the implications of scholars sharing in the creation (and not just the interpretation) of new evidence.

The need for oral history

The fact that oral techniques have made any headway at all among professional historians is due almost entirely to the reticence of conventional written sources on a number of areas that are now engaging scholarly attention. Recent political history is one such topic. Whereas in the Victorian and Edwardian periods, public figures commonly conducted a voluminous official and private correspondence, their modern counterparts rely much more on the telephone and e-mail, and when they do write letters they seldom have the leisure to write at length. There have been major public figures in recent times who left no private papers to speak of – for example **Herbert Morrison**, a leading member of the Labour Party in the 1930s and 1940s.[14] In order to fill out the evidence to the proportions appropriate to a biography, historians

have had to collect the impressions and recollections of such figures from their surviving colleagues and associates. The second
area concerns what might be termed the recent social history of
everyday life, and particularly those aspects of working-class life
in the family and the workplace that were seldom the subject of
contemporary observation or enquiry. In Britain the oral history
movement is dominated by social historians whose interest in
these topics is in many cases sustained by an active socialist
commitment, evident in their house journal, *Oral History*. Oral
historians are also acutely conscious of their obligation to make
their material available to other scholars; recordings and tran-
scripts are usually placed on public deposit, for example in the
British Library Sound Archive.

IV

The voice of the people?

> When I came to this village with my father, I was in lodgings
> as well, so there were no real home comforts to come back to
> after the pit. I remember being in one set of lodgings: there
> were six or seven other miners lodging there. It was only a
> house with three bedrooms, so you can imagine that we were
> sleeping on a rota basis.
>
> If five or six of us were on the same shift, as soon as I got
> out of the pit I'd gallop home to be the first to have a bath.
> There were no bathrooms: all you had was an old zinc tub,
> and the landlady would have a couple of buckets of water on
> the fire. If there were five or six of you together, first of all
> five of you would bath the top half of the body. Everybody
> bathed the top half of the body in a rota, and then you step-
> ped back into the bath and washed the bottom part of your
> body. What used to amuse me in those days – well, not
> amuse – what used to embarrass me was that you'd get the
> women from next door or from each side of the terraced
> house. They'd come in there, and they'd sit down in the
> kitchen, and they wouldn't bloody move – when even you
> were washing the bottom part of your body. As a youngster
> and not being used to that, I was not only shy but embar-
> rassed, because you learned the differences even in those days
> between the sexes.[15]

This narrative, collected from a retired collier in South Wales as
part of a research project on the history of mining communities,
conveys something of the qualities that recommend oral history to
historians. It is a fragment of autobiography by someone who
would never otherwise have dreamed of dignifying his reminiscences
in that way. As an individual experience that is commonplace and

yet at the same time particular, it offers a vivid insight into a way of life that now survives in Britain only in the memories of the very old. Contemporary written sources for the Edwardian period – the reports of social investigators and charitable bodies, for example – provide copious information about the homes of the poor, but it is information derived at second hand and glossed by 'expert' opinion, a description from outside rather than a product of experience. Oral history allows the voice of ordinary people to be heard alongside the careful marshalling of social facts in the written record.

The testimony that can be gleaned from informants, like the memories of most old people about their youth, is often confused as regards specific events and the sequence in which they occurred. Where it is most reliable is in characterizing recurrent experience, like the practice of a working skill or a child's involvement in a network of neighbours and kin. The routines of daily life and the fabric of ordinary social relationships were commonplace and therefore taken for granted at the time, but now they seem of compelling human interest, and oral enquiry offers the readiest means of access – as in *A Woman's Place* (1984), Elizabeth Roberts's fine study of Lancashire working-class women, based on nearly 160 interviews. What oral history also uniquely conveys is the essential *connectedness* of aspects of daily life which the historian otherwise tends to know of as discrete social facts. Through the life histories of the very poor, for instance, the way in which casual labour, periodic destitution, under-nourishment, drunkenness, truancy and familial violence formed a total social environment for thousands of people before the First World War (and later) can be vividly portrayed. Oral history, in short, gives social history a human face.

Oral history and local history

How do oral historians come by their informants? The sampling techniques of sociology have had some influence here. In a classic early attempt to incorporate the findings of oral history into a general social history, Paul Thompson took a carefully constructed sample of 500 surviving Edwardians from all classes and regions of Britain, and some of the resulting material is presented in his book, *The Edwardians* (1975).[16] But few historians have followed his example. Most recent oral history has been emphatically local in focus, and for this there are sound practical reasons. In a strictly local study all the elderly who are willing and able can be canvassed; less trust has to be placed in the reliability of the individual informant since the testimonies can be tested against each other; and the purely local references which always feature prominently in life histories can be elucidated with the help of other source materials. But it is also significant that oral history has from the outset been practised by amateur local historians. The English tradition of amateur local history (which extends back to the sixteenth century) has stressed **topography** and the world of the **squire**, parson and – more rarely – businessman. Oral history promises a sense of place and community accessible to ordinary people, while at the same time illuminating broader features of social history. Very fine work of this kind has been done under the auspices of the History Workshop movement. Raphael Samuel reconstructed the economic and social milieu of Headington Quarry near Oxford before it was enveloped by the expansion of the motor industry in the 1920s; without the rich oral testimony he collected, Samuel would have found it difficult to penetrate far beyond the stereotype of 'quarry roughs' in newspapers of the time to understand the range of trades and social networks that sustained the independent spirit of the villagers.[17] In the field of urban local history, perhaps the best oral work has been the two London studies by Jerry White, an accomplished amateur: one on a notorious Holloway street between the World Wars (Campbell Road), the other about a single-tenement block in the East End around the turn of the century.[18]

topography
The study of the physical features of a location.

squire
The general term used for a member of the gentry, the major landowner in a particular village. The term is usually reserved for those whose influence was limited to one particular locality, as opposed to nobles and aristocrats, whose landholdings might be very extensive.

Figure 11.3 The collection of oral testimony about Campbell Road in Holloway belied its reputation as 'the worst street in London'. © Topfoto/J White.

The authentic past?

Underlying the practice of oral history are two powerfully attractive assumptions. First – and most obviously – personal reminiscence is viewed as an effective instrument for *recreating* the past – the authentic testimony of human life as it was actually experienced. Paul Thompson revealingly entitles his book on the methods and achievements of oral history *The Voice of the Past*, and – notwithstanding all the reservations made in the text – the notion of a direct encounter between historians and their subject matter is central to Thompson's outlook.[19] At one level, there-fore, oral history simply represents a novel means of fulfilling the programme laid down by professional historians since the early nineteenth century – 'to show how things actually were' and to enter into the experience of people in the past as fully as possible. But many oral historians are not content with being grist to the mills of professional history. They see oral history rather as a democratic alternative, challenging the monopoly of an academic elite. Ordinary people are offered not only a place in history, but a role in the *production* of historical knowledge. In east London during the 1970s, the People's Autobiography of Hackney was an open group of local residents who recorded each other's life his-tories and published the transcriptions in pamphlets marketed through a local bookshop. Although educated people participated, no academic historians were involved; if they had been, the con-fidence of people in their own perceptions of the past might have been undermined. The idea was that through oral work the community should discover its own history and develop its social identity, free from the patronizing assumptions of conventional historical wisdom. Ken Worpole, coordinator of the group, recalls the circumstances in which it began in the early 1970s: 'producing shareable and common history from the spoken remi-niscences of working-class people seemed a positive and impor-tant activity to integrate with various other new forms of "community" politics'.[20] Local projects in oral history have served the interests of many other groups, variously based on class and ethnicity.

V

The pitfalls of oral history

However, both these formulations – oral history as 'recreation' and as 'democratic' knowledge – are problematic. The role of the professional historian itself makes for difficulties. It is naïve to suppose that the testimony represents a pure distillation of past experience, for in an interview each party is affected by the other. It is the historian who selects the informant and indicates the area

Figure 11.4 Historians have learned the techniques required to get hold of the oral testimony of witnesses to the past. But how much care is needed in dealing with first-hand accounts that are inevitably influenced by hindsight? © Topfoto/Image Works.

of interest; and even if he or she asks no questions and merely listens, the presence of an outsider affects the atmosphere in which the informant recalls the past. The end-product is conditioned both by the historian's social position vis-à-vis the informant, and by the terms in which he or she has learned to analyse the past and which may well be communicated to the informant. In the phrase made popular by the American oral scholar Michael Frisch, historian and informants exercise a 'shared authority'.[21]

But the difficulties are far from over when the historian is removed from the scene. For not even the informant is in direct touch with the past. His or her memories, however precise and vivid, are filtered through subsequent experience. They may be contaminated by what has been absorbed from other sources (especially the media); they may be overlaid by nostalgia ('times were good then'), or distorted by a sense of grievance about deprivation in childhood which took root only in later life. To anyone listening, the feelings and attitudes – say of affection towards a parent or distrust of union officials – are often what lend conviction to the testimony, yet they may be the emotional residue of later experience rather than the period in question. As one critic of Paul Thompson's work put it:

Edwardian
Relating to the reign of King Edward VII (1901–10).

Georgian
Here, relating to the reign of King George V (1910–36). The term is more usually used of the reigns of the first four Georges (1714–1830); it was only rarely used to refer to George V, and then usually in conjunction with 'Georgian' painters and writers.

Elizabethan
Although usually used to refer to the first Queen Elizabeth, it here refers to Queen Elizabeth II. There was a vogue at the start of her reign in 1952 to speak of a 'New Elizabethan Age', though the term was not current for long.

His 'Edwardians' after all, have lived on to become 'Georgians' and, now, 'Elizabethans'. Over the years, certain memories have faded, or, at very least, may have been influenced by subsequent experience. How many of their childhood recollections were, in fact, recalled to them by their own elders? What autobiographies or novels might they have since read that would reinforce certain impressions at the expense of others? What films or television programmes have had an impact on their consciousness? ... to what extent might the rise of the Labour Party in the post-war decade have inspired retrospective perception of class status and conflict?[22]

Whatever the evidence it rests on, the notion of a direct encounter with the past is an illusion, but perhaps nowhere more than in the case of testimony from hindsight. 'The voice of the past' is inescapably the voice of the present too.

The limitations of oral history

Yet even supposing that oral evidence were somehow authentic and unalloyed, it would still be inadequate as a representation of the past. For historical reality comprises more than the sum of individual experiences. It is no disparagement of the individual to say that our lives are largely spent in situations that, from our subjective perspective, we cannot fully understand. How we perceive the world around us may or may not amount to a viable basis for living, but it never corresponds to reality in its entirety. One of the historian's functions is to investigate the deeper structures and processes that were at work in the lives of individuals. The vividness of personal recall which is the strength of oral evidence also therefore points to its principal limitation, and historians need to be wary about becoming trapped within the mental categories of their informants. In the words of Philip Abrams:

> The close encounter may make the voices louder; it does not ... make their meaning clearer. To that end we must turn back from 'their' meanings to our own and to the things we know about them which they did not know, or say, about themselves.[23]

This limitation applies with particular force to the democratic or populist tendency in oral history. The idea behind projects of the 'people's autobiography' type is that an articulate and authentic historical consciousness will enable ordinary working people to take more control over their lives. But to do so they need an understanding of the forces that have actually moulded their world – most of them not of their making or directly manifest in their experience. The problem with collective oral history is that it may reinforce the superficial way in which most people think of the changes they have lived through, instead of equipping them with deeper insights as a basis for more effective political action.

Interpreting oral history

What place, then, does oral history have in the practice of historians? The problems raised here are not grounds for having nothing to do with oral history. What they suggest is rather that oral evidence, like all verbal materials, requires critical evaluation, and that it must be deployed in conjunction with all the other available sources; in other words, the canons of historical method described in Chapter 5 apply here too. Transcriptions of testimonies are not 'history', but raw material for the writing of history. They are no substitute for the work of historical interpretation.

Oral sources are in fact extremely demanding of the historian's skills. If the full significance of an oral testimony is to come across, it must be evaluated in conjunction with all the sources pertaining to the locality and people spoken of, or else much of the detail will count for nothing. Sometimes oral research itself unearths new documentary material in private hands – family accounts or old photographs – which add to the amount of supporting evidence. Jerry White describes his book on tenement life in London's East End, *Rothschild Buildings* (1980), in these terms:

> This may be primarily a work of oral history but documents have played a large part in its conception. Written sources and oral sources interact throughout: finding a new document has led me to ask different questions of the people I interviewed, and the oral testimony has thrown fresh light on the documents. The rules printed on the first tenants' rentbooks led me to ask if they were obeyed and how; finding the original plans of the Buildings made me wonder what was kept in the fitted cupboard behind the living-room door; people's memories of shopping led me to take street directories with a large pinch of salt; autobiographical details cast doubts on census classifications, sociologists' assumptions and standard historical reference works, and so on.[24]

Command of the full range of relevant sources is no less important for 'democratic' oral history. The more traditional inventory of local historians' sources – business archives, newspapers, census returns, the reports of charitable bodies, etc. – provides an entry into the economic and social context of the informants' lives and may reveal something of the historical processes that have shaped the observable changes in the locality. The limitations inherent in the amateur group project mean that, to be politically effective, it requires the participation, if not of professional historians, at least of people familiar with the methods and findings of mainstream social history.

VI

Oral history as cultural memory

histoire vérité
(French) 'Truth history', derived from the phrase *cinéma vérité*, a style of film pioneered by French directors, which attempted to show gritty and unpolished 'reality' rather than the carefully composed images of conventional cinema.

Anzac
Properly, ANZAC: Australian and New Zealand Army Corps. Anzac troops were involved in the disastrous allied landings at Gallipoli in Turkey during the First World War, where their heavy casualties sowed much bitterness towards the British planners of the operation.

Gallipoli
The amphibious landing of allied troops in 1915 at the town of Gallipoli, on the narrow Dardanelles strait in western Turkey, was one of the most disastrous allied operations of the First World War. The plan, proposed by Winston Churchill as First Lord of the Admiralty, was bold in conception but poorly planned and executed, and resulted in very heavy casualties. The troops had to be evacuated, never having been able to advance inland from the landing beaches.

However, there is an important sense in which the anxiety about the accuracy of oral testimony is beside the point. For first-hand reminiscence invites a cultural analysis comparable to the perspective described earlier for collective memory. Oral history may be less important as *histoire vérité* than as indispensable evidence of how the past lives in the consciousness of the present. From this perspective, informants are offering not so much private knowledge of the everyday as pointers to more deep-seated values and sentiments. In the case of recent public events, oral testimony is not likely to supplant or add to the written record. What it demonstrates is how those events became lodged in popular consciousness, and how their significance has been modified over a lifetime. The sense of the past that individuals carry around with them comprises a selection of their immediate experience, together with some conception of the nature of the social order in which they live. Historical biographies sometimes show how these two elements bear on each other in the thinking of leaders and intellectuals, but we know much less about their place in the historical awareness of ordinary people. Yet the way in which social groups assimilate and interpret their collective experience is a historical factor in its own right, at the heart of political culture. Hence the mental transition from 'Edwardians' to 'Georgians' and on to 'Elizabethans' is an object of study for its own sake, instead of being merely an obstruction in the way of a direct encounter with the past.

The memories of individuals are even more susceptible to reworking when they bear on public events of great moment. National morale dictates that war memories should be of a particular kind, while the collective experience of both civilians and soldiers predisposes people to conform to the accepted narratives. The twentieth-century history of Australia provides a classic instance. The participation of **Anzac** troops in the **Gallipoli** campaign of 1915 is central to the modern sense of Australian nationhood, and has been officially promoted as such since the 1920s. Alistair Thomson conducted interviews of surviving Anzacs during the 1980s. His book, *Anzac Memories: Living with the Legend* (1994), shows how men who had experienced fear, trauma and a sense of inadequacy in combat suppressed their personal memories so as to match the accepted picture of loyalty, bravery and camaraderie on the front line, which most Australians accept to this day. In other words, memory and its articulation in reminiscence produced a standardized narrative which for several decades has served to underpin Australia's sense of nationhood.

The politics of oral history are manifest as much in what is forgotten as what is remembered. Given the limited capacity that most people have for remembering the past, this is hardly surprising; but the suppression also answers to political need. Researching how workers in the city of Turin remembered the Fascist period, Luisa Passerini was struck with how they recalled the Fascist takeover in 1922–3 and the regime's collapse in 1943, but not the intervening two decades when Mussolini was firmly in the saddle: such was the force of the popular impulse to suppress the record of collusion during the period of dictatorship.[25] In another Italian example, Alessandro Portelli demonstrates how quickly crucial details can be substituted in deference to changing political priorities. Luigi Trastulli was a steel-worker killed by police during a demonstration in the Italian town of Terni in 1949. This event administered such a shock to the workers that very soon appropriate causes and circumstances were being improvised to render it explicable. Whereas Trastulli had been killed during a protest against Italian entry into **NATO**, many of the memories current during the 1970s relocated the event as part of a later demonstration against the mass lay-off of workers, a much more critical issue for most of the participants. Trastulli was also portrayed as having been pinned against the factory wall by police fire, in an image that emphasized his status as a martyr. In research of this kind the point is not to peel away the accretions and distortions until the kernel of truth is exposed. As Portelli explains,

> the discrepancy between fact and memory ultimately enhances the value of the oral sources as historical documents. It is not caused by faulty recollections ... but actively and creatively generated by memory and imagination in an effort to make sense of crucial events and of history in general.[26]

Recent commentators have identified a widespread 'memory boom' or a 'memorial culture', in which individuals seek a personal link with the public past, through genealogy, military records, old photographs and so on.[27] The demand for such a link has most political bite in the arena of identity politics. Subordinated groups often have a perspective on the recent past that is at variance with the approved national version and which is jealously preserved as a badge of group consciousness. The black residents of Brixton, Toxteth and Tottenham do not recall the riots that occurred there in the 1980s in the same terms as does

NATO
North Atlantic Treaty Organization. It is an American-led military alliance of the Western powers created in 1949 and aimed at containing and counterbalancing the threat from the Soviet Union and its allies, which responded the following year by forming their own alliance structure, the Warsaw Pact. Adherence to NATO was controversial with those who sympathized with the Soviet Union in the Cold War, or who distrusted the increasing reliance on military alliances and atomic weaponry.

'received opinion' in the nation at large. The more politically conscious the community is, the greater the need to make sense of the past in ways that are politically enabling. The conflict of memories is sharpest when the past is not yet 'over' – when the grievances and tensions that collective memory recounts are still alive today. Graham Dawson's study of popular memory in Northern Ireland shows that, despite more than ten years of truce since the **Good Friday Agreement**, the communities are almost as divided in their sense of the recent past as they have ever been.[28]

Good Friday Agreement
After nearly thirty years of 'the Troubles', an agreement was made in April 1998 between the political parties of Northern Ireland and the governments of Britain and the Irish Republic. As a result, inter-communal violence in the province was scaled down, British troops were withdrawn from the streets, and devolved self-government was restored.

The use of oral evidence by historians began as a means of restoring the particularities of human experience to their central place in historical discourse. A technique that owes its modern development to sociology and anthropology has been enlisted in support of an enterprise foreign to the generalizing, theory-oriented nature of those disciplines. In fact, the practice of oral history has had more to do with the recreational than the explanatory side of historical enquiry. Like other academic innovators, oral historians have tended in the past to advance exaggerated claims for their expertise, maintaining that they are uniquely – perhaps exclusively – qualified to recover 'lost' areas of human experience. The contribution of oral sources in these areas can hardly be denied. What cannot be sustained, however, is the notion that the historian, by listening to 'the voice of the past', can recreate these neglected strands of history with an authentic immediacy. No less than documentary sources, oral sources demand critical analysis and a sensitivity to their cultural and social context. Submitted to that discipline, what oral history reveals is a unique insight into the formation of popular historical consciousness – something that should be of abiding interest to all historians.

VII

The place of recorded reminiscence in historical enquiry is not best served by calling it 'oral history', which suggests a new specialism analogous to diplomatic or economic history. Oral history is not a new branch of history but a new *technique*. But it is nevertheless central to a new kind of historical enquiry – the study of memory. And the reason why memory is attracting so much attention is not that it represents one more topic to be historicized along with all the others, but because it is fundamental to understanding people's relationship with the past. That relationship is anything but simple. Individual recall has to be weighed against collective memory; spontaneous memory against manipulated memory; national against local tradition. We saw how the social function of oral tradition is particularly clear in pre-literate societies. Print culture and urbanization certainly complicate the picture, but they do not alter its essentials. In all societies, collective memory exists in a state of tension, because on the one hand it respectfully conserves past experience, while on the other hand it imposes the requirements of the present on the past. It is the implications of that contradiction which account for the fascination of memory studies in history.

Two final observations suggest a more penetrating explanation of the attention which historians are now giving to memory. First, if the vogue for Postmodernism has undermined the truth claims of conventional academic history (see Chapter 7), the study of memory may appeal precisely because it deals with impressions and constructions rather than addressing matters of fact. Historians who wish to be in tune with the prevalent epistemology carry much more conviction if their scholarship no longer turns on evidential proof.[29] Second, the academic history of memory has grown up alongside a burgeoning memory culture in society at large, covering such varied themes as family history, industrial archaeology and the attention given to the minutiae of royal history. Raphael Samuel regarded these popular manifestations of memory as more vital and more rewarding than most of the output of academics.[30] Indeed some historians detect a crisis of authority, as historians vie with the lay popular culture of memory for attention.[31] To speak of a struggle for survival overstates the case, but both the challenge of Postmodernism and the alleged crisis of authority remind us that memory has profound implications. It would be strange if historians did not play their part in memory studies, both to illumine their own research and to contribute to the lay understanding of what is, after all, a fundamental aspect of culture.

Further reading

Geoffrey Cubitt, *History and Memory*, Manchester University Press, 2007.

James Fentress and Chris Wickham, *Social Memory*, Blackwell, 1992.

Pierre-Nora, 'Between memory and history: *Les Lieux de mémoire*', *Representations*, XXVI, 1989.

Jan Vansina, *Oral Tradition as History*, James Currey, 1985.

Paul Thompson, *The Voice of the Past: Oral History*, 3rd edn, Oxford University Press, 2000.

Robert Perks and Alistair Thomson (eds), *The Oral History Reader*, 2nd edn, Routledge, 2006.

Sherna B. Gluck and Daphne Patai (eds), *Women's Words: The Feminist Practice of Oral History*, Routledge, 1991.

Raphael Samuel and Paul Thompson (eds), *The Myths We Live By*, Routledge, 1990.

Alessandro Portelli, *The Death of Luigi Trastulli and Other Stories: Form and Meaning in Oral History*, SUNY Press, 1991.

Notes

1 James Fentress and Chris Wickham, *Social Memory*, Blackwell, 1992, p. 59.
2 Jan Vansina, *Oral Tradition: A Study in Historical Methodology*, trans. H.M. Wright, Routledge & Kegan Paul, 1965.
3 Jan Vansina, *The Children of Woot*, Wisconsin University Press, 1978, p. 19.
4 Donald R. Wright, 'Uprooting Kunta Kinte: on the perils of relying on encyclopaedic informants', *History in Africa*, VIII, 1981.
5 Jan Vansina, *Antecedents to Modern Rwanda: The Nyiginya Kingdom*, Wisconsin University Press, 2004.
6 Dan Todman, *The Great War: Myth and Memory*, Hambledon Continuum, 2005; Malcolm Smith, *Britain and 1940: History, Myth and Popular Memory*, Routledge, 2000.
7 Fentress and Wickham, *Social Memory*, pp. 92–6.
8 Tim Judah, *The Serbs: A History*, Yale University Press, 1997, pp. 29–47, 164.
9 James Sharpe, *Remember, Remember the Fifth of November: Guy Fawkes and the Gunpowder Plot*, Profile, 2005.
10 Pierre Nora, 'Between memory and history: *Les Lieux de mémoire*', *Representations*, XXVI, 1989, pp. 7–9.
11 Pierre Nora (ed.), *Les Lieux de mémoire*, 7 vols, Gallimard, 1984–92.
12 Staughton Lynd, interviewed in MARHO, *Visions of History*, Pantheon Press, 1983, p. 152. See also his *Rank and File: Personal Histories by Working-Class Organizers*, Beacon Press, 1973.
13 Jules Michelet, *Le Peuple*, 1846, quoted in Paul Thompson, *The Voice of the Past: Oral History*, Oxford University Press, 1978, p. 40.
14 Bernard Donoughue and G.W. Jones, *Herbert Morrison*, Weidenfeld & Nicolson, 1973.
15 Christopher Storm-Clark, 'The miners, 1870–1970: a test-case for oral history', *Victorian Studies*, XV, 1971, pp. 65–6.
16 Thompson describes his sampling procedure more fully in his methodological work, *The Voice of the Past: Oral History*, 2nd edn, Oxford University Press, 1988, pp. 124–31.
17 Raphael Samuel (ed.), *Village Life and Labour*, Routledge & Kegan Paul, 1975.
18 Jerry White, *The Worst Street in North London: Campbell Bunk, Islington, Between the Wars*, Routledge & Kegan Paul, 1986, and *Rothschild Buildings: Life in an East End Tenement Block, 1887– 1920*, Routledge & Kegan Paul, 1980.
19 Thompson, *Voice of the Past*.
20 Ken Worpole, 'A ghostly pavement: the political implications of local working-class history', in Raphael Samuel (ed.), *People's History and Socialist Theory*, Routledge & Kegan Paul, 1981, p. 28.
21 Michael Frisch, *A Shared Authority: Essays on the Craft and Meaning of Oral and Public History*, State University of New York Press, 1990.
22 Stephen Koss, review of Paul Thompson's *The Edwardians* in *Times Literary Supplement*, 5 December 1975, p. 1436.
23 Philip Abrams, *Historical Sociology*, Open Books, 1982, p. 331.
24 White, *Rothschild Buildings*, p. xiii.
25 Luisa Passerini, 'Work ideology and consensus under Italian Fascism', in Robert Perks and Alistair Thomson (eds), *The Oral History Reader*, 2nd edn, Routledge, 2006, pp. 53–62.
26 Alessandro Portelli, *The Death of Luigi Trastulli and Other Stories: Form and Meaning in Oral History*, State University of New York Press, 1991, p. 26.

27 Jay Winter, 'The memory boom in contemporary historical studies', *Raritan*, XXI, 2001, pp. 52–66; Paula Hamilton, 'Sale of the century? Memory and historical consciousness in Australia', in Kate Hodgkin and Susannah Radstone (eds), *Contested Pasts: the Politics of Memory*, Routledge, 2003, pp. 136–52.

28 Graham Dawson, *Making Peace With the Past? Memory, Trauma and the Irish Troubles*, Manchester University Press, 2007.

29 Hodgkin and Radstone, *Contested Pasts*, editors' introduction, p. 2.

30 Raphael Samuel, *Theatres of Memory*, vol. I: *Past and Present in Contemporary Culture*, Verso, 1994.

31 Paula Hamilton, 'Memory studies and cultural history', in Hsu-Ming Teo and Richard White (eds), *Cultural History in Australia*, University of New South Wales Press, p. 96.

12 History beyond academia

History has a life beyond the university. Popular interest in the subject is evident in television, tourism, local history and reading tastes. This chapter considers the relationship between these popular forms and the academic kinds of study which have been the focus of this book until now. History beyond academia is now referred to as 'public history'. Does it undermine historical scholarship, or should all approaches to the past be welcomed as dimensions of a common historical culture?

In 2000, the historical reality of the Holocaust was put to the test when a leading 'revisionist' historian, David Irving, claimed that Deborah Lipstadt, an American academic, and her publisher, Penguin Books, had libelled him by describing him as a 'Holocaust denier' who suppressed and distorted the documentary record. In order to rebut the charges, the defence needed to prove both that Irving was dishonest in his use of evidence, and that the historical events which he denied had actually taken place. As a result, the evidence of professional historians was as central to the case as the arguments of legal counsel. One historian, Richard Evans, was retained specifically to investigate the validity of Irving's research procedures by tracing his statements back to the sources on which they were purportedly based. For three months the court heard a mountain of evidence of this kind. The verdict, delivered in a 350-page judgement, was an unequivocal defeat for Irving: he was found to have flouted accepted research methods and to have manipulated the evidence to suit his political prejudices. The case not only diminished the credibility of Holocaust denial; it also showed that what professional historians do matters – that some events in the past can be authenticated beyond reasonable doubt, and that society has a vested interest in the maintenance of scholarly standards.[1] But this was a highly unusual case. Historical evidence is not often cited in court, and even less often on such a critical issue. Where else, then, should we expect to find the public impact of historical scholarship?

I

That is not a new question, but today it is addressed under a new heading: *public history*. The term covers every channel for the appreciation and investigation of the past outside the universities – everything which contributes to a historical culture in the broadest sense. For this reason public history is inevitably imprecise. Four quite distinct versions are in play, each with a bearing on the public role of the historian.

The range of public histories

First, public history is often treated as a catch-all category for all public forms of representation of the past, in all media. It therefore covers historic objects and buildings, and history as it is presented in print (including fiction), and on film, broadcasting and the Internet. Ludmilla Jordanova succinctly defines this version of public history as 'all the means, deliberate and otherwise, through which those who are not professional historians acquire their senses of the past'.[2] Everything that becomes lodged in the popular mind is included, irrespective of its accuracy, and regardless of who has fashioned it. The second usage of public history places ordinary people centre stage. In this definition they not only consume the past but research it along lines which reflect their class or community interests; they are sometimes said to 'own' the past. Public history in this sense is a resoundingly democratic counter to the elitist world of academia: as one American protagonist has put it, public history 'promises us a society in which a broad public participates in the construction of its own history ... It seems to answer the question of "whose public?" "whose history?" with a democratic declaration of faith in members of the public at large to become their own historians and to advance their knowledge of themselves.'[3]

The third definition recognizes the role of professionals in advising and facilitating providers of history in the public sphere. Museum curators are the most obvious example, but conservation officers responsible for the built environment are another. It is at this point that academic historians can be said to have a clear cut function, cooperating with museums and acting as heritage consultants. Their claim to do a self-conscious 'public history' dates back to the USA during the 1970s. At first this was little more than an employment pitch for qualified historians who could not find university teaching positions. But as public historians many of these disappointed academics soon acquired recognized competence in museums, national parks and local history societies. They marketed themselves as experts in partnership with any organization with a stake in historical representation. In America there has for some time been a recognized career path for public historians and a house journal (*The Public Historian*); evidence of a higher profile than in Britain.

Lastly, public history is dispensed by professional historians addressing the public on the strength of their recognized expertise, without partners or intermediaries. Though historians have acted in this way for as long as history has been written, it is the least considered facet of public history today, since most definitions of the genre assume a much more fluid relationship between expert and public. Indeed it is maintained by some that public history has no room for the expert.[4] But the dissemination of academic scholarship is just as 'public' as the organizing of exhibitions or oral history projects. Academic writing for entertainment reaches hundreds of thousands of readers. Historical commentary on issues of topical concern reaches a smaller audience, but one whose critical take on current affairs is significantly enhanced. This is public history as a civic resource.

One of the reasons why the place of academic historians in public history is so unclear is because it varies according to which kind of public history is under discussion. At one extreme historians are barely tolerated as interlopers in a grass-roots enterprise. At the other they stand as the best available source of reliable historical information, but at the risk of appearing throwbacks to an outdated elitism. In the first of my four categories, historians are largely invisible in a medley of popular tastes and expectations. In the second, they sometimes advise – and more rarely initiate – a local research project, but are frequently on the periphery. Only in the third and fourth categories do historians have a recognized role.

II

Heritage and history

Much of the rhetoric of public history is pitched in terms of 'heritage'. This is perhaps the most advantageous viewpoint from which to assess the current scope of public history. Heritage has a much more extended provenance than public history. During the nineteenth century it was an important support for Europe's many aspirant nations. It provided the cultural evidence of a national consciousness deeply embedded in the people, expressed in folk traditions and in national schools of music. During the twentieth century, heritage was more narrowly defined as conservation – especially of the built environment. Today the agenda of heritage in Britain has broadened out once more. On the one hand, it is identified with 'high culture', stately homes and royal tradition (particularly in the policies of the Department of Culture, Media and Sport and the leading projects of English Heritage). On the other hand, heritage has been partly democratized, as communities claim recognition for their own distinctive heritage. Heritage has also become increasingly commercialized, which means that it reaches far more people, but also risks being no more than an adjunct of the tourist industry.

Despite the democratizing tendencies of community history, heritage has not lost its association with History (with a capital H). The choice of historic buildings for display is heavily tilted towards the dwellings of the rich and powerful. Of course they were more likely to endure into the present, but that is not the whole explanation. There is no shortage of houses of the middling sort – farmers, clothiers and the like – from the pre-industrial era, but these do not carry the same popular appeal. Stately homes are often presented in a way which emphasizes the elegance and taste of the past owners, without revealing much about the source of their wealth or their place in the wider society. The traditional equation of heritage with the 'core' national history of kings, queens and over-mighty subjects is re-affirmed.

However a very substantial part of 'heritage' is accounted for by the museum sector. The origins of museums lie in the private collections of wealthy members of the elite. The foundation of the British Museum in 1753 established the concept of the public museum, by allowing public access and receiving public funds, but that was the extent of the public's role. Not until the late twentieth century did museums accept that the public might have legitimate views about their acquisition and display policies. The rise of social history (see Chapter 3) shifted the emphasis of many museums to include the 'everyday': the history of women, workers, ethnic minorities and so on. Being a real presence in the community, these groups sought a voice in planning new initiatives. Consulting community representatives is now an established procedure for all historical collections, and in a few instances the community is in the driving seat. In Cape Town during the 1990s, for example, the District Six Museum was developed on the site of an urban community which had been forcibly removed by the apartheid government to make way for a whites-only area. The museum gathered together street signs, photographs and personal details. Former residents recorded their memories long after the opening of the museum, achieving a palpable sense of continuity with a vanished past.[5] Elsewhere authority is usually retained by the curatorial staff, but consultation with community representatives is *de rigueur*, and far from being a formality.

History in and by the community

Public history is most remote from professional expertise in the case of community history by amateurs. The germ of the idea lay in History Workshop during its early years in the 1970s, when both the journal and the annual conferences featured amateur historians drawing on local research (see pp. 57–8). Today the emphasis is on collective research, employing a variety of research methods. Documentary research remains important. But visual sources – especially photographs – often count for more, because they seem to offer direct access to the past for those unfamiliar with historical discourse. Oral sources are even closer to the community ideal. An early (and influential) example was the People's Autobiography of Hackney in the 1970s (see p.268). Residents of all ages interviewed each other about their working lives, dating in some cases back to the beginning of the century; the interviews were then reproduced in a local publication, which in turn prompted further recordings and group discussion. The distinction between the untutored and the professional recedes when oral history is the principal medium of investigation. There has been modest public funding for history projects which promote social inclusion, and in these cases there will usually be academic participation.[6] But in essence this is an avowedly democratic enterprise. History here is not so much a profession as an activity in which all can take part. Members of the community not only carry out research, they bring into play what they know from their individual and social experience.[7]

III

Historians in public

It has not been easy for historians, traditionally confident of their standing, to accept that there are other effective providers of history for popular consumption. Sour grapes is a predictable reaction. But there have also been significant objections on principle. A great deal of slapdash information about the past circulates in print and on TV. Historians, with their hostility to unfounded beliefs about the past, have sometimes found themselves in the thankless position of challenging statements which have already achieved popular currency. But the most telling objection by historians has been that the priorities of heritage lend themselves to an unacceptable degree of present-mindedness. The favoured evocations of the past sit all too comfortably with the political mood of the present. State-financed initiatives show too close an identification with historical elites (the monarch, the landed class, etc). Community projects are often motivated by a desire to uncover episodes which answer to their current concerns with agency and victimhood. In such projects there is too little enquiry and too much celebration, as David Lowenthal has said.[8]

Today, on the other hand, there is less of a stand-off between academic historians and public historians, because the opportunities for fruitful cooperation are more clearly understood. For example, academics are sometimes deeply sympathetic to the democratic aspirations of community history. A real empathy is possible, especially if they share a common social background. In Birmingham, Carl Chinn has for several decades collected the oral testimonies of the least advantaged, presenting them as directly as possible not only in his books, but in a regular column in the local press, and on local radio. He has become a local celebrity.[9]

Heritage can also be a field of cooperation. Heritage professionals value academically sound advice, while a growing number of historians recognize the need for public outreach. The criticisms of historians are tempered by a greater awareness of the constraints under which purveyors of the past operate outside the university sector. These factors came into sharp relief in 2007, during the bicentennial commemoration of the British abolition of the slave trade in 1807. Government funding ensured that this anniversary received exceptional attention. New permanent galleries were opened in museums in Liverpool and London; major exhibitions were held in Birmingham, Hull and the hallowed precincts of Westminster Hall. But these were only the most prominent venues: more than 200 museums marked the occasion. Historians were closely involved in planning many of the exhibitions. Their input was not restricted to the core narrative of parliamentary action. In fact their most valuable contribution was to achieve recognition of the historical contexts which bore directly on abolition; these included the scale of the slave trade in the two centuries before abolition, its impact on the British economy, the agency of slaves and freed blacks and the continuation of plantation slavery after the trade had been abolished. The specialist knowledge of historians also came into play in the sometimes heated discussions between museum curators and members of the black community. In some localities, research undertaken in preparation for an exhibition uncovered the footprint of slavery not previously known (notably in Tyneside and East Anglia).[10] An important sequel to the bicentenary was a research project at University College London which aimed to track the £20 million compensation paid to British slave-owners when slavery itself was abolished in 1833. Unlike the bicentenary of 2007, this was mainly an academic venture, but when the first results were announced in 2013, there was quite exceptional public interest, as families prominent in the public eye (including the Prime Minister's) were shown to have been beneficiaries of both slavery and the distribution of compensation.[11]

IV

Public history as a civic resource

Productive though partnerships between historians and heritage or community representatives often are, academics also have an independent role in the public sphere. If public history means the public representation and consumption of the past, then logically the dissemination of academic history qualifies. It has to be conceded that the works for which historians are best known – the endless recycling of the Tudor monarchy and the Nazi dictatorship – do not make a strong case for public utility. But academics claim their place in public history not only on grounds of sales, but because they offer something distinctive and instructive. Their claim to serve the public rests on their coverage of themes which lie outside the main thrust of public history. There is a case to be made for the focus of heritage on buildings, of museums on objects and of community history on the local dimension, but these hardly exhaust history's social role. Once the public are recognized to be citizens, and not merely consumers, many other concerns come into play. After all, citizens are called upon to have opinions about a wide swath of policies and trends, from the management of the welfare state to the conduct of foreign policy. Historical perspective is an important – even essential – adjunct to the coverage of current affairs in the media. It may warn us off re-inventing the wheel (an occupational hazard among present-minded politicians); it enlarges our understanding of the options available to decision-makers now; and it offers a means of understanding foreign or remote societies which appear to defy comprehension. If some (at least) of historians' work touches on questions of topical interest, they surely have an obligation to write for a readership that goes well beyond their academic peers and their students.[12]

To identify a significant public role for historians begs the question of communication. Historians are most used to writing monographs, textbooks and articles; how then can they reach a wider audience without the intervention of other, more media-savvy public history professionals? One avenue is the press. The editors of the quality dailies are not hostile to interventions by historians. Scholars like Eric Hobsbawm and John Keegan wrote regular columns; Linda Colley and Tristram Hunt continue to do so. The letters pages of the newspapers are also an important resource. Shortly before the general election of 2010, *The Guardian* published a letter from twenty economic historians, headed by Martin Daunton. They set out two historical lessons with a direct bearing on the response of politicians (both Labour and Conservative) to the financial crisis. First, alarm about the extent of the public debt was, they said, greatly exaggerated, since a substantial public debt had been the norm in Britain since the late eighteenth century, usually at a higher level than today. Secondly, the succession of financial crises since the late 1980s demonstrated the absolute necessity of radical financial regulation on a global scale. The impact of this intervention cannot be measured, but it was a forthright application of historical perspective to a central election issue (and one with continuing relevance today).[13]

In twenty-first-century Britain, however, print is of diminishing importance. What count are television and the Internet. Here the record of an informed and critical public history is patchy. TV carries far more history than it did twenty years ago, and it has become the prime source of popular knowledge of history. TV is of course a very broad medium, ranging from sober documentaries to soap opera in period costume. Historians are not necessarily best placed to claim their share of programming focused on the past. The most effective history on TV exploits the twin resources of archive footage and oral recall; hence it is confined to twentieth-century topics, most of all the Second World War. Photograph, film and memory are highly effective in recreating a sense of place and action, but they are less suited to the weighing of alternative explanations. It is certainly possible for TV to overcome these limitations. Programmes strongly committed to a particular viewpoint – like Niall Ferguson's controversial *Empire* series for Channel 4 (2003) – can be helpful in projecting a topic into the arena of public debate. In theory, TV is a promising medium through which to demonstrate the connections between the present and the past, especially in foreign affairs where the relevant background is not widely known to viewers. Yet such perspectives have been singularly lacking, from the invasion of Iraq to the ongoing crisis in Israeli-occupied Palestine.[14] Only very occasionally has a series fathomed the origins of a major event, like *The Death of Yugoslavia* (BBC, 1995). In the world of TV the odds are stacked against output of this quality.

Radio, on the other hand, presents a more positive picture, although its contribution tends to be underestimated. The absence of visual images allows greater attention to the spoken word, and thus to analysis and argument. Historical background to current events is much more likely to be offered on radio than on TV. Peter Laslett's analysis of pre-industrial English society and Margery Perham's assessment of Britain's colonial record in Africa were classics of public history. More recently, Jonathan Freedland's ongoing series *The Long View* (Radio 4), tracing a wide variety of topical themes to their historical antecedents, is an honourable updating of this tradition.[15]

History and policy

Lastly, no survey of the media through which history 'goes public' can be complete without the Internet. In Chapter 4, its immense potential for disseminating primary sources was discussed. But it is no less important to the historian wishing to communicate to a lay audience. The speed with which material can be posted means that the Internet is ideally suited to topical contributions that explain the bearing of history on current issues. In America this role is performed by *History News Network* under the motto 'because the past is the present, and the future too'. The Network features articles by historians which have appeared in the press all over the country.[16] In Britain, *History and Policy* offers a more carefully focused assessment of specific policies. Four hundred historians have indicated their willingness to provide policy briefings. Over 150 have contributed non-technical articles to the website; all of them have been archived and are available on line. Their subject matter ranges from pensions policy, through criminal justice and the National Health Service to economic policy. In 2006, for example, two papers were posted on the historical antecedents of the controversial Child Support scheme.[17] All this material is accessible to the public without subscription. In 2011–12 there were 132,234 visits to the site, and several papers had achieved more than 10,000 page views.[18] The impact is greater still when the page view is made by a journalist drawing on History and Policy for a background article in the daily press.

History and Policy brings into play one more role that public historians perform. Fifty years ago, Ernest May drew this inference from his studies of policy-making in the American State Department: 'if history is to be better used in government, nothing is more important than that professional historians discover means of addressing directly, succinctly and promptly the needs of people who govern'.[19] History and Policy is such a discovery. It is certainly prompt and succinct, and it cultivates informal contacts with people in government. Joint seminars are occasionally held between History and Policy, civil servants and members of think tanks. The re-launch of History and Policy in 2007 was marked by a speech by David Cannadine in which he called for historians to be appointed to all government departments. His suggestion fell on deaf ears, but that is no reason to devalue the less formal ways in which History and Policy maintains a presence in the corridors of power.

V

It has been claimed that, for all their openness to historical material, most people lack the historical awareness which would enable them to place their items of knowledge in context and in sequence: instead they are content with history as entertainment, or as support for identity. It is impossible to tell how accurate that picture is, although the weaknesses of history teaching in schools lend it some credence. Those historians who throw up their hands in despair lose sight of the possibilities inherent in the present condition of history. The situation would be dire if there was widespread indifference to history. But the reverse is the case. Historians have the advantage of being able to build on an unprecedented level of interest in the past. This in turn makes possible a growing degree of crossover between the academic and the popular. Historians who write bestsellers bear in mind the requirements of a 'good read', but that does not mean that they dumb down the content: neither Simon Schama writing on the big canvas of British history, nor Ian Kershaw revisiting Hitler's life, settled for a simple crowd-pulling formula.[20] Peter Mandler is correct to talk of 'this re-engagement of historians with the public'.[21] The visibility of historians seems assured. What is less clear is how effectively they are performing a genuine public role – as interpreters of heritage, as consultants to community history and above all as a source of insight into the world which responsible citizens attempt to understand.

Further reading

Ludmilla Jordanova, *History in Practice*, 2nd edn, Hodder Arnold, 2006, chapter 6 ('Public history').

David Lowenthal, *The Heritage Crusade and the Spirit of History*, Viking, 1997.

John Tosh, *Why History Matters*, Palgrave Macmillan, 2008.

Ian Tyrrell, *Historians in Public: The Practice of American History, 1890–1970*, Chicago University Press, 2005.

Jorma Kalela, *Making History: The Historian and Uses of the Past*, Palgrave Macmillan, 2012.

Paul Ashton and Hilda Kean (eds), *People and their Pasts: Public History Today*, Palgrave Macmillan, 2009.

Peter J. Beck, *Presenting History: Past and Present*, Palgrave Macmillan, 2012.

Notes

1 Richard J. Evans, *Telling Lies: History, Holocaust, and the David Irving Trial*, Basic Books, 2001.

2 Ludmilla Jordanova, 'Public history', *History Today*, May 2000, p. 20.

3 Ronald J. Grele, 'Whose public? Whose history? What is the goal of a public historian?', *The Public Historian*, III, 1981, pp. 46–8.

4 Peter Claus and John Marriott, *History: An Introduction to Theory, Method and Practice*, Pearson, 2012, p. 220; Ann Curthoys and Paul Hamilton, 'What makes history public?', *Public History review* I, 1992, pp 9–10.

5 Ingrid De Kok, 'Cracked heirlooms: memory on exhibition', in Sarah Nuttall and Carli Coetzee, *Negotiating the Past: the Making of Memory in South Africa*, Oxford University Press, 1998, pp. 63–6.

6 Madge Dresser, 'Politics, populism and professionalism: reflections on the role of the academic historian in the production of public history', *The Public Historian*, XXXII, 2010, pp. 39–63.

7 Paul Ashton and Hilda Kean, eds, *People and their Pasts: Public History Today*, Palgrave Macmillan, 2009.

8 David Lowenthal, *The Heritage Crusade and the Spirit of History*, Viking, 1997, p. x.

9 Paul Long, '"But it's not all nostalgia": public history and local identity in Birmingham', in Hilda Kean, Paul Martin and Sally J. Morgan (eds), *Seeing History: Public History in Britain Now*, Francis Boutle, 2000, pp. 133–6.

10 Laurajane Smith et al. (eds), *Representing Enslavement and Abolition in Museums: Ambiguous Engagements*, Routledge, 2011; Katherine Prior, 'Commemorating slavery 2007: a personal view from inside the museums', *History Workshop Journal*, LXIV, 2007, pp. 200–10.

11 *Independent*, 24 Feb. 2013; *The Voice*, 25 Feb. 2013.

12 John Tosh, 'Public history, civic engagement and the historical profession in Britain', *History*, XCIX, 2014, pp.191–212.

13 *The Guardian*, 3 March 2010.

14 Greg Philo and Mike Berry, *Bad News from Israel*, Pluto, 2004.

15 www.bbc.co.uk/history.

16 www.hnn.us

17 Thomas Nutt, 'The Child Support Agency and the Old Poor Law', and Tanya Evans, 'Is it futile to get non-resident fathers to maintain their children?', in www.historyandpolicy.org/policy-papers.

18 Data from Google Analytics, accessed by History and Policy, 29 July 2013.

19 Ernest May, *'Lessons of the Past': the Use and Misuse of History in American Foreign Policy*, Oxford University Press, 1973, pp. 189–90.

20 Simon Schama, A *History of Britain*, BBC, 2003; Ian Kershaw, *Hitler*, Allen Lane, 2008.

21 Peter Mandler, *History and the National Life*, Profile, 2002, p. 141.

Conclusion

The last four chapters testify to an impressive diversification in the scope of history. Underlying this diversity is a readiness to draw on the theoretical insights of other disciplines, notably political economy, anthropology, literary criticism and psychology. But my survey is far from complete. Other new departures such as the use of landscape and material culture as historical sources, the history of the body and the history of the book have been only lightly touched on in this book, because until now their impact has not been so pronounced; but in a comprehensive survey each would merit extended discussion. Together all these innovations amount to the most significant methodological advance since Ranke laid the foundations of modern historical scholarship more than a century and a half ago. As a result the content of historical study has been vastly extended, too. It now embraces social structures in their entirety, the history of collective mentalities and the evolving relationship between society and the natural environment. Although much further work remains to be done, women are now more present in the historical record than they have ever been. And for the first time historical research now extends to every corner of the globe; no culture is deemed too remote or too 'primitive' for the attention of historians.

Has history surrendered?

This record of innovation over the past fifty years is open to different readings. It can be seen as a surrender by historians to the promise of topicality offered by other, more 'relevant' disciplines – a line of attack that Elton made very much his own. According to this view, every enlargement of history's scope represents a departure from the central concern of the discipline (for Elton this remained the constitutional and administrative history of England). To the extent that the current turn to cultural themes is associated with a Postmodernist epistemology, it invites dire warnings of the end of history. A more optimistic and generous verdict would cite the occasions in the past when historians have successfully assimilated the insights of other disciplines, for example philology and the law in the nineteenth century. Everything depends on whether openness to contributions from elsewhere is compatible with upholding the essentials of historical awareness. There is certainly a danger that overarching social theories may obscure the particularity of the past, or that textual theory may wrench primary sources from their historical context, or that oral history may unwittingly read present-day attitudes into the remembered past. But these dangers are well understood, and one of the things that this book has sought to demonstrate is how historians, forearmed with that awareness, have successfully resisted the less digestible implications of innovations from outside the discipline. One thinks of E.P. Thompson's long campaign against the determinist tendencies of Marxism, or the carefully qualified welcome given to modern textual theory by Appleby, Hunt and Jacob. A great deal of the excitement of historical study derives from its pivotal position where the concerns of many other fields converge. Historians make those concerns their own by submitting them to the disciplines of historical context and historical process. They relinquish those intellectual positions that stand above or outside history; the rest they assimilate, and in so doing enrich the subject beyond measure.

A *fragmented discipline?*

But the enlargement in the scope of historical enquiry presents one undeniable problem: history has become a discipline with very little apparent coherence. During the nineteenth century it was possible in practice to fence off history from other disciplines and to confine its brief to the narrative presentation of political events. The rise of economic history in the early twentieth century would have imposed greater strain on this convention had it not been for the fact that political and economic history tended to remain in separate compartments. But today the situation is very different. Not only has the range of approaches to the past expanded, with the maturing of social history and the arrival of cultural history. More and more research is conducted on the frontiers *between* thematic specialisms, and the traditional claim of political history to be the core of the subject is almost impossible to sustain any longer; history has become a house of many mansions, with numerous doors and passageways inside.

History has always been inimical to the definitions of the logician. But now more than ever it can only be adequately characterized in terms of paired opposites. It concerns both events and structures, both the individual and the mass, both mentalities and material forces. Historians themselves need to combine narrative with analytical skills, and to display both empathy and detachment. Their discipline is both recreation and explanation, both art and science; in short – to return to one of the starting-points of this book – history is a hybrid which defies classification. These distinctions should be seen not as warring opposites but as complementary emphases, which together hold out the possibility of grasping the past in something like its real complexity. Nothing is to be gained from defining history in terms of lucid absolutes – except perhaps rhetorical support for some new approach whose credentials have yet to be established. A great deal will be lost if, in the interests of a spurious coherence, historians close their eyes to whole dimensions of their subject.

The purposes of history

Last but not least, the diversity of current practice reflects a central ambivalence in the function of history. For as long as men and women retain any interest in human nature and human creativity, they will recognize that every manifestation of the human spirit in the past has some claim on their attention, and that history is worth studying as an end in itself. Some of the new approaches during the past fifty years are recognizably part of this humanistic tradition. The study of collective mentalities is concerned in the first instance to recreate the emotions and intellect of people living in conditions very different from our own, so that their humanity can be more fully realized. Oral historians in Britain and other industrialized societies are committed to the recovery of everyday experience in the recent past as something of value in itself.

But the innovative strain in recent historiography has also been strongly influenced by the conviction that the record of the past holds lessons for contemporary society. The almost total retreat from topical concerns which characterized the historical profession in the first half of the twentieth century has ended. What gives most cause for optimism about the future of historical studies is that more and more historians are now investigating themes of topical relevance. They do so not as a propaganda exercise, but in the conviction that there are valuable insights to be learnt from the findings of historical scholarship. No doubt those insights are less clear-cut than the champions of 'scientific history' would care to admit. If society looks to historians for 'answers' in the sense of firm predictions and unequivocal generalizations, it will be disappointed. What will emerge from the pursuit of 'relevance' is something less tangible but in the long run more valuable – a surer sense of the possibilities latent in our present condition. For as long as historians hold that end in view, their subject will retain its vitality and its claim on the support of the society in which they work.

Index

Note to readers: Illustrations are shown by a reference in *italics*.

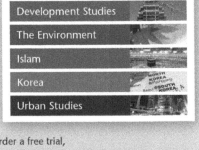